FLUX

FLUX

8 Superpowers for Thriving in Constant Change

APRIL RINNE

BK

Berrett–Koehler Publishers, Inc.

Berrett-Koehler Publishers, Inc.
1333 Broadway, Suite 1000
Oakland, CA 94612-1921
Tel: (510) 817-2277
Fax: (510) 817-2278
www.bkconnection.com

ORDERING INFORMATION

Quantity sales. Special discounts are available on quantity purchases by corporations, associations, and others. For details, contact the "Special Sales Department" at the Berrett-Koehler address above.

Individual sales. Berrett-Koehler publications are available through most bookstores. They can also be ordered directly from Berrett-Koehler: Tel: (800) 929-2929; Fax: (802) 864-7626; www.bkconnection.com.

Orders for college textbook / course adoption use. Please contact Berrett-Koehler: Tel: (800) 929-2929; Fax: (802) 864-7626.

Distributed to the U.S. trade and internationally by Penguin Random House Publisher Services.

Berrett-Koehler and the BK logo are registered trademarks of Berrett-Koehler Publishers, Inc.

Printed in Canada

Berrett-Koehler books are printed on long-lasting acid-free paper. When it is available, we choose paper that has been manufactured by environmentally responsible processes. These may include using trees grown in sustainable forests, incorporating recycled paper, minimizing chlorine in bleaching, or recycling the energy produced at the paper mill.

Names: Rinne, April, author.
Title: Flux : 8 superpowers for thriving in constant change / April Rinne.
Description: First edition. | Oakland, CA : Berrett-Koehler Publishers, Inc., [2021] | Includes bibliographical references and index.
Identifiers: LCCN 2021013312 | ISBN 9781523093595 (hardcover) | ISBN 9781523093601 (adobe pdf) | ISBN 9781523093618 (epub)
Subjects: LCSH: Leadership. | Organizational change. | Success in business.
Classification: LCC HD57.7 .R57 2021 | DDC 658.4/092—dc23
LC record available at https://lccn.loc.gov/2021013312

First Edition
27 26 25 24 23 22 21   10 9 8 7 6 5 4 3 2 1

Cover and text design: Debbie Berne

For Roland and Penny,
without whom this would have never been written

And for Jerry,
my guide, muse, and partner in flux

CONTENTS

Preface ix

Introduction **Who Moved My Future?** 1

Chapter 1 **Run Slower** 31

Chapter 2 **See What's Invisible** 55

Chapter 3 **Get Lost** 74

Chapter 4 **Start with Trust** 93

Chapter 5 **Know Your "Enough"** 113 p 115 ✓

Chapter 6 **Create Your Portfolio Career** 137

Chapter 7 **Be All the More Human (and Serve Other Humans)** 160

Chapter 8 **Let Go of the Future** 177

Conclusion **Fluxing Forward** 195

Discussion Guide 207
Notes 212
Acknowledgments 223
Index 228
About the Author 234

Change is inevitable. Growth is optional.
—JOHN C. MAXWELL

PREFACE

When was the last time change hit your life?

I'm guessing it was pretty recent. Most likely earlier today, at the latest perhaps yesterday. It may have been a big change, or it may have been small. It may have been a change you precipitated, or at least opted into, or it may have clobbered you out of nowhere, beyond your control. Schedule changes, job changes, changes in your family's health or well-being, organizational changes, environmental changes, political changes, changing expectations . . . it all hits close to home.

On the one hand, change is universal and inevitable. Regardless of your age, profession, culture, beliefs, traditions, goals, or anything else, change predates humans and has shaped the entirety of history. Indeed, the primary reason you're alive is because of it!

On the other hand, change is disorienting. Too often it leaves you feeling unmoored, reeling and adrift. Too much change hijacks your ability to show up to life fully today and influences how you perceive the future.

Humans really struggle with change, *especially* change we did not choose. We resist it, we fear it, and we mistakenly believe we can control it. The more you try to keep change at bay, the more it shows up and the harder it bangs on the door. Despite our best efforts to prevent it, change happens.

And it's not just change; it's today's ever-increasing *pace* of change too. Taken together, it can feel relentless and sometimes just a bit (or way, way, way) too much.

It feels like we should have hit peak change by now, no?

But the simple fact is: around every corner—whether that corner is this afternoon, next week, next quarter, next year, or next century—there is more change. The future is *not* more stability or more certainty. The future *is* more uncertainty, more unpredictability, and more unknowns.

To thrive in this world in flux, we need to radically reshape our relationship to uncertainty and flip the script (don't worry, you'll learn what this means) to sustain a healthy and productive outlook. *Flux: 8 Superpowers for Thriving in Constant Change* shows you how to do exactly this, and how to help others do so too. It is a book to be shared, revisited, and passed along when change hits yet again. It is not a book about "change management" or any one "kind" of change. Rather, it is about reorienting one's attitude towards uncertainty and the unknown, and learning to see every change as an opportunity, not a threat—today, tomorrow, and from here on out. In other words, *Flux* is a book for these times and all time.

Part personal guidebook, part strategic roadmap, and part blank canvas for discovery, *Flux* provides a refreshing, unconventional take on navigating change today and far into the future. Each of the eight Flux Superpowers helps you see differently, grounds you in your truth, and empowers you to thrive—no matter what changes come your way.

Whether you're leading an organization or a team, building or rethinking your career, forging new relationships, seeking peace, or simply feeling unsure about what to do next, you'll gain tools and insights for how to think, learn, work, live, and lead better with a Flux Mindset. *Flux* shows you how to slow down responsibly, identify what really matters, make wise decisions, and let go of the rest. *Flux* challenges your assumptions and expectations in ways that enable you to lean into the future with hope rather than fear, and with clarity and confidence anchored in what makes you, you.

Are you ready?

WHO MOVED MY FUTURE?

"April, are you sitting down?"

In the early evening of June 6, 1994, I was standing in the foyer of a rambling Victorian-era house in Oxford, England, home to a motley crew of students from around the world. I had spent the afternoon doing laundry and packing, preparing to lead a student trip for the summer. The sun dappled the window with a view to the garden. I had one more year of college and was so excited for this next adventure.

The voice on the phone was firmer this time: "April, I need you to sit down."

My sister had called out of the blue, from halfway around the world. We were not close, and I couldn't figure out why she would be calling. I had so many things I wanted to do before departure. Didn't she know that?

"April, Mom *and* Dad were killed in a car accident yesterday. You need to come home *now.*"

I sat down. My eyes glazed over. The ground gave way beneath me. I tried to scream, but nothing came out. Then I tried again, and it shook the house.

You might imagine where this story heads: my entire world was thrown upside down (or today I would say, it was thrown into flux). My roots were uprooted; my guiding lights went dark.

In that moment, time stood still: the future was going to be wildly different than I'd imagined, or than my parents imagined, or than it had looked a year earlier, or even an hour earlier.

In that moment, my sister and I were suspended in the unknown, not really knowing what to do next.

Never did I imagine that so many other people might someday feel like that.

OUR NEW-NOW-NEXT-NEVER NORMAL

Fast-forward to today: at home and around the world, it's an era to remember. Globally, we've witnessed the worst pandemic since 1918, some of the worst economic straits since the early 1930s, the greatest food insecurity in decades, and a climate catastrophe unprecedented in modern human history. In the United States, this is compounded by social tensions on a scale not seen since 1968. Any one of these crises is enough to shake things up. All of them happening at the same time . . . is something else entirely.

We're living in a world in flux. The workplace is in flux. Climate is in flux. Organizations are in flux. Careers are in flux. Education, learning, and schools are in flux. Public health is in flux. Planetary health is in flux. Social cohesion is in flux. Financial markets are in flux. Weather patterns are in flux. Family life is in flux. Democracy is in flux. Dreams are in flux. Expectations are in flux. And I have no doubt you could add several more examples to this list. The sheer scope of what's shifting and unknown is simultaneously awe-inspiring and downright daunting.

And it's not just *what* is changing; it's *how fast* the world we've known is evolving. The pace of change has never been as fast as it is today, and yet, it is likely to never again be this slow.[1] (Pause for a moment and let that sink in. I'll wait.)

The world feels upside down not just because of a pandemic, or a catastrophic natural disaster, or the upcoming academic year, or a job in limbo. This book isn't a magic wand that—*poof!*—makes these things disappear.

What is most in flux right now?

This is a simple exercise to get your creative flux juices flowing.

1. Without overthinking it, write a list of all the things that are upside down in your life right now. Think micro and macro, from small shifts in daily routines to future unknowns.
2. Rank them, if you'd like. Do you notice any common themes?
3. What emotions come up? Excitement, anxiety, curiosity, confusion . . . these are all equally valid.
4. Notice if different kinds of flux yield different responses, or if your responses change at different times.

Hold on to this list as you read this book.

This book *is* rooted in the simple fact that *around every corner, there is more change.* The future is *not* more stable; the future *is* more uncertain.

The future itself is in flux.

Humans are not accustomed to this degree of upside-downness. We can be incredibly adaptable when we're forced to be, but on the whole, we much prefer stability and familiarity. Even people who embrace chaos tend to do so knowing that they can rely on some things *not* changing. Yet if flux is our "new-now-next-never normal," then we need to be ready for—and have the tools to flourish in—this new reality. This book is designed to help you do just that.

WHAT THE FLUX?!

Flux is both a noun and a verb. As a noun, its most common contemporary definition is "continuous change."[2] As a verb, to flux means "to cause or learn to become fluid."[3] Hence we're living in a world of flux (noun), *and* we'd do well not merely to flex our mental muscles but to flux (verb) them too.

Take a moment to observe your life and the world today. In some ways, life is unfolding at warp speed. You had a life program and now it's stalled, or maybe gone. Your company had a strategy, your team had a plan, your family had a schedule . . . and it's been flipped on its head, overnight.

Yet in other ways, it's as though the world were standing still: paralyzed, unsure of what to do or what comes next. And it's not just the world: perhaps *you* feel stuck, frustrated, anxious, and in limbo too.

Taken together, this reality—of speeding up and slowing down simultaneously, of chronic uncertainty and unknowns—can be infuriating, disorienting, and unnerving. But do not despair: it's simply time to learn how to flux.

NOT ALL CHANGE IS CREATED EQUAL

To be sure, "change" is not one-size-fits-all. There are big changes and small changes, internal changes and external changes, personal changes and professional changes, family changes and company changes, changes in nature and changes in society. Changes can be completely visible or nearly imperceptible—yet still have significant effects. The same change can be marvelous for one person and miserable for another. You may love change in your personal life, while you may hate change in your workplace. Or vice versa. And of course, it may depend on changing circumstances.

There are many kinds of change that most people undertake willingly, even joyfully: entering a new relationship, moving to a new city, starting a family, trying a new sport, and so on. However, *choosing* to change is a very different experience than having change *imposed* externally. Decades ago, renowned family therapist Virginia Satir developed a five-stage model of change, which underscored the fact that humans typically go along with change *so long as it benefits us.*[4] We willingly embrace change when we're given a choice and we like the perceived results. Or, as systems thinker Peter Senge says, "We don't resist change. We resist *being changed.*"

But here is the hook: by and large, a world in flux is about those changes you *don't* get to choose. There is no opting in; they just happen, ready or not.

In an ideal world, of course, change is a choice, both individually and organizationally. If we're *really* lucky, we're prepared for it: it's expected change. But this kind of neat-and-tidy change that's easy to deal with and often even welcome reflects only a fraction of the changes we must grapple with today. What about the rest? That's what this book is about.

In a world in flux, we must learn to be comfortable with the reality that around the next corner is more change, much of which is unexpected, beyond our power to choose, or both. It's about a shift: from struggling with such change to *harnessing and developing an eagerness to use it well.*

THE THEORY OF FLUX

A world in flux did not magically show up one day. Change has been a universal constant since time immemorial. But our understanding of it, and how we've been taught to deal with it (or not), has evolved over time, driven largely by cultural norms, expectations, and available technologies.

As with most things in life, how we think about change is influenced by how we are socialized. Where, how, and with whom did you grow up? What were you taught to believe is important, and what was frowned upon? How were you taught to define success and failure? Were you taught to fear change or to embrace it?

Each and every one of us, for our entire lives, in some way has been following a script. There's not one script, of course: there are myriad scripts, each unique to your own experience, though this can be hard to remember sometimes—especially if you feel stuck inside your own head, just trying to get through the day as more change bangs on the door and walks in, uninvited.

Your script may be shaped by being part of an immigrant family or a family that's been in your hometown for generations. Your script may be shaped by immense privilege or by accidents of birth that are the opposite of privilege and set you up to have to work harder than other people. It may be shaped by chronic pain, or trauma, or perfect health. It may be shaped by a sense of belonging, or being chronically overlooked, or outright inequality. It may be shaped by living through war, times of peace, or an existential crisis.

Although each person's script is different, everyone's script is shaped by the same forces unfurling and the universal experience of being human. And with rare exceptions, your script is clear.

For many people, your script tells you to work hard and stay the course—whatever that "course" may be. It probably tells you to get good grades, go to a prestigious university, and get hired by a prestigious company. It may tell you to follow in your parents' footsteps. For a big subset of people, your script tells you that success is at the top of a corporate ladder, so you should climb it rung by rung and become CEO. Voilà: the definition of and recipe for "making it."

This script probably also teaches you that more is better, vulnerability is a sign of weakness, and the fastest person wins—so you should run fast. It may teach you to go where everyone else is—you need to fit in!—and that no one (other than perhaps blood family) can really be trusted.

Oftentimes, your script applauds you for acquiring money and toys. It usually doesn't pay more than passing attention to Mother

Earth or ancient wisdom, however, while it does tend to see new technologies as a sort of panacea.

In many ways this script cheers you on for achieving goals set by society. By and large it doesn't ask you what you want; it takes care of that for you. Perhaps you've tried to consult your inner voice about this, but your script drowned that out. In fact, for this script to work, your inner voice must be silent.

This script doesn't tell you everything, of course—especially when you're young. For example, it doesn't tell you that a corporate ladder can also be a kind of escalator that can trap you. When you want to get off the ladder, you find you're stuck: beneath student debt, mortgage payments, an expensive car lease to keep up with your colleagues, or your next promotion. It doesn't tell you that privilege is a head start up this escalator. It doesn't tell you why it's so hard for many people to get on this escalator or how many people desperately want to get off it.

In fairness, the script just painted is a bit of a stereotype, and that's intentional. (Another twist: until recently, this was overwhelmingly a man's script.) I get that reality is far more nuanced. But the point is: *every single person* has a script. And for quite some time this script held. It's been passed down so often that it's taken for granted.

And then.

And then, the way things worked flipped upside down. A world in flux arrived. Boom.

Some of this change has been creeping up for years, yet we've been (or pretended to be) blind to it. Some of it hit like a full-speed locomotive, an instantaneous body blow. Some of it may have been hard to grasp, even if your inner voice had long felt uneasy.

Whatever the case, the old scripts broke. Your script, my script, and many other people's scripts are no longer fit for today's world— or one could say, they *are* fit for a world that's no longer there. But even so, they have a really long tail. Old ways of being and seeing the world tend to stick around long after they've lost their utility. They're still in our consciousness, and we still make decisions according to outdated filters because we haven't actually swapped them out yet.

And this is where *Flux* comes in. *Individually and collectively, we are in the early stages of writing new scripts that are fit for a world in flux.*

While the old script was written by others for you to follow, your new script is written by you, for you to become. Your new script contains what grounds you and orients you and makes you, you—even when everything else changes.

The Theory of Flux reveals the relationships between your old and new scripts, specifically how to transform an old script into a new script that's fit for today's world of constant change. This theory can be summarized in three steps, each of which is explained below and shows up throughout the book:

Step 1: Open a Flux Mindset

Step 2: Use your Flux Mindset to unlock the eight Flux Superpowers

Step 3: Apply your Flux Superpowers to write your New Script

Remember: just as everyone's old script is unique, so will your new script reflect what is uniquely you. The Theory of Flux demonstrates how *you* can best groove a Flux Mindset and develop your Flux Superpowers to thrive, no matter what change comes your way.

MINDSET ORIGINS: NERVOUS SYSTEMS, ANXIETY, AND GROWTH

Before digging into a Flux Mindset, let's explore how one's mind gets "set." Where does one's mindset come from, and what drives it?

One answer comes from our neurobiology. We humans have two major nervous subsystems that work in tandem: the sympathetic and parasympathetic nervous systems. They regulate the same set of internal body functions, but they have opposite effects. The sympathetic nervous system controls what many people know as the "fight, flight, or freeze" response and prepares the body for intense action, while the parasympathetic nervous system seeks to calm the body, sometimes known as the "rest and digest" function.

Normally, the sympathetic and parasympathetic nervous systems work together as allies; each has a set of activities that it governs. At the risk of oversimplifying, if you're being chased by a tiger, the sympathetic nervous system takes over; if you're meditating, the parasympathetic nervous system is in charge. For most activities, however, a combination of the two is in play.

Our ever-accelerating world has thrown these systems out of balance. Specifically, we perceive ever more and more dangerous stimuli, which present ever more opportunities for the sympathetic nervous system to hijack our ability to respond appropriately. We are *not* being chased by tigers, but our bodies respond as if we were. Too many perceived tigers, and we lose the ability to calm down.

Today, it's not just our individual nervous systems that get hijacked. Anxiety is now manifest at every level: individual, organizational, and societal. Many people feel anxious about their careers, family, well-being, bank accounts, children's futures, or when the next calamity will strike. We have anxiety about our organizations' values, resilience, culture, competitive landscape, and how business is done. At the broadest level, there is enormous societal anxiety around global warming, inequality, intolerance, and injustice. Moreover, digital technologies are correlated with increases in anxiety: the mere presence of your own smartphone reduces your available cognitive capacity.[5]

Leaders today face an onslaught of very good reasons to feel anxious. In my experience, anxiety and concern are part of many if not most leaders' daily lives, even if they don't express them externally. And even if you don't personally self-identify as anxious, chances are extremely good that you have a colleague, friend, or family member who does.

I can relate. For the first forty-three years of my life, I didn't know what *not* being anxious felt like. (I realized this only when I was asked to recall my first anxiety-free memory and came up empty-handed.) Not only that, but the more "successful" I became by external standards, the more anxious I felt inside. It was a never-ending and self-sabotaging spiral.

The fear, confusion, and shame that I felt led me to research anxiety further. What I learned was sobering. Close to 10 percent of the world population suffers from diagnosable anxiety, costing the global economy an estimated $1 trillion each year.[6] In the United States, this figure rises to one in every four adults, while 63 percent of college students report having felt *overwhelming* anxiety in the last year.[7]

All of this was true *before* a pandemic, protests, natural disasters, lockdowns, disinformation, melting ice caps, social tensions, or take your pick of other shocks served to accelerate the loss of any sense of normalcy.

Of course, to some degree it is natural to feel anxious when the world is on edge. But if we're looking at a future of constant change, then we must treat this as a society-wide anxiety crisis: an unspoken epidemic, which many people don't want to believe so we don't talk about it, yet the statistics and lived experiences tell another story.

In my case, the wake-up call about my relationship to anxiety was also a catalyst to better understand my own fraught relationship to change. I had been digging into flux already, but this experience blew the doors open on my learning and growth. This is also where a Flux Mindset comes in. A Flux Mindset knows how to *flux* in a world *in flux*.

STEP 1: OPEN A FLUX MINDSET

The first step in putting the Theory of Flux into action is to open a Flux Mindset. A Flux Mindset sees change as an opportunity, not a threat, by being clear and grounded in your values.

As we've seen, change is universal, but one's experience of it is personal, contextual, and rooted in your script. For instance, you may love a change that someone else hates. Or what feels like change to you might feel like the status quo to someone else. Or a change that's easy for someone else might be really difficult for you, and vice versa.

The challenge today is that in a world in flux, a vast range of scripts are breaking. It's not just you: many, if not most, people are having to radically reassess this. We're still clinging to an old, outdated script, when what's actually needed is to write a new script. Opening a Flux Mindset is where and how you begin to do this.

You can think of a Flux Mindset as the state of mind, body, and spirit that grounds you and holds you when everything else changes. In practice, a Flux Mindset has several essential elements, including core values, comfort with paradox, and the ability to see uncertainty from a place of hope rather than fear. Keep in mind that these things play out at personal, organizational, team, community, and societal levels. While our primary focus is on *your personal relationship to change and your own script*—what grounds you?—we can also imagine, for example, cases of organizational flux in which a company's core values are tested. (We'll revisit these different layers of flux throughout the book.)

My own Flux Mindset took time and effort to develop. My Flux Mindset is rooted in an unwavering faith in humanity, which is related to a commitment to service and a deep, clear appreciation for diversity. (As you'll learn, these values go back to my childhood, though I still had to learn how to align them with my script.) So when change hits, for example, or I'm racked by uncertainty, I immediately look to the wisdom of *many different cultures* (not limited to the ones I was raised in), and I reach out to *help others.* These things don't automagically resolve my situation, but they do shape my relationship to change: other cultures help me see differently, including my expectations and goals, while serving others underscores humanity's interdependence and helps me better understand my life story in context. Both tend to fill me with hope and wonder, rather than fear. Both remind me that there is no one way to "do" change. And both underscore that an effective relationship with change always begins from within. (Again, we'll pick up these ideas throughout the book.)

Table 1 illustrates how some of the elements of a Flux Mindset play out more broadly. How do you typically see, or think about, these themes today? If any of these make a light bulb go off in your head, or trigger an intense reaction (good or bad), pay attention: that's a signal that tells you something about your current script and relationship to change. I call this your "fluxiness."

Flux Mindset: Oriented towards Change
A Flux Mindset builds on the concept of a growth mindset, developed by Stanford psychologist Carol Dweck more than thirty years ago and primarily applied to children's ability to learn. A growth mindset reflects "the understanding that abilities and intelligence can be developed." It is characterized by a belief that (1) you can get smarter, and (2) effort makes you stronger.[8] This understanding drives motivation and achievement in profound ways. But it doesn't address what happens when change hits. The Flux Mindset takes that step.

One of the key insights of a Flux Mindset—indeed, what gives it such tremendous power in today's world—is its grounding. With a Flux Mindset, you are so grounded in your values and your new script that when change jostles (or even clobbers) your world, you *can't help but* see it as an opportunity. Change is no longer

Table 1. Open a Flux Mindset

HOW DO YOU SEE	OLD MINDSET	FLUX MINDSET
Your life story	Written by others, for you to follow	Written by you, for you to become
Life	A ladder to climb	A flowing river
Career	A path to pursue	A portfolio to curate
Expectations	Determined externally, by others	Determined internally, by you
Goals	Set in concrete, yet hard to attain	Emergent and often blurry, yet rich with opportunity
Measurements of success	Rungs of the ladder	Next steps and new insights
Leadership	Manage and control other people, "me"	Unleash potential in others and yourself, "us"
Power	Top-down, guarded	Bottom-up, dispersed
Peers	Competitors	Allies and collaborators
Vision	Certainty	Clarity
Change	Threat	Opportunity
Emotions associated with change	Fear, anxiety, paralysis	Hope, wonder, curiosity

threatening; it is both expected and often welcomed.

Keep in mind that being grounded isn't just about what is beneath you or what you stand on. Being grounded means having both stability and clarity. Stability gives you courage and helps

Your Flux Mindset Baseline

"Finding" your Flux Mindset isn't as easy or obvious as you might think. If it were, I wouldn't have written this book, and you probably wouldn't be reading it. One place to start is by identifying your Flux Mindset Baseline.

This baseline is less a definition of your Flux Mindset than a diagnostic for your current relationship to change: your fluxiness. It is a tool to help guide you as you read this book, to help you see what triggers you (or not), and to identify which Flux Superpowers may be most helpful. Don't worry about getting the "right" answers; there are none. Rather, pay attention to whatever comes up—including "I don't know. I've never really thought about that before!"

Values / Inner Compass

- What gives you meaning and purpose? Has this changed over time, and if so, how?
- To whom and to what do you turn in times of uncertainty?
- To whom and to what are you committed, no matter what?
- What would "make you, you" if you were stripped of all your privilege?
- What would "make you, you" if your home and most cherished possessions burned up?

Reactions

- When something takes longer than expected, do you feel agitated, or do you appreciate the delay? (Chapter 1, Run Slower)
- If something can't be measured, does it exist? (Chapter 2, See What's Invisible)
- When you take a wrong turn and end up somewhere you've never been before (and had no intention of going), do you feel frustrated or intrigued by that new place? (Chapter 3, Get Lost)

- Can the average person be trusted? (Chapter 4, Start with Trust)
- When you give someone a gift, is that a loss or gain for you? (Chapter 5, Know Your "Enough")
- What would be your professional identity if you lost your job today? (Chapter 6, Create Your Portfolio Career)
- When your smartphone is out of reach for an entire day, do you feel jittery or peaceful? (Chapter 7, Be All the More Human)
- Who and/or what do you believe is in control of your life? (Chapter 8, Let Go of the Future)

And finally:

- What one word best describes your relationship to change today?

Hold on to whatever comes up now. Come back to these questions as you read the book. See whether and how your baseline changes.

you trust; clarity enhances your vision, guides your direction, and helps you focus. Both are part of your orientation, to change and the world. Your orientation includes what is around you, above you, and beyond you. It includes knowing where help is and where potential dangers lie. It is the basis of how you navigate: a day, a situation, a new place, a delicate conversation, or change in the world at large.

Consider for a moment how different cultures have learned to orient and navigate. For example:

- For centuries, the North Star and Southern Cross have helped explorers orient and guided their journeys. What is your North Star or Southern Cross in times of flux?

- Seafaring cultures learn how to read horizons, decipher clouds, and track waves. There is no "ground" to speak of, yet these sailors are intimately oriented with their surroundings. How do you surf the waves of change?

- In yoga philosophy, *drishti* is a focused gaze whose purpose is to develop concentration and keep your balance. The object of your *drishti* can be a dot on the wall, an object on the floor, or a pinpoint on the horizon. What is your *drishti* in a world in flux?

The North Star is above you. The horizon is beyond you. Your *drishti* is in front of you. None of these things is defined by physical land, yet they all *orient* you to your landscape and *ground* you within it.

When we get overwhelmed, we often feel *disoriented*. We lose our bearings, direction, and perspective. The more change hits, the easier it is to "lose your way"—and often the harder it is to find your way back.

Think of a Flux Mindset as your newly minted **compass for change**: it grounds you, orients you, and guides you when everything around you is moving. It's your North Star, *drishti*, surfboard, and terra firma all at once. It is grounded in your core values, reflects your true self, and enables you to be yourself whatever changes may come.

If you're wondering, "So what do I *do* about my Flux Mindset?," you're in the right place. Keep reading.

STEP 2: UNLOCK YOUR FLUX SUPERPOWERS

Once you've begun to open a Flux Mindset, or at least opened yourself to the idea that it's time to forge a healthier relationship to change, you may be feeling antsy. Now what?

The next step in putting the Theory of Flux into action is to use your Flux Mindset to unlock the Flux Superpowers: the essential disciplines and practices that are fit for a world in flux, applied and integrated into your life.

The eight Flux Superpowers are:

1. Run Slower
2. See What's Invisible
3. Get Lost
4. Start with Trust
5. Know Your "Enough"
6. Create Your Portfolio Career
7. Be All the More Human (and Serve Other Humans)
8. Let Go of the Future

Each of the Flux Superpowers helps you *see* change in new ways, develop new *responses* to change, and ultimately reshape your *relationship* to change. Together, they help you live your life with hope rather than fear, wonder rather than anxiety, and curiosity rather than paralysis. As each chapter makes clear, each superpower is useful on its own, *and* together they amplify each other.

In many cases, you already have these superpowers (or at least the seeds of them) within you. But they are often hidden, buried, or invisible. They have been socialized out of you by forces, people, and institutions defending the old script. With a Flux Mindset, it's now time—and eminently possible—to uncover, rediscover, and apply them. Table 2, on the following page, provides a closer look.

The Flux Superpowers are like a Japanese bento box for the mind: each superpower is an exquisite, nutritious delicacy that can be consumed (practiced) on its own, and together the superpowers provide a nourishing, delicious full meal. Each superpower underscores your fluxiness in different and complementary ways. They represent a menu, not a syllabus.

Table 2. Scripts, Habits, and Superpowers

OLD SCRIPT / OLD HABITS	NEW SCRIPT / FLUX SUPERPOWERS
Run Faster	Run Slower
Focus on What's Visible	See What's Invisible
Stay in Your Lane	Get Lost
Trust Nobody	Start with Trust
More = Better	Know Your "Enough"
Get a Job	Create Your Portfolio Career
Technology Knows Best	Be All the More Human (and Serve Other Humans)
Predict and Control the Future	Let Go of the Future

For most people, certain Flux Superpowers will be easier (and harder) than others to develop, depending on what you bring to the table and the nature of your script. Similarly, each Flux Superpower can hold different weight for each person at different times in their life. For someone struggling with burnout, for example, learning how to run slower will likely be more important at the outset, while someone struggling with feeling out of control may wish to focus on letting go of the future. (As you learn to run slower, you'll become more adept at letting go, and vice versa.) Regardless, none of the Flux Superpowers requires anything you don't already have within you: no fancy technology, no genius IQ, not even an app.

The relationship between the Flux Superpowers and Flux Mindset is similar to a hub-and-spoke structure: the Flux Mindset is the hub, and the eight Flux Superpowers radiate from it (see

Figure 1. Flux Mindset and Flux Superpowers

Figure 1). The superpowers exist independently of one another, yet they are connected through the hub. When your Flux Mindset is opened, the Flux Superpowers can get to work.

Perhaps you've already noticed that there's an unconventional twist to this: the Flux Superpowers are superpowers only if you have opened a Flux Mindset and believe that a new script is your best path forward. If you are stuck in the old script, then you will see the Flux Superpowers as liabilities, or unhinged somehow. You will say that to run slower is to be lazy, or to let go of the future is to give up. But this is not what the new script says at all.

Similarly, the new script does *not* say that you should never run fast or use technology at times. Nor does it imply that jobs don't have merit or that we shouldn't work hard. These charges take the Theory of Flux entirely out of context.

Rather, the new script—and by extension, the Theory of Flux—recognizes that we've been running far too long and too fast after things without stopping to consider whether doing so is wise or sustainable, or what we really even want. What are you running after, and why? Whose goals are you working towards, and do they truly reflect your best self?

The Flux Superpowers don't manifest in the ways we've typically been taught, because they are part of a new, emerging script. But Flux Superpowers are just as much disciplines as their erstwhile counterparts, the Old Habits (that die hard). There is just as much (and some would say, far more) discipline involved in running slower than running ever faster on the hamster wheel. There is just as much (and again, some would say even more) discipline in letting go as in hanging on to assumptions that are past their prime. Peace is not passivity. These aha's can be jarring, especially if you've got the old script etched in your mind. But with a new script, look out, world!

So let's talk about that new script now, shall we?

STEP 3: WRITE YOUR NEW SCRIPT

The third and final step of putting the Theory of Flux into action is to apply your Flux Superpowers to write your New Script. Your new script enables you to transform your relationship to change and bring your best self to the world.

Just as each person's old script is unique, based on each individual's life experience, so will your new script reflect what is uniquely you. That's one of the most exciting things about your new script: *only you* can write it! No one can write it for you, and no one can write the same script as you. It's a custom fit!

I can't predict exactly what your new script will say, but here are a few ways in which I often see Flux Superpowers translate into new scripts that are superadapted for a world in flux:

- When you learn to run slower, you begin to crave a calmer pace. Silence becomes a friend.

- When you learn to see what's invisible, you discover marvelous new universes of opportunity—and that the old script made you blind to things you genuinely care about.

- When you learn to get lost, you begin to feel delight when things *don't* go according to plan, when plans change, or when you have no clue what will happen next.

- When you learn to start with trust, you yearn for more trust. You're better equipped to earn trust and allow others' trustworthiness to shine through.

- When you know your "enough," you begin living in abundance and take better care of yourself and others.

- When you learn to create a portfolio career, you immediately stop seeing work merely as "having (or getting) a job." You no longer fret about losing a job and can position yourself confidently towards the future of work.

- When you learn to be fully, wholeheartedly human, your relationships with other people (and your mental health, and your sleep) improve. You're finally able to recalibrate your relationship with technology too.

- When you learn to let go of the future, you find it looks brighter than ever.

Sounds pretty awesome, doesn't it? And that's not all.

Over time, these things—your new script, your Flux Superpowers, and your Flux Mindset—mutually reinforce one another. The more you develop one, the stronger and clearer the others become. You might think of this along the lines of 1+1=11.

The more you practice and hone your Flux Superpowers, the better you groove your Flux Mindset. By nurturing and cultivating your Flux Mindset, the more you can put your Flux Superpowers to full use.

I like to think of your Flux Mindset as a booster rocket for your life and your relationship to change. Your Flux Superpowers are rocket fuel. Both things are essential to bring your new script to life. They work in tandem: offering a never-ending, ever-evolving, incredibly exciting (and even out-of-this-world) journey through flux.

So whether you're sizing up your career or taking a hard look at your values, rethinking a product design, leading an entire organization's transformation, trying to inspire your colleagues, or simply trying to show up more fully in the world, applying your Flux Superpowers to write your new script empowers you to *flux better*.

MY JOURNEY TO FLUX

Ever since that pivotal June afternoon when my sister called, I've been fascinated by how we adapt to change: individually, organizationally, and societally. My crash course in grief included anxiety and panic attacks, as well as rebuilding my life and finding meaning—all different ways of adapting to change. Later I was exposed to futurism and complexity theory, which also seek to better understand and adapt to change . . . yet whose starting points are a world away from grief. Through it all, I continued to find inspiration and insight through travel, through learning about other cultures and what connects us: our shared humanity. I began to layer, mix, and blend insights from very different places.

My starting point was bumpy, to say the least. Shortly after my parents' deaths, I developed an irrational-yet-fundamentally-real fear that I had less than a year to live. If the two people closest to me had disappeared without warning, why wouldn't that happen to me too—or anyone? And if I were to die tomorrow, would my existence on this earth have mattered? Never mind that I was twenty: it might as well have been a full-blown midlife crisis.

Less than two years after my parents died, I graduated from college, which threw me into yet another kind of tailspin: it was time to enter the "real world" (as if I hadn't had enough reality) and make something of myself. Not only that, I had to fulfill my parents' wishes for me and honor their legacy. I had to know exactly what I was supposed to do and then do it to perfection: beyond what they or anyone else could imagine. I felt like I had to do all of this as quickly as possible, too, because I might die tomorrow.

Right?

I was so wrong.

As we'll explore in the coming chapters, in many ways this time in my life planted the seeds for *Flux*. When my parents died, I had a grand total of zero Flux Superpowers, and my Flux Mindset was anything but open. I ran a massive flux deficit. I was tightly wound in the old script and didn't know many people who had written their own new scripts. My parents were open-minded, and even a bit rebellious, but they were living their own old scripts too.

My relationship to change—and especially, opening my Flux Mindset—has improved as I've experienced change from more directions. When my parents died, enormous change was thrust on me: life changes, family changes, future changes. I had no choice: I had to deal with these upheavals, like it or not, difficult or not,

The new script for leadership in flux

If you're reading this book, you're likely both a leader and a seeker. But what kind of leader?

The old script has a fairly narrow definition of leadership: leaders are the people at the top of the ladder. Leaders manage, direct, command, and often control the actions of others. Leaders are expected to have answers, hold power firmly, and pursue the spotlight. In a business setting, leaders crush the competition.

But in a world in flux, and with a new script in hand, what makes a good leader discernibly changes—in terms of both hallmark characteristics and who qualifies as a leader. Being a "great leader" under the old script is no guarantee of great leadership when the world flips upside down. In fact, the old skills can be handicaps. It all depends on your relationship to change: your ability to lead *yourself and others* in, through, and beyond flux.

For example, a 2019 study by Leaders on Purpose found that the top leadership skill needed today is comfort with risk and ambiguity. The best leaders can live with, navigate, and trust ambiguity in ways that others can't.[9] In other words, great leadership in flux seeks the opposite of certainty. Rather, the goal is clarity of vision, which also means knowing when to take leaps of faith that defy old-script metrics.

Moreover, the new script makes it clear that many people are leaders, not just those making their way towards the top of the ladder. Leadership in a world in flux can come from any direction: it is not confined to the top. It harnesses the principles of "new power" of networks, ecosystems, and collective wisdom.[10] (Remember: The strongest node in a network isn't the biggest, fanciest, oldest, or most credentialed one. It's the *most connected* one.) Flux leaders seek to lead *with* others, not lead *by* themselves.

For example, Greta Thunberg would fail almost all old-script leadership metrics: she's young and scrappy, and cares little about what other people think. However, her clarity of vision about catastrophic climate change and her desire to galvanize others—not for her own benefit, but to achieve a collective goal—make her the kind of leader that the new script understands.

To get started assessing your own flux leadership capacity, and how you may wish to improve it, here are a few fire-starter questions:

On a scale of 1 to 10, how would you rate your personal ability to lead in flux today? How would your best friend?

Do you tend to think in terms of "me" or "we"?

How do you feel about sharing power with others?

How would you rate your organization's ability to flux? Are certain topics trigger points? Are select people, teams, or departments fluxier than others?

Five (or two, or ten) years from now, what kind of leader or seeker do you want to be? Of what kind of organization?

Keep these answers nearby as you read this book.

tragic or not. My Flux Mindset began to crack open. Since that time, I have also sought out change, sensed change coming, and witnessed change in myself and many others. Each of these experiences has taught me that *every "kind" of change, welcome or not, opens one's Flux Mindset further.* The more change is thrown your way, the stronger your Flux Mindset can become—if you lean into it.

As my Flux Mindset cracked open, I began to consider my Flux Superpowers. It felt overwhelming. I had *so much* to learn. So I opted to focus first on the superpower I couldn't ignore: how to let go of the future. Losing my parents also meant losing what I thought my future would look like . . . until it didn't. But gradually, as the years passed, I started experimenting and imagining and talking to new people, and in the process began to see just how poorly my old script fit my personality. I began to paint a different picture of my future: different career paths, different priorities, different ways of being. When society said turn right, I learned to listen to my inner voice—which often nudged me to turn left.

Mind you, there was no perfect science to this back then—nor is there today. But the more I practiced, the better I got. Today, I can paint dozens of different pictures of my future (or any future!). And yet, as only one future ultimately unfolds, I've become adept at letting go of the rest (which is to say, most possible futures and most of the time).

Around the same time, I began testing my luck with trust and getting lost. There is nothing like senseless tragedy to feel like the world can't be trusted. Yet what kind of future would it be to live trapped in fear and mistrust? Not the future I wanted. So I started digging into my old script again and realized I had trust backwards. I started cracking open—both to heal my bruised heart and to see if trust *just. might. work.* I have never looked back. (As you'll see, starting with trust does not mean naive trust, nor does it mean things go according to plan. It simply sets a different default that allows you to greet change with confidence.)

My ability to get *really, really* lost got a jump-start thanks to two forces: emotions and travels. My parents' deaths were the first deaths I'd ever known. My first funeral was theirs. Emotionally, I was in over my head without a compass, roadmap, *drishti*, or whatever else. Day by day, I learned new ways to gain my bearings, from journaling to discovering wonder (rather than fear) in the depths of my soul. Later, as I ventured from one far-flung corner of the planet to another, I found wonder (rather than fear) in not knowing who I would meet on any given day or where I would rest my head that evening. Time and again, I saw that we create fear, or make fear go away, depending on the stories we tell ourselves.

Today, more than two decades later, I have a portfolio career that reflects my new script. Developing this superpower took quite a few iterations. However, although my career journey has been unconventional by most metrics—one might characterize it as jumping off a new professional cliff every few years—my guiding, and *grounding*, question remains the same: *If I were to die tomorrow, what would the world need me to do today?*

(This question comes with an added bonus: each year on my birthday, I still marvel that I am alive.)

Other superpowers took longer to identify and hone. I'm still working on every Flux Superpower every day. Writing my new script is a lifelong quest. But I've learned that although nothing is certain, I'm probably *not* going to die tomorrow . . . so what better quest to invest in for life?

YOUR ROADMAP TO FLUX

Over the past twenty-five-plus years, I've had numerous opportunities to reflect on my own journey to flux—not least, what tends to work and what doesn't—and to guide others through change too. A few observations and insights tend to stick out. I think of these things as landmarks for navigating your own change landscape and writing a new, flux-forward script: your roadmap to flux.

- **Values come from many places.** One's faith, commitment to service, dedication to a cause beyond individual self-interest or "winning," and love of children and humankind are all frequently cited.

- **Your relationship to change begins within.** Many people get their relationship to change backwards. They focus on "change management strategies" or "investing in uncertainty" in the external world. Yet they fail to recognize that every single strategy, investment, or decision you make fundamentally depends on, and is filtered by, your internal world: *your mindset.* (Do you see change from a place of hope or fear? That's not strategy; that's mindset.) Take care of the internal part first—that is, your relationship to change—and the external dynamics make sense and have clarity they lacked before.

- **No one except you can write your new script, nor can you write anyone else's script for them.** There's a lot we can learn from one another, especially those who have already written their new script, but no one can ever be "fully you" except you.

- **Learning to flux is exhilaratingly hard work.** It pays off, for you *and* the world, in more ways than perhaps anything else you'll ever do.

Life will give you plenty of opportunities to practice opening your Flux Mindset and developing your Flux Superpowers. Don't overthink things: start with whatever change-related challenge is facing you at the moment. And no matter what, remember: these aren't skills just for today, or just this year, or just the issue that flipped your world upside down yesterday. These are superpowers you can harness *forever.*

HOW TO READ THIS BOOK

The structure of *Flux* is simple: each chapter is a Flux Superpower. You can read these chapters in whatever order you wish; from beginning to end works well, though it is not required. You'll find references to the other superpowers throughout, so head wherever your curiosity pulls you. Each chapter contains exercises and questions to help you develop and practice a given superpower, strengthening your Flux Mindset and seeding your new script in the process. At the end of each chapter are five questions that distill key themes and provide a pause for additional reflection.

This book enriches our language by offering a nascent lexicon for flux. Your new script and the Theory of Flux are part of this foundation. Constant change, an ever-faster pace of change, and navigating unknowns are things many people have been *feeling*, but on the whole we still lack a rich vocabulary to talk about them. Of course, simply defining a problem doesn't solve it, but it's hard to surface a meaningful conversation about something if we don't have the right words. This book serves to raise awareness and spark discussions about learning to flux, together.

Flux is the term of our times and of the future. *Flux* is also a book for our times and for the future. May it help you and everyone whose lives you touch.

CHAPTER 1

RUN SLOWER

Human beings run faster when we've lost our way.
—ROLLO MAY

Take your pick of reasons to run. New and unexpected change happens every week, if not multiple times a day. It could be a new schedule that disrupts a routine that took ages to get right. Or a team that's behind schedule. Or a time-sensitive opportunity on the horizon. Or not knowing how long you can make your rent payments. Or worrying about your safety. Or your family's or friends' safety. Or a melting planet.

Should you walk, sprint, or simply stay put?

Individuals and organizations alike are struggling to answer this question. In the workplace, human resources leaders often argue that when uncertainty looms, it's necessary to "fire fast." When you're not sure where revenue will come from, one of the easiest things to do is reduce your team. After all, salaries are the single-largest line item for most organizations' budgets.

Yet if we dig into the research, we learn that the opposite is true: since 1980, companies that delay layoffs as long as possible perform better over time than companies that fire fast.[11] Why?

It turns out that not only is top talent hard to replace, but layoffs are devastating to the morale and productivity of the team that remains.[12] Organizations that place economic efficiencies over fundamental fairness end up showing their true cards. Values and trustworthiness are hard to recoup.

The lesson here is not that layoffs should never be made or that we should never take swift action. It's that responding quickly doesn't necessarily mean responding wisely. In a world in flux, fastest doesn't always finish first.

THE SUPERPOWER: **RUN SLOWER**

To thrive in a fast-paced world, slow your own pace.

In an upside-down world that coaxes, cajoles, and coerces you to run ever faster, your key to true success and growth is to do the opposite: learn how to run *slower*.

The old script says we must run faster to keep up. But a world in flux has different race conditions because the finish line keeps shifting. Whether it's business demands, home and family priorities, responsibilities to juggle, relationships to nurture, or relentless uncertainty to decipher: the faster we run, and the more we run without resting or reflecting or even paying attention, the worse our results will be over time.

Yet for most people, running faster remains our default. We're stuck in the old script, and it does not bode well. Especially if we're running faster alone.

When we learn to run slower, the outcomes are better across the board: wiser decisions, less stress, greater resilience, improved health, a stronger connection with our emotions and intuition, presence, focus, and clarity of purpose. Paradoxically, slowing down actually gives us *more* time, which leads to less anxiety. Slowing down enhances our productivity in ways that matter and sends burnout to the dustbin. In reality, there are *many kinds of growth that can come only with rest.*

It took me ages to learn to run slower. For much of my life, I ran as fast as I could: towards goals set by others, away from things I feared, but without giving much thought to why. When my parents died, I wanted to run as fast as I could away from the situation . . . and yet I didn't. I stood my ground, and that began my practice of this superpower. It would take many more years to really understand the dynamics of what was unfolding, both internally and in my relationship with the outside world.

Today I can run much slower than I used to, though there's still plenty of room for improvement. Through trial, error, and deliberate practice, I've learned to cherish the power of the pause. I'm more present and less anxious. It's humbling to admit, but I can see so many things that I simply ran past before. Some things I used to fear have even become sources of joy.

To be clear, running slower does not mean stopping, laziness, stagnation, lack of purpose, or (perhaps the most startling objection) not caring. Nor can it be solved by merely taking a vacation, downloading an app, or seeking a "one-and-done" quick fix (ironically, this will bring a world of misery because what you seek to "fix" is constantly changing). In reality, running slower means plenty of motion and inquiry—at a sustainable pace. It means caring enough to quiet the mind and focus on what really matters.

Of course, there are times when running faster is the right thing to do: swerving to avoid oncoming traffic and signing up for a pandemic vaccination are two things that come to mind. And when we're in the flow—completely immersed in what we're doing—we may feel as if we're more alive, moving and thinking faster than ever.

But on the whole, we are hampered and harmed far more often by our minds racing when we'd rather be calm. We spend our time in constant pursuit of expectations set by others, then wonder where our time (and our hopes, dreams, and desires) went.

We are running chronically ever faster and, in so doing, running right past life itself. But it doesn't have to be this way, and right here is where to start.

How fast are you running?

This is a two-part exercise. First, answer the following honestly:

Do you feel like you're running too fast?

From whom or where does your "need for speed" come?

If you slowed down enough to shift your attention, what do you think you'd discover?

If you knew that you'd die tomorrow, for what purpose or towards whom would you run?

Bonus question: Did you have difficulty "pausing" long enough to do this exercise?

Second, on a piece of paper, draw four concentric circles (like a target with a bull's-eye) and label them as follows:

The inner circle is **your personal quest**: your relationship with yourself, your personal goals, and how you wish to show up in life.

The second circle is **your personal relationships**: with friends, family, and loved ones.

The third circle is **your role(s) in organizations**: your professional responsibilities, expertise, colleagues, etc.

The outer circle is **your role(s) in the world**: for example, as a citizen, a consumer, a climate advocate, a traveler, etc.

Jot down where you're running too fast. Which circles do they fall within? Are any circles empty?

Next, write why. Where does the desire to run too fast come from? Are you driving yourself to do more, or are others driving you? When did the pressure to run faster begin? (Did you notice it at that time?) You might also jot down your typical coping mechanisms and whether they have helped.

Now look at the whole picture. Which areas of your life need to slow down most? Do any of them feel easier to handle than others?

Finally, consider who else could benefit from this exercise—colleagues, family members, and so on—and share it with them.

THE OLD SCRIPT AT WARP SPEED

In 2010, researchers at Harvard University revealed that 47 percent of our waking hours are spent thinking about what *isn't* going on.[13] At the time, smartphones were only three years old. We were just beginning to adjust to mobile devices that within a decade would become not only our telephones but our televisions, teachers, bank tellers, transportation providers, food procurers, travel agents, dating services, laundromats, confession booths, and so much more. And yet each of these apps, each button on your smartphone, is another distraction: another opportunity to veer your thoughts elsewhere, away from the magic of life unfolding right in front of you.

Today our on-demand economy has exploded, along with insta-everything expectations, 24/7 lifestyles, and the perception of being "always on." Today, we take it for granted that Amazon will deliver the next day, if not sooner; we hail a car to pick us up and get frustrated if it takes longer than three minutes; and we outsource tasks in the spirit of "optimizing" our lives by saving five minutes. Never mind that this activity used to bring us joy or in contact with family or friends; it's far better to preserve that time for being "productive."

But here's the rub: we're miserable from all this running. Millennials are dubbed the Burnout Generation, having internalized the idea—which is reinforced by society, our education system, and often our peers and parents—that our self-worth is directly derived from how much we work. Thus, we should be working *all the time.*[14]

Yet Millennials are the tip of the iceberg. Executives and managers report ever-increasing demands on their time. Leaders are concerned about the well-being of their teams at the same time that they're under pressure (and rewarded) to prioritize quarterly returns over long-term health. Teachers have more to teach, to more students, with more difficult circumstances and fewer resources year after year. Ministers, caregivers, and others committed to service are totally spent. Parents "optimize" their children's playtime. The list goes on.

The seed of this problem is planted when we're young and told that we can, and should, "do it all." (This is often a nuance of the old script.) On the one hand, this message encourages ambition and achievement: great! At the same time, it leaves you feeling forever as though you're falling short: you don't do enough, earn enough, or have enough. (More on this in chapter 5, Know Your "Enough.") The implicit message is: *You're not enough.* So keep going and run faster.

This leads to a kind of internal persecution: not that you're not capable, but that if you just work harder, *you can be better at everything!* Paradoxically, this message results in what psychoanalyst Josh Cohen calls "a strange composite of exhaustion and anxiety, a permanent state of dissatisfaction with who we are and what we have. And it leaves us feeling that we are servants rather than masters of . . . the unending work we put into achieving our so-called best selves."[15]

While each person's life circumstances are unique, this run-ever-faster reality is pervasive across contemporary culture. Women and men alike aspire to "have it all" and "make it." You're running fast to keep up with monthly bills or your neighbors' display of wealth (real or not), while your neighbors are doing the same thing. The crux is: all this running is unsustainable and making us crazy, yet somehow we can't seem to stop. But nobody else is going to stop the merry-go-round.

There's an inextricable link between your ability to slow down and your ability to thrive. Yet this is an increasingly fraught balance to strike because we inhabit a world—a system—that is *designed,* intentionally or not, to thwart our doing so.

YOU ARE NOT A TO-DO LIST

But it doesn't have to be this way. Even better, not every place or culture is hell-bent on running faster and always-doing. Have you ever considered not-doing?

Not-doing doesn't mean merely not working. We often lump activities like meditation and journaling in a sort of "doing nothing" bucket. But these things are very much "doing": you're engaged, occupied, thinking. When I say not-doing, I mean really *doing nothing*. No specific action, no distractions, no goals. And importantly, trusting that the sky will not come crashing down. In fact, it might even be lighter and brighter when you actually stop to appreciate it.

Niks, Anyone?

In the Netherlands, *niksen* is the socially acceptable and culturally celebrated concept of not-doing.[16] The term literally means "to do nothing," or to do something specifically without any productive purpose. It's about "daring to be idle."[17]

The benefits of *niksen* are profound. Dutch researchers have found that people who regularly *"niks"* have lower anxiety, improved immune systems, and even an enhanced ability to come up with new ideas and solve problems.[18] The key is to *niks* regularly (even two minutes a day is a start), without intention and without considering whether it's productive.

> Doing nothing often leads to the very best of something.
> —WINNIE THE POOH

Wu Wei

Chinese Buddhism has embraced the concept of *wu wei* (無爲), meaning "lack of exertion" or "action through least action," since 700 BCE.[19] *Wu wei* is central to the philosophy of Taoism. *Wu wei* is different from *niksen* in that its goals are clearly strategic: it's a sort of selective passivity that focuses on adjusting ourselves to a given situation rather than frantically seeking to control it. *Wu wei* can be achieved only when you've slowed down enough to truly gauge the situation at hand.

Wu wei is often compared to being "in the zone" or a state of flow. It's like water, trees, or moss. Not only do these things bend, mold, and adjust themselves to the shape of their surroundings—wind, rock, or soil—but their strength and resilience comes from a slow-growth process. Their power comes from not rushing.

When my parents died, my world simultaneously ground to a halt and tripled in speed. On the one hand, there were so many things to figure out; on the other hand, time stood still. There was nothing to do and everything to do. I was faced with a gaping hole that I could fill with busyness, or with grief.

In retrospect, the most helpful thing I "did" was not-doing. As a young person who wanted nothing more than to graduate and "get going" with life, taking a semester off and an extra year to graduate was hard. Friends graduated while I grieved. My sister, Allison, did even better: she put an indefinite X through her calendar (which ended up lasting almost two years). Allison and I stood in the thick, tragic truth of our situation and re-rooted, each in our own ways given our respective life experiences. We didn't distract ourselves; we dug into our souls, and that made all the difference.

In the twenty-five-plus years since then, the world has sped up while humanity's ability to slow down and not-do has stalled. In the face of collective anxiety and doubt worldwide, the best thing we can do is incorporate *not-doing* into our lives. This can mean pausing, daydreaming, or sitting still. It's the simple yet profound act of holding yourself in the great space that is the unknown, in order to discover what you've been running too fast to become.

Not-doing is when you overcome all things.
—LAO TZU

PRODUCTIVITY: FOR WHAT AND FOR WHOM?

Somehow, a lot of people have landed in a world of exhaustion with a resounding thud. All too often, work is allowed to fill whatever time we give it. Why?

Technology certainly is one culprit, affording insta-always connectivity in our pockets. Meanwhile, contemporary mass-market consumerism and free-market capitalism fuel notions of never having enough, being enough, and—by extension—working hard enough. That's how consumerism thrives: *by making sure we never see ourselves as enough.* Yet whether you accept this messaging, indeed *if you even see it,* is a function of your mindset. Are you questioning this system, or are you too busy hustling on its hamster wheel to notice that you may be running right past life?

My path to running slower has been circuitous and perplexing at times. I have gotten much better at it and recognize it is a lifelong practice. But for a long time, I had more questions than answers.

In the immediate aftermath of my parents' accident, I was torn in two directions. On the one hand, I wanted to *run as fast as I could* away from what had happened. On the other hand, I'd been stopped in my tracks and brutally reminded of the fragility of life. Should I run faster into life, because mine could end soon too? Or should I hit the pause button and get clear about exactly what I was running towards, away from, or for?

I opted for the latter, despite some mentors encouraging me to stay the course, go straight to graduate school, or get a job at a consulting firm or a bank. From their perspective, I was credentialed and primed to get my career underway pronto. Ready, set, go!

Yet I also could not stop wondering: *What are we racing for? And why?*

The old script was all around me. Not only did I feel the pressure to conform personally, I saw my peers rushing to climb the corporate ladder. And I kept second-guessing what my parental sounding board might have said. Would I build something I truly believed in, or was I destined to be a cog in a wheel of someone else's dream? Would I choose my path, or would it be chosen for me?

At twenty-two, I wanted nothing more than to contribute to the world, especially in ways that would have made my parents proud. But how could I do that without knowing what really mattered to me—and how could I do that without slowing down enough to take stock of the question?

The insights of this story extend far beyond my situation, though here's how things played out back then: I skipped Wall Street and landed a job researching and guiding hiking and biking trips, beginning in Italy and progressing from there. For almost four years, I traveled with a backpack and without a permanent address, fueled by insatiable curiosity to understand how the rest of the world lives. I got into crazy trouble, learned firsthand about global development, and earned a black belt in cultural diplomacy and self-sufficiency. I earned far less than I would have on Wall Street, but I spent far less too. I lived at the pace of wherever I was, and my entire future changed as a result.

Learning to run slower precisely when society told me to run faster made all the difference. It felt risky to pause, with my irrational-yet-full-blown fear that I might die tomorrow. But it felt far riskier to not even try. Ever since that time and continuing to this day, I regularly ask myself and have asked hundreds of others: *If you were on your deathbed tomorrow, what would you wish you'd done?* No one has *ever* answered, *Run faster.*

Keep in mind, this isn't just about how this plays out for you or me individually. Collectively, the push to run faster is also destroying the planet. We're caught in a never-ending cycle of rushing, producing, consuming, and grasping for more. In this quest, we're burning ourselves out *and* burning ourselves up.

The faster we produce and consume goods, the more we damage the environment. The more we look for happiness and satisfaction outside ourselves—a new car, a new dress, almost anything that allows us to "buy and display our way out of sadness," as psychology professor Tim Kasser says—the more likely we are to be depressed.[20] We're taught to consume, consume, consume—and please don't think about the side effects, thank you very much.

Yet did you know that before marketing ate the word, to consume meant to *destroy*, as in "consumed by fire," and to *squander*, as in "to spend wastefully?"[21]

For today's leaders, the stakes of running fast are high. At risk is not only one's well-being, business success, and health of the economy. The survival of earth's life-support systems and the welfare of future generations are up for grabs as well. Against this backdrop, learning to run slower could solve a lot of other problems too. It's almost completely at odds with the old script, yet it's our best shot at staving off collapse.

INSTEAD OF PRODUCTIVITY, OPTIMIZE FOR PRESENCE

There is a better way to rethink our relationship to productivity, sustainability, and a world in flux. And guess what? It's right in front of us, and it's part of the new script.

For starters: imagine for a moment that rather than optimizing for productivity, we optimized for presence. (Lest you worry this sounds a bit woo-woo for your business, career, or lifestyle, I assure you it is not.) Allow me to explain.

The old script is obsessed with optimizing for speed, efficiency, and productivity. If you can shave five seconds off your daily routine, or cram one more call into a jam-packed afternoon, that's victory. The more meetings one can have, the greater one's sense of worth or self-importance. Keep busy! Success! Progress!

For a long time, even after I'd started writing my new script, I didn't question this busyness. I went along with it, on extra-busy days even joyfully. But the more I observed, the more undeniable the disconnect was. And when I slowed down to deepen my observation, I was dumbfounded. Hold on: What are we *really* doing? How in the world have we persuaded one another—and ourselves—that more meetings will somehow make our legacy more important? How have we convinced ourselves that saving five minutes will somehow save our soul?

With the new script, rather than measure meetings, you can gauge presence: your ability to be *fully in* a moment, experience, or decision. One meeting in which everyone is fully present is worth more than a thousand meetings in which people are distracted.

Ultimately, presence is about attention and response. These things are different yet closely related: you respond to what you're paying attention to. When you're running fast, you're unable to pay full attention. When you're scattered, you pay attention to the wrong things, which often botches your response. For example, you may respond out of fear rather than love, or contempt rather than compassion, or shut down a conversation that would otherwise ignite your curiosity. In short, you bungle both the question and the answer. When the problem is misunderstood—or worse, missed completely as we race past—the solutions will continue to elude all of us.

And yet, the crux of the solution is simple: slowing down improves your chances of getting the issue and your response right. But that's not all: you also discover that time is what you perceive it to be. *When you slow down, you actually have more time.*

So how does one learn to optimize for presence? Fortunately, there are many ways to begin. Some may seem mundane and others quirky. Try whichever ones pique your interest, without overthinking! I find that the more bizarre a new practice seems, the more off-kilter current habits usually are.

- **Stillness practice:** Start with thirty seconds, then one minute, two minutes, up to five minutes (or longer) of utter stillness. This is not meditation; it is even simpler. It's sitting, stilling your mind, and seeing where it wanders. Don't judge; just notice. Is your mind able to unwind, or does it speed up?

- **Silence practice:** Silence—whether the silence of nature or the silence at the end of a breath cycle (*kumbhaka*)— helps quiet the mind. Silence can be found almost anywhere: you may have to search a bit, but it is there. Find five minutes to bathe in silence daily. Pay attention to the emptiness. Notice what hangs in the space between you and sound. What is it calling you towards?

- **Patience practice:** Cultivating patience is one of the most difficult yet most powerful ways to run slower. Pick something that you know will take time—say, waiting for an appointment—and deliberately don't fill that waiting time with social media apps, calls, word games, or whatever else. Just be . . . and wait. Do you feel tested, or freed?

- **Not-to-do (or to-don't) list:** To-do lists help us run faster and stay on the hamster wheel. A not-to-do list does the opposite. Draft both versions and see which one feels more fluxy. (I find that a combination of both can work well, so long as what's on my to-do list actually matters.)

- **Micro-sabbaticals:** Brainstorm a list of opportunities to pause, whether for a moment or for a month. The simple act of drawing up this list can help relieve tension. It creates a sense of space rather than rushing and serves as a reminder of the many shapes of slowing down.

- **Nature bathing**: Nature is a microcosm of constant change and an unparalleled tutor for running slower. Find the nearest spot of wilderness—a forest, lake, or open field—and absorb the environment through all five senses. This isn't hiking, birding, or camping; this is simply being in nature. The Japanese call this *shinrin-yoku,* or "forest bathing."[22]

- **Technology Shabbat**: Once a week, disconnect from the use of all technology with screens: smartphones, computers, tablets, and television.[23] If that feels like too much, start with a few hours and build up to a day. Use the time for quiet personal reflection, perhaps with an old-school pen and paper.

Running slower shifts your focus of attention from outside to inside, with a goal to *really listen* to what's going on internally. Not turning away, looking away, or running away. This is presence: how you connect with your true self and learn that so many of the answers you seek are inside . . . *if* you can slow down long enough to hear them.

PROTECT THE ASSET

The first time I heard this phrase was in China, listening to a panel of international entrepreneurs who had experienced massive health scares talk about coping when health thwarts your best-laid plans. The punchline was: no matter what your mindset, your body still keeps the score.[24] We can't keep treating conditions like exhaustion, anxiety, and burnout by merely exercising and eating better. We must address the underlying sources of these conditions and meaningfully, consistently slow down.

"Protecting the asset" acknowledges that when your mind is wound up, your body is wound up too, and neither functions well. Grooving a healthier mindset also requires addressing the somatic aspects of one's relationship with speed. And there is no way for *anyone* to heal at speed. Quite the contrary: running ever faster ultimately kills. So we *must* slow down.

The first step in protecting the asset is assessing how your body is holding on to, and embodying, speed. I think of this as a micro health check-in with myself. *How am I feeling? Which parts of my body are racing? Which are speaking up, and what are they saying?*

This isn't about judging yourself, and it's definitely not about trying to change the sensations. This is strictly about paying attention and seeing what comes up. We often associate pain in the neck, shoulders, or lower back with stress. But—no joke—pain and sensations can show up *anywhere*: in your elbow, foot, or lungs. Heartache is real: not only aching for others but aching for your own well-being.

Pay attention to the discomfort. Sit with it and start to dig deep, to understand what's behind it. Write about it. Do you try to "work through" distress by ignoring it, or do you give it the time it deserves?

Our bodies communicate with us constantly, yet we often ignore their signals. In a world in flux, your body's signals may feel even more confusing, yet they are all the more important to understand.

Your most powerful somatic tool is your breath. It's like a Swiss Army knife, because it does so much. It is also the bridge between your inner and outer worlds, and between body and mind. As you navigate constant change, a committed breathing practice—even a few minutes a day—becomes essential.

Yoga can also help. In the twenty-first century, most people think of yoga as a physical practice. Yet for the first 3,000 years of its existence, it is generally understood that there were no *asanas* (physical poses). There were only breathing (*prana*) and meditation while seated. The word *yoga* itself means "union": of body and mind, and of the individual with everything else. The goal of yoga is to still the fluctuations of the mind, which practitioners throughout history realized involved bringing the body into alignment. The body is but a vessel through which we calm our minds and connect with others.

More recently, Sensory Awareness Training (SAT) has become popular. SAT helps enhance your awareness of your senses. It includes a range of exercises, from "five senses check-ins" (spending one minute wholly focused on each of your five senses), developing "mental snapshots" (look around, close your eyes, and see how much you remember), and going barefoot.[25]

Beyond formal constructs, there is a range of simple yet powerful personal exercises and habits that can help you run slower and protect the asset:

- Eat slower, thoroughly noticing and relishing each bite.

- Walk slower, paying attention to the details on your path: the patina of a building, the texture of flowers, the eyes of the people you encounter. Even better, walk with a young child and let them set the pace. Follow their explorations.

- Walk instead of drive, drive instead of fly: slow down your pace of travel.

- Dance rather than walk to a destination. Rather than putting one foot in front of the other, let your entire body guide you. (Stares from others are worth it: you may even spark a dance party!)

RUNNING FROM OURSELVES

Many humans today have a primal fear of slowing down. There's the perceived fear of social stigma, disbelief, and condescension from others if we get off the fast track. There's the potential loss of our value to society, for if we aren't always on, then what are we?

Adding to this conundrum, the more someone takes on, the harder it can be to let go. Broadly speaking, today's society is one of grasping: for status, wealth, and certainty of the unknown. The bigger one's pyramid of activities and accomplishments, the bigger one's sense of self, even if deep down that person is miserable.

The missing link of this conversation is that "getting more done" is not the same as progress, value, or worth. As philosopher Tias Little says, "From a spiritual perspective, moving fast and checking things off of a to-do list is *the opposite* of progress."[26] According to Little, we've become trapped in a "speed vortex" of technology, society, and expectations. We're caught in "life's speed lanes" rife with restlessness and frustration. Many people are actually addicted to this speed. But our jam-packed schedules don't necessarily mean we're growing; quite possibly, we're running to escape from ourselves.

This speed gets trapped in the body and affects your ability to think, focus, dream, and create. It keeps you from simply being. It compromises your nerves, connective tissues, and glands. It hampers your physiology and brain chemistry. Your body keeps score while your brain tries to justify a pace that's working against you.

I had a glimpse of running slower after my parents' deaths, yet that was one piece of a more complicated puzzle because I was still running from myself. More than a decade later, even though I'd slowed down to grieve, I still lived a "fast" life: working long hours, traveling for business to twentyish different countries each year, and for pleasure to even more, and throwing my all into everything that I could. On the outside, I was doing it all (or at least an awful lot). Yet inside, I was still wracked with anxiety. The more I achieved externally, the more anxious I felt internally. My roots were thin, and I knew that at some point they could splinter, and no amount of external (financial, professional, reputational, etc.) security or reassurances from others could break that fall.

Ultimately, I found my way to cognitive behavioral (CBT) and eye-movement (EMDR) therapies, where I discovered just how deep my anxiety and addiction to speed ran. This discovery was nothing short of life changing. Yet equally revealing is what it led me to observe in many others, in a wide variety of settings and cultures: there is an almost perfect correlation between anxiety and accomplishment.

I have been part of leadership circles in which every single person (representing a range of cultures) feels anxious and unable to properly address it. I regularly see high achievers at their breaking point, who simply keep running because they don't know what else to do—and are too frightened or too fully on autopilot to stop. Even those who *are* clear on their personal purpose are often addicted to speed and flirt with burnout regularly. Needless to say, this is no way to live, nor does it bode well for organizations or society to flourish. The imperative to run slower is urgent.

THINK SLOW(ER) AND DELAY JUDGMENT

> Slow is smooth. Smooth is fast.
> —NAVY SEAL ADAGE

Running slower doesn't only improve your emotional and physical well-being. It also helps you make better decisions and get better results.

On a day-to-day level, how we think—and how quickly we respond—affects our personal and professional relationships: whether you spark or defuse an argument, make a wise investment, mend a friendship, or win a game. Over time, your ability to gauge timing has a profound impact on how your life unfolds, period.

Research has shown, time and time again, that whenever possible it's best not to hurry. In other words, the longer you can wait, the better.[27] This is *not* procrastination; this is about your ability to observe, assess, feel, process, take action . . . and pause, in order to get the best outcome possible.

Running slower is naturally aligned with the concept (and book) *Thinking Fast and Slow,* popularized by Princeton professor and Nobel Prize–winner Daniel Kahneman. Kahneman reveals how we listen too much to people who think fast and shallow and too little to people who think slow and deep.[28] All too often, we frantically get through the day without reserving time to think, learn, and unlearn—yet this is exactly what we need to do in order to think more clearly.

When we're running fast, we automatically fall into fast-thinking mode: we react quickly and opt for what's familiar or intuitively comfortable. But as Kahneman shows us, being fast on your feet may make you sound smart, but it doesn't make you wise.[29] Opting for what's familiar means you miss what's new, *and* it does a very poor job preparing you for flux!

Your ability to think slower is directly related to how fast (or slow) you respond, with strikingly similar results. As Frank Partnoy, author of *Wait: The Art and Science of Delay,* says, "The amount of time we take to reflect on decisions defines who we are . . . A wise decision requires reflection, and reflection requires a pause."[30]

Partnoy has explored delay in the context of everything from Wimbledon tennis to Warren Buffett's investment portfolio. It turns out that elite athletes' ability to "first observe, second process, and third act—at the last possible moment—also works well for our personal and business decisions."[31] This requires an ability to slow down *and* to slow down time. For tennis players, this is the split-second pause between seeing and hitting the ball. For fighter pilots, it's the OODA (observe-orient-decide-act) loop.[32] For the rest of us, it's the pause between hurting someone's feelings and offering an authentic apology.

And yet, in today's fast-paced world, the ability to delay judgment is all the more at risk. As an example, in my role as a startup adviser I have seen numerous entrepreneurs race after venture capital. It doesn't matter whether their idea is wonderful, wild, or mediocre. They race after funding as if the VC industry (and their personal prestige) were closing shop tomorrow.

And yet, in my experience, entrepreneurs who take money from the first person or firm that offers funding all too often find themselves distraught down the road. Neither the founders nor the investors took the time to fully understand one another's ethos, expectations, or mission. They let numbers outweigh integrity. They were blinded by the promise of quick returns rather than inspired by the fact that creating value takes time.

This stands in sharp contrast to the concept of Slow Money: "patient capital" that prioritizes investment in long-term, sustainable systems over making a quick buck and fleeing.[33] When change hits, what kind of investment would you prefer?

Running slower helps you think slower and delay judgment, both of which empower you to manage your time—rather than time managing you—and bring your best self to life.

> On average, bad things happen fast and good things happen slow.
> —STEWART BRAND

FROM FOMO TO JOMO

In 2004, Harvard Business School student Patrick McGinnis coined the terms FOMO and FOBO in a blog post about social theory.[34] He posited that HBS students were overwhelmingly plagued by FOMO (fear of missing out) and FOBO (fear of better options), which led

Leadership fast and slow

- Think about your *typical* decision-making style. Do you tend to decide fast or to contemplate?

  If you move quickly, do you consider your potential blind spots?

  If you move slowly, do you have a filter for when the time is right?

- Think about your leadership style. Do you expect your colleagues and partners to adopt your pace? Why or why not?

- Reflect on a situation in which a decision took longer than expected. What did you observe, process, and learn during the delay? How did this affect your actions?

to insane social schedules and behavior that contradicted the students' supposed intelligence.

In the years since then, FOMO has gone mainstream. Today it's a term you'll hear fifteen-year-olds and fifty-year-olds use with ease. Society-wide, we're petrified of missing out.

The thought process goes roughly like this: hyperconnected technologies make it easier for people to share what they're up to and for others to see, hear, and know about it. As we are exposed to ever more people, places, and activities, our brains react with: look at all that you're *not* doing! Even multitaskers are only *truly* doing one thing, in one place, at one time. FOMO and FOBO make our brains unravel. And when it comes to our pace of life, it's all exacerbated by a fear of slowing down. If we slow down, then we fall behind, lose out, and the FOMO/FOBO cycle begins again.

McGinnis acknowledges that FOMO is crazy, yet it is real. Originally, he suggested an alternative: fear of doing anything, or FODA (which he characterized as a paralytic state). FODA never really caught on. Instead, it was superseded by a more optimistic phenomenon: JOMO. Fear of missing out becomes *joy of missing out*.[35]

We can flip our FOMO and make it positive. Rather than running faster and fretting about everything we're *not* doing, we can run slower and rejoice about it instead.

In an interview with *Essentialism* expert Greg McKeown, McGinnis suggests a three-step process to start unpacking your FOMO.[36]

1. Notice the next time you are feeling FOMO.

2. Ask yourself, "Is this jealousy, or could it be revealing something deeper that I am called to do?"

3. Block time on your calendar in the next week to explore this sentiment in more depth.

I struggled with FOMO and FOBO for years before gradually realizing how rotten both made me feel. In my quest to overcome them, a very simple exercise was among the most powerful: the practice of *creating and holding space to notice*. I still do this frequently, and it helps every single time.

When we suffer from FOMO, life becomes a Tetris game to fit as much as possible into a given day. Creating and holding space to notice is the antithesis. Here's how you can start:

- Notice how you feel in the empty spaces in between
- Notice your breath
- Notice the space between notes of music
- Notice the space between the leaves on the trees
- Notice the space that opens up when you notice, period

When you develop the superpower of running slower, you open space for JOMO to creep in. You may discover whatever envy you once felt melting into compassion, pity, and kindheartedness. Today, I love being in the flow, but I rejoice in unstructured space, whether on my calendar or in my soul. Once you experience JOMO, it's hard not to want to help others run slower and feel it too.

WHAT ROSES?

Skeptics of running slower, not-doing, and JOMO say, "Ah, I get it. So we should just stop and smell the roses more?!" While I do believe that the world would be a better place if we appreciated the beauty of nature more, this framing sells this superpower's potential woefully short.

Of course, life isn't always about being slow. There are times to fly like the wind, to rush into one's passion, or to burn the midnight oil for one's dreams. These are moments to cherish, even as they exhaust your reserves.

The far bigger challenge and concern, however, is that we do not—and *cannot*—have meaningful conversations, develop truly innovative solutions, or fully express or receive love when we are rushing around. As George Butterfield, whose travel company's tagline is "Slow Down to See the World," says: "These things aren't happening *because they can't* at 700 miles an hour! Where are the conversations about this frenzy in our schools and organizations, or around the supper table?"[37] Not only do we miss the roses entirely (what roses?!) when we're running too fast, but also future generations continue our traditions of burnout, hustling, and unsustainable business . . . to the point of collapse.

As we look towards a future in flux, this racing ever faster looks all the more bizarre and all the more dangerous. In a world in flux, we must run slower: not to finish, but to flourish.

1. In which areas of your life do you feel you're running too fast? *teaching, NF St NF carlgwing, cooking*

2. From whom or where does your "need for speed" come? Are you driving yourself to run faster, or are others driving you? *avoidg boredom @ home $ to renovate, mother III*

3. When did the pressure to run faster begin? Did you notice it at that time?

4. What are your typical coping mechanisms? Which ones *Alanon* have been most useful? Which ones need to be replaced or retired? *listn radio in bed alone church prayer, quiet, wisdom*

5. If you slowed down, what do you think you'd discover? *→ love marriage,*

Notice how your thinking may have evolved in the course of reading this chapter. Integrate these insights into your new script.

CHAPTER 2

SEE WHAT'S INVISIBLE

The real voyage of discovery consists not in seeking
new landscapes, but in having new eyes.
—MARCEL PROUST

I have worked in South Africa at various points in my career. My
first exposure, many years ago, was collaborating with microfinance
institutions and policymakers focused on financial inclusion. More
recently, I did a nationwide survey of the country's sharing economy to better understand who was participating and how the concept was viewed in the Rainbow Nation.

As I traveled—when I got into taxis, went into shops, and
observed locals—I would often hear "Sawubona." *Sawubona* is
a standard Zulu greeting. Zulu is the largest ethnic group in the
country, and *sawubona* is how you say hello.

The word *sawubona* is gentle, melodic; it rolls off the tongue. I
became fascinated by it. I asked people I met about it and did more
research. It turns out that although *sawubona* translates to hello,
its meaning goes far deeper than a casual greeting.

Sawubona literally means "I see you." I see all of you: your dignity and your humanity. I see your vulnerability and your pride, your
dreams and your fears. I see your agency, your power and potential.

I see you and I value you. I accept you for what you are. You are important to me, and you are part of me.[38]

In the Zulu tradition, seeing is more than the simple act of sight. *Sawubona* makes another visible in a way that "hello" does not. It's an invitation to witness and truly, fully be in the presence of one another. The customary response to *sawubona* is *shikoba*, which means "I exist for you."

When we say hello, what do we really mean? Is this ability to see beyond sight innate in us, or is it something we must learn?

And what happens when we do?

THE SUPERPOWER: **SEE WHAT'S INVISIBLE**

When life feels blurry or the future is uncertain, shift your focus from what's visible to what's invisible.

As children, we are often taught to look straight ahead and focus: on a goal, a destination, or a specific achievement. Learn how to read, excel at sports and extracurriculars, and graduate at the top of your class. These milestones are largely determined by the cultures, norms, and expectations of the society you're raised in. They serve as orientation towards the future.

As children grow older, their skills and horizons may expand, yet in many ways their scope of focus narrows. Before long, children become teenagers, then young adults who are expected to track into careers that build expertise in one domain but leave little room for dabbling beyond it. By and large, adults also track into social circles designed to keep us within our comfort zones and communities of choice. We track into an institutional ecosystem—from consumer culture to educational curriculum, from public health to political parties—that makes sure we have certain knowledge and dismisses, ignores, or seeks to hide the rest.

In this process, each person is trained—whether consciously or not—to *see* certain things. What you see is baked into your script; what I see is baked into my script. And in so doing, each of us is also trained—again, whether by choice or by default—to *not see* other things. We grow certain roots and dismiss others. This is a universal phenomenon: it isn't a critique of any particular culture or point of view. Every culture and every person is faced with this reality. Not a single person sees the full picture. The best anyone can do is become aware of, and then learn to see, what they are missing.

Don't get me wrong: social norms serve an important purpose. Norms help ensure that individuals grow up with values, skills, relationships, and the capacity to contribute to society. Norms help keep order and stability. Yet by and large, any set of social norms represents only one way of seeing and being in the world: one slice of an infinitely broader human spectrum.

But when the world flips upside down, this narrow focus can wreak havoc. It can rip your roots from the ground. Indeed, the greater the change or the narrower one's focus, the more disruptive the upheaval—and the fewer options one has to regain balance.

When my parents died, I went temporarily blind. My eyes were open, but I could not *see*. I felt unmoored, with grief and uncertainty enveloping me like fog. I fumbled along, unsure of the next step, wondering where the guardrails were. I was missing what was lost and now invisible. It took time for me to learn how to see differently, see beyond, and see what's invisible. As I did, however, the fog lifted. It wasn't that I could just see again: I could see *better*. My vision had drastically improved.

Today, a lot of people—perhaps you too—are missing what is no longer. There is a void: an absence of what was and an unknowingness of what comes next. You may sense this, or find it hard to identify. You may struggle to imagine, much less see, a different future at all. You may feel like a shadow of yourself, unable to see who you really are and wish to be. According to the old script, these things are invisible. Yet they are very much alive.

Each of us is inspired by what we see. But in a world of constant change, that principle only gets us so far. How do we move beyond what we *can* see and find inspiration in what we *can't*? How do we learn to see differently and make the invisible, visible? This is all directly tied to writing your new script.

Indeed, a world in flux demands a new script in which you, I, and all of humanity can see more broadly. We can see what's on the periphery, what appears upside down or inside out, what we've been blind to, and what we've been trained to believe isn't there.

Learning to see what's invisible doesn't mean losing focus or ignoring what's visible. Quite the opposite, in fact: it's the ability to adjust your gaze, see the full picture, and *really* understand what's what. When you learn to see what's invisible, it becomes easier to embrace change today *and* a future chock-full of unknowns.

YOUR SOCIAL AND CULTURAL ORIENTATION SHAPES WHAT AND HOW YOU SEE

The Himba people of northwestern Namibia have an astonishing ability to focus on small details. They are a seminomadic tribe that grazes livestock and counts wealth by the number of cattle they own. Traditional Himba have an almost preternatural capacity to concentrate: they hold their attention and ignore distraction far more easily than more "modern" cultures.[39] Could the Himba's exceptional vision come from their need to identify each of their cattle's markings, or could it be that the absence of modern tech in daily life makes them less easily distracted?

The Iroquois tribes of North America believe that all people, animals, and animate and inanimate natural objects possess an invisible power called *orenda*. *Orenda* is a collective power of nature's energies; each and every thing that has it can communicate its will and influence its experience in some way.[40] Storms, rivers, rocks,

You are what you see ... and so much more

Pause for a moment and think about what and how you *really see*. Consider, for example:

When you meet someone for the first time, what is the first question you ask them?

In a job interview, do you spend more time talking about the professional experience that's on the candidate's résumé or the lived experience that's *not* on it?

When you meet someone for the first time, do you feel they can be trusted?

Do you believe that if something cannot be measured, then it does not exist?

Do you believe that capitalism is empowering or oppressive?

Does empty space inspire you, bore you, or scare you?

Do you believe that expressing one's vulnerability is courageous or wimpy?

Have you faced organizational challenges that were "hard to see" according to traditional strategy models?

If you could drive with only one set of headlights, would you choose high beams or fog lights?

Do you sense that something is missing in your life, or waiting for you, but can't quite identify what?

If any of these questions intrigues you or rings true, this chapter is for you.

and birds possess *orenda*, along with human beings. *Orenda* is also an essential part of the Iroquois vision quest, a rite of passage that gives each member of the tribe a personal guardian spirit. How does whether we believe power is visible or invisible affect how we show up in the world?

In Japan, *satori* (悟り) is the Zen Buddhist term for awakening. It is derived from the Japanese verb *satoru*, meaning "to know or understand." *Satori* relates to the experience of *kenshō*, "seeing into one's true nature." *Ken* means "seeing," and *shō* means "nature or essence." Might having a rich vocabulary, traditions, and encouragement to see inside oneself help the Japanese acknowledge (at least some of) what's invisible? Might it help them embrace change?

No one script is better than another. The Himba, Iroquois, and Japanese traditions are simply different scripts, written by different cultures. However, they all acknowledge what's invisible and, in so doing, shine light on new ways of understanding.

How we see runs deep and wide, regardless of which kind of society we live in. Our social constructs determine how we raise children (by parents, relatives, "aunties," or an entire village), how we cooperate, how we organize economic activity, and, in turn, how economics organizes us.

For example, generally speaking, people in Japan, China, and much of Asia tend to be more collectivist, while people in the West tend to be more individualist. Net-net, collectivist societies value collective interdependence, community well-being, and "we" over individual independence and "me." Collectivist cultures typically stress cooperation among community members and problem-solving together, while individualist cultures leave these things to one's own wherewithal. These are sweeping statements, and of course there are some exceptions, but overall there is broad consensus on these differences.

The point is: these social orientations fundamentally influence how we see. For example, people who live in collectivist societies tend to prioritize the context of a social situation and the big picture when solving problems. They home in on the overarching relationships and interplay of systems beyond any individual's control. When asked to describe a picture, they spend more time explaining the background and surroundings.

In contrast, people in individualistic societies tend to focus on separate elements and especially the main image of a picture. (Even children's drawings focus on the "me." Drawings by children in collectivist societies tend to include more holistic context. Our social orientation starts young.) Individualists tend to consider situations as fixed, and whatever change comes about is the result of individual effort and willpower.[41]

In addition to culture, one's profession also affects how one sees. To take but one example from agriculture: Growing rice is far more labor-intensive and requires greater cooperation than growing wheat. Growing rice relies on complex irrigation systems spanning many different farms. Collaboration among neighbors is essential; no single rice paddy thrives on its own. In contrast, wheat farming depends on rainfall rather than irrigation. Growing wheat takes about half the amount of human labor. Wheat farmers don't need to collaborate with one another much and can focus on their own crops. Yet wheat farmers tend to cooperate more than shepherds, who by and large oversee their flocks independently (albeit with a clear set of culturally accepted grazing norms).[42]

So what does any of this have to do with flux?

When change hits, we default to our social and cultural scripts. What you, I, or any person sees—and doesn't see—is a result of this script. But if you can't see what grounds you, it is much harder to move forward. It can be scary to take your next step or gauge your best direction.

An upside-down world gives everyone an opportunity to consider a new range of solutions and perspectives, and to update our scripts. You deserve to see *everything:* what's visible and invisible. Tangible and intangible. What's right in front of you and what you can barely imagine. Why? Because the broader your vision, the more potential solutions you have at hand. The more holistic your worldview, the greater your capacity to help, to serve, to innovate . . . and to thrive.

CHECK YOUR PRIVILEGE AND YOUR OPTIONS

In learning to see what's invisible, privilege is a thorny stumbling block. Privilege blinds: It limits people's perceptions of what's in their script. It keeps them from seeing the full picture and what's in the wings.

Privilege isn't one-size-fits-all. There's privilege you're born with, privilege that accrues from who you know, hard work, and sheer luck. For example, different kinds of privilege attach to getting a college degree, being able to afford college, having encouragement or role models to attend college, living somewhere with access to quality education, and being born with a healthy body and mind capable of study and imagination.

Overcoming the blindness induced by privilege requires learning about the inequities that privilege brings with it. But simply learning about privilege isn't enough. It takes deliberate action to make the invisible, visible: calling out privilege, even if it's uncomfortable.

A similar tension exists with options. An option is something one has the power, right, opportunity, or freedom to choose. All things being equal, the more options people have, the better positioned they are to deal with change and uncertainty.

Optionality is the ability to keep as many options open as possible. You increase your optionality by keeping an open mind, having a Plan B (and C, D, and E), and expanding your peripheral vision to include more possibilities.[43]

Life presents new options to every person, every day. Many are small and not life changing. But in times of great change, more options arise, including more life-changing ones. The ones that make you say "What if?" and "If not now, when?"

Greater privilege is typically associated with more options. Yet there's a hook: if you haven't learned how to see what's invisible, then privilege will actually blind you. The more you perceive to have on the line, the greater your perceived risk of loss.

What does your worldview make visible . . . and keep invisible?

Take a moment and consider who and what shaped your worldview most: from the values that your parents or caretakers instilled in you, to where you lived and went to school, who your friends are, your profession and ambitions, and your beliefs about the future. Here are a few questions to get started:

What does fear look like, or feel like, to you?

Were you taught to fear change or embrace it?

Were you told to be quick to trust or quick to mistrust?

Were you encouraged to hang out with people who are like you or different from you?

How might privilege have blinded you or kept you from seeing the full picture?

What was erased from your view of the world? What was left out of your script?

It is easy to see the branches of trees moving, but it takes practice to see the wind. —Social entrepreneur and executive Elaine Genser Smith

Privilege and options play out in every corner of life. In my case, losing my parents made the privilege of *having* parents glaringly clear and took several options (from family structure to future expectations) off my table. At the same time, it underscored my privileges of health, education, race, and curiosity, and opened up *new* options (such as building a "family of choice" and career horizons I'd never thought of before) that would not have come about otherwise.

The punchline is: to thrive in constant change, aim to make choices that keep your options open, including the options to change how you think and what you prioritize. Some of your options are likely invisible to you today, and others may be clouded by privilege. Yet when you can check privilege at the door, you can see a richer, more meaningful future ahead of you.

HOW DO YOU SEE OTHERS? CONSUMER VS. CITIZEN

Have you ever stopped and *really thought* about the word *consumer*? Chances are, probably not. The word is typically thrown around without concern.

Many people consider *consumer* a term of art to describe ourselves and almost every aspect of our daily lives: from the products and services we design and purchase and use, to how we nourish our bodies, to how we learn and play, to the news and information we—surprise!—*consume*. The term isn't limited to classic "consumer goods" like breakfast cereal, smartphones, and cars; we now "consume" education, health care, entertainment, and even elections.

Today's society is hyperconsumer-driven. But it wasn't always this way.

Indeed, for most of human history, the word *consumer* wasn't used to describe, much less denigrate, any person. Today's hyperconsumer culture dates back only one-hundred-ish years, to the advent of mass marketing. Mass marketing was itself a result of the newfound plethora of products developed in the Industrial Revolution—which transformed society in countless positive ways yet, at the same time, ever so subtly shifted our sense of worth.[44] Previously we were seen as human beings, whose job was to contribute to society and help others. With the advent of consumer mass marketing, we became seen as consumers, whose principal job is to consume. A new, consumer-driven script was born.

And yet, as we saw in chapter 1, the original meaning of "to consume" is "to destroy"—as in "consumed by fire." Until recently, consumption did not boost gross domestic product (GDP); it killed you. In English, consumption is another word for tuberculosis. In Latin, *consummare* means used up, wasted away, finished.

Roughly one century later, this consumer destruction proceeds apace: our pocketbooks are depleted, and the planet is at risk of wasting away.

We're told to keep following this old, crusty, dangerous script in order to keep the economy intact. Consume, consume, consume! Some people have even begun to believe that their purchasing decisions have a greater impact on society than their voting decisions.[45] Let that sink in.

In today's world, we're *seen* first and foremost as consumers: or as futurist Jerry Michalski says, as "gullets with eyeballs and wallets."[46] So long as we continue to consume, we're told, all will be well in the world.

But all is not well whatsoever.

When we're treated as mere consumers for long enough, it affects how we think and behave, which also affects how we see. For example, we see our purchases as more important than our votes and what defines our self-worth. At the societal level, we chase metrics like GDP that measure only economic activity "seen" as dollars and cents. GDP does not "see" a wide range of extremely valuable activities that underpin our economy and well-being, such as the "invisible labor" of parenting and volunteering, and the "invisible value" of shared (rather than owned) resources.[47]

When we follow the consumer script, we also train our eyes to *not see*: to not see the full effects of what we buy, to not see those who are struggling. We even stop seeing when there are better paths forward.

In our race to consume, we've lost track of what really matters. And when massive change arrives, jolting us to the core, our wake-up to this reality hits hard. In the cracks of whatever broke, what was previously invisible comes into view.

In many ways, many people are in the midst of this wake-up today. We're taking off our blinded-by-the-old-script goggles and asking: Why didn't we *see* what was happening—to each of us, our families, our communities, and people halfway around the world? If we *did* see it, why didn't we do something about it? For we are all participants, willingly or not, in a global consumer catastrophe.

One way out of this mess is to start seeing one another—and treating one another—as citizens and humans, rather than as consumers. (I mean citizens not in terms of passports and borders but as participants and change agents in society.) This is a new script with a subtle yet profound shift: no longer merely passive purchasers and clickbait targets, we become proactive contributors. Together, we lead responsibly rather than follow blindly. We open our Flux Mindsets to develop this superpower and write our own new scripts.

In your new script, start by asking: Would *you* prefer to be seen by others as a consumer, or as a citizen and catalyst for good? Beyond "buying stuff," what would you like your legacy to be?

In my experience, simply waking up to how you are seen (and not seen) is a big step. But once you do, you start seeing ways to take action all over the place: from which companies you support to the words you use, from how you think about online shopping to what you pay attention to while walking down the street. Initiatives like the Citizen Shift are emerging to build awareness and harness such efforts worldwide.[48]

For leaders of consumer-centric organizations: this is the time to revisit your marketing strategies and business models. This is the time to make sure your mission aligns with the new script—and if it doesn't, it's time for a new one.

THE EMPTY SPACE

In the wake of #BlackLivesMatter, #MeToo, and a broader reckoning of systemic injustices and inequalities, Harvard Business School professor Laura Huang found herself reviewing recommended first-year MBA reading lists and curricula. What she found was not surprising, yet it was entirely disquieting: *all* of the lists were overwhelmingly dominated by white male authors.

Meanwhile, Todd Sattersten, coauthor of *The 100 Best Business Books of All Time*, was in the midst of a personal reckoning. He considers himself progressive yet wondered: How many authors included on the list were people of color? He'd tried to identify the most popular books but hadn't paid attention to demographics. The answer was equally disturbing: zero.[49]

Mandates and calls for greater diversity in the business world and beyond are not new, yet the needle has barely budged. By and large the voices of women, Blacks, Latinxs, and other minorities are still difficult if not at times impossible to be found . . . or rather, to be *seen*.

It's not that they're not out there. It's that for too long, they've been ignored, relegated to the sidelines, and written out of the script.

And critically, there is a clear and resounding prerogative for diversity, equity, and inclusion (DEI) in the new script.

Women and people of color have been showing up for ages *and* doing the hard work. Unmistakably visible, yet unseen. Full-throated voices, muted. Some of the best and brightest idea generators, concealed in the light of day. Marginalized on the periphery. Occupying the empty spaces.

When we look only front-and-center—at today's CEOs, "climb to the top of the ladder" power structures, and "know how to play the game" metrics—not only are we seeing just a fraction of the full picture, but also what we're looking at is pretty stale. This is the old script at work. Yet in reality, *on the periphery* and *in the empty space*, is where real action, meaning, and progress are found. (And as you'll learn in chapter 6, climbing a ladder is passé.)

As a futurist, this dynamic makes sense to me because in one way or another, the forces that shape the future are *always* on the periphery before going mainstream. For years, "mainstream leaders" believed that mobile phones would never overtake traditional landlines. Mobile phones were marginalized. Yet today there are nearly twice as many mobile devices as people on the planet, and landlines are fast becoming relics.

Mainstream thinking also deemed a pandemic a peripheral threat—until the coronavirus infected hundreds of millions and body-slammed the global economy in just a few months. Indeed, sometimes what's on the periphery can go mainstream at warp speed.

My point here is simple: we need to drastically improve our ability to see, and appreciate, what's on the periphery and in the empty space. Not only because a just, equitable society demands it; this is also where truly innovative ideas come from.

Empty space is the ideal place, indeed perhaps the *only* place, where there is enough oxygen to breathe life into new possibilities.

Laura Huang saw this. She knew that all around the white men who are at the center of traditional MBA curricula are extraordinary yet underrepresented experts on business strategy, finance, investment, organizational theory, management, and leadership.

So she created The Well-Balanced MBA Reading List featuring women and people of color (and yes, white men to balance things out).[50] Their perspectives are fresh. They come at business and life from the side flank. Their goal isn't to "hit the bull's-eye": they know that's already past its prime. They're writing a new script that includes a bigger, more inclusive future of business and beyond.

LEARNING TO SEE

In many ways today's world is one giant case study of learning where to look and, fundamentally, *how* to see. When change hits, those who can see what's on the edges, in the empty space, and where new solutions are to be found are better positioned to navigate uncertainty and be responsible leaders. But it's one thing to talk about this superpower and another thing to actually develop it. So let's look at a few simple ways to get started.

Expand Your Peripheral Vision

Peripheral vision is the ability to see objects, movement, and opportunities outside your direct line of vision. You can think of peripheral vision as the awareness of everything you're *not* looking at.

Today, most people are hyperfocused on what's front and center: the task at hand, the next thing on the to-do list, this quarter's returns, or just getting through the day. We often don't notice what's on the periphery or horizon. Perhaps you don't feel like you have the time, or you're not sure where to look. Yet there's an entire universe of new insights and aha's within your grasp . . . *if* you can see it.

Peripheral vision isn't just about fresh ideas or finding answers. It turns out that when you're anxious, your peripheral vision shrinks. This can happen if you're anxious about work, grades, finances, expectations, relationships with friends and colleagues, or just about anything. The effect is the same: your scope of reality, comfort, and creativity narrows. This is called "tunnel vision" for good reason.[51]

Expanding your peripheral vision opens up new horizons, surfaces solutions, *and* reduces anxiety. Yet it doesn't happen automagically; it's a skill you must develop and a superpower you must practice.

Our ancestors used their peripheral vision far more than we do today. Peripheral vision evolved to catch movement, not to pay attention to details (that's the job of central vision). In other words, peripheral vision is good at detecting *that* something enters our field of vision, but it is weak at distinguishing whether that thing is red or blue, soft or hard, friend or foe. Our ancestors simply needed to identify "incoming alert!" and then passed things over to their central vision colleagues.

Yet today, our peripheral vision has atrophied. As a species, humans now spend enormous amounts of time in front of screens, we've sliced our time into fractions, and the risk of a tiger in hot pursuit is slim. Our survival once depended on the quick response of our peripheral vision. But today we hover over our devices, poring over messages and texts on screens smaller than a slice of bread.

In other words, we've let our peripheral vision lapse precisely when it would serve us well.

Thankfully, we can get it back. We can regroove this ability and put booster rockets on it.

To go back to basics, try this simple exercise:

Hold your hands in front of your face. Put your thumbs on your ears. Pivoting on your ears, spread your fingers out to the sides and move them backward until you can't see them anymore. Then begin to wiggle your fingers and move them forward until you see them on your periphery. *That's your peripheral vision.* Pay attention to it. What do you see that you didn't notice before?

You can also practice this while blinking, moving your head from side to side or in circles, or while walking, reading, or doing any other activity that restricts your attention.

Or go upside down. Hang from a tree, do a handstand, or simply reach for your toes. Then look at wherever you are from this new vantage point. Don't overthink it. Do you see the same scene, differently? What had you not noticed right side up?

I have done handstands for more than forty years.[52] What began as childhood gymnastics has turned into a full-fledged passion for an "upside down perspective" and a core part of my personality. Practicing handstands helps me shift my view and *see* better. They increase my flexibility and mental acuity. And they're fun.[53] What's not to like?

Expanding your peripheral vision isn't a silver bullet. But it can help you see *more*, see *better*, and soften your anxiety. It's a great place to start.

(Re)assess Your Intention

There are endless ways in which invisible value is hidden today. Oftentimes, whether you see or don't see it depends on your intention as you look.

For example, whether we see people—and treat people—as consumers or citizens boils down to intention:

- If you want people to buy your products or click on your ads: that's seeing them as consumers.

- If you want to help, create, be of service, and help others reach their potential: that's seeing them as citizens and collaborators.

Whether we see ourselves as passive or active participants in life comes down to intention as well:

- If you rely on the old script or believe that what you do won't make a difference, then you'll probably stay put, keep quiet, and fear what comes next.

- If you open a Flux Mindset and believe that your Flux Superpowers can be developed, then you see—and are already harnessing—your agency for change.

And whether we seek answers and find solutions depends on . . . you guessed it: intention!

- If you ask with an intention to judge or criticize, your mental door is already closed.

- If you ask with an intention of curiosity, however, you're likely to learn something new (including how to ask better questions and question your assumptions).

Reassessing your intention is a critical step in opening a Flux Mindset *and* developing this superpower. As Jane Goodall said, "What you do makes a difference. You have to decide what kind of difference you want to make."[54] What kind of difference do you wish to make in a world in flux? What are your intentions today?

MAKE THE INVISIBLE, VISIBLE

Developing the ability to perceive beyond what's visible front and center is a superpower for today's world. It enables you to discover your roots, spark new insights, develop new solutions, and show up fully in life. It lowers your anxiety, awakens your inner voice, and brings you in closer touch with others. It gives you clarity of vision for whatever changes come your way.

All too often, we don't realize how much we *don't* see, whether it's not seeing our own gifts and abilities, or not seeing systemic injustices, or not seeing beauty that's all around us. The more you're stuck in the old script, the less you can see. Ultimately, you become blind to the truth and the fullness of life.

But as you write your new script, this changes completely. Indeed, seeing what's invisible represents the difference between hope and fear. Between thoughtful observation and paralysis. Between knowing when to act and when to wait. Between building an oppressive system or an inclusive system. Once again, it's a difference that can make all the difference.

SEE WHAT'S INVISIBLE: REFLECTIONS

1. Do you tend to trust your head or your heart more?

2. When your peers tell you to turn right, do you ever want to turn left instead?

3. Can you detect invisible patterns?

4. How aware are you of the rules that govern your life? How explicit are they?

5. How has privilege (or lack of privilege) affected your script? What kind(s) of privilege?

Again, notice how your perspective may have shifted as a result of reading this chapter. Pay attention to how it can show up in your new script.

CHAPTER 3

GET LOST

Lost really has two disparate meanings. Losing things
is about the familiar falling away, getting lost is about
the unfamiliar appearing.
—REBECCA SOLNIT

Bukovina is not on most travelers' itineraries. Tucked in the north-
eastern corner of Romania, near Moldova and Ukraine, Bukovina is
a sleepy pocket of rolling landscape dotted with Orthodox churches
and monasteries. Built between 1487 and 1583, these religious
structures are covered inside and out, floor to ceiling, with brilliant
frescoes. For centuries candle smoke dimmed the frescoes' colors
and ultimately snuffed out their visibility to the outside world.

After the collapse of communism and the Romanian Revolution,
Bukovina slowly began to reemerge. I'd heard fables about these
frescoes in my college art history class and dreamed of visiting.
A few years later—still long before smartphones, GPS, organized
tourism, or Airbnb—and after a marathon Tolstoy-esque train ride,
I found myself in the town of Suceava (*soo-chah-vah*), the closest
jumping-off point for the monastery circuit.

From Suceava, I hitchhiked along muddy roads traversed more
by donkeys than cars. I caught taxis when I could, but transport was
thin. Locals, most of whom were farmers, looked at me with a mixture of curiosity, delight, and pity. I rode in sputtering Russian-era

cars and wagons filled with hay. Smiles and pointing were our common languages. The frescoes were more extraordinary than I'd imagined. The landscape was calming.

Walking along a quiet lane one day, lost in my thoughts, someone shouted, "Hey! Lady! Hey!"

I turned to my right and saw a quintessential Romanian grandmother: a human cannonball with ruddy cheeks and a kerchief firmly knotted under her chin. She had flung open her wooden shutters and clearly wanted my attention.

I stopped and stared. What was I supposed to do? For that matter, where *was* I?

The old woman continued, "Hey! Lady!" in a thick-yet-melodic accent. I cautiously responded, "Hello . . . ?"

"Lady, are you lost?"

I paused. On the one hand, I had no idea where I was. Romania, yes, but technically I was very much lost.

On the other hand, I felt more alive than ever. I was riding in wheelbarrows, eating *mamaliga cum brinza* (steamed polenta with milky-fresh melted cheese), and seeing frescoes hidden for centuries. In those moments, I was anything *but* lost.

Grandma didn't wait for my answer. "Lady! Lady! You *must* be lost. Come in here *now!*"

Two minutes later, I'm in the middle of a Romanian family dinner. It's as though I've arrived from the moon. Grandma's children and grandchildren surround me, simultaneously firing questions in Romanian-spiced English: Why was I in Bukovina? What is America like? Would I like more *mamaliga*?

As stomachs filled, the conversation turned to why I was traveling alone. The family was convinced that I not only was lost geographically but also had lost my husband—because why else would a woman travel alone? (Never mind any other traveling partner or gender.) It wasn't judgment; it was genuine curiosity, tinged with worry. *She's lost and we must help her!*

In rural Romania, traveling alone was simply unheard-of. It wasn't that this family didn't believe that I could; rather, they were baffled by why I would want to. I didn't fit their script whatsoever. They had fought hard for their country's recent independence from Russia and all that entailed, but individual independence still revolved around community, and wanderlust was a different concept altogether.

Usually when I was met with questions like "Where is your husband?" on the road, I would chafe. "Don't assume I'm not capable!" I would mutter under my breath. But this meal taught me something different, about the Theory of Flux and how multiple scripts can evolve at the same time.

The family was concerned for my well-being for reasons far from my mind, while I was worried about things distant from theirs. Our views on getting lost were completely different and equally valid.

We had different roots and orientations. Our old scripts were wildly different, and we were at different points on our respective journeys to a new script. Nevertheless, we could share our respective views and learn from one another's navigation styles. In the process I discovered a new slice of what makes me, me.

When we'd finished our last drop of homemade *tuica* (plum brandy), the son drove me to the train station. But he didn't just drop me off. He escorted me to the ticket office, purchased my ticket, walked me to the train, got on the train with me, ensured that my seat was to my liking, and commanded my seatmate to look out for me.

For once, I didn't chafe. I relished every minute. Getting lost was found.

In the landscape of change, getting lost is how you find your way.
Humans' relationship with getting lost is complicated. Although
many people would agree that getting lost is half the fun of life, the
old script sees it as failure. Getting lost is a liability that's perceived
to involve loss of some kind: I've done something wrong, I've fumbled, and life will somehow be less as a result.

But in an upside-down world in which new changes hit every
day—when familiarity is itself in flux—getting lost is part of a new
script. In this world we are uprooted, disoriented, and unmoored
constantly. Whatever compass you're using has gone kaput. What's
more, this new landscape of change isn't something you, or I, or
anyone gets to choose. Flux just is.

Once you've opened a Flux Mindset, getting lost becomes a virtue: a secret weapon and stroke of genius not only to embrace being
lost but to actively seek out the unfamiliar and stretch beyond your
comfort zone as well. Getting lost doesn't mean lacking direction
or being foolish—that's just the old script at work again. Rather,
it means being completely comfortable with what you don't (and
may never) know.

Fundamentally, this superpower boils down to your response:
Does getting lost make you feel comfortable or distressed? Curious
or anxious? Can you get out of your own way, or do you trip over
your own feet?

My own experience with getting lost is multifold. Losing my
parents and then forging new relationships, losing and then finding my way through several career chapters, losing hope and then
finding meaning, all coupled with travel adventures (and misad-
ventures) from Bukovina to Bolivia to Bali: each of these experiences has helped me regrind my lens on change. They've helped me
see that getting lost is a gift. If you never get lost, you never actually
find your way, and your new script can never fully shine.

Thankfully, in a world of more change, you're going to get lost often. We all are, and you know the reason why: because the old script is breaking. It is no longer fit for purpose. And as your Flux Mindset opens, you'll learn how to get lost in the best of ways: how to be comfortable in discomfort, find familiarity in the unfamiliar, see what you were *really* looking for . . . and ultimately weave all of this into your new script.

THE LOST UNIVERSE

There are as many ways to get lost as there are people. Getting lost goes far beyond taking a wrong turn.

- You can get lost in your natural environment: in the wilderness or at sea.
- You can get lost in your built environment: the wrong address, road, or landmark.
- You can get lost in your digital environment: new apps and technologies (ironically, even those designed to help you navigate).
- You can get lost in time.
- You can get lost in your thoughts.
- You can get lost in an idea.
- You can get lost in a book.
- You can get lost in your emotions.
- You can get lost learning something new.
- You can tell others to get lost.
- And various people and organizations may be helping you get lost. (For more on this, head to chapter 4, Start with Trust.)

Getting lost, finding yourself

Recall a story about a time you got lost or disoriented. It could be in a foreign country, a parking lot, or your own home. Don't overthink it.

Think about how you responded to being lost at that time. What feelings came up? Did you feel fearful and frustrated, or curious and adventurous?

Think about how you *would like* to react to getting lost. Go back to your story. Were you telling it from the perspective of your old script or new script? Can you retell it from a vantage point of hope and discovery?

Sometimes these experiences have magnificent results. You may discover new things and become more aware of your surroundings. You can reorient your compass. You're able to see and experience more, and more vividly. You learn new skills and widen your perspective in ways that fundamentally transform you. Getting lost can bring you alive.

Yet other times, getting lost can be frustrating or dangerous. In times past, losing sight of the trail or shore meant great peril. Today, for many people, disorientation triggers anxiety and fear. In the business world (with old-script rules), getting lost is shunned and stigmatized: it's seen as compromising efficiency and productivity.

When we optimize for efficiency, getting lost is the ultimate *in*efficiency. But not only that: in the process, we sap creativity out of the picture and send the misguided signal that the path ahead is clear. In reality, it is anything *but* clear. Indeed, if the goal is truly innovative solutions, or fresh thinking, or simply being resilient, then getting lost is essential.

LOST ≠ LOSS ≠ FAILURE

Part of why many people struggle with getting lost is that they confuse it with, or substitute it for, loss. I can relate. When my parents died, I *was lost* beyond measure. I'd lost my footing, my sounding boards, and the home I'd grown up in. The ground beneath me had cracked and given way. I worried that I would soon lose my sister, my health, and my curiosity too.

But loss and lost are different, and neither means failure (though the old script goes to great lengths for you to believe otherwise). While my life had clearly changed and was "less" my parents, it was not somehow destined to be doomed. True, it would be wildly different from what I'd ever imagined, but it was also an invitation to go somewhere new. I was lost and going to get more lost, whether I wanted to or not. *And in the process, I could write a new script of my own.* I'd have adventures. New doors might open. I might gain new superpowers. In fact, getting lost might turn out to be not only the antithesis of failure but the best outcome ever.

TRADE-OFFS AND SCARCITY

Many people also struggle with getting lost thanks to trade-offs and scarcity thinking, hallmarks of the old script. Trade-off thinking says that the only way I can win is if someone else loses (and vice versa: if you win, I must lose), while scarcity thinking is rooted in the belief that no matter how much there is, there will never be enough. In both cases, the loss-lost-failure cycle repeats.

But hang on . . . says who?!

Trade-offs and scarcity thinking are problematic even in the best of times. But the headaches they cause are compounded in a world in flux, because we're applying traditional metrics (the old script!) to a radically changed reality. This goes far beyond the feeling of being "lost" due to a job loss or disrupted schedule.

Today, every single person—young and old, rich and poor, around the world, and across the political spectrum—has lost some part of life as they've known it. Globally, the ground has shifted beneath *everyone's* feet—and it is far from settled. It may be the loss of loved ones, a source of income, a favorite restaurant, vacation plans, or hope for the future. For many, it's the simple-yet-crucial loss of a sense of normalcy. (Even an abysmal status quo is at least familiar.) Under such circumstances, any script that says "stay in your own lane" sounds ludicrous. It's prime time to get lost.

GROWTH BEYOND YOUR COMFORT ZONE

When I was growing up, my dad was a geography teacher and my best friend. Our family didn't have much in terms of money or physical possessions, but my dad had abundant curiosity. At our kitchen table I had a plastic place mat, like many kids do, to contain spills. On my place mat was a map of the world. In the morning over breakfast, my dad and I would play (what we called) the capital game. He'd name a country, and over time I learned the capitals. Names like Addis Ababa, Ulaanbaatar, and Ouagadougou were magical to say, and I began to dream of visiting these far-off lands one day.

As I explored new (to me) corners of the globe while munching cereal, my dad would drill three things into my head.

- First: "The world is bigger than your own backyard. Go explore it! You might even find it has some of the answers to the questions you ask at home."

- Second: "The world doesn't exist to serve you. You're incredibly lucky to go to school, and that good fortune gives you a responsibility to give back."

- And to wrap up: "Remember, the more different someone looks than you, the more interesting they are to get to know. Why would you want to hang out with people who look like you, sound like you, and eat the same things as you?! That sounds pretty boring to me. Now, go have a good day at school."

Growing up, I assumed all kids had the same breakfast lesson. Years later I learned that this isn't the case, which sent me on a quest to understand: Does this advice hold up beyond childhood? Does getting lost by stretching beyond one's comfort zone make a meaningful difference in the real world?

The answer is a resounding yes. What's more, it doesn't require getting straight A's, earning a lot of money, or traveling long distances. Most of all, it's grounded in common sense.

Diversity invites consideration of different options, opinions, ideas, and points of view. Diversity stretches our imaginations, creativity, and curiosity. It underscores our interdependence and makes us stronger. Diverse teams, boards, and organizations have higher rates of innovation, resilience, and returns over time.[55]

But that's not all. Beyond day-to-day benefits, periods of great change demand fresh perspectives. In other words, more diverse teams and individuals exposed to more diversity are more *ready* for a world in flux.

> Ninety percent of people get lost because they don't go far enough.
> —ANONYMOUS

NOT LOST. JUST TEMPORARILY MISPLACED.

Humans have developed a remarkable array of approaches to navigate the unfamiliar. Time and again, across cultures and continents, we are reminded: we are less lost than temporarily misplaced. The point of life is not to not get lost per se but to grow through finding your bearings. When the ground beneath you shifts, you can steady and reorient yourself.

What follows is a selection of perspectives and tools from different people, lifestyles, and corners of the planet about getting lost. Some relate to getting lost in travel, others lost in thought, and still others lost in life. Some manifest culture-wide, others within a given country, region, or organization. Each one underscores the diversity of what works and probes the question of what makes you, you. Which ones might shed light on your new script?

Do You Know Your *Wēijī* from Your *Wabi Sabi*?

In the West, the word *crisis* typically conjures up images of doom and destruction: at best, discomfort; at worst, Armageddon. The word comes from the Greek word *krisis*, meaning the act of judgment or determination. In this view, a world in flux is crisis on steroids. Dystopia has arrived; we might as well throw in the towel.

In China, crisis is viewed differently. The Chinese word for crisis is *wēijī* (危机). *Wēijī* is composed of two symbols: *wēi*, which represents "danger," and *jī*, which represents a turning or "change point." Crisis is a challenge, but one that demands awareness, sparks curiosity, and opens possibility.

Two different scripts seek to explain a phenomenon that has unmoored humanity for millennia. What if more people in more places knew about *wēijī*? It wouldn't eliminate crisis, of course, but it could reshape how we wrestle with change. It could insert a dose of hope to temper the fear.

Traveling east from Greece and west from China, we arrive in Tibet and then India: places of the bardo. The bardo is a space of imagining, a gap between worlds. In the bardo is where transition and transformation happen.[56] It is a daunting, awe-inspiring, otherworldly place where we might reimagine ourselves, our dreams, society, the future . . . or all of them.

In Buddhism, the bardo is an intermediate, liminal state between death and rebirth. It's the in-between phase between one state of existence, one way of being, and another. In the bardo, death doesn't mean only one's physical death. It can also mean the end of a lifestyle, an illness, or a state of mind.

Keeping this concept of bardo in mind, consider the word *apocalypse*. The original meaning of apocalypse (from Greek *apokálypsis*) isn't "disaster" but "revelation and unveiling." An apocalyptic time is one of great truth and transformation.

Now connect the scripts of the bardo and apocalypse to today's world. We might say that humanity is in a collective bardo right now, as we navigate new unknowns and existential threats. Seen through the bardo's light, however, this is less a challenge to be feared than an opportunity to unveil a new and vastly better world.

What if more people in more places knew about the bardo and what apocalypse really means? It wouldn't magically—poof!—eliminate uncertainty, but our ability to thrive in the in-betweens of change would fundamentally improve.

Traveling east from China, we reach Japan. The land of the rising sun is also famed for its aesthetic about change and impermanence. *Wabi sabi* and *kintsugi* celebrate those forces outright.

Wabi sabi are syllables that roll off the tongue. *Wabi sabi* is the love of imperfection and the transitory nature of all things. *Wabi sabi* represents the path to wisdom and success in Japan—in other words, making peace with our ever-aging selves and our ever-changing world.[57] *Wabi sabi* doesn't attempt to keep things as they are, nor is it thrown off-kilter when they don't go as planned.

Kintsugi ("golden joinery") is the Japanese philosophy of seeing beauty in what's broken. It is best known as the art of repairing broken pottery, in which the seam that binds the broken pieces is more beautiful than the original work.[58] Both *kintsugi* and *wabi sabi* see—and *appreciate* and *encourage*—change as healthy, positive, even aspirational. Yes, change is messy. But wouldn't it be a better world if we cheered one another along through the hard stuff rather than trying to disguise it? Change can't be pretended away.

Western language has no equivalent—and really, no comparable scripts—for *wabi sabi* and *kintsugi*. Linguistic gaps may remain, but that doesn't prevent you from authoring your new script. Imagine incorporating these concepts, as more people in more places take comfort in what they stand for . . . and a new script for society begins to emerge.

> My barn having burned, I can now see the moon.
> —SEVENTEENTH-CENTURY JAPANESE POET MIZUTA MASAHIDE

The Power of *Bildung*

It's not just different cultural *concepts* of change that we can learn from. From time to time, progressive cultures have built *structures* to help people embrace massive change as well. You might think of this as creating helpful containers for getting lost . . . and for new scripts to emerge.

In the late nineteenth century, Nordic countries (Norway, Denmark, Sweden, and Finland) were poor places adjusting to the widespread changes brought about by the first Industrial Revolution (which was in its own way a tumultuous new script at the time). Government and community leaders recognized that thriving in a newly industrialized world would take much more than merely adopting a compulsory, lockstep education system. It would require a deeper understanding of one's inner world, values, and web of relationships that shape life.

So they created *bildung*: an educational ecosystem to help people explore these themes and their own personal growth. (*Bildung* is a German word that, like *wabi sabi* and *kintsugi*, has no equivalent in English.) In effect, these institutions built scaffolding for citizens standing on shaky inner ground. Roughly 10% of the population took *bildung* retreats, for free, for up to six months; this was enough for the *bildung* ethos to spread widely across society.[59]

Bildung reimagines not only educational curricula but also how students of all ages *see* the world and think about getting (or feeling) lost. It helps people write and interpret their own new scripts. It recognizes the importance of deep listening and resilience. It sees education first and foremost as the ability to navigate complexity and change.

Imagine what an updated, global *bildung* network fit for the twenty-first century could achieve!

UNCERTAINTY BY ANOTHER NAME

Think of a time when you've been truly befuddled. You probably started sleuthing the answer by looking close at hand: drawing on what you already know, plus Google searches with familiar terms.

But do you ever stop to consider what a discipline about which you know very little (or even nothing) might be able to teach you? True, this can be a bit chicken-and-egg—after all, you don't know what you don't know—yet entirely rewarding to give a whirl. And it doesn't have to be only things you don't know about.

For example, what would experts from entirely unrelated fields say about constant change?

A biologist would probably point towards evolution as constant, unrelenting change—and the superpower of species adaptation. A linguist may focus on etymology: the word *uncertainty* derives from the Latin verb *cernere*, which means "to distinguish or discern one thing from the rest." Our ability to deal with uncertainty is rooted in our ability to discern what's what—and how they are related.[60] An astronomer whose research on stars and galaxies is rife with unknowns aims to develop better ways to *estimate* uncertainty. Anthropologists may harness astronomy, too, as they research how cultures throughout human history have developed stories, metaphors, and rituals that shape our view of the world, how we orient ourselves, and whether we fear change or embrace it.

Biologists, linguists, astronomers, anthropologists—to say nothing of historians, neuroscientists, psychologists, sociologists, and myriad others—struggle with change, research change, and have developed views on change. They get lost in change in different ways *all the time.* There is no single answer, or solution, yet each of these disciplinary scripts helps fill in gaps and overcome fears about not knowing.

Different domains of expertise provide unique perspectives on change. Think of these as enriching the soil of the ground that you stand on and orient from. The closer you can stand in the shoes of another and experience change from their perspective, with their carefully drafted script in hand, the better you can understand a bigger picture, including where your own challenges with navigating change may come from and how you might embrace them.

You're *both* fortifying your foundations and helping one another get comfortable getting lost.

Amitav Ghosh is a best-selling Indian author of novels that span time, place, and culture. His view of why some people fear change and others do not is compelling. Ghosh says, "I come from a part of the world where we didn't have very rosy expectations of the world or the future. We knew there would be a lot of upheavals, and we witnessed these upheavals at first hand, so in that sense I think Westerners had a belief in stability and the promise of the future that I didn't share.

"I have a philosopher friend who says: All projections of the future are fundamentally projections of power," Ghosh continues. "This is why it's almost always the white guys who make those projections, because they're really projecting a disappearance of power into the future. I don't know anything about the future."[61]

In those few short lines, Ghosh speaks volumes about our complicated relationships with change. Some cultures have witnessed or experienced change—getting lost, in many ways—so often that it's become normalized. For these cultures, constant change *is* the script. Flux is the rule; stasis is the exception. We might think of nomadic cultures as an extreme version of this: when you move and rebuild your home several times a year, your whole life long, you naturally develop a mindset of permanent impermanence. Change is your norm.

At the other end of the spectrum, cultures that have experienced long periods of stability tend to be the most fearful of change. This fear is baked into the script. Moreover, the more tools we have to prevent ourselves from getting lost superficially—from GPS to budget-tracking apps—the easier it is for this fear to get buried. But this fear doesn't go away; it festers. Deep down we still believe we can control uncertainty, and the future . . . and as we've seen, this is what gets us in trouble.

When you open a Flux Mindset and learn to celebrate getting

lost, this celebration becomes a piece of your new script. Until then, it may torment you: keeping you from making wise decisions, opening up to new opportunities, or being fully yourself.

Cultures that normalize getting lost are far better placed at navigating a world in flux, with or without GPS. I'm not saying nomadic life is easy or that experiencing upheaval inoculates you against fear. Not at all. Rather, cultures that see constant change as the rule rather than the exception and have integrated this into their scripts are able to groove mindsets that adapt rather than control. How fluxy is that?

CODDIWOMPLING

Have you ever had an urge to travel but didn't know where to go?

Have you ever wanted to try something new but didn't know quite what?

Have you ever chafed at having to "have a plan?"

Have you ever wondered if there is more to life than "making it?" Are you even clear on what "it" actually is?

If any of these ring true, then welcome to the world of coddiwomple.

Coddi-*what?*

Coddi*womple*. A delightful word that when said well might make you blush.

Coddiwomple is an essential entry in the Flux Mindset lexicon, though it's still difficult to find in most dictionaries (which by and large overrepresent the old script). It means *to travel in a purposeful manner towards an as-yet-unknown destination.*[62]

Coddiwomple exemplifies not just getting lost but *being lost, excitedly and intentionally*, from the outset. You can coddiwomple your way into a dream job that you didn't know existed (if this intrigues you, then head to chapter 6 on portfolio careers), or you can coddiwomple your way through the adventure of a lifetime. Coddiwompling is driven by purpose, courage, and authenticity. But it breaks with tradition—and the majority of today's life coaches—by letting go of the old script's maxims: that "making it" is a fixed milestone, and "getting there" is a predetermined destination.[63] In a coddiwomple world, "it" and "there" are constantly evolving, ever changing—*and that is the essence of life.*

A coddiwompler has peace of mind because she's not waiting to "become" someone or for something else to happen. She has left the old script at the side of the road and is forging her own path. She's comfortable getting lost because, well, she knows that's where the truly worthwhile opportunities are. She's constantly incorporating new information about *what is and could be* in her new script, rather than selling herself short on *what was* in the old script. A coddiwompler is the personification of flux.

LADY, ARE YOU LOST?

On any given day, everyone is lost in some way. Yet when change hits, feeling lost can shift to feeling unmoored. Opening a Flux Mindset helps you regain your bearings while harnessing the strength that comes from getting lost.

There are many more ways you can get lost proactively in your daily life beyond what has already been shared. Here are a few easy, tried-and-true suggestions to help you build this superpower:

- Adopt the mindset of a traveler. Even if your adventures are limited to one room, your backyard, or your neighborhood: What do you carry with you? What do you *really* know (versus think you know, or wish you knew about your environs)? What do you *not* know but could benefit from learning or exploring?

- Notice the first emotion triggered when unexpected change arrives. Do you see a crisis or an opening? Do you see an apocalypse or a bardo? Spend time with these feelings and consider why they are your default. What happens if you try an alternative?

- Think like a coddiwompler. What does your purposeful manner of travel to an as-yet-unknown destination look like?

- Turn off your GPS. Orient yourself with your surroundings, as a human.

- Blindfold yourself. Explore your home or backyard blindfolded. Eat dinner in the dark. Move slowly, stop frequently, pay attention, listen. Mentally map your movements (or where food is on your plate), then test your accuracy afterwards.

Getting Lost has overlaps with every other Flux Superpower, so you'll see it again. For now, remember: getting lost is an opportunity to get found, to get comfortable in discomfort and familiar with the unfamiliar. It's part of your new script, based on your unique life journey in an ever-changing world.

GET LOST: REFLECTIONS

1. When you become disoriented, do you typically feel frustrated, fearful, or curious?

2. Do you tend to see detours as hassles or adventures?

3. When you were growing up, were you encouraged to hang out with people who are like you or different from you? What were those people like? What did you learn?

4. When faced with uncertainty, who or what grounds you and helps you find your way?

5. To what extent do other cultures or traditions factor into your worldview? How are these scripts different from yours? How did you learn about them?

Keep noticing. Keep paying attention. Keep integrating these aha's into your new script.

CHAPTER 4

START WITH TRUST

**The best way to find out if you can trust somebody
is to trust them.**
—ERNEST HEMINGWAY

Today's global trust crisis makes headlines so often it's almost
cliché. A global trust barometer has fallen to its lowest levels ever.[64]
Our trust in corporations, government, media, and academe seems
fundamentally broken. Worse, we increasingly mistrust one another.
Consider but a few ways in which this plays out all too often:

- We don't trust government leaders or CEOs to be ethical.
- We don't trust the media to report the truth.
- We don't trust corporations to put the needs of society
  before this quarter's returns.
- We don't trust someone who looks different, eats
  different foods, or wears different clothes than we do.
- We don't trust employees to show up to work on time or
  to not steal intellectual property.
- We don't trust a neighbor to respect our peace and
  privacy.
- We don't trust children to be capable of learning or
  playing safely on their own.

- We don't trust banks to see us as more than our account balance.
- We don't trust the education system to prepare the next generation for tomorrow.
- We don't trust where our food comes from, and we don't trust the companies that produce it.
- We don't trust *anything*, so we paper over our mistrust with legal contracts and lawsuits.
- We don't trust *you* to know what's best for you.
- And if this weren't enough, today there is an *active undermining* of trust underway, fueled by individuals and organizations who wish to wreak havoc and divide society.

Despite myriad laws and the regulatory, certification, and oversight organizations that are supposed to enforce them, humans are struggling with trust at every level. We distrust, or mistrust, far too many of our institutions, our leaders, our colleagues, our peers, our policymakers, our neighbors, and even (though thankfully a bit less) ourselves.[65]

We've lost our bearings and urgently need to reestablish trust as our North Star: individually, organizationally, and societally. Without it, the future is beyond bleak.

If it is any consolation, today's struggles with trust are not new. Trust has been a challenge throughout history. Rachel Botsman, trust expert and author of *Who Do You Trust?*, notes that there are more academic papers on the definition of trust than on any other sociological concept (including love).[66]

Botsman defines trust as "a confident relationship to the unknown."[67] Dictionaries call it "assured reliance on the character, ability, or truth of someone or something" or "dependence on something future or contingent; hope." Clearly confidence, hope, and uncertainty play starring roles. Together, this is called our horizon preference and affects how we perceive the world: when we have a high level of confidence—about ourselves, our surroundings, and the future—it's easier to trust. When we have a low level of confidence about any of these things, our trust wobbles. Our hope turns to fear.

Trust is not just about confidence and hope, however. It's also about intention.

When fully expressed, trust is an invitation to repair and strengthen relationships, an invitation to express your credibility, your reliability, your authenticity, and your values. When a request to "trust me" is used as a vehicle to curry favor or to get something from someone else that advances my own self-interest, it is suspicious and will likely backfire. Trust and self-interest are inversely correlated: all else being equal, the greater your true intention to help others without personal benefit, the greater your trustworthiness (and the greater the "benefit" of being trustworthy).

This book is a gesture of trust, and this chapter reflects a longer journey into trust that was jolted into hyperdrive when my parents died. All of a sudden, I *had* to trust in order to rebuild and survive. And I had to do this at precisely the same time that in many ways the world I *had* trusted melted before my eyes.

I had to trust others to guide me, including many people I'd never met before. I had to trust my grief, my heart, and my inner voice to not lead me astray. Perhaps most of all, learning to trust meant trusting love—and that loving someone did not mean they would unexpectedly die too.

This journey was neither smooth nor predictable. I met more than a few people who took advantage of me and my grief along the way. But again and again, I saw that such people were the exception, not the rule. *Most* people are fundamentally good: they greet life, and others, with good intent. Each time I was reminded of this, I became a little bit more grounded: more capable, more confident, and less anxious whenever change hit.

I began to see not only how the old script of mistrust, fear, and always being on guard was not helping me rebuild myself but also how harmful and counterproductive it is for humanity, period.

As the years passed, layers of trust formed. Years of solo travel cracked me open to trust in new ways on a near-daily basis: where to stay, whom to talk to, how much to pay, whether to accept an invitation. I began to rebuild a "family of choice" on the very principles of trust and vulnerability. Members of this extended family made leaps of faith and trust, together. Over time, our root systems intertwined.

Today as a futurist, when it comes to trust, I'm constantly on the lookout for what's around the corner. On the one hand, new technologies have vastly expanded our ability to connect with one another, and in the process to forge trust with people you may have never known otherwise. On the other hand, a wide range of companies and organizations have subtly persuaded us that they themselves are trustworthy—which, we're learning, is a leap of faith we make at our individual and collective peril. The more a company blasts out advertisements saying, "Trust us, we've got this!," the less you should actually trust them.

Trust is the glue that holds people and society together: it is the master enabler of humanity and a safer, wiser world. Nevertheless, it can take years to build and be lost in a second. You know when it exists yet can't point to it as you would a person or piece of furniture. It can only be earned, not given, even though many people try otherwise.

In so many ways, humans have slid down a slippery slope of mistrust, often without even noticing what's happened. But it doesn't have to be this way. How do we find our way back?

When trust seems broken, assume good intent.

Growing up, most children are taught: do not speak to strangers.

Growing up, most children are told: when the school bell rings, even if you're completely absorbed in what you're doing and learning, you must switch gears.

As adult professionals, we're asked to sign nondisclosure agreements (NDAs) and log in and out of time clocks. New technologies track our keystrokes and facial expressions.

Take another look at these examples and the longer list at the beginning of this chapter. Together, they cover a huge range of activities that govern much of how we live, work, raise our families, and think about the future. We have *internalized and normalized* the assumption that humans can't be trusted. It's not that you mistrust everyone automatically; rather, the default for many people is that the *average individual* cannot be trusted. In the process, mistrust becomes not only how we orient our daily lives but also an invisible yet pervasive constraint on our individual and collective dreams.

Is this the way you wish to live your life, or how you wish to be seen by others?

When it comes to trust, the old script is like death by a thousand cuts. Day in and day out, we are reminded: people are not trustworthy. We cannot and should not trust one another. All else being equal, you cannot and should not trust me, and I cannot and should not trust you.

But hang on: What are we *really* achieving here?

We're snipping the human connections and community that used to be the fabric of trust. We're normalizing mistrust, disconnecting from each other and even from ourselves. We're parching ground that was fertile, making it impossible for life—and trust—to take root and thrive.

And that's not all. We're also destroying curiosity, exacerbating inequality, and expending a ridiculous amount of time, money, and energy to keep these systems in place. (More on this in a bit.)

But remember: this is the old script, and in a world in flux, it's crumbling before our eyes.

In a world in flux, it becomes glaringly clear that trust is the glue that holds relationships, organizations, and cultures together. When the world flips upside down, trust is how you anchor and right yourself. Trusted relationships help you ride the rapids of change with confidence. Mistrust surrounds you with fear and cuts you off from others.

Starting with trust doesn't mean being naive (again, this is the old script at work). Nor does it mean there aren't bad apples in society. The brilliant twist of this superpower is quite simple: treat untrustworthiness as the exception, rather than the norm. The effect is astonishing.

When it comes to trust, the new script isn't actually that new. In reality, it's timeless. It draws from universal human consciousness and indigenous wisdom that have been passed down for millennia. But as we "industrialized" the economy, "modernized" the world, and poured money into consumer mass-marketing campaigns, we also changed the script . . . and gradually this wisdom receded from collective consciousness. But this "new" script has always been there, and it is now time for us to rediscover it. It's time to change the script back, starting with a few observations:

- Humans are naturally creative, curious, and trustworthy.
- Hamster wheels are not only not designed for humans, they are harmful to humans.
- Plundering natural resources is not okay.
- Trust is not built by marketing campaigns. Trust happens when we care for one another, look out for one another, and celebrate one another.

As with all of the Flux Superpowers, starting with trust—and embracing this new script—can only happen if you have opened a Flux Mindset. The old script believes that assuming good intent is foolish. With the old mindset, ironically, trusting someone is seen as a flaw in *your* character (not the other person)! But if you believe the new script and want to forge a more humane future, then starting with trust quite possibly reflects the most powerful of the superpowers to be fluxed.

MISTRUST DESTROYS GENIUS

Think about the last time you were invited into a team brainstorm but told you had to "stay in your lane" and couldn't think beyond the topic you were assigned. Or maybe you were told you'd asked a "stupid question," or that colleagues in another department don't know what they're talking about. Each of these instances is peppered with mistrust.

Systems designed from mistrust shut down our curiosity, shut us off, and disconnect us from one another. We kill the very things that otherwise bring our brilliance alive.

When we design from mistrust, we often destroy the genius that's in the room.[68] Rigid job titles and management hierarchies do a great job of this. So does compulsory education: we make kids study in lockstep fashion regardless of their curiosity. (History at 8 a.m.! Math at 9! Do not color outside the lines, and do not write a poem when you should be solving equations!) No wonder so many brilliant kids have a hard time with school. True, society is trying to ensure a basic level of knowledge (and a discussion of the challenges of today's education systems is beyond the scope of this book). But the bigger point is: by and large, children's curiosity and genius get stamped out, little by little, day by day—with a subtext of *"we don't trust you."*

Why do we do this? Why don't we design in a way that *unlocks* genius—as children and adults, as professionals and parents, as innovators and instigators—and blows the lid off your Flux Superpowers? Let's explore some of the reasons why, and what to do about it.

BREACHES OF TRUST BY (OUTDATED) DESIGN

Professionally, my most bitter taste of (mis)trust came as a lawyer. Whether the goal was more inclusive finance, more sustainable business, or simply making sure someone kept up their end of a deal, the tools of choice were the same: contracts, liability legalese, and lawsuits. I don't remember a single pause to consider what a contract would look like between trusted parties; the default was mistrust, and the harsher the threat of legal action, the greater the perceived likelihood of compliance. I grew increasingly aghast: Where was the human connection? I went to law school to help empower people, yet the practice of law seemed designed to divide and seed distrust among them.

My point is *not* that contracts and legal norms don't matter. Quite the opposite: the rule of law and the ability to uphold it have never mattered more. What I *am* saying is that we have papered over fundamentally human connections with legalese, and in the process we have snipped the very relationships that hold society together.

Yet law firms are but the beginning. When you really dig in, you find *perceived* breaches of trust everywhere—but *not* because most people are untrustworthy! Rather, we have designed so many things from the premise of mistrust of the average individual[69] that we've crowded out the space for authentic trustworthiness to show up. There are far too many examples to list them all here, but consider this sampling (and keep reading for more details):

- Exorbitant executive pay is a breach of trust.

- Advertising is often a breach of trust. Marketing campaigns proclaim "Trust us!" without providing full transparency. Companies stalk and surveil customers,[70] mining their information to sell more stuff while keeping them in the dark about what's really going on.

- Incentivizing and rewarding people using measures that gloss over the real implications of their work—whether that means increased stress, environmental damage caused by the products they're hired to make and sell, or prioritizing short-term profits over long-term well-being—are breaches of trust.

- Investment funds that invest in the firms doing these things are breaching the trust placed in them.

INEQUALITY BREEDS MISTRUST

Are you more likely to trust a CEO whose salary is in line with his team members, or one whose salary is exponentially greater than theirs? Why?

Are you more likely to trust a company that shares its profits with employees and opens its accounting books for public review, or one that keeps these details closed?

Are you more likely to trust someone who is rich, or someone who is poor? Why?

Inequality and mistrust are correlated. Within and among organizations, societies, countries, and cultures: the greater the inequality, the greater the mistrust.

In the United States, in 1958, the average CEO salary was eight times greater than the salary of the average worker. In 1965, this ratio had grown to 21-to-1, in 1989 it was 61-to-1, in 2018 it was 293-to-1, and in 2019 it had ballooned to 320-to-1.[71] That means the typical CEO earns 320 times as much as the average person who works for him and is perfectly content with this arrangement. Yet think about this from a worker perspective: Where is the trust? If CEOs are out for their own payday, they are not authentically out for trust. Moreover, by approving such a structure, the company—including its board of directors—is fostering a culture of mistrust. It's also botching other efforts aimed at resilience and sustainability (which we'll take up in chapter 5, Know Your "Enough"). And there's more: companies with greater salary inequality tend to be less well managed.[72]

The connection between mistrust and inequality isn't only an American problem. It's a global nemesis, with extra damage to places with colonialist history. Part of colonialism's role was *and still is* to keep a wall of mistrust between natives and colonizers, between locals and foreigners. Breaking down trust not only creates an "us vs. them" mentality, it also legitimizes structural inequality. This system sowed the early seeds of mistrust long ago; today's exorbitant executive pay is one of its many weeds that continues to fester.

Incentive-based compensation is a powerful, useful tool. It is used successfully by organizations worldwide. But too much of anything can be toxic, and when we find ourselves in a world in which approximately 2,100 people (the world's billionaires) have greater financial wealth than the poorest 4.6 *billion* people combined,[73] it's impossible not to acknowledge that this system has missed the mark.

ANCIENT WISDOM, TIMELESS TRUST

Before we slide too far down the slope of mistrust, let's take a step back into history, in order to better understand what came before us and to help us step forward into a brighter future.

In our modern-day struggles with trust, we can in fact learn a great deal from ancient and indigenous wisdom, which are in reality very much alive today and contain invaluable clues for how to flux.

Indigenous wisdom is rooted in trust and relationships: between people and the environment, between seasons and activities, between work and life, and among past and present and future.

For most of human history, people spent their days observing nature and gradually came to understand: When do fish run? When do seasons change? Where do birds lay their eggs? How do stars move?

For most of human history, people also lived in community, on the commons.[74] We managed common resources—watersheds, land, food, shelter—with a communal mindset. No resource was for one to take and another to be denied. We learned to think ahead: if you find eggs in a nest, you don't snatch them all—because you want there to be birds next year.

This wisdom was hard-won. It took patience, diligence, focus, and trust over millennia. From First Peoples in Australia to the First Nations in Canada, the Quechua in the Andes, and thousands of other tribes around the world, this ancient wisdom continues to hold the story of humankind.

Yet all of this was nearly ripped to shreds by the dual forces of colonization and consumerism, because indigenous wisdom presented a threat to their objectives.

Colonialism and consumerism, each in its own way, often labeled indigenous community management practices as heresy. Colonialists maligned and stigmatized indigenous wisdom as "primitive." Consumer-driven mass-marketing pitches seek to blind us to its timeless common sense. (Remember the consumer vs. citizen riff in chapter 2? It's a major part of our trust crisis too.) We become blinded to the point that we believe these misrepresentations are perfectly normal. A company that sells our intimate details in exchange for the ability to share our photos? Sure! A company whose CEO earns 1,000 times more than everyone else? Okay! These may (or may not) be misrepresentations or trade-offs we have agreed to; regardless, they are massive breaches of trust.

Moreover, this reality undermines our trust not only of organizations but also of one another. Mistrust has a remarkable ability to creep. Once we've normalized it, we often don't even notice it's there. But when you take a step back and look at what we've done—through surveillance capitalism and overprotection of intellectual property[75], or simply fearing a child climbing on a jungle gym—it's really weird. Common sense says we can do so much better than this. Indigenous wisdom *knows* we can.

As we seek to regain trust in the twenty-first century, this timeless wisdom is one key to get there. It is part of a "new" script that in reality long predates the old script. We don't need to find new solutions: we need to regain our bearings, reconnect with ourselves and one another, and rediscover what we've always known.

Trust, truth, and ancient cultures

More than 3,000 years ago, sages in India were at work on a number of Sanskrit texts that form the backbone of Indian traditions today. One such work was the *Yoga Sutras*, attributed to the sage Patanjali.[76] In this opus, Patanjali outlines a series of universal ethical restraints and observances, known as the *yamas* and *niyamas*. The second *yama* is *satya*, or truthfulness. Its root, *sat*, translates as "true essence or nature."

According to *satya*, trust can come only by being truthful. Practicing *satya* requires a total commitment to truth: being truthful with ourselves and with others, in our words, actions, and intentions. When we are not truthful, we disconnect from our higher selves: our minds become confused and we cannot trust ourselves. With *satya* we can trust our inner wisdom *and* the outside world—including a world in flux.

Roughly a millennium later (and still in India), the *chakra* system emerged as part of another ancient text, the *Vedas*.[77] *Chakras* are the seven energy centers within the human body, typically represented by a spinning disk or wheel that runs along one's spine. The health of your *chakras* is directly connected to the health of your mind, body, and spirit.

The first *chakra*, known as the root *chakra*, grounds you and governs your sense of security. The second *chakra*, known as the sacral *chakra* or *svadhisthana*, means "the place of the self" and governs your emotions—including your right to feel.

If you are unable to trust, you are unable to feel. Trust is what opens you up to experience, engage, learn, and feel alive. When you are unable to feel, *everything else* in your system—including your personal power, identity, confidence, compassion, voice, perception, and intuition—can become blocked or, worse, cut off altogether. Trust is the fulcrum around which your potential revolves.

Halfway around the world and nearly two millennia later, the Toltecs of Mesoamerica further leveled up our understanding of trust. Popularized in *The Four Agreements* by Don Miguel Ruiz, the Toltecs held that truth—and trust—were at the center of all else.[78] The first agreement is: *be impeccable with your word*. What is impeccable but being truthful and trustworthy?

THE NEW SCRIPT: DESIGN FROM TRUST

The old script of mistrust is like death by a thousand cuts, many of which we've now witnessed. In contrast, the new script of trust offers enormous opportunity—indeed, a super-superpower—for those who can embrace a Flux Mindset. When we start with trust, responsibly, we create abundance, connection, and solidarity. Consider the following:

- Wikipedia is a global online encyclopedia that allows *anyone in the world* to edit it.[79]

- Netflix's employee expense policy is five words long: *Act in Netflix's best interests.*[80] No fancy HR handbooks, no per diems, no forms to sign. Just five words.

- BlaBlaCar is a global intercity ride-sharing platform that operates across Europe, Asia, and Latin America. Travelers heading in the same direction use it to share rides. They don't know each other in advance but often make fast friends. BlaBlaCar transports more than four times as many people as the entire European train network and is valued at more than $1 billion.

- Microfinance is the provision of small loans to economically active poor people with no collateral. Traditional banks deem such customers "unbankable," yet microfinance clients' repayment rates are consistently as high or higher than any other type of loan.

- Early natives in Argentina mastered the art of horse gentling, known as *doma india.*[81] For them, the traditional practice of taming a horse by "breaking" it is not only cruel but also leads to a far less capable animal. (It was only much later, when Europeans arrived in South America, that breaking horses began.)

- In Kibera (an urban slum near Nairobi, Kenya) and countless neighborhoods worldwide, neighbors share ingredients. One family provides the salt, another provides the flour. This is done without ledgers or IOUs. "What's available" is not limited to your cupboard but, rather, extended to your community.

- Open-source software is software that anyone can use, study, modify, and share. It's developed in a collaborative, public manner—in other words, it's the antithesis of intellectual property zealously protected by legal moats. Some of today's most powerful and popular programs are open source. Moreover, the concept extends far beyond software: open-source projects, products, and initiatives exist in almost every sector, harnessing the principles of open exchange, transparency, and collaborative participation.

Online encyclopedias, ride sharing, HR departments, software development, financial services: these are wildly different examples. Yet what do they all share in common?

They are all designed from trust,[82] a fundamental building block of the new script.

These systems, models, products, and services are created from a fundamental belief that most humans are trustworthy, have good intentions, and are hardwired for human connection. Not *all* people: *most* people![83] Designing from trust acknowledges that bad apples exist, but treats them as an exception rather than the rule.

Designing from trust frees the genius that mistrust tried to destroy. Open-source software and Netflix's HR norms trust people to figure things out and make new discoveries together. They turn the fear of scarcity into abundance born from trust.

These examples are counterintuitive at first. They force you to see just how far down the rabbit hole of mistrust you may have gone, often without realizing it. You might even feel embarrassed.

But once you've gone beyond that and really thought about what these examples represent, you want more. You want to join. You become an ambassador for trustworthiness. *You crave more trust: to be trusted, to trust others, to live in a world that's designed from trust.* (Just imagine. It'd be awesome, no?)

I first learned about design from trust thanks to Jerry Michalski. Back in the 1990s, Jerry was a technology trends analyst. As he researched companies, he was shaken by consumerism's hold on our lives. Over the years, he saw how the way we're treated as consumers (rather than as citizens, creators, collaborators, or simply *humans*) involves many breaches of trust. Later, he grew those insights into Design from Trust.[84] I came to trust Jerry, and his way of thinking, so much that I ended up marrying him.

THE NEW SCRIPT: LEAD WITH TRUST

I can hear you now: "I get the concept. But as a leader, *really*, what does it look like to start with and design from trust?" Here's a snapshot of what to do, where to begin, and what to aim for on the horizon.

It Sucks to Hide Everything

As you've seen (and almost certainly experienced firsthand), companies are doing all kinds of things that prevent them from be(com)ing trustworthy.

When you design from mistrust, you have to hide information: from employees, from customers, from friends, ironically from whomever you wish to placate (or, in less-inspiring terms, from whomever you wish to co-opt). If you have exorbitant compensation structures, you've foreclosed the ability to have a candid, open conversation rooted in trust. You might launch a "trust us!" marketing campaign—but that is a clear-cut signal of untrustworthiness for workers and customers alike.

Here's a good filter for whether your company is trustworthy: if it *can't* share salary information transparently, if it runs marketing campaigns designed to persuade rather than empower customers, or if it keeps workers in lockstep lanes, then there's a good chance it's not.

It takes nontrivial actions to overcome these barriers and become a truly trustworthy organization. On the upside, there are myriad ways this can happen.

A good baseline is to conduct a "trust audit": identify all of the places where trust is high, low, or nonexistent. Can you map these? Do you have an inkling of how mistrust crept in? Do you apply policies designed from mistrust to colleagues you have no reason *not* to trust?

For starters, err on the side of openness. Think open books: let all employees see budgets, salaries, and metrics.

Then, go further: let employees set salaries and bonuses, working together. Trust that if you delegate down and provide enough information, they'll get the job done well—*and reciprocate the trust.* You've just freed their genius and turned scarcity into abundance: when people feel trusted, they're not only more creative but more positively productive as well.

Then, keep going down this path of trust: walk the talk and foster workplace democracy. Give all employees company shares. Establish a cooperative structure for at least some portion of your operations.

Some additional questions that may come up and are worth answering along the way:

- When it comes to metrics, not everything can be measured by numbers. How do you measure trust?
- If your organization's culture and sustainability are fundamentally rooted in people and relationships, then how do you measure their health?
- Do you assume the good intent of others? If not, then why would you hire that person in the first place?

The Paradox of Vulnerability and Trust

You're the CEO of an organization. I say "vulnerability." What does it mean to you? What does it mean to your colleagues?

You and your life partner are talking about "vulnerability." What does it mean to you? What does it mean to your partner?

You may find that your answers are completely opposite. In a business setting, vulnerability is often associated with weakness. Yet in a personal setting, vulnerability is one of the most treasured traits we can have. It is what allows us to love, be loved, and show up fully as ourselves.

With the old script, we saw vulnerability as a liability to design *out* of systems.

With the new script and in a world in flux, we need to responsibly design vulnerability *into* systems in ways that actually *boost* resilience, *allow for* change and evolution, and wake up that part of our humanity that wants to connect and do the right thing.

In the new script, *vulnerability is an asset, not a liability.* We transcend the barrier of lawyers freaking out and telling us that we can't be vulnerable on any dimension or that we're doomed if we show any weakness. In large measure, what lawyers are *actually* freaked out about—and I say this as a recovering lawyer myself—is that some of their fees will disappear.

BUT THIS FEELS SO . . . WEIRD!

If any of this feels counterintuitive, contrarian, awkward, or even scary, you're not alone. It's hard to let go of old scripts and ways of thinking that you've relied on for years, or to acknowledge they're badly broken. They don't merely need to be fixed; they demand wholesale transformation—and that is one of the most exciting, worthwhile, and fulfilling parts of your leadership journey.

In times of low trust, high-trust leaders and organizations are even more attractive. In a world in flux, trust is your moral compass and differentiator. Trustworthiness distinguishes you from the old script of "business as usual." Trust is what keeps customers coming back (without a marketing budget!) and bolsters your longevity. Today, this opportunity to differentiate yourself in ways that really matter is bigger than ever.

Keep this in mind, as well: starting with trust isn't just about you. Consider the power of collective intelligence, collaborative sense-making, and the power that emerges when we *collectively* start with trust. Think about how you can be an advocate for this with others and what you can forge together. Think of the new (yet timeless!) ways of working, living, collaborating, creating, understanding, learning, leading, and *being* that are finally unlocked.

IN FLUX WE TRUST

In a world in flux, a culture of mistrust isn't merely frustrating, inefficient, or unjust. In an environment of constant change, without trust among people, society begins to break. It is impossible to manage ongoing uncertainty without trust: it's as if we've thrown our compasses *and* life jackets overboard while a storm rages at sea, even while many people on the boat recognize that our individual and collective survival depends on them.

We are in the early stages of this boat capsizing. Depending on whom you talk to, the cracks in the hull are already clear. Those who feel most threatened by the cracks—or whom a culture of mistrust serves well—are the least likely to see them. This complicates the landscape of uncertainty: Will humans *ever* see eye to eye?

Yet, to heed Leonard Cohen's well-worn phrase, these cracks are precisely how the light gets in and a brighter future has a fighting chance. Today's reality is both a wake-up call and an opening to transition. It's an entry point to rethink and redesign how we live, work, relate, and see one another. And we can—we must—rethink, and unlearn, and relearn, and begin again . . . with trust.

START WITH TRUST: REFLECTIONS

1. Can the average person be trusted? Why or why not? What influences your response?

2. Are you usually quick to trust or quick to mistrust?

3. Do you trust yourself? When does your trust in yourself falter most?

4. If something can't be measured, does it exist?

5. When you ask people to "trust you," how does it feel?

CHAPTER 5

KNOW YOUR "ENOUGH"

Greed is a little bit more than enough.
—INDONESIAN POET TOBA BETA

I still remember the day. I was seven years old, sitting at the sun-dappled kitchen nook that my father had built. My chin barely grazed the tabletop, and my mother led the conversation.

"April, you've just learned how to add, subtract, multiply, and divide. You like numbers. We have an idea that we think will help you learn even more. From today, we're putting you in charge of your own budget."

At the time, I couldn't quite process what this meant. What about my allowance? Was this like a budget for pocket money, or for *everything*?

It turns out, my parents were quite serious. If not everything, I was in charge of *almost* everything: from school supplies to underwear to "fun money." I could earn as much as I wanted, though the going rates for seven-year-old labor weren't especially lucrative. My parents were public school teachers; money was chronically, uncomfortably tight.

Unsurprisingly, I became entrepreneurial and resourceful fast. I began using whatever skills I had to make ends meet: I learned how to sew and sold simple clothes. I washed cars, cleaned our neighbors' homes, and mowed lawns. I learned how to budget, what loans and compounding interest are, and eventually how financial markets work.

At the same time as I hustled and learned, I lived in a limbo of not knowing if I would have enough. My parents made it clear that if I couldn't make ends meet, I shouldn't ask them for help. My mother's daily mantra was self-sufficiency and independence, yet my seven-year-old self sometimes felt abandoned, as if I'd been thrown into the deep end without a safety float.

When I went to college, I was shocked when my friends would simply ask their parents for money. They were eighteen and had never had to budget?! I was both horrified and a tad envious.

And then my parents died. Almost immediately, I had to ask: What did enough *really* mean?

- Enough love to survive?
- Enough security to feel safe?
- Enough money to take care of myself?
- Enough joy to remember what's good in life?
- Enough patience to see a better tomorrow?
- Enough courage to take the next step?

In the years since that initial reckoning, this concept of enough has only become richer and more complex for me. Beginning with my work in global development and travels throughout frontier markets, I began to question, directly and often uncomfortably, what is:

- Enough compassion for humanity?
- Enough income to pull someone out of poverty?
- Enough food, water, housing, and health care to thrive?
- Enough commitment to help others in need, wherever they may be?

In today's consumer-driven world, we are plagued by a stubborn script that proclaims "More is better" and taunts you for never doing, earning, or achieving enough. This script is old and crusty, but it remains very much alive. Among its more popular manifestations is that *you will never have enough*:

- Power to make a difference
- Prestige to feel important
- Money to be rich
- Choice to be satisfied
- New toys to outshine your peers or neighbors
- Success, period.

And as we race to acquire more stuff, we leave essential priorities on the table such as:

- What is enough equality?
- What is enough integrity?
- What is enough well-being?

At the end of the day, too many people struggle to answer: *Am I enough?* (You may even be wondering if Know *Your* Enough is a typo for Know *You're* Enough. I assure you it is not.)

It's all rather out of control. But pay attention: by and large, these are echoes of the old script. They begin to dissolve when you write a new script centered on enough. This script is sustainable, inspiring, and human-centric. It helps you redefine your metrics of success, brings contentment, and transforms how you think about what you have, do, and aspire to become.

In a world relentlessly striving for more, know your "enough."

The ancient Greek root word of enough is *enenkeîn*, which means "to carry." For much of human history, how much a person could carry was enough. The concept is rooted in human scale. Other early languages, from Latin to Old English to Albanian, similarly focused on enough's sufficiency and satisfaction: enough meant having reached, attained, or met one's needs. Not more, and not less.

Today, *enough* is both an adjective and an adverb. Whether in terms of quantity or quality or scope, enough still maintains a focus on sufficiency and satisfaction: not more, and not less.

Yet somewhere along the way, despite definitions, there was a shift. Mentally, emotionally, and practically, a large proportion of humanity dropped the norm of "enough to satisfy" and picked up a new mantle: perpetual insufficiency, insatiability, and "never enough."

A big chunk of this shift can be traced to the advent of modern consumerism. The consumerist script relentlessly succeeds in convincing individuals and society as a whole that more is better. The more you own, the greater your "worth." The more you earn, the greater your importance. The more followers you have, the more . . .

Seriously?!

This script has also put us, collectively, on a hamster wheel that's racing ever faster to nowhere. (Cue chapter 1, Run Slower.) Even people with myriad accomplishments and accolades still crave "more."

A mindset of "more" measures by numbers and relative power: "You are what you measure." "If you can't measure it, it doesn't exist." You earn more than Jack, you're less successful than Olivia, your house is bigger than Frank's, your IQ is lower than Julia's, and so on. Yet what does this really say about you—and the values behind these metrics?

This "cycle of more" and the script that powers it can be quick to take root and surprisingly difficult to let go. The truth is: no amount of physical stuff can *ever* replace your inner sense of worth, but it *can* easily bankrupt you (and harm the environment in the process). Yet the old script persuades you of the exact opposite. This is how today's consumerism is *designed*: the goal of "more" can never be fully satisfied, which keeps you tethered to the hamster wheel, clicking on ads and buying things that never fully satisfy.

But hold on. This is a script. And it's not a script that many people would opt into, if they actually paused and thought about it. Who wants to live for an unattainable goal set by others, that's exhausting and expensive, and often brings more jealousy than joy?

The new script sees through the mirage of more and says, enough is enough.

With your Flux Mindset opened, you can begin to reset your metrics and write a new script. This shift—from an interminable quest for more to a clear understanding of your enough—is simple yet profound.

Knowing your enough does not mean being miserly, uncharitable, or living in scarcity. If that's your reaction (or your fear), you've misunderstood this superpower entirely. Knowing your enough is in fact the opposite of these things: it gives you room for generosity and plenitude.[85] (A great irony of this superpower is that in a world focused on more, you'll never find enough. Yet in a world focused on enough, you'll immediately find more.)

Knowing your enough brings clarity about what really matters. When you know your enough, you have less anxiety and your ability to thrive expands a lot. Honing this superpower unleashes your full potential to the world.

Knowing your enough sees through the futility of comparison and empowers you to develop your own metrics of "enoughness" rooted in internal satisfaction, meaning, relationships, resilience, discovery, and helping others. Such metrics transcend a price tag.

They don't diminish the success of others: I am not "more" fulfilled than you, or vice versa, if we're clear on our respective enoughs. To the contrary, we're more capable of lifting one another up.

And here's the crux: in a world in flux, when change knocks you upside down, your enough matters. A LOT. If you're hustling on the hamster wheel and aren't clear on your enough, expect a world of pain when change hits: not only the pain of being knocked off the hamster wheel and not knowing where to turn, or the angst of feeling insufficient by societal standards (which you nonetheless opted into), but also the discomfort and risk of maintaining an "ever-more" lifestyle. Put another way, when change hits, the more you need—or the further away your enough lies—the less flexibility you have to adapt.

But it doesn't have to be this way, and this chapter explores how people, organizations, and cultures around the world are figuring this out every day.

TODAY'S TENSION: TOO MUCH VS. NOT ENOUGH

To be clear, there is a huge difference—and a lot of tension today—between people who have more than enough and those whose basic needs are not met. It is a completely different conversation with someone who wants to simplify their life and someone who worries about feeding their family or having a roof over their head.

As we learned in chapter 2, privilege keeps people from seeing the full picture. Privilege tends to limit your script, your perceptions of what's in the script, and your beliefs about how that script could change. Whether you have "more than enough" or "not enough" is inevitably to some degree a function of your privilege—regardless of whether that privilege is due to hard work, other people, or sheer luck.

What is your enough?

- How do you define "enough" today? Do you define it differently *p 117* for yourself versus other people? Why or why not? *relationships* *future* *open mind, empathy*
- How do you define your self-worth? What metrics do you use? *discovery* *£*
- What do you have "more than enough" of today?
- What do you have "not enough" of today? *discovery, balance$*
- What sentiment usually comes up when you think about enough: frustration, inspiration, anticipation, fear, joy, or *freedom* something else?
- What is your "enough" that will help you create a better world? *-*

Keep these answers close at hand while reading this chapter.

While it's impossible to strip you of your privilege within the pages of this book, it is nevertheless essential to check your privilege at the outset, in order to truly develop this superpower. To help you do so, consider the following in the context of whatever privilege you may have:

- What does it mean to have more than enough money, but less than enough humanity?
- What does it mean to have too many clothes, but not enough fresh air to breathe?
- What does it mean to have too many things on your to-do list, yet not enough time to think?

More than enough is too much. Not enough is precarious. Neither is fit for flux.

Knowing your enough means both paring back excess and lifting up those in need. Knowing your enough means appreciating that your individual enough is contingent on society's enough. An example can bring this dynamic to life.

Around the world, people are worried about the effect of automation on the workforce. Will my job be eliminated? If the vocation I've trained for becomes obsolete, what will I do? Careers are in flux, expectations are in flux, and the future of work is in flux. *Will there be "enough" work for "enough" people to earn "enough" income to have a decent "enough" standard of living?*

In Sweden, the national government's strategy is to "protect people, not jobs." The Swedish government has made it clear that no job (including yours) is guaranteed: a new technology (or a pandemic, changing tastes, or myriad other forces) may result in your job becoming obsolete. However, the government *does* guarantee that if your livelihood is disrupted, your well-being will be protected. This is done via income support and retraining, and is paid for by taxes.[86]

Pause for a moment and think about the implications of Sweden's policy. Losing a job is never easy, and especially not during times of great change and uncertainty. Your brain may go into crisis mode: struggling to be creative, resisting acknowledgment of what's happened, and perhaps even shutting down entirely. You've lost your professional identity (we'll pick this up in the next chapter) and along with it a piece of your old script.

Yet what if you knew that, although you may not earn "more" prestige from the promotion you'd expected or "more" income as the most senior person on the team, you still had enough of both to move forward? You could free your brain from worrying about what is no longer and focus instead on what is to come.

This is not a book about public policy; however, the policy implications of enough are remarkable. They affect productivity, future-readiness, organizational culture, social stability, and individual and collective well-being. In countries with limited or no flexible labor policies, it's no wonder that people fear automation.

In the absence of basic income guarantees, affordable access to health care, and future-forward retraining programs, it's easy to envision—even doing everything you're supposed to—slipping towards "not enough."

LEADING WITH ENOUGH

If you and I were having a real-time conversation, this is the point where a question or two around leadership might arise. You're a leader and a seeker, but what does leadership in a world of enough look like?

As we saw in the introduction, the old script has a narrow definition of leadership. But with a Flux Mindset and a new script, leadership takes on new and expanded relevance, not least because what makes a great leader evolves in a world in flux.

Leading from a place of enough looks quite different from what many self-styled leadership gurus stuck in the old script suggest. This superpower goes beyond dismantling hierarchies or establishing diversity, equity, and inclusion (DEI) initiatives. It has implications for responsible leadership and longevity, as well as sustainability and trust. It also has a few surprises.

Let's begin with that last bit about trust. Go back to what we learned in chapter 4: within organizations and societies alike, *the greater the inequality, the greater the mistrust*. If, as a leader, your salary is dramatically greater than your colleagues, then unfortunately you have established a culture of mistrust *and* put yourself on a path *away from* enough.

Ask yourself, and then ask your colleagues: Are you more likely to trust a CEO whose salary is in line with his team, or one whose salary is vastly greater? Why?

Next, consider your legacy. What do you want to be remembered for? *Why* do you do what you do?

Leading with the old script in hand, you might answer this question in terms of more: maximize profits, create a bigger company, have a bigger house, or build a big yacht. But this would be woefully out of touch.

Leadership with the new script and a Flux Mindset would answer in terms of paying everyone enough, ensuring everyone feels safe and valued, and treating others as peers rather than subordinates.

Go back to your legacy. When you're gone, people won't remember whether you had "more." They will remember how you treated them.

In 2018, visionary architect Kevin Cavenaugh gave a TEDx talk titled "How Much Is Enough?"[87] In it, he noted that Milton Friedman won the Nobel prize in economics in 1976 for, among other things, espousing the notion that greed is good. Yet, Kevin wondered, what might have happened if a leader with Toba Beta's perspective ("greed is a little bit more than enough") had won the Nobel prize back then instead, and we'd spent the past forty-plus years building an economy that both values innovation and technology and also ensures we rise together with enough?

Forty years later, we are witnessing the effects of this short-sightedness. In our quest for growth, profits, efficiency, and "more," we've been blind to (or simply looked away from) the impacts on relationships, inequity, and inequality. While we've kept marketing departments busy and earnings reports in line, we've sold consumers (or, better word: humans) short.

Kevin puts it this way: "As a property developer, one approach to rent is to make as much money as possible out of every square foot. I call these properties 'greedy buildings.' Another approach is to ensure housing for all. This means creating beautiful, affordable buildings that humans love to inhabit and are enough to meet their needs. This is the legacy I want to leave."[88]

It's not that Kevin doesn't care about money or profitability. Quite the opposite. But the lens through which he views these things is rooted in enough, which makes a profound difference.

In both Kevin's and my own experience, *if you're not having a conversation about enough, then you're leaving value (including money!) on the table.* And here's why:

Conversations about more tend to focus on transactions: how to do more deals, monetize more interactions, and make more money. The time frame is short: the sooner money can be made, the faster you can cash out. In this world, people are consumers: they are mere means to a monetized end. There is no genuine care for their well-being beyond their ability to pay.

Conversations about enough, on the other hand, center on relationships: how to cultivate lifelong friendships, build sustainable and human-centric enterprise, and nourish the planet. The time frame is long: this is about lifetime leadership and evergreen legacies, with humanity at the core.

Leading with the old script and a "more" mindset treats relationships as transactional. Monetizing relationships can kill them outright (at best, it saps them of meaning).

Leading with enough means nurturing relationships above all

else: not for money, but for their inherent and often incalculable value.

Relationships endure and sustain; deals are done and put on a shelf. Which do you want to be remembered for?

THE ECONOMICS OF MORE

Assessing the full effects of capitalism, consumerism, and modern-day mass marketing on human behavior is its own book series. This book is not that endeavor. But let's briefly scan the economic landscape and identify a few key landmarks that will guide our path to enough.

Going back a couple millennia, did you know that the root of the word *economy* isn't industry or quarterly returns? It's the Greek word *oikos*, which means "home" or "household." In Greek, *oikonomia* (economy) means abundance.[89]

Next, fast-forward in history to prior to the 1980s, when it was common practice for companies to share their profits with workers. Back then, the average store clerk or factory worker could expect to have job stability and a nest egg for retirement. Of course, there were differences between countries, cultures, and company size, but on the whole for developed economies, this structure held true. Ensuring that all workers had enough—to care for their family today and plan for the future—was considered smart, responsible business.

Since the 1980s, however, this model has gone sideways. The 1980s ushered in an era of cost-cutting, outsourcing, and automation in the name of higher efficiency, productivity, and bottom lines. The script shifted from ensuring that all workers had enough to: As long as there are "enough" quarterly returns for investors and market analysts, why should "enough" for anyone else matter?

The effects of reframing the old script in this way are astounding and disturbing.

Since the 1980s, profit-sharing with rank-and-file workers has all but disappeared, particularly in large companies. Paradoxically, this is precisely the era in which profit-sharing with company executives began.[90] The slice of workers for whom holistic well-being is taken into account narrowed to a fraction of what it had been. And ever since, the corporate world has jumped on the "more" bandwagon and not looked back.

Fast-forward again, to today, when 2,153 billionaires hold greater wealth than the 4.6 *billion* people who constitute 60 percent of the world's population combined. The twenty-two richest men in the world have more wealth than all of the women in Africa.[91] Global inequality has gone bonkers in the pursuit of more.

But inequality isn't only in terms of global development. It lurks in every country, city, neighborhood, and backyard—with countless troubling ripple effects.

As we saw in chapter 4, inequality breeds mistrust. Moreover, systemic inequality normalizes a "more" mindset while rendering invisible those without "enough." This imbalance increases until we reach a breaking point. Many people would say that point is nearing now.

To be clear, it's not that capitalism is inherently flawed. Capitalism is a powerful and useful tool when used responsibly. Our challenge is that the current *flavor* of capitalism, as set forth in the old script, is toxic: it is addicted to more and allergic to enough.

The old script keeps your eyes glued to your screens and your wallet empty. It reminds you that your job is to buy more, consume more, and that *you. will. never. be. enough.*

Yet hold on a minute. Who wrote this script?! Is this really what you believe? Have you asked your inner voice about it?

For many years I took the old script for granted too. It was what I was taught in school, all the way through capital markets classes at Harvard. But when I tried to apply it to the real world, it fell short. I couldn't reconcile it with my observations and experiences, at home and worldwide.

Sure, venture capitalists remain hell-bent on maximizing financial returns, lawyers continue to seek tax-efficient structures, and venerable economists are petrified by the prospect of "de-growth." But respectfully, each of these stakeholders is arguing with a tattered, outdated script.

At the same time, I've seen firsthand how $25–$100 is enough funding to start a micro-enterprise in some parts of India (and other emerging economies), how one car is enough mobility for several people when effective car-sharing is in place, and how one neighborhood has more than enough resources to go around when neighbors open their closets and cupboards. Concepts like Doughnut Economics take these ideas further, casting a practical vision for long-term, society-wide sustainability at scale.[92]

The economics of more don't square, yet large swaths of today's society are shackled to their expectations and the old script. Yet if we apply *oikos* and write a new script, we can see *real* abundance and reap the benefits of enough.

THE PSYCHOLOGY OF MORE

As the best-selling author of *Drive: The Surprising Truth about What Motivates Us*, Daniel Pink has had a front-row seat to research and experiments about the psychology of more. What he found is revealing.[93] Most people are motivated by autonomy, mastery, and purpose. They like to be self-directed, to improve, and to do the right thing, and they are motivated when more of these outcomes are available. Most people are *not* motivated by more money. Paying people *enough* is important, but beyond that its effect is negligible.

Yet think about how we structure compensation packages and develop metrics. We brag about making more money, but we rarely celebrate self-direction or nonmonetary satisfaction over salary.

And it's not just salary: we're also addicted to success. As you saw in chapter 1, anxiety makes us run faster, and the more we take on, the harder it is to let go. We grasp for more: more status, more wealth, more certainty. Ironically, the more successful we're seen to be, the more we worry about being "enough."

Yet this goal can't be met. We can thank the "hedonic treadmill" for this.[94] When I'm on the hedonic treadmill (which I like to imagine is perched next to the hamster wheel), the satisfaction I get from success wears off quickly, like a drug high. To keep up, and avoid lapsing into sentiments of "not enough," I must run towards the next reward. I may even sacrifice my own well-being with overwork to keep the feeling of success alive.

As investor and author Morgan Housel says, "Enough is realizing that the opposite—an insatiable appetite for more—will push you to the point of regret."[95]

Think about the last time you felt really proud of an accomplishment. How long did that feeling last?

What is most bizarre (until you sit and really think about it) is that even supersuccessful people are envious of people they see as more successful. Why? Because "more" is viewed in comparison with others in your reference group, whether that group is millionaires, teachers, or stay-at-home parents.[96] In other words, the pursuit of more is futile. You will never reach your destination, because the mile marker will keep changing. And changing. And changing.

That is, until you fall ill, find yourself trapped by golden handcuffs, or are on your deathbed. At that point you realize that chasing ever more isn't the point of life, nor does it give life meaning. Externally your life looks full, but internally your spirit feels bankrupt. You wonder: what's the point?

Metrics and values

Metrics measure what we value. How we spend our time is how we spend our love.

- Whom do you admire more: someone who spends his time getting himself to the top, or someone who helps others reach their dreams? How do *you* spend your time?
- Which metric do you prefer: how someone spends their time or how they spend their money?
- What do you value, and how does that reflect your values?

When the world is upside down, in some ways it's easier to ask this question. When you do, you're heading straight towards a Flux Mindset. Knowing your enough means having internal clarity. With this superpower, you're able to quiet the noise that taunts you about being not enough and embrace the fact that *you are*.

FROM MORE TO ENOUGH

As the old script peels away and you take stock of today's reality, your new script begins to emerge. This script recognizes that:

- There is a big difference between "too much" and "not enough."
- Your enough depends on whether your worldview is one of abundance or scarcity.
- Our current system is *designed* to keep people craving more, even as people yearn to be accepted as enough.
- Today's society has dangerous proxies for enough. The more you try to buy your way to love or fulfillment, the more alone and insufficient you're likely to feel.

- Inequality and basic security (income, food, housing, health) are catalysts for enough.
- There is no such thing as too much love, too much compassion, or too much humanity.

When you open a Flux Mindset, you're able to embrace this script. When the world is upside down and tomorrow is anyone's guess, if you know your enough, you're ready to flux.

Now let's explore a few easy-to-grasp ways to start making this happen. Enough is enough!

Subtract before Adding

A mindset grooved towards more has an incredible propensity to creep. This goes beyond simply craving more success. We begin to believe that all of life is improved by addition. A new friend, a new car, a new role, a new house, a new dress, a new toy, a new trip, a new insight: all of these things should make our lives better, happier, and more fulfilling. Right?

So very wrong.

New ideas, a new relationship, or a new haircut can undoubtedly boost your spirits and may even change your life. But the addition of each one also adds to your to-do list and increases the demands on your finite time.

What if, instead of adding to reach your "more," you subtracted to find your "enough?"

The ways you can subtract are almost endless. Start small. Here are some favorites:

- Unsubscribe from one newsletter.
- Remove an app from your phone.
- Gently end a negative relationship.
- Gracefully decline one invitation.
- Cancel one subscription.

- Let go of feeling guilty for an obligation.
- Cut one workday free of meetings each week.
- Sell the exercycle (or pick-your-choice-of-appliance) that you haven't used in a decade.
- Donate one item of clothing that you haven't worn in ages.
- Retire one hobby, club, or group that's no longer inspiring you.
- Turn off the television. Eliminate background noise.
- Empty your cup instead of filling it.
- Shed a mindset that is holding you back.
- When you are tired, rest.

Subtracting not only simplifies our lives. It also creates time, space, and resources to focus on what really matters . . . which actually *boosts* your chances for fulfillment and success.

Give

Generosity is the spirit of giving liberally. Being generous means knowing the joy of giving to others. Authentic generosity isn't book-keeping: it seeks nothing in return.

In the old script, people who chase "more" see generosity as "less." If my goal is to have more than someone else, why would I give something away?

But in a world in flux, as we've seen, this old script blows up. With a Flux Mindset and your new script, generosity is a super-power enabler.

As Adam Grant showed in his seminal book *Give and Take*, the most successful people are the most generous people who also know when and how to ask for help.[97] Generous leaders understand that having the greatest impact on the world means *giving* the most *of* ourselves, not *acquiring* the most *for* ourselves. To be more, give more.

Yoga and subtraction

In yoga philosophy, *brahmacharya* is the principle of nonexcess.[98] Historically, practicing *brahmacharya* included abstaining from sex. (The thinking went: individuals were to conserve their sexual energy and use it to further their yogic path.) That condition didn't last long in the modern era, however, and today *brahmacharya* means living in moderation.

When you strip away everything that is not authentically you, and everything that keeps you from experiencing the truth of who you are, you are able to bring more of your true self to life. By subtracting what you are *not*, you become all that you *are*.

A potlatch is a gift-giving feast practiced by the First Nations peoples of Canada and other indigenous tribes in North America. The word *potlatch* comes from the Chinook Jargon language and means "to give away," or "gift."[99] In a potlatch, leaders give away their wealth: *wealth is expressed by giving it away* to others in the community. We're not talking about token donations or giving away thousands while keeping millions for yourself. A potlatch means giving away the very resources that keep you alive.

A potlatch system prevents any one family from accumulating wealth, strengthening relationships and social harmony in the process. Yet look deeper: from a potlatch perspective, the more you give away—the more vulnerability you express—the more powerful and revered you are.

For anyone with the old script, a potlatch can seem absurd. But with an open Flux Mindset and a new script, the potlatch system represents wisdom beyond words. It is an ancient tradition with timeless value.

Potlatch forces us to rethink our views on wealth. Wealth is not something that an individual holds; rather, it is shared with the

The risk of mis-FIRE-ing

In recent years, the Financial Independence, Retire Early (FIRE) movement has indeed caught fire.[100] Around the world people are learning to live frugally, save aggressively, and escape the hamster wheel (including often uninspiring jobs).[101]

On the one hand, FIRE could be seen as the ultimate enough: a sort of allergic reaction to more. On the other hand, however, FIRE has come increasingly under criticism for what it glosses over: meaning and motivation.[102] Early retirement will not give your life purpose if you didn't have it before; in fact, it may exacerbate your feelings of insufficiency (to say nothing of how a lack of livelihood may roil you in times of great change).

Insofar as FIRE can help people rethink their enough and expand their options mindfully, it can be transformational. But beware of the risk of misfiring: without meaning and motivation, your best FIRE intentions could go up in smoke.

community. The value of the items that a leader potlatches isn't lost; it is simply distributed. Ultimately that value is returned, many times over.

In times of great change, when the world is in flux, we need each other more than ever. We need one another's support, wisdom, guidance, presence, and occasionally a shoulder to cry on. We need one another's generosity.

Knowing your enough means knowing that the more you give, the better you make others' lives. The better you make others' lives, the more they can contribute to the world. The more they can contribute to the world, the more your life is improved . . . and the cycle continues.

What's your personal potlatch?

Know Your Happiness from Your Contentment

Ancient and indigenous cultures almost never use the term *happiness* when they describe what it means to be well. Rather, they use some form of the word *contentment*. Why?

Start by considering what makes you happy. Perhaps it's seeing a loved one, or nice weather, or good news. Chances are it's due to some factor beyond you: an external circumstance, person, or event.

Now consider what makes you content. (If you equate contentment with happiness, this may be your first signal to learn more.) Contentment comes entirely from within.

In other words, attaining "happiness" will always be outside your control. Moreover, it will be fleeting. Just as you attain it, it's taken away. (Can you think of a time, place, or situation in which happiness stuck around forever? My hunch is: no.) So you start seeking it again, and the cycle repeats. This doesn't mean you shouldn't strive to be happy . . . just beware of its limits.

Contentment, on the other hand, is entirely within your power. Moreover, it can be permanent if you understand where it comes from and how to harness it.

The word *contentment* comes from the Latin root *contentus*, which means "to hold together" or "to contain." It was used originally to describe containers, and later people as well. If a person is content, she feels complete and held together—*within herself.* In other words, contentment is a state of "unconditional wholeness," regardless of what is happening externally.[103]

Notice the overlaps between contentment and enough. Both are rooted in internal satisfaction and sufficiency. (Peek again at the Greek word for enough, *enenkeîn*, at the beginning of this chapter for a refresher.) Knowing your enough brings you one step closer to contentment. Not needing to be more, and not desiring to be less.

Bhutanese culture has a special word for this mindset: *chokkshay*, which translates as "the knowledge of enough." In Bhutan, *chokkshay* is considered the highest achievement of human well-being: "It basically means that right here, right now, everything is perfect as it is, regardless of what you are experiencing outside."[104]

Enough, contentment, and *chokkshay* are all part of the new script. They are designed for a world in flux. When change hits, enough and contentment ground you. They provide stability and essential orientation. They are easier to reach *and* to maintain than the pursuit of either happiness or ever more. Enough and contentment are determined by you, and cannot be altered by anyone other than you. Indeed, they reflect the essence of what makes you exactly, perfectly, flux-fully you.

Drop the Superhero Capes

The old script teaches people (both consciously and unconsciously) to substitute material possessions for emotional security. Don't feel loved enough? Buy a new sweater. Don't have enough confidence? Get plastic surgery. Don't feel important enough? Drive a fancy car. Never mind that each of these things may put you in debt. They are capes, or patches, for whatever parts of you feel insufficient.

These old-script capes aren't limited to what you look like or possess. They also extend to how you show up in the world.

I first heard about "superhero capes" in Glennon Doyle's outstanding TEDx talk, "Lessons from the Mental Hospital."[105] She wasn't talking about cars or nose jobs so much as the universal discomfort and messiness of being human, and how so many people are wrapped in superhero capes that don't really reflect their true selves. We hold ourselves out to be someone we're not. We profess to be "more" than we feel inside. Yet these superhero capes don't free us to achieve superhuman feats. To the contrary, they can bury us, cover us, and keep our true selves (and our inner voices) hidden. I, too, spent much of my life wearing a cape.

Superhero capes allow the pretense of perfection.

Perfectionism is the inability to let expectations go. It's also the enemy of enough (specifically, *good enough*).

When you truly realize this, you're able to drop your cape, leave your perfectionism at the door, and embrace enough. And here's the most amazing surprise: in so doing, you also discover a sweet spot. It lies somewhere between your best efforts and perfection. If you've genuinely given something your best shot yet worry that it's still not perfect, that's okay. That is human. That is brilliant. Get it out into the world and let other humans help make it better. Together, this is more than enough.

KNOW YOUR ENOUGH AND THAT YOU ARE ENOUGH

> He who knows that enough is enough
> will always have enough.
> —LAO TZU

At the end of the day, knowing your enough means also fundamentally knowing that *you are* enough, just as you are, right here and right now. (It's not a typo. Both your and you're matter.) A Flux Mindset understands this intuitively. You are not defined by your purchases, nor am I stuck chasing ever more. Your worth comes from within.

Knowing your enough is dramatically easier when you can harness other Flux Superpowers, particularly when you See What's Invisible (chapter 2) and Start with Trust (chapter 4). Together, these Flux Superpowers reveal a world of abundance, not scarcity. They show your Flux Mindset in earnest action.

Knowing your enough makes navigating change, uncertainty, and the future so much easier. The younger and sooner you (and your kids) know your enough—*and* know you *are* enough!—the better. Helping others identify and understand their enough brings you, and them, one step closer to a sustainable, humane, and flux-ready world.

I sure wish I'd known all this when I was seven.

KNOW YOUR "ENOUGH": REFLECTIONS

1. Is more really better? Why or why not?

2. When you give someone else a gift, is that a loss or gain for you?

3. How do you define "enough" today? Do you define it differently for yourself versus other people? Why or why not?

4. How do you define your self-worth? What metrics do you use?

5. Think about someone who exemplifies "enough." What makes you think this?

CHAPTER 6

CREATE YOUR PORTFOLIO CAREER

You don't want to be the best at what you do,
you want to be the only one.
—JERRY GARCIA

Ever since high school graduation nearly thirty years ago, every four-ish years, something shifts. Almost like clockwork, I shed a skin. I get restless and need to level up. I'm ready to grow new roots or change direction. Sometimes it's a major shift: leaving the practice of law, for example, or ditching grad school to guide hiking trips. Other times it's more subtle. Regardless, it becomes time to reorient my compass and write a new chapter in my book of life.

Early on, in my twenties, people gave me all kinds of flak for this. They said my résumé made no sense and forebode that my future would crash. I felt like something was wrong with me because I was interested in so many things and wouldn't settle on one pursuit. How could I possibly pick just one area of focus, even though everyone else was laser-focused on climbing corporate ladders and staking out their domain of expertise?

Fast-forward to today: broadening one's career focus no longer seems so strange, yet we still largely lack the language and infrastructure to develop this kind of career. Globally, labor policies and expectations remain rooted in units of work we call "jobs." The implicit expectation—and often, the goal—is that you will work for someone else, for a long time, and not veer from that path (at least not willingly). True, there are many ways to work and build a career, but the vast majority still revolve in one way or another around this script.

Yet this old script is giving way, and these expectations are increasingly inconsistent with reality . . . more so every day.

For the past several years, I've given keynotes on the future of work. I've spoken about the rise of independent workers and free-lancers, the growth of remote work and digital nomads, the effects of automation, and the implications of all of this on education and public policy. The coronavirus pandemic made it clear that the future of work isn't in the future: it is now. We blew through ten-year forecasts for remote work and "work from anywhere" in two quarters. Meanwhile, unprecedented unemployment left millions of workers wondering what's next, schools and universities scrambling, and no clear path forward.

Professionals wonder: What does all this mean for my career?

Parents wonder: What does all this mean for my kids?

Leaders of organizations wonder: What does all this mean for our team, strategy, culture, and the organization's future, period?

My hunch is that you may be asking all of these things too. The old script was already crumbling, but in many ways it was easy to mask. Then the pandemic lit it on fire, and all of a sudden we realized just how outdated it is. Now each of us—you, me, and talent across the board—must write a new script for our careers, livelihoods, and professional purpose. Yours may have been in draft mode already, and with a Flux Mindset, it can get the kind of attention it deserves.

For success and satisfaction in a world in flux, treat your career as a portfolio to curate rather than a path to pursue.

Serial entrepreneur Robin Chase sums it up well: "My father had one career his entire life. I will have six careers in my lifetime. And my kids will have six careers *at any one time*."

Alex Cole spent ten years in entertainment, another ten years in marketing, and ten years in consulting before finally launching his latest venture in his early fifties: a yoga studio, co-owned with his wife and daughter. The studio recently had its tenth anniversary party, so he's thinking about what's next. *That's me!*

Diane Mulcahy thinks of her seasons as verbs. She's a financial whiz, strategist, lecturer, and author who crafts each quarter differently. This also allows her to split her year between the United States and Europe, where she holds dual citizenship.

Binta Brown left a successful legal career advising Fortune 100 companies to launch her own firm representing musical artists, while she plays the saxophone and produces documentaries along the way.

Mari Nakama is a project manager and trainer at a scientific research company. She's also a fitness instructor, designs her own clothes, and co-runs a pottery studio with her partner. Each role nurtures her in a different way.

As a professor of marine conservation, Enric Sala saw himself "writing the obituary of ocean life." So he left academe and pivoted to full-time conservation, leading research teams and working with governments to create first-of-their-kind marine-protected areas.

Each of these people has a portfolio career.[106] Their careers have not been straight lines but a series of twists, turns, pivots, and jumps—sometimes because they needed to or were nudged to, and often because they wanted to. They have sensed that there was more to do, learn, build, and try in life, and they rose to those occasions.

Wow — that's me!

The new professional script is not about pursuing a singular path. A Flux Mindset knows that the career of the future looks more like a portfolio: a diversified professional identity, with resilient roots and customized to you.

Practically speaking, a portfolio career typically leads to:

- Diversification of income sources, which actually can provide *more* security than a traditional job.
- Ownership of your career. Unlike a job that someone else gives you, a portfolio can't simply be taken away.
- An expanded professional community.
- Over time, more meaning and flexibility in what you do.
- A unique professional identity that evolves and thrives in a world in flux.
- Making yourself un-automatable (or automation-proof).

Creating a portfolio career does not mean lacking ambition or not having a "real job." In reality, portfolio careers are quietly yet quickly becoming the most sought-after livelihoods of all.

I now see that back in my twenties, I was interested in a portfolio career but had few options to express it. Thankfully, that's no longer the case.

Today, this goes far beyond individual preferences. When the old script of jobs, employment, and career paths is fraying before your very eyes, and the future of work itself is in flux, a portfolio career offers resilience and a proactive strategy to thrive in your career, rather than being tossed around by the winds of change.

WHAT EXACTLY IS A PORTFOLIO?

When we think about a portfolio, most people usually think of finance, business, or art:

- **Investors** use a portfolio approach to diversify risk. Traditional financial advisers recommend a portfolio that includes equities, bonds, and cash.
- **Venture capitalists** build portfolios of investments, based on their level of risk.
- **Executives** often use portfolio theory (pioneered by BCG's product-portfolio matrix in the 1970s) to analyze their business units, strategy, and foresight.[107] The purpose of their portfolio is to manage risk and return into the future.
- **Office managers and HR leader**s use portfolios to stay organized.
- And, of course, an **artist** throws open her portfolio to show works she's really proud of—the canvas of her life.

A portfolio career takes inspiration from these different usages. Portfolios can be sequential (one role or vocation at a time) or simultaneous (multiple roles and activities at once). Career port-folioists often create professional niches and lifestyles that are more complete, personalized, modern, adaptable, and personally rewarding than any single role could be.

The term *portfolio* comes from the Italian words *portare* (to carry) + *foglio* (sheet of paper). In other words: How do you carry your most important papers? What contains your book of life?

In my case, each of my professional hats is the equivalent of a sheet of paper, a sketch, or an investment. My portfolio includes speaker, futurist, adviser, lawyer, hiking guide, global development executive, investor, yoga practitioner—and soon, book author. Most of my pages now last longer than four years, though my level-ing-up-every-so-often continues unabated.

Importantly, one's portfolio isn't limited to only professional roles: it includes capabilities that are customarily left off your résumé yet fundamentally make you, you. For example, my status as an orphan, globetrotter, insatiable handstander,[108] and mental-health advocate are included in my portfolio.

Similarly, portfolioists are clever and resourceful about skills development. When I was a hiking and biking guide, some people ribbed me for not taking my career seriously. What they didn't see was that as a guide, not only was I usually working eighteen-hour days—first up and last to bed—but also every day I was learning how to project-manage, accommodate differences, balance budgets, build teams, ensure safety, create serendipity, forge lifetime friendships, *and* make sure everyone had fun. Guiding provided a practical mini-MBA on the trail that would have been hard to replicate in a traditional classroom.

Moreover, one's portfolio isn't strictly about "being your own boss." Ultimately, *creating* a portfolio *empowers* you to do this, but your portfolio itself should include every role you've ever had—including jobs with a boss, jobs you hated, and jobs where you followed the old script. (My portfolio includes these things too. The jobs I hated still taught me a lot.) A portfolio is a container where *all* of your skills and capabilities, wherever and however you learned them, can be mixed together.

Several years after people gave me flak for my "unconventional" résumé, those very same individuals resurfaced on my radar. I still remember the day, and the conversation could not have been more different. They said, "We see what you're up to now. On second thought, how can we do that too?"

FROM PATH TO PORTFOLIO

For most of the twentieth century, a model career path looked like a ladder, an escalator, or perhaps an arrow. The old script was firmly in place and the message was clear: progress up the ladder, rung by rung, each promotion lifting you another step towards your eventual goal at the top. The arrow would fly far and in a straight direction. The escalator would continue to move. If all went well, your future could be preordained, ideally near the bull's-eye of targets established by family, society, and other external metrics.

For this ladder or escalator to work, large numbers of people needed to believe that they could climb it successfully. So we developed a linear view of career progression, which went more-or-less like this:

- Study hard and get good grades.
- Go to college or vocational school. Specialize in an employable discipline or trade.
- Get a job.
- Do said job well, for a long time.
- Get promotions.
- Retire.

This linear way of thinking worked all right for a long time. There were enough jobs and plenty of work to be done. Most workers went to the same office or place at the same time every day. They followed the script: stay on the path and avoid detours. Most people strayed from their career path only unexpectedly; career changes were generally seen as unfortunate mishaps. Résumés with strange detours were liabilities. The corporate ladder remained firmly in place, with promises of a corner office, fancy title, and prestige at the top.

Along this linear path, individuals became defined by what they "do." Your sense of self-worth got wrapped up in what rung of the ladder you occupy. Once you landed a job and started working your way up, you—and many others—didn't pause to consider what might happen if the ladder teetered or broke, or if someday you no longer wanted to be on it.

Yet in recent years, this ladder is most definitely teetering, and the old script is in tatters. Consider these *pre-pandemic* stats:

- Since 2008, 94 percent of net new job creation in the United States has *not* been full-time employees.[109]

- Forty-three percent of recent college graduates hold jobs that don't require a college degree. Nearly two-thirds of them remain underemployed after five years.[110]

- Independent workers and freelancers—that is, people with no one "job" or professional affiliation—are growing three times as fast as the rest of the labor force. In 2017, 47 percent of Millennials were already freelance.[111] By 2019, 35 percent of the entire American workforce (including 53 percent of Gen Z) was.[112] By 2027, it is expected that freelancers will outnumber employees, period. Keep in mind: freelancers include Ivy League CXOs who want more flexibility, as well as lower-skilled workers hustling to make ends meet.

- Seventy-seven percent of full-time freelancers report having a better work-life balance than they would in a traditional job.[113] Eighty-six percent of all freelancers (and 90 percent of new ones) say that the best days of free-lancing are ahead.[114]

- It's harder to get to the top. And more people are realizing the top isn't where they want to be.

Although many of these stats are from the United States, the trends they represent are global. Freelancer growth rates are somewhat lower in many countries, but the overall growth trajectory is similar.

These shifts are driven by the one-two-three punch of corporate action, individual awakening, and technological innovation. Both push- and pull-side dynamics are at work:

- *Corporations are driven to reduce costs and increase profits and efficiency.* Full-time employees are, on average, more expensive and less flexible than independent workers.

- *Individuals are waking up to the reality that today's corporate system is fundamentally designed for financial profit over human flourishing.* Whether it's overwork, workism, bullshit jobs,[115] or simply feeling undervalued, workers are fed up. They want to spend their waking hours in meaningful, worthwhile ways. Moreover, increased human longevity means talent can (and often wants or needs to) work longer than ever before.

✓ Yeah
Josie

- *Technology is a booster rocket.* It makes it easier to source talent, earn income, create a brand . . . *and* automate jobs out of existence.

To all of this we can add the Pandemic Accelerant, which put these shifts into hyperdrive.[116] Alongside unprecedented unemployment, companies are pushing to automate faster—not least because machines don't get sick or protest—without a full appreciation of the human implications of doing so. As future of work strategist Heather McGowan says, "We'll be getting there—wherever *there* is— with fewer people": fewer blue-collar workers, fewer white-collar professionals, fewer recent graduates, fewer employees, period.

But hang on:

- If jobs that are here today are gone tomorrow, then how do you stave off a perpetual cycle of unemployment?

- If you've defined yourself by your professional identity, then how do you avoid an identity crisis precipitated by a career in flux—or simply losing a job?

- If your kids ask for advice about what they should study or how they should "get a job," after reading this chapter so far, what do you tell them?

For all of these questions, a portfolio career is part of the answer. It is your—and yes, your kids'—superpower to thrive professionally today, tomorrow, and throughout the future of work.

REDEFINING YOUR PROFESSIONAL IDENTITY FOR A WORLD IN FLUX

For centuries, one's professional identity—as a tradesman, farmer, nurse, soldier, monk, or scholar—shaped one's entire life. Our script embodied our vocations, so much so that many surnames are occupations: Cooper, Miller, Sawyer, Smith.

In recent times we've seen an evolution from "I-shaped people" (with deep expertise in one topic) to "T-shaped people" (having both breadth and depth of exposure and expertise), "Pi(π)-shaped people" (who have depth in more than one area), and even "X-shaped people" (with breadth, depth, diversity, and the ability to stretch into new domains).[117] A world in flux is a world for π- and X-shaped people. You may already sense this shift, or already be a "π thinker," but didn't realize there's a name for it. Rest assured you are not alone. This is an incredibly empowering shift.

The future of work is fluid, not fixed. Your professional future is similarly fluid, not a predetermined path. You are no longer bound to an old script, given to you (or taken away from you) by someone else. It's time for a new script—and your unique, bespoke professional portfolio.

BUILDING YOUR PORTFOLIO

When jobs, employment, professional development, and the future of work itself are in flux, a portfolio career offers a more likely path to thrive. But how does one actually write that new script? And what does an identity fit for this future look like, anyway?

Developing a portfolio career involves two phases: creation and curation. Let's take each of these in turn.

Step 1: What's Already in It?

First things first: whether or not you realize it, you already have a portfolio career. You just haven't necessarily been strategic about it. This exercise helps you get started. It takes time, but it's worth it.

Pull out a piece of paper (or a blank Google document) and into it put the following:

- Every role you've ever had, paid or unpaid
- Every skill you have that helps others
- Every topic you know comfortably more about than other people do
- Your superpowers, according to you
- Your superpowers, according to others (we're surprisingly blind to some of our own superpowers!)
- Any new skills you've learned in the past six months
- Any capabilities or activities on your résumé or LinkedIn profile that you genuinely enjoy, whether or not they've been part of a "job"

- Any capabilities, skills, or experiences that are *not* on your résumé yet have helped you get to where you are today

Take this list and put it aside. Sleep on it, and tomorrow take another pass at filling it out. Be expansive. Did you list *every* skill, including those you've never been paid for? Did you include every topic, including those beyond what the old script would call your "domain of expertise?"

Some people like to think about their portfolio like a bento box, with each skill in its place. Others think about it like a jungle gym or a lattice, rather than a ladder. I like to think about it as a flower. Every few years, I create a new petal by gaining a new skill or stretching into a new or adjacent space where I can use my skills (more on that below). Over time, my career flower becomes bigger, more colorful, more interesting, and more valuable. In all of these iterations, I'm rooted in what makes me, me—and I continue to evolve.

Step 2: Be(come) the Only

Once you've assembled what's in your portfolio today, then the real fun begins. The following steps are part personal *ikigai*, part professional *jiu-jitsu,* and part responsible risk management. It's also about making yourself automation-proof for the years ahead. You're charting your unique career landscape and horizons.

Ikigai is a Japanese concept that means "reason for being." It translates as life purpose or meaning, or what makes one's life worthwhile.[118] It's why you jump out of bed in the morning. It is also your highest calling. Your *ikigai* is *uniquely you.*

Ikigai is often depicted as the intersection of four circles:

- What you are good at
- What you love
- What the world needs
- What you can be paid for

Portfolio careers vs. the gig economy

A portfolio career is not the gig economy, though "gigs" can be part of a portfolio.

The gig economy usually conjures up images of hustling, race-to-the-bottom platforms for short-term gigs. (Think Instacart, Grubhub, or Fiverr.) This is distinctly different from a portfolio approach.

With a career portfolio, you intentionally craft a portfolio full of skills and capabilities. Your portfolio evolves and grows over time. Some of what's in your portfolio at any given time may include gigs that, on their own, may qualify as part of the gig economy. But what matters is that you are deliberately curating these skills, services, and opportunities as part of a flexible and future-forward career.

This is where your portfolio can shine. No two people have the same *ikigai* because no two people are the same!

A career portfolioist does the hard work of figuring out what the world truly needs, maps that to a range of skills she possesses and enjoys, and folds that into a business model that allows for ongoing adaptation. The point is not to reach "the top" of a ladder, the end of a path, or a specific salary. The point is ongoing fulfillment and joyful contribution to the world.

Go back to Jerry Garcia. *Don't be the best. Be the only*. What is your only? The key to one's "only" is that it's not about one skill. It's about *your unique combination* of skills, capabilities, interests, and dreams. This is your unique new script.

For example, you may be trained as a lawyer, love history and cooking, and take long bike rides on the weekend. There are savvier lawyers, more knowledgeable historians, more adventurous cooks, and speedier bicyclists than you. But is anyone a better legal adviser to travel companies leading cycling trips focused on food, wine, and history worldwide than you? Probably not.

Passion: not mandatory, but highly recommended

Debates often flare up around the role of passion. Some people doubt that they could earn money doing what they love. Others wouldn't want to, because monetizing a source of joy—turning a passion into a profession—can change their relationship to that joy. In the "passion economy," something you love doing can become something you have to do.

That said, knowing what you are truly passionate about is worth its weight in gold. As any challenging time makes clear, having a passion makes getting through *anything* easier—and elimination of that passion can be brutal.

If you don't have a passion, don't worry. Pay attention to what piques your curiosity and follow that. Keep following it. Notice what emerges. Follow the sparks.

If you do have a passion, nourish it. Share it with others. And never take it for granted.

Or you're a finance wonk who loves physics, photography, and cares for your elderly parents. Or an engineer who loves orchids, helping youth learn how to code, and Bernese mountain dogs. (The more specific you can be, the better. Not that you're guaranteed to find a perfect match, but it makes your "only" easier to define.)

The point is: your *ikigai* is unique, and it can play out in myriad ways, each of which is exciting for its own reasons. A portfolio career isn't about doing one thing for many years, hitting a wall, and then wondering what to do next. A portfolio career contains multitudes: of possibilities, combinations, and opportunities.

Step 3: Cross-Pollinate

With a portfolio career, you rarely stay in your own lane. You're a cross-pollinator. You take a useful skill or expertise and parlay it into opportunities elsewhere, often in a completely unexpected arena. You translate across problems, roles, teams, and industries. You use your compass's orientation to discover new insights. In the process, you create new value, help others level up, and inspire them to write their own new scripts too.

The old script says: get a job and do what others tell you to.

The new script says: create a portfolio of roles and do things no one else dreamed of.

The old script says: if you go to law school, then be a lawyer.

The new script says: a law degree is one of the most malleable, powerful degrees that exists. It invites creativity. Do more with it.

In my case, many of my colleagues today don't realize that I am trained as a lawyer. Some of them are incredulous when they find out: "But you're nothing like a typical lawyer!" I managed to filter out the bigger-picture potential of a legal background early on, so although I haven't practiced law in decades, I still draw on this skill set almost every day. It has been one of my most effective sources of cross-pollination.

Go back to Robin Chase. You are likely to have six or more careers, perhaps even at the same time. Cross-pollinate *within* your portfolio too.

Every time you cross-pollinate, you're collecting and synthesizing new knowledge along the way. You're simultaneously honing your compass and strengthening your roots. When done well, it's an upward spiral, and you improve everything you touch along the way. You bring new insights to siloed sectors that badly need them. You help others see not just the forest and the trees but what is *beyond* the forest. You remind them that the path forward is not to be found in the trees but *between* them: the space that's right there in front of us, yet which we all too often miss.

To cross-pollinate effectively, it's essential to understand the old script and to redirect resistance to portfolioist thinking in a productive way. More often than not, the source of resistance is fear, lack of awareness, or both. People working from the old script and mindset often get confused by portfolio careers. They assume that each move means starting from scratch. The attitude is one of "Why on earth would you do that?!"

Meanwhile, anyone who has opened a Flux Mindset and is writing their new script sees portfolio careers as an evolution: each move is an improvement, addition, expansion, and adventure that aligns with your evolving self. The attitude is an enthusiastic "Let's get started!"

Step 4: Redefine Your Identity

When you have wrapped your arms around your portfolio, you're ready to take this step.

Embracing a portfolio career means transcending any one identity, story, or narrative about yourself.

With a Flux Mindset and a portfolio career, you are no longer defined by "what" you do. You are not defined by a title, a specific salary, or a corner office. You are not defined by one profession. While you have many skills, you are not defined by them.

Rather, you harness *all* of your capabilities and continuously reimagine how they can be combined and offered in new ways, creating new value and opening new doors.

Your portfolio reflects your roots. It *is* your new script, your foundation for the future, and an ever-evolving identity that fits *you.*

Step 5: Curate, Forever

Once your portfolio is sufficiently established, you can shift to curation mode. This is your ongoing, evergreen career: it is the script that, so long as you are breathing and thinking, you will continue to write. Depending on whether the investor, executive, manager, or artist portfolio perspective resonates most with you, curation can take a few different forms:

The evolution of "What do you do?"

"What do you do?" tends to be the first question people ask when meeting someone new. (It's practically baked into the old script.) We ask children what they would like to do when they grow up. Of course, we're inquiring about goals, values, passions, and dreams . . . and these are laudable intentions. But in a world in flux, does this make sense? Or if a robot makes my job obsolete, melting my professional identity with a single swipe, then what do I "do"?

"What do you do?" fundamentally asks the wrong question. "What motivates and inspires you?" is better. Best of all, however, is to ask questions that solicit learning more about a person's unique script— what makes them who they are, despite whatever changes may whipsaw the world.

Thankfully, there are many different paths of inquiry to pick from today. Here are a few favorites. Which others would you add?

- What brings you here today?
- Who has most inspired you in life?
- What are you most grateful for?
- What are you most proud of?
- Who is the greatest teacher you ever had?
- Which six people, living or dead, would you invite to an intimate supper party?
- How would you describe your inner compass?
- What is your *ikigai*, or reason for being?
- What question do you wish more people asked you?

- Investor: rebalance your portfolio
- Executive: modernize your portfolio
- Manager: organize and upgrade your portfolio
- Artist: update and expand your portfolio

The essential point of portfolio curation is that it mirrors your growth, so long as you proactively take care of it. In a world in flux—and the future of work—a curated portfolio career provides an unparalleled combination of flexibility, stability, longevity, and meaning.

PORTFOLIO CAREERS AND THE FUTURE OF EDUCATION: WELCOME TO LIFELONG LEARNING

Universities continue to make the promise to "help graduates get a job." Yet as we saw, 43 percent of recent college graduates hold jobs that don't require a college degree, and nearly two-thirds remain underemployed after five years. What kind of promise is that?

Career services centers continue to focus largely on attracting employers to campus. Yet as we saw, more than half of Millennials are independent workers (rather than salaried employees), and more young adults are likely to be their own boss than ever before. Why are career services advisers still so focused on the old script?

By and large, educational institutions today appear to have not received the future of work memo, or if they did, they did not read it thoroughly. LOL!

True, many colleges and business schools offer courses on entrepreneurship. But they miss the mark when it comes to the reality of many students' professional journeys. They fail to offer dedicated services to help students be their own boss, and they have yet to harness the (super)power of portfolio careers.

If you're a young adult or a parent, this is a bright red flag for the future of education—and all the more reason to take this chapter seriously.

Portfolio careers are for all ages, and the sooner we can open a Flux Mindset to create them, the better for all: students, graduates, families, the workplace, and society as a whole.

Borderless portfolios

Curating a portfolio career isn't only about what you do or how you do it. Where your portfolio can thrive matters as well.

In recent years, several countries have been rethinking how to foster welcoming environments for career portfolioists and beyond. In 2014, Estonia (a member state of the European Union) launched e-Residency, a credible digital identity that allows you to conduct business globally as if you were Estonian, regardless of where you are actually based. It is not a passport or a visa, yet Estonia's e-Resident growth rate now outpaces its birth rate. I have been an e-Resident since 2015, and the program works remarkably well.[119]

More recently, Estonia and several (at last count more than two dozen) other countries across Europe, Latin America, the Caribbean, Asia, and Africa have launched digital nomad visas (DNVs). DNVs permit foreigners to live and work in-country up to twelve months (and in a few cases, two years). Previously there were only two options: arrive as a tourist for up to ninety days or apply for permanent residency. Tourist visas created a straitjacket of sorts—you had to duck across the border every ninety days, which created a lot of hassle, as well as a gray area for policymakers—while permanent residency was the goal of only a tiny fraction of visitors.

DNVs make it extremely easy to look beyond where you live: taking a portfolio career global, and adapting and expanding it along the way.

If you're twenty years old today, there's little reason why you should not have already hung your professional shingle online. This represents the first piece of your portfolio. (If you're thirty years old, this is even more true. Ditto for fifty years old. And if you have a child who's twenty years old, consider this your joint call to action.)

Here's the crux: it has never been easier, cheaper, or made more common sense to start your own business. You're not signing away your professional life; you're simply learning the basic how-to's of technology, branding, and business acumen. Whether it's for childcare services, custom T-shirts, Gen Z expertise, or *whatever you love to share with other people,* the experience of hanging your own shingle will teach you more than almost any formal course. Learn by actually doing it! Moreover, the experience will open other doors. It becomes part of your portfolio, and you can always upgrade, reinvent, or combine it with other folios down the road.

Portfolio careers transform not only how you think about your career but how you think about learning and growth, period. To echo Heather McGowan, "The future of work is learning, and the future of learning is work" and "Learning is the new pension. It's how you create your future value every day."[120] Portfolio careers are aligned with both. In a world and workplace in flux, *you will never stop learning. Ever.*

Insofar as "What do you do?" is the classic question of the old script, "What are you learning?" becomes a quintessential question of your new script.

Gone are the days when people will study for a profession and do that profession for life. Even if you stay in the same industry, given the pace of change, chances are good that it will transform within a generation. Anyone who believes that they are somehow immune from these changes will face the rudest wake-up of all.

With a portfolio career, you're awake to a future of work in flux. You see how your unique blend of skills—your portfolio—mitigates your risks of professional obsolescence and empowers you to widen your range. You can be both a generalist and a specialist, and you know which one is appropriate in a given situation. You see how a portfolio career is a natural catalyst of lifelong learning and vice versa. As you identify new additions for your portfolio, you also true up your *ikigai.*

So what are you waiting for?

WORKING TOGETHER: TWENTY-FIRST CENTURY GUILDS

Crafting a portfolio career isn't only about what you do or how you do it. With whom you do so matters as well.

Career portfolioists have colleagues, partners, and professional peers just as people with a linear career path do. But thanks to new technologies, there are more options to meet new people and collaborate than ever before. Twenty-first century guilds are one of the most useful such options.

The guild concept is not new. Guilds date back many centuries and have long served to bring people focused on the same craft or trade together, to keep quality high, and to pass on the trade's skills and practices to others. Blacksmiths, carpenters, cobblers, and accountants were among the many professions with guilds. While guilds took a back seat (and at times were actively undermined) as industrialization, corporations, and single-employer work rose in prominence, they never disappeared—and they are now making a comeback.

Modern guilds serve many purposes, from (in today's terms) vocational training to business development, networking, and mutual aid.[121] Guilds help their members learn and develop expertise in the profession. They help members network, collaborate, and source other types of expertise beyond the guild. Guilds also serve as an informal gauge of reputation and trust: a sort of collective orientation. For example, Enspiral is a guild of 150+ individuals from around the world who spawned multiple ventures together, wrote an open-source handbook about their collaborative practices, and use participatory co-budgeting to further support Enspiral membership.[122]

As portfolio careers and more diverse work arrangements take root in the twenty-first century, guilds are a vehicle to accelerate learning, professional community, and responsibility. They are fit for flux.

YOU ARE SO MUCH MORE THAN YOUR CURRENT JOB DESCRIPTION

Back in 2012, the phrase Generation Flux was used to describe the kind of person who excels in a fluid, chaotic workplace.[123] Today, thriving as a GenFluxer means having a career portfolio too.

At its core, a portfolio career reflects how you see yourself *and* what you do in the world. It is *your* script. The shift from a linear, conventional career path to a unique and ever-evolving career portfolio strengthens your roots and boosts your resilience. With a portfolio, your professional development is no longer an exercise in anxiety and change management, remedied by a course here or glorified by a promotion there, yet constantly at risk of being lost or hijacked by forces beyond you. In contrast, your portfolio career reflects your Flux Mindset *at work.*

Portfolio careers still face challenges, primarily from people and public policies stuck in the old script. But these are shifting little by little (and occasionally, a lot), and the fact is: *portfolio careers align with the future.* Already today, every job is temporary, whether we admit it or not. The future—including the future of work—will favor those who can think beyond jobs, create portfolios, and know how to flux.

library, story time — children + adults
reading to + *~ nanny, woofg . do*
move

be
caring for weak, sick *thrift stores ? alone /*
together

1. What would be your professional identity if you lost your
job today? *Counsellor, actor, yoga T?*
Senior fitness, food prep, AIM L teachg

2. How would you describe your greatest career aspiration?   *lvg in*
Could you draw it? *— Land CostaRica*   *Italy*

3. What's the first thing you ask when you meet someone
new (other than their name)? *— tell me about urself*
I've said enough, Did so @ GNG H union   *atelier*
4. Does the idea of changing roles every few years excite you   *&*
or scare you? Why? *— excites, scaffoldg*
· magical
5. If you could be anything, what would it be?   *meaning*
— so who loves, gives   *ful*
shares,

CHAPTER 7

BE ALL THE MORE HUMAN (AND SERVE OTHER HUMANS)

Find the human in everything we do. *eg. when ~~it truly works~~ any more*

—AILISH CAMPBELL, AMBASSADOR OF CANADA TO
THE EUROPEAN UNION

human

Amazon's Alexa is more than an artificial intelligence–powered virtual assistant: she is a new family member. In China, pedestrian lanes specifically for mobile phone users have been established, along with a new term to describe the phenomenon: "heads-down society."[124] In 2019, teenagers spent an average of six hours and forty minutes per day on their mobile, tablet, and TV screens. Assuming they sleep, that's more than 40 percent of their waking hours.[125] Keep in mind, of course: these stats were *before* a shift to work-from-home, remote learning, and online lessons blew screen time through the roof.

Yet it's not just screen time. Automation is also proceeding at a breakneck pace. From e-commerce and driverless vehicles to text recognition and disease diagnosis, increasingly a wide range of activities and expertise that used to take intensive labor or many steps can now be done quickly, efficiently, and on almost any schedule by automated technology. It's not that automation itself is new, but the *pace* at which it is taking root—without consensus around best practices or ethical rules—is mind-boggling. Again, this was underway *before* a pandemic hastened the race to automate and shoved such concerns aside. The reasoning goes: If a machine can't get sick, protest, or struggle to pay its bills, what could possibly be the downsides?

Yet it's not just screen time and automation. We continue to see on a daily basis how technology can connect us . . . and divide us. Studies show that more screen time correlates with higher levels of depression among adults.[126] Sixty percent of young people have witnessed online bullying, and most do not intervene.[127] We use technology both to learn and to escape; to unite and to alienate; to share our feelings and to mask them; to better ourselves and to compare ourselves, often with debilitating results, with everyone in the world.

Humans spend ever more time with technology and ever less time with other humans. We are interdependent: we face borderless challenges, from climate change to intolerance, yet we fundamentally lack borderless solutions. At the same time that we can connect with more people and learn more things than ever before in human history—with a mere click, swipe, or touch of a button—we are more divided and disconnected: from one another, and often from our very own selves. We are alone, together.

THE SUPERPOWER: **BE ALL THE MORE HUMAN (AND SERVE OTHER HUMANS)**

In a world with more robots, your key to thrive is to be all the more human—and to use your humanity to help others.

In ways that are both glaringly clear and nearly invisible, technology has gradually crept into almost every aspect of our lives. Often, new technologies are helpful: they make things easier, faster, or cheaper to do. But alongside their efficiency is a more subtle and problematic message: that technology itself *is* the answer. It is humanity's savior. An algorithm knows better than you do.

The ripple effects of this narrative are widespread: little by little, humans are cut off from their confidence (technology does it better), feelings (technology gladly numbs them), and agency (just keep clicking, that's your only job!). Often without noticing, it becomes vexing to imagine "who I am" without my devices close at hand.

This messaging is overlaid on an even older script that reminds us to be tough. Whether it's beating your competitors, not crying when you're sad, leading with ego, or striving to meet expectations set by others, the old script requires you to present a clean-scrubbed version of yourself to the world. Show up as *others* wish you to be, not as you authentically are. And win at all costs.

And yet, what is this messaging actually doing?

Little by little, it's substituting someone else's truth for your own. We're pitting human against human, disconnecting from ourselves and one another. We're snipping the threads that form the fabric of humanity. And we're heading down a rabbit hole of anxiety, depression, and loneliness.

Thankfully, this is not the only way to live. Or to relate to technology. Or to relate to other people.

Today's world in flux reveals the shortcomings of this way of thinking, in spades. As you open a Flux Mindset, you're able to see beyond the trappings of the old script towards a reality in which you—and society as a whole—puts "human" back in humanity.

As you develop this Flux Superpower, your relationship to technology is reset. It's not that you become a technology Luddite or tech-hater. That's not the point at all. Rather, you harness the positive power of today's new technologies with the inner wisdom that *none* of them are as powerful as the "technology" of awakened human consciousness.

As you practice this superpower, a new script emerges with you in the author's chair. This new script invites you to show up fully, stand in your own truth, and unlock your full being. It celebrates vulnerability as a sign of inner strength, not weakness. It doesn't seek power *over* others but shares power *with* them, recognizing the extraordinary wisdom of our interdependence.

With a Flux Mindset opened and your new script underway, you're able to reconnect with others *and* your inner voice, make wiser decisions, find more sources of joy and equanimity than you can imagine right now, and edge ever closer to your full potential. Who wouldn't want that?!

> To be yourself in a world that is constantly trying to make you something else is the greatest accomplishment.
> —RALPH WALDO EMERSON

HUMANITY AND THE BRAIN

Waking up to flux demands a reconciliation of the evolving relationships *between* humans and technology and the human implications *of* technology. It requires a moral compass, rooted in the fact that humans aren't algorithms. It requires the superpower of being fully human.

As you've seen, human response mechanisms are affected by technology as well as emotions, not the least of which is fear. Traditional thinking is tuned to form and certainty. Our limbic system is wired such that we become afraid of what we don't know, whether that unknown is a minor detail or a macro force beyond our control. Marti Spiegelman, Harvard-trained scientist, Yale-trained graphic designer, leadership adviser, mentor, and initiated shaman, puts it well: "Our attachment to the known creates our fear of the unknown, yet our human genius is to constantly engage the unknown in service to our creative evolution. With our fear reactions out of control today, we push away our greatest resource, and it looks for all the world as though we've forgotten how to be fully human."[128]

Marti goes on to explain that fear sits in the part of the brain where the ego sits. Rather than allowing ego to be simply the natural home of our personality, we begin to believe it's responsible for our survival. As a result, anything that threatens our ego threatens our very survival[129]—and this is where we get twisted up. When you let your awareness focus only on your ego, you begin to believe everything is about your ego and your ego is responsible for everything, even your biological survival. You also wind up cutting yourself off from real-time incoming sensory data, leaving yourself in the precarious position of having access to only past information. In other words, we cut ourselves off from the now.

This quickly turns into a slippery slope: when we cut ourselves off from incoming sensory data, we cut off our ability to know through direct experience what is actually happening in the world around us. In this way, we cut off our ability to know what has triggered the fear circuit. The more we don't know, the more afraid we become, and the more we cut ourselves off from knowing.[130]

Ultimately, you—and we—cut ourselves off from the essence of being fully human.

SERVICE AND SUFFERING

By and large, in today's society we're *not* taught how to suffer. Rather, we're told that the goal is to be free from pain and suffering. If you experience these things, you've failed somehow.

This is one of the many ways in which the old script and new script collide head-on. The old script says: Be tough. Even if you're in the pit of despair, don't show it. Hide your feelings. But when feelings are buried, it's impossible for others to help.

In contrast, the new script says: Be real. Show up fully. Let others know how they can help. Ask others how you can help them too. This *is* service and how we show up for one another.

Being fully human isn't about being free from suffering. Being fully human means being wholly aware of your senses and your humanity: fully present and thoroughly, unabashedly yourself. This includes being comfortable with your discomfort (and occasionally being public about this) to harness it for greater growth.

Being fully human is also about showing up for others. When you're able to help others, you put interdependence into action. When you manifest a shift in awareness "from me to we," you unleash your individual capacity *and* our collective potential *and* make it easier to respond mindfully to change.

Today, we are faced with unprecedented opportunities to put this Flux Superpower into action. There are countless examples to draw from, few of which is as potent as grief.

In one way or another, the coronavirus pandemic caused each and every person alive today to lose some piece of the world as they'd known it. But not only that: the vantage point into whatever you thought the future would be has also shifted, and in many cases disappeared outright. What was is no longer, and what's coming is anyone's guess.

Individually and collectively, we are grieving the loss of what was and what may not be tomorrow. Although our losses may look and feel different—losing a job or a dream, a loved one or a daily schedule, a sense of normalcy or expectations—no one is untouched.

And this isn't just about the effects of a pandemic! Or a natural disaster, or a lost job, or lost love. This is about the universal, timeless reality of loss and how we deal with it. It's about whether we embrace grief or try to suppress it. Whether we are frightened by our feelings or can fully welcome them, even the Debbie Downers. Whether we try to short-circuit our pain or recognize that the only way out is through.

Before my parents' deaths, I had never been to a funeral. Their accident happened prior to Facebook and smartphones, so there was zero expectation for me to grieve publicly (nor were there online platforms to share my grief). As far as I knew, there was no right or wrong way to grieve. The point was to simply be human: to walk through the fear, sadness, uncertainty, and suffering. I showed up as I was, and I cracked open. To this day I remain in awe of how other people—who had no obligation or expectation to do so—showed up too. They were fully human, and as a result, they helped me discover my own humanity . . . and what "grief support" truly means.

Today, grieving publicly online is common. For many people, online platforms are an essential tool in their own grieving process (even if I still struggle to imagine being "expected" to grieve my parents' deaths publicly). Sharing your grief can help you feel less alone and allows others to support you. But the digital world also broadcasts the risk of expectations around how one "should" grieve online, which in turn can lead to burying grief out of guilt, worry, or numbed feelings. Weeding out the genuine support from whatever callous shaming may show up can be incredibly hard to do, especially in the pit of sadness.

Pause and think about your own approach to grief, as a person and as a leader. Are you leery of supporting others in the depths of their grief? Is your approach more akin to "I'm so sorry" and "just be strong," or do you walk through the fires of sadness and suffering with them? Are you attuned to both individual and collective grief?

Being fully human means showing up with emotions, empathy, and ethics. With integrity, intuition, and imperfections. Serving others means showing up with the ability to celebrate wins and mourn losses, with one another and for life—which technology will never have the heart to do.

> When "i" is replaced with "we," even Illness
> becomes Wellness.
> —MALCOLM X

YIN YOUR YANG

Yin and yang are universal symbols of harmony. Their origin story comes from Chinese mythology: yin and yang were born from chaos when the universe was first created.[131] When yin and yang are in balance, an organism, system, or the entire world can thrive. There are many variations on this theme of harmony: light and dark, joy and despair, peace and conflict . . . to name a few.

Yin and yang are complementary forces and energies. They root, ground, and direct you in complementary ways.

Every person has aspects of both yin and yang. Yang energy is considered bright, linear, active, sharp, and laser-focused. It is associated with male energy. Yin energy, on the other hand, is soft, holistic, round, and keenly aware of the many relationships in play. It is often called female energy. This doesn't mean that all men are yang and all women are yin; instead, each of us has both energies, in different proportions.

Yang is about domination. Yin is about collaboration. Yang sees nature as something humanity controls. Yin sees nature as something humanity serves.

To thrive, yin and yang energy must be in balance with each other. This principle holds for individuals, organizations, ecosystems, and society as a whole.

The old script oozes yang. It has left yin out of the narrative. Today, we urgently need to yin our yang and get this harmony back.

Part of why we're in such a mess today is because we're suffering from a yang overdose.[132] For too long, official yang leadership has been at the helm without the balance of yin. Consider that in business, only 7.4 percent of Fortune 500 CEOs are women (in 2000, that figure was 0.4 percent).[133] In politics, most countries have never had a female head of state, and the percentage of female political leaders today hovers around an all-time high of 10 percent. Only four countries (less than 2 percent) have at least 50 percent women in their national legislatures.[134]

On any scale, these metrics are wildly imbalanced. *Yang* is running the show.

Yet what we fail to realize is that a *yang*-led world cannot reach its full potential without sufficient *yin*. Moreover, this imbalance inflicts great harm: on people, relationships, the environment, and the future.

The new script is not another rant for more women in leadership roles, equal gender pay, and parental leave policies (though all of those things would help). The new script is a call to action at a more basic level: to realize that every single person—from community leaders to CEOs, parents, teachers, managers, you-name-it—who doesn't address their *yin-yang* imbalance is selling themselves short and contributing to a less equitable, less productive, less vibrant society. The longer this imbalance persists, the more it festers.

On the upside, humans are completely capable of recalibrating. Getting "back to balance"—*yinning* your *yang*—is entirely within reach.

One of the most common concerns I hear is that *yang* leaders feel threatened about giving up their power. When one believes that control and domination are the only path forward, this is understandable—and ultimately destructive. But again, this is the case only if you adhere to the old script.

Anyone who believes that patriarchy (meaning a system governed by men and *yang*) is the opposite of matriarchy (a system governed by women and *yin*) does not understand how these systems work. In a patriarchal system, women are typically excluded because of its culture of inferiority, hierarchy, and exclusive power, all of which are consistent with *yang*. If a man believes that matriarchy is *the opposite system*, then naturally he would be fearful of it because it signals his own exclusion and loss of power. In other words, doom.

But this understanding is wholly off the mark. Matriarchies are *not* the mere opposite of patriarchy. Whereas patriarchy is hierarchical and exclusive, matriarchy is egalitarian and inclusive. Matriarchies are based on *yin* values: relationships and nurturing *of all*, women and men alike.[135]

When women enter a patriarchal system, they are excluded. But when men enter a matriarchal system, they are included . . . because matriarchies reflect a culture of equality, shared power, and *yin*. Men have no reason to fear this. In reality, women and men alike have every reason to embrace it.

The new script understands this, and a Flux Mindset—regardless of gender—embraces it.

When men and women alike *yin* their *yang*, everyone can be more balanced and more fully human.

The Yin Effect and VUCA

VUCA stands for volatile, uncertain, complex, and ambiguous. A VUCA world is a world in flux. Our response to flux, and to VUCA, could be much improved by learning to *yin* our *yang* as well.

VUCA comes from the military and has quickly made its way into business. It makes sense: both settings feature competitive landscapes and battlefields, domains in which a *yang* overdose is particularly acute and the old script is firmly in place.

Yet as we've seen, much of the flux we're struggling with today is internal, personal, and interpersonal. It's uncertainty that no amount of "crush your competitor" strategy will resolve. Moreover, "crush your competitor" isn't actually what people want! Many people are hungry for human connection. We're yearning for peace, both internally and among peoples. We wish for decency, dignity, and shared humanity.

What if we applied *yin-yang* balance to VUCA? What if we overlaid a new, flux-forward script on traditional complexity studies? We could expect to see the following:

- More collective and collaborative leadership models, rather than top-down hierarchical structures.
- More transformational leaders whose goal is to lift others up, rather than transactional leaders whose modus operandi is punishment or reward.
- Inclusivity operationalized.
- A shift from seeking "power over" to sharing "power with" and giving "power to" others. We might even learn that power is gained not by hoarding it but by giving it away. (We also saw this in chapter 4.)

As Nilima Bhat, leadership expert and coauthor of *Shakti Leadership: Embracing Feminine and Masculine Power in Business*, says, we would understand that "the only win is win-win."[136]

Yin and *yang* ground us in our full humanity, in equal measure. Both are essential to thrive in flux.

BOOST YOUR DQ

If you're in the United States, Canada, China, or any of the twenty-seven countries where Dairy Queen operates, you may be wondering what flux has to do with a Turtle Pecan Cluster Blizzard. In this case, DQ has nothing to do with ice cream. It means *digital intelligence*.[137]

For a long time, it was broadly assumed that one's IQ, or intelligence quotient, was the best predictor of general success. Your IQ is your raw intellect, according to a series of testing questions based on abstract reasoning, math, vocabulary, and common knowledge (assuming a white upper-class background, alas). Some years later the concept of emotional intelligence, or EQ, emerged. EQ is your ability to understand, care about, and forge relationships with people. EQ doesn't measure what facts or equations you know; rather,

Do you DQ?

The Digital Intelligence Institute is an organization committed to helping people boost their DQ. While much of the institute's focus is on children, enhancing one's DQ is essential for all ages.

Here are some initial questions to assess your current DQ:

Do you know how much time you spend online each day?

Do you know which individuals and organizations have access to your online information (and which information)?

Do you actively manage your digital footprint?

Do you know what your digital citizen rights are?

Can you identify cyberbullying? If so, do you take action to call it out?

Do you believe you maintain an appropriate balance with technology?

What happens to your emotions and overall sense of well-being when you disconnect from technology? (Can you recall the last time you went completely offline for more than a day?)

Do you feel that you're able to show up "fully human" online?

More information is available at dqinstitute.org and dqtest.org.

it measures if you "know" how to connect with other humans. It quickly became clear that one's EQ is as important as, if not more important than, IQ in determining one's overall success in life. Whether you have meaningful relationships, feel loved and supported, and are a champion of humanity is more a result of your EQ, not necessarily your IQ (although both help).

The IQ + EQ script did its thing fairly well for a long time. But in today's digital society, there is increasing concern that technology is getting the upper hand and potentially compromising both our

IQ (the internet can quickly provide answers we previously worked hard to solve) and our EQ (disconnecting us from meaningful relationships). We need to update this script.

Digital intelligence, or DQ, is part of the new script. To truly succeed in the twenty-first century—and a world in flux—humans need to boost their DQ.

Before you race to conclude that having a high DQ means knowing how to code or build apps, don't worry: it does not. DQ is an overarching concept that encompasses a range of competencies to engage responsibly in the digital world.[138] DQ includes skills related to digital safety, digital identity, digital literacy, digital rights, and digital communications. Having a high DQ means, for example, that you know when and how to put your device down and have a face-to-face conversation. It means responsibly managing your screen time, calling out cyberbullying, and knowing when you may be at risk of digital identity theft.

In today's technology-driven world, it is all too easy to believe that technology will solve our problems. Fundamentally, having a high DQ means knowing that technology is only a means; it is neither a solution nor an end in itself. DQ is a human-centric compass for the digital world. It is an essential pillar of your new script.

> Let us pray that the progress of robotics and artificial intelligence may always serve humankind. We could say, may it "be human."
>
> —POPE FRANCIS

HOPE AND CONSCIOUSNESS

Professor Brené Brown has helped crack stereotypes and shed stigma around vulnerability as much as any human living today. She reminds us that courage comes from *cor*, the Latin word for "heart." The original meaning of courage was not found on battlefields or in marketplaces. Rather, it means *speaking your truth, from the heart.*[139] Courage is found within—and it's something no robot or AI can do.

Before my parents died, I was hardly a student of vulnerability or courage. I rarely spoke those words (and truth be told, I doubt I would have been able to define "vulnerable"). Then, their tandem deaths cracked me in a way I did not know was humanly possible. Vulnerability wasn't a choice; it was reality. Courage wasn't an option; it was essential to getting through my days.

I couldn't have figured this out on my own. Others showed me the way. When I broke open, a favorite professor of mine, Judy Raggi-Moore, showed up. Not only did she open her heart to my grief, she opened her entire family and home to me. She, her husband, Danny, young daughter, Jessica, and mother, Francesca, became my new, extended "family of choice." I now have a second sister and a third grandmother. Judy and Danny didn't replace my parents; they complemented and, in some ways, amplified them. They made sure that my preexisting family relationships remained in place while helping me regain my bearings and heal. I was expected to celebrate holidays with them, as a full family member and not a spare wheel. I was allowed to grieve in peace, while a piece of the rug that had been ripped from underneath me was stitched back together, stronger. Judy and her entire family showed me what it means to fully embrace one's humanity. They *all* became integral parts of my new script.

What Judy did came from the heart. She didn't think her way through it. She *felt* a need to help and took action. And she acted out of love, not fear.

Many years later I began to study consciousness, thanks to Marti Spiegelman, and what I had experienced earlier (but had struggled to understand) became clear. With training in neurophysiology *and* the fine arts *and* indigenous wisdom, Marti is amply qualified to see the insights—and the disconnects—among how we think, feel, see, and behave.

According to Marti, each and every person has internal wisdom that is far superior to any computer. (She's not talking about quantum computing here; this is wisdom about humankind and how to live, hard-earned over millennia and irreplaceable by algorithms.) As humans marched our way towards the "modern" era, nudged by consumer mass-marketing and distracted by the "attention economy," this hard-earned wisdom was set aside.[140] We forgot about it as we gawked at advertisements persuading us that our path to success is paved with likes, followers, and ever more stuff.

Yet this isn't real consciousness. In humans, real consciousness is dependent on our ability *to perceive*—to know the world through the senses—and our capacity to be aware of every detail that is perceived.[141] So if our conscious capacity is dependent on our ability to know the world through our senses, then today our brain has overridden all five. *We're left being fully conscious . . . of nothing.* Instead, we've replaced perception and awareness with words and others' scripts, which filter our perceptions. As Marti says, we talk about the world because we no longer feel the world. We explain our feelings in words because we've lost the ability to perceive them: to sense and simply be aware of them. (Think about the difference between explaining an experience and having an experience. See what I mean?)[142]

Real consciousness represents an ancient, even timeless, script. Your new script is how you regain it.

When the old script is in hand, it is incredibly easy (and often expected of you) to forget what it means to truly know through your sensory experiences. Instead, we seek to explain what we know through language. As a result, our *thinking* goes into overdrive while our *being* gets stuck. With a new script, however, standing in your authentic truth means reconnecting with your inner voice and wisdom, harnessing them into action, and bringing your best to others—quite possibly without ever saying a word.

ROOTED IN HUMANITY, ORIENTED TOWARDS SERVICE

If you're stuck in the old script, you'll see a quest to be more human as naive, and a goal to serve others as a waste of time. But if you have opened a Flux Mindset and truly understand the forces in play, you'll run towards this superpower.

As you navigate a world of ever more change, would you prefer to live a script written by an algorithm or with your own head and heart? Would you prefer to have the support and friendship of others or to go it alone? Would you prefer to leave a legacy shaped by apps or trusted relationships?

Times of great change, like we're all in today, offer an unparalleled opportunity to rediscover our shared humanity and interdependence. A world in flux highlights the need to pause and rethink your relationships with technology *and* with other people. When change hits, an app will not give you meaning or love you. It will not show you the path forward. Humans will. And the more fully human we can be as we navigate more change ahead, the better.

> Human beings are a work in progress that mistakenly think they are finished.
> —DAN GILBERT

BE ALL THE MORE HUMAN (AND SERVE OTHER HUMANS): REFLECTIONS

1. Do you tend to think in terms of "me" or "we"?

2. Do you maintain an appropriate balance with technology? Why or why not?

3. How would you characterize your *yin-yang* (im)balance today?

4. What happens to your emotions and well-being when you disconnect from technology? (Can you recall the last time you went completely offline for more than a day?)

5. Do you feel that you're able to show up "fully human"? Why or why not?

CHAPTER 8

LET GO OF THE FUTURE

> When I let go of what I am, I become what I might be.
> —LAO TZU

When my parents died, a piece of my future died too. While they hadn't pressured me to follow a particular career, they did have high hopes and dreams for me. Were those hopes and dreams still alive without them? Were they the right hopes and dreams for me, and how should I know?

Once the initial shock wore off, I began having frequent nightmares and panic attacks. My nocturnal psyche would convince itself that my parents were alive and well, and recent experiences were but a bad dream. Then I would awake and relive my sister's phone call all over again. Panic, anxiety, disbelief. Wash, rinse, repeat.

After a while, I began not dreaming at all. This relieved the edge of pain, but what is a future without dreams?

Fast-forward many years to today, when a future without dreams feels uncomfortably close for too many people.

Perhaps you had a job you loved, and then you lost it. But you didn't just lose a job: you lost a piece of your identity, your extended family of colleagues, and a key reason you woke up motivated every day.

Or maybe it's your child who dreams of going to college, and now neither of you is sure it's worth the expense and unknowns—or if it's even possible.

Or you worked hard for years on a project that was just about to launch. It was to catapult your career. But the launch went sideways or, worse, had to be scrapped.

Or this situation describes not you but a member of your team or community.

Or perhaps it wasn't a project but a lifestyle. You'd been experimenting for years to juggle work and family in order to "have it all." You'd finally found something resembling balance and it was sustainable . . . until change hit.

Perhaps your careful financial planning finally paid off: you'd quit your job and had tickets to travel the world, but then your itinerary became untenable.

Or perhaps little by little, living month-to-month sapped your energy to dream.

Each of these scenarios comes down to one fundamental question: When the world you've come to know suddenly melts, or flips upside down in ways you neither expected nor desire, how do you keep your dreams alive?

THE SUPERPOWER: **LET GO OF THE FUTURE**

Letting go of the future enables a better future to emerge.
From a young age, many people are led to believe that humans can predict and control the future. The messaging goes: Work hard and you'll get a good job. Jump through the right hoops and the right doors will open. Make plans that will go as expected. These instructions aren't bad, but each one assumes a predictable, controllable world . . . which couldn't be further from reality today.

This old messaging is an illusion. Certainty is an illusion. The fact is, *no one knows* what tomorrow holds and *no one* can control the future. The old script describes how things are "supposed" to play out in a static, fixed, unchanging world. But that world is long gone and is not coming back.

Today's world in flux demands a new script that understands: the ability to let go of your *perception* of control is where *real* control is to be found.

Letting go of the illusion that you can control external circumstances releases you to focus on what you *can* control: how you respond. Letting go of everything you *don't* need frees up time, space, and resources for what you *do*.

To be clear, letting go doesn't mean giving up or somehow failing (though adherents to the old script struggle greatly to understand this). The ability to let go is in many ways the ultimate Flux Superpower. It may be counterintuitive, yet therein lies its potency.

Letting go gives you control of what really matters, empowers you to move forward, and reminds you to live fully *right now*. With a Flux Mindset, you turn fear and frustration about tomorrow into fuel for your purpose, potential, and inner peace today.

STUCK IN THE PAST, FEARING THE FUTURE

Human beings are incredibly good at living in the past and the future. As neuroscientist Amishi Jha says, "The mind is great at time travel."[143] In fact, we spend the majority of our time in this mode. We reminisce about the past (waxing nostalgic, regretting a decision, or simply remembering what was) and seek to forecast the future of our dreams while avoiding our fears.

Reminiscing about the past and forecasting the future—especially when it "must" work out or unfold a particular way—can deter you from living today. Time spent reliving yesterday or trying to predict tomorrow is time spent missing life itself. You are fully alive only in the present. Right here, right now.

Of course, I don't mean that reflection and planning don't matter. Remembering happy times can lift our spirits, and preparing for what's next is both responsible and often essential. Memory and anticipation are among the greatest joys of life.

What I *do* mean is that all too often we get *stuck* in the past and future and can't get ourselves back to now. We end up spending our lives somewhere else. We forget our incredible capacity to engage the unknown and instead creep towards a future driven more by fear of it than the possibility of something better. Our minds default to a negativity bias: we tend to have more negative thoughts than positive ones, which stay in our memory longer and affect our decision-making more. When this cycle plays out over time, the results can be disastrous. We need stronger mental muscles to both ground ourselves in the present, so that we can appreciate and learn from life right now, *and* lean into the future with a level head.

A world in flux is your time, our time, *the time* to do just this.

AFRAID TO LET GO

One of the most interesting and unexpected insights on my journey through flux is that when we talk about letting go, we always talk about letting go of the past: an old grudge, a regret, a love story, or a moment that is now gone. Occasionally, we'll talk about letting go of something in the present: perhaps a source of stress, a toxic relationship, or a bad habit. But we never—really think about it, never (!)—talk about letting go of the future.

Of course, some people are excited about the future. But even they know that the future has countless unknowns and nothing is guaranteed. Many people, however, fear the future—and in so doing, they get stuck . . . paralyzed . . . fixated on a situation they can't control. The more you grasp for what is beyond your reach, or what is no longer working, the more frustrated you become.

And yet, this is exactly when you should be letting go. But no one talks about it, no one teaches it, and certainly no one celebrates it. Why not?

CONTROL: PERCEPTION VS. REALITY

If you've spent your life following the old script, the chances are very good that you're geared to fight for control, chase success, and yearn for external recognition. If this is all you've been taught, it's hard to fathom any other way of being. Yet this is far from the full truth; there is more than one way to be, to think, and to succeed.

Some people are also blinded by privilege. As we saw in chapters 1 and 2, privilege limits our perceptions of what's in the script. In some ways privilege gives you more choice, while in other ways it limits your choices. Specifically, the more privilege you perceive yourself to have (or the more choices you technically have), the more fearful if not petrified you are of making the wrong choice, and the harder it is to let go.

And yet, here is the great paradox: only those who are able to let go are those with real power and freedom. Those who can see through privilege are powerful in a way that those with privilege will never understand, unless they let go.

Of course, there is a huge difference between being forced to let go and choosing to let go. When change hits and you're forced to let go, that's usually when resistance and fear show up. But when you choose to let go proactively, it can be a profoundly liberating and empowering experience.

Letting go offers another fantastic opportunity to learn from other cultures with humility and respect. Humans have struggled with issues of attachment and control since time immemorial. What can we teach one another in the hopes of improving *everyone's* ability to let go?

Aparigraha is a Sanskrit term that translates into nonattachment, nongrasping, and nonpossessiveness. In the cultures in which it prevails, including Hinduism and Jainism, *aparigraha* is the highest form of human strength. It's a superpower—with or without flux.

Aparigraha is the ability to let go of everything that does not help you be your best self. It includes the ability to let go of expectations and fears about the future. Fear shatters your ability to be present, and when left unchecked, it leads only to more fear. Anger and anxiety are manifestations of this fear. It's a never-ending cycle of self-sabotage and a double hijacking: it both saps your mental energy towards fear and prevents you from spending that time in productive ways. This is called "ironic mental processing": when we try to avoid thinking about something, our brain tries to help us *not* think about it by constantly checking in with us to see if we're thinking about it. Not only does this not work; it's actually counterproductive.[144]

Personally, I experienced both fear and ironic mental processing for so long that I thought I would go crazy. Even before my parents died, I had an affinity for worry. My mom struggled with depression for much of her adult life, and there was a constant sense of walking on eggshells at home; my earliest memories include it. When she and my dad died, my propensity for self-sabotage grew. It was only once I began to explore the ideas in this chapter that I began to see a kinder, wiser way to live—and so much to let go.

Today I envision living in a society in which the role model of success is the person who can let go: of fear, anxiety, and expectations about the future. It's not only that you *can* do this; it's that you *choose* to do this. You do this because you know that letting go makes you free: free from living a life based on someone else's view of the world, free from the illusion that you can control what happens next, and free from becoming unhinged when change hits. In this freedom, what seemed impossible before is now within reach.

> If you realize that all things change, there is nothing
> you will try to hold on to.
> —LAO TZU

THE NEW SCRIPT: 3 SHIFTS TO FLUX

Letting go of the future doesn't mean dropping it like a hot potato. Rather, it means *reframing* your relationship to the future and whatever change may come. There are three main ways this new script can be written:

1. **A mindset shift: from predict to prepare.** This shift recognizes that it's impossible to predict the future, nor is any one future guaranteed to play out. Rather, a whole bunch of different futures are possible, and your best approach is to be as prepared as possible for the prospects coming your way. Resist the urge to predict what "will" happen and invest your energy in crafting initial responses to what "could" happen instead.

Immediately after my parents died (and long before I'd connected any of these dots), I would sit and write down all of the different ways that my future might unfold. Maybe I'd teach or maybe I'd start my own business. Maybe I'd get married and maybe not. Maybe I'd have kids and maybe not. Maybe I'd live in Timbuktu or Thailand, or maybe I'd stay close to home. Then I would look at these scenarios, and I would ask, "Could I find peace and joy again?"

In each of these wildly different scenarios, I concluded that I could. Each was full of change and uncertainty and massive unknowns, yet each offered a path forward. When I could let go of trying to predict what would happen, this allowed a whole bunch of different-yet-fulfilling futures to emerge.

2. An expectations shift: from "things will go to plan" to "plans will change." Even if you can let go of your desire to predict, your brain may still default to the assumption that your plans will work out (and if they don't, then you've failed). This mismanagement of one's own expectations is the root of much suffering and second-guessing.

Think about a recent experience in which things didn't go as planned. How did you respond: Were you angry or anxious, or did you take it in stride? How might you have responded better, or prepared differently, if you'd known that your well-laid plans would change?

Flipping your mental switch to treat change as the general rule, rather than the exception, improves everything: your ability to pivot, your foresight, and your compassion towards others as we all navigate today's landscape of uncertainty.

> Plans are of little importance, but planning is essential.
> —WINSTON CHURCHILL

3. A shift in focus: from known to unknown. All too often, when solving problems or navigating change, people look to be better prepared should the same thing happen again. This isn't a bad strategy per se, but it's incomplete. What about things that *haven't* happened yet?

The future is only a concept; we can never truly know what it will be. True, history is an amazing teacher, yet today's changes include factors that are new to the human experience. For the most part, surprise and unknowability don't show up in today's models. Yet we know that what got us here isn't necessarily going to be what will ensure you, or I, or anyone thrives in the future.

When you shift to being in awe of life's mysteries, rather than

Scenario map your life

Scenario mapping is a favorite tool of futurists. It's a type of forecasting that maps out many different possible scenarios, given a particular situation, with the goal of providing smart, grounded ideas of what the future *might* hold. In practical terms, it's a powerful mechanism to guide the shift from prediction to preparation.

While scenario mapping is commonly used by companies and organizations, it can be helpful in a wide range of settings: from assessing the future of a given sector (e.g., education), concept (e.g., capitalism), or business shift (e.g., work from home) to understanding how your own reality might change (e.g., the future of your career or your kids' education) and options to respond. Think of it as part secret weapon and part magic wand for navigating life in a world in flux.

Any future scenario has pros and cons. The best scenarios are those that feel feasible to you. Scenarios are basically thought experiments; if your sixth sense says, "Yes, even if some aspects are a bit wild, this sounds like it could happen," then stick with it.

Scenario maps are typically drawn with two axes that represent two key themes (i.e., four quadrants to explore together).

Any range of issues can be selected. For example: A decade from now, will a four-year college degree be the customary credential, or will there be new options better geared towards today's world? Will your company's growth be driven by humans or automation? Personally, what *may* change in your life—and what would you *like* to change about it? Play with a range of factors that speak to you.

Once you've identified your themes and drawn your axes, let go and imagine the possibilities. In each of the four quadrants, describe a range of possible outcomes, ripple effects, obstacles, and responses. Let your curiosity drive the design. Highlight those that seem most effective, and notice when your intuition says, "Pay attention *to this!*" Be serious but not so serious as to thwart your creativity.

How can this exercise help you rethink your response to unknowns—wherever they come from?

expecting the past to repeat itself, your horizon literally and figuratively expands.

REAWAKEN YOUR AGENCY

Letting go of the illusion that any one person can control the future frees every person to focus on what they *can* control: how they respond to change. In other words, letting go of the future demands that you reawaken your sense of agency: that feeling of being in charge of your life. Empowering agency is a core pillar of your new script.

Agency often includes a much longer list of things than you might at first write out. It includes your ability to learn, create, decide, and grow. It includes everything from your ability to vote (or not), to responsibly manage your screen time (or not), to apply the "law of two feet"—which says that in any situation in which you're neither learning nor contributing, use your two feet to find a place where your participation is more meaningful—and leave an unfulfilling job or end an unfulfilling relationship (or not), to whether you respond with kindness or with animosity. Agency is also closely related to seeing what's invisible: when you learn to see what's invisible, you discover even more ways to apply your agency.

Expressing your agency doesn't guarantee that you'll get your way, but it does give you a voice. *You can't control the outcomes, but you can control whether and how you contribute to them.*

Agency has never been more important—and yet, collectively, we've done an extraordinarily good job of stamping it out across society. Education systems teach students to "study for the test" rather than embark on a quest for true learning; consumer mass-marketing machines persuade us that our only real job is to buy, not to think; technologies numb us to our feelings as we scroll and swipe. Each of these examples reveals how agency, subtly and even unconsciously, can shift to the recesses of human consciousness.

But agency is still there: your agency, my agency, and our agency together. Agency has never left, and so long as you are alive, you cannot lose it. Now more than ever, it's time to reclaim it, own it, and use it fully.

THE "PROBLEM" WITH CHANGE

Problems are basically unwelcome change. Something happened that you wish had not, or something didn't happen that you wish had. This something may have happened five minutes ago or five decades ago. The "problem" is some kind of change that you wish would disappear.

Today more than ever, it seems, humans are in perpetual problem-solving mode. Long-standing problems, brand-new problems, complex problems, problems society thrusts on us, and problems we create, whether by aiming for the wrong goals, provoking others, or failing to see our blind spots. The elusive search for happiness seems woefully and mistakenly dependent on having resolved problems. (Yet as we learned in the last chapter, this misses the mark too.)

Oftentimes, you may find yourself faced with problems you simply can't solve on your own. Things you would love to fix and that perhaps someday will be resolved. But in the here and now, they're intractable and beyond your control.

Think about a specific problem you're grappling with at the moment. Perhaps it's new work dynamics or new family dynamics. A new supply-chain partner or a new schedule. Declining revenues or declining confidence. Or a relationship that's been faltering for years.

In such situations, society often teaches you to fight, and that if you don't fight, you fail.

And yet, this is not the complete story. Of course, there are times when fighting is the right thing to do: human rights, a livable planet, social justice, and fundamental fairness are good examples of this "good trouble." But there is a different, very large and distracting set of problems we often bludgeon by fighting, which would benefit more from a different stance: acceptance.

For now.

Acceptance does *not* mean failure or being passive. (Again, the old script struggles to see this. But that myopia is exactly what makes that narrative outdated.) Acceptance means being present, with a twist: rather than spending your strength feeling anxious about the change itself, use that strength to lean into the change in your response.

When you're able to accept change by letting go of the illusion that you can control it, remarkable things can happen. You find peace, clarity, and even previously unfathomable aha's. Your imagination lights on fire.

When you allow yourself to let go of what you were trying to control, a whole new universe of possibility opens up. When you stop preoccupying your mind with what's not working, you create space to manifest what could be. To invent something new, or to make any kind of change—in your daily life, in an organization, or in society—requires first the ability to *imagine* that things could be different. It invites your *intention* to see differently, rather than a *resolution* that a particular outcome "must" happen.

Think back to the ways in which your life has changed recently. What have you accepted? What are you still resisting? What have you let go of, and what did that create space for?

WORRY LESS ABOUT WORRYING

For most of my life, I was enveloped in a fog of worry. My earliest memories are of my mother worrying that I would die of severe food allergies. (Her fear wasn't entirely misplaced: my allergies kept me frequently ill and my pediatrician busy.) By the age of five, I'd learned to worry about money, because it was perpetually in short supply. By elementary school, I chronically worried that other kids didn't like me. After school, I worried about whether and when to go home, in the hopes of avoiding an increasingly inevitable family argument.

Then my parents died, and my worry went into overdrive. Generalized anxiety became nightmares and panic attacks. Sometimes I would feel completely unmoored by grief, cracked open in a way I wanted desperately to understand. Clearly, my parents' accident wasn't just a bad dream. This was my new reality. But now what? My rational and irrational brains constantly dueled over what was "worth" worrying about. The answer was usually: everything.

It wasn't until my forties that I learned that a perpetual, chronic state of worry isn't normal. It happened unexpectedly, when I was asked to describe my earliest memory of *not* feeling worried . . . and I couldn't recall a single one. True, I could travel and speak and stretch beyond my comfort zone, but these things were easy compared with quieting the bird of anxiety that chirped incessantly on my shoulder about anything, everything, or nothing at all. Indeed, on the very best days I would worry about the fact that there was nothing to worry about.

The day I realized that I had zero sense of what it felt like to be worry-free was a wake-up call. Back then, I knew enough to know that worry and anxiety feed on themselves, becoming a vicious and never-ending cycle. But I hadn't realized how deep this wound had cut personally, and I didn't know how to heal it.

Overcoming chronic anxiety is in many ways a lifelong endeavor. It's a gradual rewiring of the brain. It's also one thing to say "Worry less about the worry" and another to actually do so.

One of the most useful practices I've come across for this is to ask yourself, "What's the worst that could happen?," and then flip the rhetoric on its head. Let me explain.

When it comes to change, humans can be prone to catastrophize. I can hear you now: the "worst that could happen" is actually pretty bad. The answer is a series of negatives: What you would lose, what would not be there, or what would be empty? It's implicit in how the question is framed: *the worst*.

I get it. Change is damn scary. It clouds your horizons and paralyzes your courage. But it only tyrannizes you if you let it.

What if you flipped the question and asked instead, "What's the *best* thing that could happen if I shifted from resisting change to yielding to it? What's the *best* thing that could happen if I let go of my expectations about the future?"

Might you discover that you're more capable than you ever dreamed possible? Might you finally see doors that have been waiting to be opened?

Might the worst that could happen be never knowing what could have been?

When my parents died, "the worst that could happen" didn't seem nearly as bad as what had already happened. It took time for "the best that could happen" perspective to sink in, though as soon as it did, it felt like the earth shifted beneath my feet. My ground became solid yet gentle. I could keep my parents' memory alive *and* feel genuinely excited about the future.

Little by little, I developed habits to deal with my anxiety. My fear of the future continued to get the upper hand from time to time, but I learned to pay attention to what the fear was saying. I started using this simple yet powerful three-part process that I continue to use today:

1. **Notice it.** Stop and catch myself when I slip into anxiety and fear. What just happened? Where do I feel it in my body? Am I re-running worst-case scenarios? If possible, give my feelings a name—even personality. But don't judge; just notice.

2. **Welcome it.** Rather than berate myself about how I should "not" feel, own these feelings in this moment. Realize that they come from a place of care. Can I find a slice of gratitude for them within?

3. **Use it.** Finally, flip my focus of attention. What is this fear or anxiety asking me to let go of? How is it opening me up to what really matters? Does my response align with my values? Who has *real* control, me or my fear?

This approach isn't about trivializing the hard stuff or forgetting about loss. Suffering and challenges are part of your story, my story, humanity's story. The key is to not let fear of the future hijack your life script or prevent you from living today.

Ultimately, your mindset determines your well-being. A Flux Mindset knows how to let go of the worry and lean into the wonder of what could be.

BEGIN AGAIN

The human brain is hardwired to plan for the future, yet let's be honest: *no one* knows how the future will unfold. I say this as a renowned futurist! The more we try to predict and control, or boast about knowing "for sure," the more the future slips through our fingers.

Then again, life has always been this way. No one can *ever* know exactly what any day holds, much less a week, a year, a decade, or an entire generation. But therein is the real beauty and even awe: when every day is new and unknowable, every day is also an opportunity to begin again.

Every. Single. Day. To. Begin. Anew.

This reality isn't unique to today: a world in flux and a faster pace of change simply make it clearer.

And when every day is full of change, and every day also offers a new opportunity to begin again, the way to reconcile this tension— between your desire to plan and an unknowable future—is to take things one day at a time. As Dr. Judson Brewer, director of research and innovation at Brown University's Mindfulness Center, advises, "Do what needs to get done today, and then take care of tomorrow, when it comes: tomorrow. When it comes to information, the closer to now you stay, the more clearly you will be able to think."[145]

If today feels like too long a horizon, consider this hour, this minute, this second. The key is to stay grounded in the present moment and recognize every opportunity to begin again.

After my parents died, I was stuck in what felt like interminable not-knowing. I so badly wanted to plan, yet I couldn't possibly know what was going to happen. Waking me up every morning was the same question: What in the world should I do?

Gradually I learned to boil this down to the here and now. Each morning, I had two choices: I could get out of bed and see what happens, or I could curl up in a ball and never know. Many days, crawling into a corner and disappearing sounded really good. But a little voice would chirp: *Don't you want to know what today holds?*

Over time, the simple act of getting up and putting one foot in front of the other became less of a deliberation and more of a small daily victory. My mantra became: "I want to know, but I have to learn." I wrapped my head around the reality that there are some things we simply cannot know. It felt unfair, even cruel, yet I realized I could destroy myself if I kept trying to pin down what was beyond my—or anyone's—grasp.

And this led to the most helpful realization of all: there is beauty in not knowing. Not knowing encourages curiosity, wonder, and awe, all of which are in short supply today. When it's impossible to know, then it is time to let go . . . and begin again.

HOLD THE FUTURE GENTLY

When change hits, the ability to let go—of expectations, of what to do in this uncertain future, and even of the need to know—makes all the difference. People who grasp on to "what was" or believe they can control what happens next are easily derailed. But those who can let go of what-was-yet-is-no-longer, and give the future the space and oxygen it needs to emerge, will thrive.

Letting go of the future is about flow, not grasping. Working with life rather than against it. Fluxing rather than feeling stuck. Seeing the future not as a sinkhole of uncertainty or an impenetrable brick wall but more akin to water: pliable, yielding, taking the shape of its container, impossible for human hands to hold for long. A form that is at once gentle and supple, yet can carve through prehistoric rock.

As water holds the shape of its container, powerful yet at ease with its temporary state of being, holding the future gently is how you embrace—and thrive—in flux.

> All that you touch you Change. All that you Change changes you. The only lasting truth is Change.
> —OCTAVIA BUTLER

LET GO OF THE FUTURE: REFLECTIONS

1. When you make plans, do you generally expect that they will work out or not?

2. Mentally, where do you spend most of your time: in the past, the present, or the future?

3. Describe something that you recently let go of. How did it feel? How did it go?

4. How does "not knowing" make you feel?

5. Have you ever scenario mapped your life? If so, how did it go? If not, would you like to? Why or why not?

FLUXING FORWARD

Life is flux.
—HERACLITUS

So here you are: You've read the pages of this book that appealed to you, in whatever order felt right to you. You're doing your best to open a Flux Mindset, unlock your Flux Superpowers, and write your new script that's fit for today's world. You can sense this is a big shift for your mind, your body, and your soul. You know it will help you as a leader, a professional, an entrepreneur, a parent, a community member, and—most of all—as a human being. But you're still wondering: What else? What *next?* What do I actually *do* now?

You've landed in the right place. But first, let's get our bearings and better understand what you've learned thus far. This will make it much easier to cast a meaningful vision forward.

Perhaps the single most important thing to remember (which is all too easy to forget) is that absolutely everything that you do affects how you navigate change. You get better at whatever you practice. If you practice fear, you get better at being fearful. If you practice flexibility, you become more flexible. If you practice hope, you invigorate your capacity for hope.

Part of "what's next" is seeing flux *as a practice.* Opening a Flux Mindset and strengthening your Flux Superpowers doesn't happen overnight. Being truly fluxy is a lifelong endeavor: it requires practice, practice, and more practice. The goal is improvement, not perfection. And the upshot? Every day (and especially today!) gives you plenty of opportunities to do so.

You've also seen that *Flux Superpowers amplify one another.* While each superpower stands on its own, when they are combined, the result is that much more powerful. For example:

- It's easier to let go when you start with trust.
- It's easier to start with trust when you can see what's invisible.
- It's easier to see what's invisible when you're running slower.
- It's easier to run slower when you can be fully human. And so on.

When it comes to practicing flux, start with whichever Flux Superpower feels closest at hand, and know that the others will enhance it (and vice versa) over time.

Similarly, you can start with whatever change is closest at hand. One of the real gifts of flux is that it's *scale-free*: it can be applied to any unit of size, scope, or scale. Individually, we can talk about your daily schedule in flux, your family in flux, your career in flux, or your dreams and expectations in flux. Organizationally, we can talk about offices in flux, HR in flux, or strategic planning in flux. Societally, we can talk about politics in flux, cities in flux, climate in flux, and so on. And when the entire world is in flux, a Flux Mindset has almost endless utility.

In this light, it's clear that this book is just the beginning. Each of the Flux Superpowers may merit its own book. There may be a series to launch: Leadership in Flux, Work in Flux, Relationships in Flux, Trust in Flux, Careers in Flux, Learning in Flux, Risk Management in Flux, Cities in Flux, Politics in Flux, Public Policy in Flux, Expectations in Flux . . . what you've begun to tap into in this book extends far beyond any one change, any one person, or any one time.

But right now, let's come back to today, and you. The basic premise of *Flux* is that in a world of constant change, we need to radically reshape our relationship to uncertainty and flip the script to sustain a healthy and productive outlook. We do this in three steps:

Step 1: Open a Flux Mindset
Step 2: Use your Flux Mindset to unlock the eight Flux Superpowers
Step 3: Apply your Flux Superpowers to write your New Script

The ability to "flip the script" is key. Your new script is fit for today's world and empowers you to thrive in constant change. But it doesn't happen on its own: it requires an understanding of your old script and how it has shaped your *current* relationship to change.

Everyone's relationship to change is unique, because it is fundamentally rooted in our life experiences—no two of which are the same. The crux of *Flux* is: What grounds you, roots you, and orients you when change hits? What values provide you with the clarity and stability that enable you to see change as an opportunity, rather than a threat? How committed to these values are you? How do these values affect how you react when whatever you thought was going to happen—a particular career, partner, daily schedule, family member, product launch, new hire, or election cycle—doesn't?

(This may be a good moment to revisit your Flux Mindset Baseline in the Introduction and see whether and how your answers have changed.)

While each person approaches *Flux* with a different history and personality, there are four actions I've found that are natural catalysts for strengthening a Flux Mindset and applying your Flux Superpowers. You can do each of them right now.

First: Take *Flux* into your life and work. There are many ways to do this at home, in the office, and on the road. However, the best place I've found to *start* is outside. Get into nature: it's the epitome of flux and our best teacher of constant change.

Back in 500 BCE, Heraclitus was already onto this: nature is never-ending change, yet it is also a constant in a sea of change. Nature pays little heed to the changes that rock your world. The seasons change, trees bear fruit, flowers bloom, and animals hibernate . . . just as they always have. Moreover, nature is constantly shifting and becoming something different from what it was before. Atoms in motion are changing; cells are dividing; air and energy are moving. "Like a river, life flows ever onwards, and while we may step from the riverbank into the river, the waters flowing over our feet will never be the same waters that flowed even one moment before."[146] Among nature's countless examples of flux:

- Caterpillars go through chrysalis and become butterflies: *A bug becomes goo, then sprouts wings and flies?!*

- Bamboo spends more than a year developing roots and rhizomes below ground before going through an incredible growth spurt: *A plant that grows three feet (one meter) per day to become stronger than steel and quite possibly the strongest material on earth?!*[147]

- Waves ebb and flow, producing both idyllic vacation spots and destructive hurricanes: *A tsunami of change!*

Nature also has a deep connection to indigenous and ancient wisdom. Looking at our most wicked problems, from sustainability, to community building, to ecosystem management, time after time I am struck by how humans today would have a far better, richer understanding of flux if we'd followed ancient wisdom and understood its relationships to nature *and* to change. Quite possibly we would have made better decisions that would have allowed us to inhabit a world in which:

- Success is measured in terms of relationships and sustainability, including our relationship with Mother Earth.

- Planning includes and prioritizes future generations, such as the Seventh Generation Principle, which states, "In our every deliberation, we must consider the impact of our decisions on the next seven generations."[148]

- Fear is an emotion to hold gently, not a monster to run away from.[149]

- Our inner wisdom is tapped and trusted, rather than contingent upon external validation.

- The future is not to be predicted, but when you are in touch with your inner wisdom, you can excel at *sensing* where things may be heading.

Pause and consider your current relationship to nature and what you did (or didn't) know about indigenous wisdom before picking up this book. Are you able to *really pay attention* to nature's nuances? Had you heard about the Himba people's extraordinary sight, or thought about how *kintsugi* could be applied to your life? Did you know what a potlatch is, or what the words *enough* and *contentment* actually mean?

When you spend time in nature, you learn about constant change directly from the source. Indigenous wisdom is one of humanity's greatest treasures. Both nature and indigenous wisdom bring your Flux Superpowers alive: they help you learn to see things that were invisible to you before and to trust nature's voice. Watch, listen, learn, and apply these insights to your own life and work. Take your Flux Mindset to the next level; write the next chapter of your new script.

> But don't be satisfied with stories,
> how things have gone with others.
> Unfold your own myth,
> without complicated explanation,
> so everyone will understand the passage,
> We have opened you.
> —RUMI

Second: Take *Flux* into your organization. Much of this book's focus is on individual capacities, but that is just the beginning. When we adapt and apply the Superpowers to organizational culture, we find positive linkages with everything from business model structure to strategic planning, performance metrics, and diversity, equity, and inclusion (DEI) efforts that go beyond surface conversations to yield substantive change.

For example, ask yourself the following questions about your company or organization (or if you are not currently working, assess the first company or organization that comes to mind):

- What does a corporate strategy of "enough for all" rather than "more for some" look like? What about a strategy that can run slower and consider longer-term time horizons beyond quarterly returns?

- What happens when a company treats its customers as citizens rather than consumers?

- Practically speaking, what does a social contract that's rooted in trust and enoughness include? What about company compensation and ownership structures?

- How does the ability to flux affect the organization's view of what is risky and what is responsible?

I have heard, time and time again, how many organizations are not fit for constant change. Even so-called agile organizations get stuck in outdated policies, misread markets, and cause friction (or worse) within their teams. Often, leaders say they want innovation but make choices that resist it.[150]

There is undoubtedly another book specifically for organizational flux, plus workshops, diagnostics, and more. But there is plenty that this book can already spark, especially when it comes to *Flux* as a sort of organizational manifesto and a tool for team collaboration.

Whether you work in the private, public, or social sectors, whether you work for a for-profit, nonprofit, or for-benefit organization, and whether you work full-time, part-time, as an employee, as a contractor, are self-employed, or a career portfolioist: imagine what that organization would look like aligned with all eight Flux Superpowers. Imagine if *your organization and all of your colleagues* knew how to Run Slower, See What's Invisible, and Start with Trust. Imagine if *the entire team* could Be All the More Human and encouraged you to do the same. Imagine an *organizational* new script fit for a world in flux.

If this sounds appealing, the starting point is simple: share this book and start having *Flux* conversations with your colleagues!

If you're leading an organization, convene the entire team and explore your old scripts together. Assess your Flux Mindset Baseline (in the introductory chapter) and share your answers. See who else is interested in writing their new script. (My experience shows that relatively few people have thought about this, yet once they do, almost everyone wants to author their own.) Partner up to flux better together.

Go one step further: craft a new script for the organization that includes everyone's voices in equal measure.

At the end of the day, any organization is only as successful (or as hampered) as its people, and change is no exception. An organization whose talent has harnessed their Flux Superpowers will be much better prepared for a future full of change than a team that's still clinging to its old script.

> **You can make change. Or it can make you.**
> —GEORGE MACIUNAS, FOUNDER OF THE
> FLUXUS ART MOVEMENT

Third: Take *Flux* into your family. As you've seen, one's relationship to change begins from the inside out. The Flux Superpowers are useful at any age, and the sooner we can develop them, the better. In an ideal world, children would be raised with a healthy relationship to change. They would groove a Flux Mindset young and have Flux Superpowers for life. In fact, I've lost track of how many parents have expressed to me their desire to make this happen.

Moreover, many young people—especially young adults—want a different way of living, working, and being. They see that the old script is broken, and they want a new script: a new roadmap to orient and guide their lives that is fit for today's world. Many young adults *don't* want to get on the escalator, and they're hungry to know what else is out there. This book can help, and so can you.

Again, the starting point is simple: talk to your kids about *Flux*. Tell them honest stories about difficult changes in your life. Have open conversations about which kinds of change are hardest, and which Flux Superpowers would be most helpful. Depending on how old your children are, talk about what a new script could look like.

When you bring *Flux* into your family, you also open the door for conversations about empathy, interdependence, and privilege. What is the reality of your flux versus someone else's? This is a wonderful way to help kids understand humanity's interconnect-edness, individually and societally.

Privilege (or lack of it) shapes your view of flux and cuts both ways. Some kinds of privilege allow you to sail through some kinds of change unscathed. Yet some kinds of privilege can also saddle you (not least, on the escalator of the old script) and make it *harder* to embrace change.

Privilege comes in many forms: emotional stability, financial wealth, the color of your skin, a loving family, and a safe home are all forms of privilege, and they can all trigger different responses to change. Growing up in an abusive or dysfunctional family may make it harder to trust. Never having enough may make it hard not to crave more. Paradoxically, being surrounded by privilege makes it (often much) harder to let go, even when it's in your own (and the world's) best interest.

It's only when you become aware of your (and others') privilege *and can imagine a fulfilling life without it* that you can fully lean into flux. A Flux Mindset demands that you look within, understand your own privilege (or lack thereof) and how it keeps you from embracing change. This may sound like a tall order, but it's one that every person should aspire to—not least because even privilege that's often taken for granted (such as having parents, your health, or a job) can change at a moment's notice.

> A self that goes on changing is a self that goes on living.
> —VIRGINIA WOOLF

Fourth: Take *Flux* into the world. At the broadest level, you can become an ambassador of flux. You can be part of a *Flux* community—and help build that community—to rewrite our collective scripts. You can be a catalyst for new thinking about the "life cycle of flux": for example, how does our Flux Mindset evolve as we age? You can catalyze how we talk about change too: this is the only way we'll see true transformation at scale.

Indeed, writing this book revealed how feeble our current language is for navigating flux. Just as we struggle with constant change, we also struggle to express it. We have words like *resilience* and *adaptability*, but actually *being in the vortex of flux?* Not so much.

And yet it is difficult to talk about something, much less genuinely connect with others about it, without the right words to describe what "it" is. This conundrum isn't unique to flux; it's a common reality for topics that are awkward or stigmatized, or we'd rather avoid. It's especially frustrating when there is an enormous amount to be learned, but we're cut off from that information: for example, when yoga philosophy is seen as woo-woo by the business world, or when indigenous wisdom is marginalized by quants.

This is your opportunity to help break down these barriers to give voice to what matters, and to recognize *just how much* we have to learn from one another. We are in an ideal, and increasingly urgent, moment to develop a robust flux vocabulary: a lexicon (fluxicon?) that helps raise awareness and bring people together, which in turn can be a catalyst for the Flux Superpowers to take root.

Beyond talking about flux better, you also have the chance to level up your own "flux capacity" to forge a brighter future for all. For example, how can the Theory of Flux inform the way we craft metrics to measure the health and well-being of society? Is there a new GDP for flux? (I reckon there is.) What does it look like to build something truly transformational whose full effect will not be felt in your lifetime? This also points back to indigenous wisdom, which carries so many of the answers we seek (and so much of what we've always known). It is a process of rediscovery on a global scale.

> It must be obvious . . . that there is a contradiction in wanting to be perfectly secure in a universe whose very nature is momentariness and fluidity.
> —ALAN WATTS

For champions of humanity, this is an opportunity of a lifetime. As old scripts crack, and your Flux Mindset opens, your Flux Superpowers emerge: you're able to run slower and calmer, see what's invisible and make it visible, let go of a future no longer fit for purpose, and remain present while building what's next.

This is learning to flux, and there is no better time to practice than now. Your new script is just around the corner.

Are you ready? Let's go!

DISCUSSION GUIDE

Flux is intended to help individuals and organizations reshape their relationship to uncertainty and change, in order to sustain a healthy and productive outlook. Throughout the book, call-out boxes are provided to prompt self-reflection, curiosity, and conversation. Many of the callout boxes include questions and exercises designed to help you open a Flux Mindset and develop your Flux Superpowers. Below is a selection of those questions (plus a few extras!) curated to help assess your "fluxiness" and spur meaningful discussions. They can be used with your friends, colleagues, family, team members, leadership circles, mastermind groups, and even strangers. They are appropriate for individual consideration as well as one-on-one and small-group settings. Enjoy!

For even more questions, ideas, and inspiration, please head to **fluxmindset.com**.

Your Flux Mindset Baseline

1. What kinds of change do you love? What kinds of change do you hate?
2. What gives you meaning and purpose?
3. To whom and to what do you turn in times of uncertainty?
4. To whom and to what are you committed, no matter what?
5. Growing up, were you taught to fear change or embrace it?
6. What "makes you, you"? How much is due to accidents of birth (privilege or lack of it)?
7. What one word best describes your relationship to change today?

Run Slower

1. When something takes longer than expected, do you tend to feel agitated or to appreciate the delay?
2. In which areas of your life do you feel that you're running too fast?
3. When did the pressure to run faster begin? Did you notice it at that time?
4. From whom or where does your "need for speed" come? Are you driving yourself to run faster, or are others driving you?
5. What are your typical coping mechanisms? Which ones have been most useful? Which ones need help?
6. If you slowed down, what do you think you'd discover?

See What's Invisible

1. Do you tend to trust your head or your heart more?
2. When your peers tell you to turn right, do you ever want to turn left instead?
3. Can you detect invisible patterns?
4. How aware are you of the rules that govern your life? How explicit are they?
5. How has privilege (or lack of privilege) affected your script? What kind(s) of privilege?

Get Lost

1. When you take a wrong turn and end up somewhere you've never been before (and had no intention of going), do you typically feel frustrated, fearful, or intrigued by that new place?
2. Do you tend to see detours as hassles or adventures?
3. When you were growing up, were you encouraged to hang out with people who are like you or different from you? What were those people like? What did you learn?
4. When you are faced with uncertainty, who or what grounds you and helps you find your way?

5. To what extent do other cultures or traditions factor into your worldview? How are these scripts different from yours? How did you learn about them?

Start with Trust
1. Can the average person be trusted? Why or why not? What influences your response?
2. Are you usually quick to trust or quick to mistrust?
3. Do you trust yourself? When does your trust in yourself falter most?
4. If something can't be measured, does it exist?
5. When you ask people to "trust you," how does it feel?

Know Your "Enough"
1. Is more really better? Why or why not?
2. When you give someone else a gift, is that a loss or gain for you?
3. How do you define "enough" today? Do you define it differently for yourself versus other people? Why or why not?
4. How do you define your self-worth? What metrics do you use?
5. Think about someone who exemplifies "enough." What makes you think this?

Create Your Portfolio Career
1. What would be your professional identity if you lost your job today?
2. How would you describe your greatest career aspiration? Could you draw it?
3. What's the first thing you ask when you meet someone new (other than their name)?
4. Does the idea of changing roles every few years excite you or scare you? Why?
5. If you could be anything, what would it be?

Be All the More Human (and Serve Other Humans)

1. Do you tend to think in terms of "me" or "we"?
2. Do you maintain an appropriate balance with technology? Why or why not?
3. How would you characterize your *yin-yang* (im)balance today?
4. What happens to your emotions and well-being when you disconnect from technology? Can you recall the last time you went completely offline for more than a day?
5. Do you feel that you're able to show up "fully human"? Why or why not? Is there a difference between your offline and online experiences in this regard?

Let Go of the Future

1. When you make plans, do you generally expect that they will work out?
2. Mentally, where do you spend most of your time: in the past, the present, or the future?
3. Describe something that you recently let go of. How did it feel? How did it go?
4. How does "not knowing" make you feel?
5. Have you ever scenario mapped your life? If so, how did it go? If not, would you like to? Why or why not?

Organizational Flux and Leadership

1. How would you rate your organization's ability to flux? Are select people, teams, or departments "fluxier" than others? Why do you think that may be the case?
2. What typically happens in your organization when there is an unexpected delay or disruption?
3. Think about your leadership style. Do you expect your colleagues and partners to act quickly, to stay the course, and/or to agree with your decisions? Why or why not?

4. How do you feel when trying to meet expectations set by others? How do you feel when setting expectations for others?
5. How do you feel about sharing power with others?

And finally . . . What other questions does *Flux* raise for you?

NOTES

1   For example, the effects of the First Industrial Revolution took more than one hundred years (i.e., several generations) to be fully felt. Today's Fourth Industrial Revolution will take a fraction of that.

2   *Cambridge Dictionary*, s.v. "Flux," https://dictionary.cambridge.org/us/dictionary /english/flux (accessed December 26, 2020).

3   *Merriam-Webster*, s.v. "Flux," https://www.merriam-webster.com /dictionary/flux (accessed December 26, 2020).

4   Steven Smith, The Satir Change Model, October 4, 1997, https://stevenmsmith .com/ar-satir-change-model/ (accessed December 27, 2020).

5   Adrian F. Ward, Kristen Duke, Ayelet Gneezy, and Maarten W. Bos, "Brain Drain: The Mere Presence of One's Own Smartphone Reduces Available Cognitive Capacity," *Journal of the Association for Consumer Research* 2, no. 2 (April 2017), https://doi.org/10.1086/691462 (accessed September 26, 2020).

6   Dan Chisholm, Kim Sweeny, Peter Sheehan, Bruce Rasmussen, Filip Smit, and Pim Cuijpers, "Scaling-Up Treatment of Depression and Anxiety: A Global Return on Investment Analysis," *Lancet Psychiatry*, April 12, 2016, https://doi .org/10.1016/S2215-0366(16)30024-4 (accessed September 25, 2020).

7   American College Health Association, "Fall 2018 National College Health Assessment," https://www.acha.org/documents/ncha/NCHA-II_Fall_2018_ Undergraduate_Reference_Group_Data_Report.pdf (accessed September 25, 2020); Nicole J. LeBlanc and Luana Marques, "Anxiety in College: What We Know and How to Cope," *Harvard Medical School Health Publishing*, May 28, 2019, https://www.health.harvard.edu/blog/anxiety-in-college-what-we-know-and-how-to-cope-2019052816729 (accessed September 25, 2020).

8   Carol Dweck, *Mindset: The New Psychology of Success* (Ballantine, 2007).

9   Leaders on Purpose, "The CEO Study: A Longitudinal Study of the Leadership of Today and Tomorrow," 2019, https://www.leadersonpurpose.com/ceo-research (accessed September 25, 2020).

10   Jeremy Heimans and Henry Timms, *New Power: How Power Works in Our Hyperconnected World—and How to Make It Work for You* (Doubleday, 2018).

11   James Guthrie and Deepak Datta, "Dumb and Dumber: The Impact of Downsizing on Firm Performance as Moderated by Industry Conditions," *Organization Science* 19, no. 1 (2008), https://econpapers.repec.org/article /inmororsc/v_3a19_3ay_3a2008_3ai_3a1_3ap_3a108-123.htm (accessed September 23, 2020).

12   Jennifer Senior, "More People Will Be Fired in the Pandemic. Let's Talk about It," *New York Times*, June 14, 2020, https://www.nytimes.com/2020/06/14/opinion/layoffs-coronavirus-economy.html (accessed September 23, 2020).

13   Steve Bradt, "Wandering Mind Is Not a Happy Mind," *Harvard Gazette*, November 11, 2010, https://news.harvard.edu/gazette/story/2010/11/wandering-mind-not-a-happy-mind/ (accessed September 20, 2020).

14   Anne Helen Petersen, "How Millennials Became the Burnout Generation," BuzzFeed, January 5, 2019, https://www.buzzfeednews.com/article/annehelenpetersen/millennials-burnout-generation-debt-work (accessed September 27, 2020).

15   Josh Cohen, "Millennial Burnout Is Real, but It Touches a Serious Nerve with Critics. Here's Why." NBC News, February 23, 2019, https://www.nbcnews.com/think/opinion/millennial-burnout-real-it-touches-serious-nerve-critics-here-s-ncna974506 (accessed September 27, 2020).

16   Olga Mecking, "The Case for Doing Nothing," *New York Times*, April 29, 2019, https://www.nytimes.com/2019/04/29/smarter-living/the-case-for-doing-nothing.html (accessed December 29, 2020).

17   Sophia Gottfried, "Niksen Is the Dutch Lifestyle Concept of Doing Nothing—and You're About to See It Everywhere," *Time*, July 12, 2019, https://time.com/5622094/what-is-niksen/ (accessed September 27, 2020).

18   Benjamin Baird, Jonathan Smallwood, Michael D. Mrazek, Julia W. Y. Kam, Michael S. Franklin, and Jonathan W. Schooler, "Inspired by Distraction: Mind Wandering Facilitates Creative Incubation," *Psychological Science* 23, no. 10 (October 2012), https://doi.org/10.1177/0956797612446024 (accessed September 27, 2020).

19   The School of Life, "Wu Wei: Doing Nothing," https://www.theschooloflife.com/thebookoflife/wu-wei-doing-nothing/ (accessed September 26, 2020).

20   Tim Kasser, *The High Price of Materialism* (Bradford, 2002); Tim Kasser, interview for The True Cost, https://truecostmovie.com/tim-kasser-interview/ (accessed September 27, 2020).

21   *Merriam-Webster*, s.v. "Consume," https://www.merriam-webster.com/dictionary/consume (accessed December 26, 2020).

22   Qing Li, "'Forest Bathing' Is Great for Your Health. Here's How to Do It," *Time*, May 1, 2018, https://time.com/5259602/japanese-forest-bathing/ (accessed December 29, 2020).

23   Tiffany Shlain, "Tech Shabbats," Let It Ripple, https://www.letitripple.org/about/tiffany-shlain/technology-shabbats/ (accessed December 30, 2020).

24   Bessel van der Kolk, *The Body Keeps the Score: Brain, Mind, and Body in the Healing of Trauma* (Penguin, 2015).

25   Patrizia Collard and James Walsh, "Sensory Awareness Mindfulness Training in Coaching: Accepting Life's Challenges," *Journal of Rational-Emotive & Cognitive-Behavior Therapy* 26 (2008), https://doi.org/10.1007/s10942-007-0071-4 (accessed September 26, 2020).

26   Jason Crandell, "How Speed Gets Trapped in the Body with Tias Little," Yogaland podcast, January 21, 2019, https://www.jasonyoga.com/podcast/episode137/ (accessed September 27, 2020).

27   Frank Partnoy, *Wait: The Art and Science of Delay* (PublicAffairs, 2012).

28   Daniel Kahneman, *Thinking Fast and Slow* (Farrar, Straus and Giroux, 2013).

29   Kahneman.

30   Frank Partnoy, *Wait.* (PublicAffairs, 2012).

31   Frank Partnoy, "Waiting Game," *Financial Times*, June 22, 2012, https://1icz9g2sdfe31jz0lglwdu48-wpengine.netdna-ssl.com/wp-content/uploads/2012/08/Novak-Djokovic-Waiting-Game.pdf (accessed September 20, 2020).

32   Frank Partnoy, "Act Fast, but Not Necessarily First," *Harvard Business Review*, July 13, 2012, https://hbr.org/2012/07/act-fast-not-first (accessed December 29, 2020).

33   Woody Tasch, "Inquiries into the Nature of Slow Money," Slow Money Institute, May 2010, https://slowmoney.org/publications/inquiries-into-the-nature-of-slow-money (accessed September 27, 2020).

34   Patrick McGinnis, "Social Theory at HBS: McGinnis' Two FOs," *Harbus*, May 10, 2004, https://harbus.org/2004/social-theory-at-hbs-2749/ (accessed September 20, 2020).

35   Rosie Bell, "JOMO," BBC, July 21, 2019, https://www.bbc.com/worklife/article/20190718-jomo (accessed September 26, 2020).

36   Patrick McGinnis and Greg McKeown, "Less Is More: The Power of Essentialism," FOMO Sapiens podcast, season 4, episode 17, July 2020, https://hbr.org/podcast/2020/07/less-is-more-the-power-of-essentialism (accessed September 26, 2020).

37   George Butterfield, interview by author, July 22, 2020.

38   Exploring Your Mind, "Sawubona: An African Tribe's Beautiful Greeting," October 17, 2018, https://exploringyourmind.com/sawubona-african-tribe-greeting/ (accessed September 19, 2020).

39   David Robson, "The Astonishing Vision and Focus of Namibia's Nomads," BBC, June 26, 2020, https://www.bbc.com/future/article/20170306-the-astonishing-focus-of-namibias-nomads (accessed September 26, 2020); Jan W. de Fockert, Serge Caparos, Karina J. Linnell and Jules Davidoff, "Reduced Distractibility in a Remote Culture," PLoS ONE 6 (October 2011), https://doi.org/10.1371/journal.pone.0026337 (accessed September 26, 2020).

40   *Merriam-Webster*, s.v. "Orenda," https://www.merriam-webster.com/dictionary
/orenda (accessed December 26, 2020).

41   David Robson, "How East and West Think in Profoundly Different Ways," BBC,
January 19, 2017, https://www.bbc.com/future/article/20170118-how-east-and-
west-think-in-profoundly-different-ways (accessed September 26, 2020).

42   Esther Hsieh, "Rice Farming Linked to Holistic Thinking," *Scientific American*,
November 1, 2014, https://www.scientificamerican.com/article/rice-farming-
linked-to-holistic-thinking/ (accessed September 26, 2020).

43   Shane Parrish, "Preserving Optionality: Preparing for the Unknown," Farnam
Street, March 2020, https://fs.blog/2020/03/preserving-optionality/ (accessed
September 26, 2020).

44   Frank Trentmann, "How Humans Became 'Consumers': A History," *Atlantic*,
November 28, 2016, https://www.theatlantic.com/business/archive/2016/11/how-
humans-became-consumers/508700/ (accessed September 26, 2020).

45   Dave Donnan, "The Kearney Global Future Consumer Study," A.T. Kearney, 2017,
https://www.kearney.com/web/consumers-250/article/?/a/influence-vs-affluence-
the-changing-menu-of-food-choices-article (accessed September 26, 2020).

46   Rick Levine, Christopher Locke, Doc Searls, and David Weinberger, *The Cluetrain
Manifesto*, 10th anniversary edition (Basic Books, 2009).

47   Diane Coyle, "Rethinking GDP," *Finance & Development* 54, no. 1 (2017), https://
www.imf.org/external/pubs/ft/fandd/2017/03/coyle.htm (accessed September
26, 2020).

48   The New Citizenship Project, "This Is The #CitizenShift," https://www.citizenshift
.info/ (accessed January 2, 2021).

49   Todd Sattersten, "I've Been Thinking . . . (#13)," June 18, 2020, https://
toddsattersten.com/2020/06/18/ive-been-thinking-13/ (accessed November
6, 2020).

50   Laura Huang, "The Well-Balanced Meal MBA Reading List," June 26, 2020,
https://laurahuang.net/the-well-balanced-meal-mba-reading-list/ (accessed
September 26, 2020).

51   Bernhard A. Sabel, Jiaqi Wang, Lizbeth Cardenas-Morales, Muneeb Faiq, and
Christine Heim, "Mental Stress as Consequence and Cause of Vision Loss," *EPMA
Journal* 9 (2018), https://doi.org/10.1007/s13167-018-0136-8 (accessed September
26, 2020).

52   April Rinne, "Handstands," https://aprilrinne.com/handstands (accessed
October 31, 2020).

53   Judi Ketteler, "If Life Has You Down, Do a Handstand," *New York Times*, May 4,
2017, https://www.nytimes.com/2017/05/04/well/move/if-life-has-you-down-do-
a-handstand.html (accessed October 31, 2020).

54 Jane Goodall, "Make A Difference," Jane Goodall Institute, November 16, 2015, https://news.janegoodall.org/2015/11/16/make-a-difference/ (accessed February 25, 2021).

55 Paul Gompers and Silpa Kovvali, "The Other Diversity Dividend," *Harvard Business Review*, https://hbr.org/2018/07/the-other-diversity-dividend (accessed September 16, 2020); McKinsey, "Diversity Wins," https://www.mckinsey.com /featured-insights/diversity-and-inclusion/diversity-wins-how-inclusion-matters (accessed September 16, 2020).

56 Joanna Macy, "Entering the Bardo," *Emergence Magazine*, https:// emergencemagazine.org/story/entering-the-bardo/ (accessed September 14, 2020).

57 The School of Life, "The History of Ideas: Wabi-sabi," https://www.youtube.com /watch?v=QmHLYhxYVjA (accessed September 14, 2020).

58 The School of Life, "Eastern Philosophy: Kintsugi," https://www.youtube.com /watch?v=EBUTQkaSSTY (accessed December 26, 2020).

59 David Brooks, "This Is How Scandinavia Got Great," *New York Times*, February 13, 2020, https://www.nytimes.com/2020/02/13/opinion/scandinavia-education. html (accessed September 14, 2020).

60 Manisha Aggarwal-Schifellite and Juan Siliezar, "Three Takes on Dealing with Uncertainty," *Harvard Gazette*, July 10, 2020, https://news.harvard.edu/gazette /story/2020/07/3-takes-on-dealing-with-uncertainty/ (accessed September 14, 2020).

61 Amitav Ghosh, "What the West Doesn't Get about the Climate Crisis," Deutsche Welle (DW), https://www.dw.com/en/amitav-ghosh-what-the-west-doesnt-get-about-the-climate-crisis/a-50823088 (accessed September 14, 2020).

62 *The Adventure Diary*, "Coddiwomple," https://adventurediary.co/coddiwomple-definition/ (accessed September 14, 2020).

63 Nancy Osborn, "The Theory of Coddiwomple," TEDxOrillia, May 16, 2019, https://www.youtube.com/watch?v=h4ReT52nJA8 (accessed September 14, 2020).

64 Edelman, "2020 Edelman Trust Barometer," https://www.edelman.com /trustbarometer (accessed September 19, 2020).

65 Rutger Bregman, *Humankind: A Hopeful History* (Little, Brown, 2020).

66 Rachel Botsman, "Trust-Thinkers," Medium, July 26, 2018, https://medium .com/@rachelbotsman/trust-thinkers-72ec78ec3b59 (accessed October 4, 2020).

67 Botsman.

68 Jerry Michalski, "Trust Unlocks Creativity (and Genius)," Jerry's Brain, https://bra.in/9v2mVe (accessed September 19, 2020).

69 Jerry Michalski, "Design from Trust," September 21, 2018, https://www.youtube .com/watch?v=6di2OBPKmkc (accessed September 19, 2020).

70 Shoshana Zuboff, *The Age of Surveillance Capitalism* (Public Affairs, 2019).

71   Moreover, between 1978 and 2019, CEO pay grew by 1,167%, while compensation of typical workers grew by just 13.7% over the same period. See Lawrence Mishel and Jori Kandra, "CEO Compensation Surged 14% in 2019 to $21.3 Million," Economic Policy Institute, August 18, 2020, https://files.epi.org/pdf/204513.pdf (accessed January 2, 2021).

72   Nicholas Bloom, Scott Ohlmacher, Cristina Tello-Trillo, and Melanie Wallskog, "Better-Managed Companies Pay Employees More Equally," Harvard Business Review, March 6, 2019, https://hbr.org/2019/03/research-better-managed-companies-pay-employees-more-equally (accessed December 30, 2020).

73   Oxfam International, "Time to Care," January 20, 2020, https://www.oxfam.org/en/press-releases/worlds-billionaires-have-more-wealth-46-billion-people (accessed September 16, 2020).

74   ExO World, "Jerry Michalski on Trust," April 15, 2020, https://youtu.be/rlo8d7F5hdo?t=256 (accessed September 19, 2020).

75   Shoshana Zuboff, The Age of Surveillance Capitalism: The Fight for a Human Future at the New Frontier of Power (PublicAffairs, 2019).

76   David Gordon White, The Yoga Sutra of Patanjali: A Biography (Princeton University Press, 2014).

77   Frits Staal, Discovering the Vedas: Origins, Mantras, Rituals, Insights (Penguin Global, 2009).

78   Don Miguel Ruiz, The Four Agreements: A Practical Guide to Personal Freedom (A Toltec Wisdom Book) (Amber-Allen, 1997).

79   Matthew Wall, "Wikipedia Editing Rules in a Nutshell," BBC News, April 22, 2015, https://www.bbc.com/news/technology-32412121 (accessed December 30, 2020).

80   Patty McCord, "How Netflix Reinvented HR," Harvard Business Review, January 2014, https://hbr.org/2014/01/how-netflix-reinvented-hr (accessed December 30, 2020).

81   CNN Staff, "The Philosophy of Doma India," CNN, October 9, 2014, https://www.cnn.com/2014/10/09/sport/horse-yoga-argentina/index.html (accessed December 30, 2020).

82   Jerry Michalski, "Why You Love Design from Trust," July 24, 2019, https://medium.com/@jerrymichalski/why-you-love-design-from-trust-f9afdfc08e2e (accessed September 19, 2020).

83   Jerry Michalski, "Not Naïve Trust," August 22, 2016, https://www.youtube.com/watch?v=e-2NaSxJPJk (accessed September 19, 2020).

84   Jerry Michalski, "Design from Trust," https://www.designfromtrust.com (accessed September 19, 2020).

85   Juliet Schor, Plenitude: The New Economics of True Wealth (Penguin, 2010).

86   Peter Goodman, "The Robots Are Coming, and Sweden Is Fine," *New York Times*, December 27, 2017, https://www.nytimes.com/2017/12/27/business/the-robots-are-coming-and-sweden-is-fine.html (accessed September 16, 2020).

87   Kevin Cavenaugh, "How Much Is Enough?" TEDx Talks, April 2018, https://www.ted.com/talks/kevin_cavenaugh_how_much_is_enough (accessed September 16, 2020).

88   Kevin Cavenaugh, interview by author, July 14, 2020.

89   Dotan Leshem, "Retrospectives: What Did the Ancient Greeks Mean by *Oikonomia?*," *Journal of Economic Perspectives* 30 (2016): 225–31, https://pubs.aeaweb.org/doi/pdf/10.1257%2Fjep.30.1.225 (accessed September 16, 2020).

90   Robert Reich, "When Bosses Shared Their Profits," *New York Times*, June 25, 2020, https://www.nytimes.com/2020/06/25/opinion/sunday/corporate-profit-sharing-inequality.html (accessed September 16, 2020).

91   Oxfam International, "Time to Care," January 20, 2020, https://www.oxfam.org/en/press-releases/worlds-billionaires-have-more-wealth-46-billion-people (accessed September 16, 2020).

92   Kate Raworth, *Doughnut Economics: Seven Ways to Think Like a Twenty-First-Century Economist* (Chelsea Green, 2017).

93   Daniel Pink, "Drive: The Surprising Truth about What Motivates Us," RSA, April 1, 2010, https://youtu.be/u6XAPnuFjJc (accessed September 16, 2020).

94   Thomas Oppong, "The Hedonic Treadmill: Why People Are Never Happy and How You Can Change That," Mind Cafe, April 23, 2020, https://medium.com/mind-cafe/the-hedonic-treadmill-why-people-are-never-truly-happy-and-how-you-can-change-that-c1743ee9f7e5 (accessed December 26, 2020).

95   Morgan Housel, "Fat, Happy, and in over Your Head," Collaborative Fund, September 17, 2019, https://www.collaborativefund.com/blog/fat-happy-and-in-over-your-head/ (accessed November 6, 2020).

96   Joe Pinsker, "The Reason Many Ultrarich People Aren't Satisfied with Their Wealth," *Atlantic*, December 4, 2018, https://www.theatlantic.com/family/archive/2018/12/rich-people-happy-money/577231/ (accessed September 16, 2020).

97   Adam Grant, *Give and Take* (Viking, 2013).

98   Rolf Sovik, "Brahmacharya: The Middle Path of Restraint," Yoga International, https://yogainternational.com/article/view/brahmacharya-the-middle-path-of-restraint (accessed September 16, 2020).

99   U'Mista Cultural Society, "Potlatch," https://umistapotlatch.ca/potlatch-eng.php (accessed December 26, 2020).

100   Steven Kurutz, "How to Retire in Your 30s with $1 Million in the Bank," *New York Times*, September 1, 2018, https://www.nytimes.com/2018/09/01/style/fire-financial-independence-retire-early.html (accessed September 16, 2020).

101 Anne Tergesen and Veronica Dagher, "The New Retirement Plan: Save Almost Everything, Spend Virtually Nothing," *Wall Street Journal*, November 3, 2018, https://www.wsj.com/articles/the-new-retirement-plan-save-almost-everything-spend-virtually-nothing-1541217688 (accessed September 16, 2020).

102 Charlotte Cowles, "A FIRE That Burns Too Male and Too White," *New York Times*, June 7, 2019, https://www.nytimes.com/2019/06/07/business/fire-women-retire-early.html (accessed September 16, 2020); Vicki Robin, "My Life with FIRE," https://vickirobin.com/my-life-with-fire/ (accessed September 16, 2020); Vicki Robin, *Your Money or Your Life* (Penguin, 2008).

103 Daniel Cordaro, "What If You Pursued Contentment Rather Than Happiness?," *Greater Good Magazine*, May 27, 2020, https://greatergood.berkeley.edu/article/item/what_if_you_pursued_contentment_rather_than_happiness (accessed November 1, 2020).

104 Cordaro.

105 Glennon Doyle, "Lessons from the Mental Hospital," TEDx Talks, May 31, 2013, https://www.youtube.com/watch?v=NHHPNMIK-fY&vl=en (accessed September 16, 2020).

106 April Rinne, "The Career of the Future Looks More Like a Portfolio Than a Path," Quartz at Work, February 27, 2018, https://qz.com/work/1217108/the-career-of-the-future-looks-more-like-a-portfolio-than-a-path/ (accessed September 18, 2020).

107 Bruce Henderson, "The Product Portfolio," Boston Consulting Group, January 1, 1970, https://www.youtube.com/watch?v=EezmRPE3fpQ (accessed September 18, 2020).

108 April Rinne, "Handstands," https://aprilrinne.com/handstands (accessed October 4, 2020).

109 Lawrence Katz and Alan Krueger, "The Rise and Nature of Alternative Work Arrangements in the United States, 1995–2015," National Bureau of Economic Research Working Paper No. 22667, September 2016, https://www.nber.org/papers/w22667 (accessed September 18, 2020).

110 Melissa Korn, "Some 43% of College Grads Are Underemployed in First Job," *Wall Street Journal*, October 26, 2018, https://www.wsj.com/articles/study-offers-new-hope-for-english-majors-1540546200 (accessed September 19, 2020).

111 Upwork and Freelancers Union, "Freelancing in America 2017," October 17, 2017, https://www.upwork.com/press/2017/10/17/freelancing-in-america-2017/ (accessed September 19, 2020).

112 Upwork and Freelancers Union, "Freelancing in America 2019," October 3, 2019, https://www.upwork.com/press/2019/10/03/freelancing-in-america-2019/ (accessed September 19, 2020).

113 Upwork and Freelancers Union, "Freelancing in America 2018," October 31, 2018, https://www.upwork.com/press/2018/10/31/freelancing-in-america-2018/ (accessed September 19, 2020).

114 Upwork, "Freelance Forward 2020," September 2020, https://www.upwork.com /documents/freelance-forward-2020 (accessed December 29, 2020).

115 David Graeber, *Bullshit Jobs: A Theory* (Simon & Schuster, 2018).

116 Uri Berliner, "Jobs in the Pandemic: More Are Freelance and May Stay That Way Forever," National Public Radio, September 16, 2020, https://www.npr .org/2020/09/16/912744566/jobs-in-the-pandemic-more-are-freelance-and-may-stay-that-way-forever (accessed September 19, 2020).

117 David Clifford, "Forget about T-shaped people. We need X-shaped people." TEDx Talks, September 24, 2019, https://www.youtube.com/watch?v=EezmRPE3fpQ (accessed September 18, 2020).

118 Yukari Mitsuhashi, "Ikigai: A Japanese Concept to Improve Work and Life," British Broadcasting Corporation, August 7, 2017, https://www.bbc.com/worklife /article/20170807-ikigai-a-japanese-concept-to-improve-work-and-life (accessed September 19, 2020).

119 April Rinne, "One of Estonia's First 'E-Residents' Explains What It Means to Have Digital Citizenship," Quartz at Work, April 1, 2018, https://qz.com/ work/1241833/one-of-estonias-first-e-residents-explains-what-it-means-to-have-digital-citizenship/ (accessed December 30, 2020).

120 Quoted in Thomas L. Friedman, "After the Pandemic, a Revolution in Education and Work Awaits," *New York Times*, October 20, 2020, https://www.nytimes .com/2020/10/20/opinion/covid-education-work.html (accessed October 30, 2020).

121 John Hagel, "From the Gig Economy to the Guild Economy," July 21, 2020, https://www.johnhagel.com/from-the-gig-economy-to-the-guild-economy/ (accessed September 19, 2020).

122 Enspiral Network, "What's Your 'Meaningful Work' to Do in the World?," https:// www.enspiral.com/ (accessed December 30, 2020).

123 Robert Safian, "This Is Generation Flux: Meet the Pioneers of the New (and Chaotic) Frontier of Business," Fast Company, January 9, 2012, https://www .fastcompany.com/1802732/generation-flux-meet-pioneers-new-and-chaotic-frontier-business (accessed December 26, 2020).

124 Tiffany May, "For Chinese Pedestrians Glued to Their Phones, a Middle Path Emerges," CNBC & *New York Times*, June 8, 2018, https://www.cnbc. com/2018/06/08/for-chinese-pedestrians-glued-to-their-phones-a-middle-path-emerges.html (accessed September 17, 2020).

125 Common Sense Media, "Media Use by Tweens and Teens, 2019," https://www .commonsensemedia.org/research/the-common-sense-census-media-use-by-tweens-and-teens-2019 (accessed September 17, 2020); Kristen Rogers, "US Teens Use Screens More Than Seven Hours a Day on Average—and That's Not Including School Work," CNN Health, October 20, 2019, https://www.cnn. com/2019/10/29/health/common-sense-kids-media-use-report-wellness/index. html (accessed September 17, 2020).

126 K. C. Madhav, Shardulendra Prasad Sherchand, and Samendra Sherchan, "Association between Screen Time and Depression among U.S. Adults," National Institutes of Health, August 16, 2017, https://www.ncbi.nlm.nih.gov/pmc/articles /PMC5574844/ (accessed September 17, 2020).

127 Children's Society, "Safety Net: Cyberbullying's Impact on Young People's Mental Health Inquiry Report," https://www.childrenssociety.org.uk/sites/default /files/social-media-cyberbullying-inquiry-full-report_0.pdf (accessed September 17, 2020); DoSomething.Org, "11 Facts about Cyberbullying," https://www .dosomething.org/us/facts/11-facts-about-cyber-bullying (accessed September 17, 2020).

128 Marti Spiegelman, interview by author, October 9, 2020.

129 Spiegelman.

130 Spiegelman.

131 John Bellaimey, "The Hidden Meanings of Yin and Yang," TED-Ed, https://ed.ted .com/lessons/the-hidden-meanings-of-yin-and-yang-john-bellaimey (accessed December 26, 2020).

132 Jerry Michalski, "Why I Do What I Do," June 2, 2011, https://www.youtube.com /watch?v=2dx-6I9Sc6A (accessed January 2, 2021).

133 Emma Hinchliffe, "The Number of Female CEOs in the Fortune 500 Hits an All-Time Record," *Fortune*, May 18, 2020, https://fortune.com/2020/05/18/women-ceos-fortune-500-2020/ (accessed September 17, 2020).

134 Rachel Vogelstein and Alexandra Bro, "Women's Power Index," Council on Foreign Relations, May 22, 2020, https://www.cfr.org/article/womens-power-index (accessed September 17, 2020).

135 Heide Goettner-Abendroth, "Matriarchies Are Not Just a Reversal of Patriarchies: A Structural Analysis," *Feminism and Religion*, February 16, 2020, https:// feminismandreligion.com/2020/02/16/matriarchies-are-not-just-a-reversal-of-patriarchies-a-structural-analysis-by-heide-goettner-abendroth/ (accessed September 17, 2020).

136 Nilima Bhat, "Shakti Leadership: Why Lead with Only Half Your Power?" EVE talk, July 26, 2019, https://www.youtube.com/watch?v=BSCgYrC2jO8 (accessed September 17, 2020).

137 DQ Institute, "Digital Intelligence (DQ)," https://www.dqinstitute.org/ (accessed September 16, 2020).

138 DQ Institute, "Digital Intelligence (DQ) framework," https://www.dqinstitute.org/ dq-framework/ (accessed September 16, 2020).

139 Brené Brown, "Courage: To Speak One's Mind by Telling All One's Heart," February 14, 2019, https://brenebrown.com/blog/2019/02/14/courage-to-speak-ones-mind-by-telling-all-ones-heart/ (accessed September 17, 2020).

140 Marti Spiegelman, interview by author (part of a group conversation), August 19, 2020.

141 Marti Spiegelman, interview by author, October 9, 2020.

142 Marti Spiegelman, "For Our Well-Being," Leading from Being, May 3, 2020, https://www.linkedin.com/pulse/our-well-being-marti-spiegelman-mfa/ (accessed December 29, 2020).

143 Amishi Jha, "How to Tame Your Wandering Mind," TEDx Talks, March 2017, https://www.ted.com/talks/amishi_jha_how_to_tame_your_wandering_mind (accessed September 26, 2020).

144 D. M. Wegner, "Ironic Processes of Mental Control," Psychology Review 101, no. 1 (January 1994), https://doi.org/10.1037/0033-295X.101.1.34 (accessed September 26, 2020).

145 Judson Brewer, "Anxiety is Contagious. Here's How to Contain It," Harvard Business Review, March 18, 2020, https://hbr.org/2020/03/anxiety-is-contagious-heres-how-to-contain-it (accessed September 25, 2020).

146 Lindsay Baker, "Why Embracing Change is the Key to a Good Life," BBC, October 8, 2020, https://www.bbc.com/culture/article/20200930-why-embracing-change-is-the-key-to-a-good-life (accessed November 7, 2020).

147 Newsweek Staff, "Stronger Than Steel," Newsweek, April 12, 2008, https://www.newsweek.com/stronger-steel-85533 (accessed September 17, 2020).

148 Indigenous Corporate Training, "What Is the Seventh Generation Principle?" https://www.ictinc.ca/blog/seventh-generation-principle (accessed December 26, 2020); Ken Homer, "The Seven Generations vs. the Seventh Generation," Collaborative Conversations, https://www.kenhomer.com/single-post/2018/09/17 /The-Seven-Generations-vs-the-Seventh-Generation (accessed December 30, 2020).

149 First People, "Two Wolves: A Cherokee Legend," https://www.firstpeople.us /FP-Html-Legends/TwoWolves-Cherokee.html (accessed December 29, 2020).

150 Jennifer Mueller, Creative Change: Why We Resist It . . . How We Can Embrace It (Houghton Mifflin Harcourt, 2017).

ACKNOWLEDGMENTS

This book has taken more than twenty-five years to form. It has been a joy, an honor, and an adventure to write. My gratitude for the people, perspectives, and cultures that helped shape it stretches far beyond these pages. I'll do my best to share as much as I can here—it's a lot of Flux to remember!

This book would have never seen the light of day if it weren't for my parents, Roland Eugene Rinne and Penny Jo (Loffler) Rinne. In life and after life, they have been signals and guideposts for flux. What really matters? What would Dad say? I miss you, and I'm delighted that *Flux* can help keep your spirits alive.

I'll never be able to thank enough the people who saw me through the darkest depths of my parents' deaths. Above all, my sister, Allison (Rinne) Douglas, helped me see what is, and is not, and to this day is an unwavering inspiration. Mom's identical twin sister Paula Yingst, younger sister Donna Flinders, and the entire extended Loffler family surrounded me with love from the moment I got the phone call until this very day. Nieces Ella and Amelia keep flux and future generations front of mind. Roger and Barbara Rinne and Stefan, Roger, and Carolyn Douglas, thank you as well.

My extended families of choice brought love in the most beautiful ways I could ever have imagined. The Raggi-Moores—Judy, Danny, Jessica, Francesca (Nonna), and Frances (Meema)—added a whole new, full layer of family, love, and belonging. My heart has had a safe place to land ever since. Linda Nelson, Steve and Terry Casey, and the No More Cru showed me that love and joy can show up anywhere. Baine and Sally Kerr taught me what it means to empower others and gave me an early glimpse of listening to my inner voice. Mom and Dad's closest friends kept tabs on me and my parents' memories alive.

My dad was a teacher and my best friend. I was fortunate to have several teachers early on who saw my potential (even when I struggled to see it myself) and to whom I looked up (even when life looked down). From elementary school to law school, and both inside and outside the classroom: Karen Crosson, Patty Weed, Thomas Lancaster, Priscilla Echols, Jody Usher, Ngaire Woods, Elizabeth Warren, Jonathan Zittrain, Jon Hanson, and Laurent Jacques powered my curiosity, encouraged me to see what was beyond the test or title of the class, and in their own ways helped me lay a foundation for my new script to emerge.

I now understand why authors talk about "birthing" a book: ideas gestate, writing is both labor and great joy, and the end result is an act of love that changes you forever. I can't imagine having better delivery partners than the Berrett-Koehler team. BK represents how publishing should be done. Steve Piersanti is an author's dream editor. He spent (by my guesstimate) hundreds of hours helping make this manuscript stronger, and each round of revisions opened my eyes further to the book's potential. Jeevan Sivasubramaniam, Katie Sheehan, Kristin Frantz, Valerie Caldwell: the BK dream team! Thank you *all*. Mark Fortier and Jessica Pellien, thank you for helping introduce *Flux* to the world with extraordinary kindness, wit, and savvy. Elan Morgan, Debbie Berne, and Joaquín González Dorao, thank you for your creativity and ability to visualize my fluxy ideas to be shared with the world. Ariane Conrad, Ed Frauenheim, John Kador, Stewart Levine, Tim Brandhorst, Carla Banc, the TEDxFrankfurt team, and the BK Authors community: thank you for being catalysts for this journey as well.

Mental health has played a subtle and not-so-subtle role within these pages, both personally and in my sensing a broader societal reckoning with flux. Ross Cohen, Bryna Livingston, and Marlys Kvsager: thank you from the bottom of my heart. Wholehearted thanks also to the YoYoYogi community for opening the door to bridge yoga philosophy with today's world in flux. Alex, Terri and Kristi Cole, Tori Griesing, Isabel Allen, Galen Fairbanks, and Rachel Meyer: you all rock.

I've always sought to have colleagues who are also friends: people who care about one another beyond the task at hand and celebrate one another's life journeys as they unfold. My colleagues at the Harry Walker Agency personify this affection. Don and Ellen Walker, Amy Werner, Meghan Sheehan, Lily Winter, Tiffany Vizcarra, McKinsey Lowrance, Nicki Fleischner, Elizabeth Hernandez, Carolyn Boylan, Molly Cotter, Emily Trievel, Beth Gargano, Suzanne Manzi, John Ksar, Ruben Porras-Sanchez, Gus Menezes, Mirjana Novkovic, Dana Quinn, Miranda Martin: thank you all (and anyone I may have missed as this went to print)!

My portfolio career has allowed me to create a more diverse professional community than would have otherwise been the case. These colleagues have given me a seat at the fifty-yard line of flux in more sectors and organizations than I ever could have pulled off on my own and have consistently helped stretch my brain, challenge my own assumptions, and walk the talk. Over the years many of my colleagues at Airbnb, Allen & Overy, AnyRoad, Butterfield & Robinson, Institute for the Future, Jobbatical, nexxworks, Sharing Cities Alliance, Trōv, Unsettled, and Water.org have become dear friends as well. Change? Bring it on!

No single community has had a more significant effect on my personal-professional journey through flux than the Young Global Leaders at the World Economic Forum. YGLs are a never-ending source of inspiration, as well as a petri dish for what does (and doesn't) matter. I'm certain I'll miss a few who should be mentioned, but here's my best-effort list of YGLs who helped bring this book to life, directly or indirectly: Hrund Gunnsteinsdóttir, Geraldine and James Chin-Moody, Lisa Witter, Niko Canner, Raju Narisetti, Amy Cuddy, Elaine Smith, Brett House, Valerie Keller, Nilmini Rubin, Binta Brown, Aaron Maniam, Nili Gilbert, Robyn Scott, Kristen Rechberger, Enric Sala, Dave Hanley, Geoff Davis, Julia Novy-Hildesley, Ailish Campbell, Peter Lacy, David Rosenberg, Cori Lathan, Adam Werbach, Adam Grant, Drue Kataoka, Lucian Tarnowski, Hannah Jones, Ian Solomon, John McArthur, Werner Wutscher, Eduardo Cruz . . . you are all bright lights for flux. And the YGL team of yesterday and today: John Dutton, Mariah Levin, David Aikman, Eric Roland, Kelsey Goodman, Merit Berhe, Shareena Hatta . . . thanks for wrangling us all together.

There are so many people who provided ideas, feedback, perspective, and inspiration—occasionally without even knowing it—and helped bring this book to fruition. Marti Spiegelman, Kevin Cavenaugh, Heather McGowan, Mara Zepeda, Vanessa Timmer, Juliet Schor, Gary and Heidi Bolles, Julie Vens de Vos, Peter Hinssen, George Butterfield, David Kessler, David Nebinski, Allegra Calder, Mike Macharg, Estee Solomon Gray, Astrid Scholz, Manisha Thakor, Jonathan Kalan, Michael Youngblood, Karoli Hindriks, Jerry's Retreaters, and the Relationship Economy eXpedition (REX) and Open Global Mind (OGM) groups have provided insights and inspiration over many years, as well as during the writing process. Joy Batra, Saskia Akyil, Anne Janzer, Chris Shipley, Laura Fronckiewicz, Ann Lemaire, Clark Quinn, Rollie Cole, and Stephi Galloway provided invaluable feedback on my draft manuscript. Dear friends Marta Zoppetti, Daniela Gangale, Jay Turner, Sharon Jones, Jenny Ellickson, Jane Stoever, Anna Tabor, Jen Harrison, Trisha Anderson, Lea Johnston, Gaurav Misra, Noah Messing, Stirling Spencer, and the wonderful members of University College's Middle Common Room (MCR) in 1993–94 have cheered me on since before I knew this book would see the light of day. Sigh: this is when I start genuinely fretting about leaving someone out.

I launched the Flux Mindset eXplorers Club (FMXC) as a collaborative quest to navigate change. FMXC continues to be a never-ending source of joy, diversity, showing up, and learning and sharing together. Huge thanks to each and every member. (If you'd like to join, please head to fluxmindset.com and sign up!)

Last, yet in so many ways first, thanks to Jerry Michalski in more ways than I can count. Thank you for believing in me, for your unwavering support and love, for understanding my quirks (often better than I do), for your big ideas and extraordinary ability to help me distill mine, and for being such a stellar partner in life, love, travel, and, of course, flux.

INDEX

*page numbers in **bold** type refers to chapters*

abundance, 128, 135
acceptance, 187–88
advertising, 101
agency, empowering, 186–87
Amazon Alexa, 160
ambiguity, comfort with, 24
ancient wisdom, 7, 103–4, 107, 133, 173–74, 198–99
anxiety, 9–10, 13 Table 1, 17, 22–23; about the future, 177, 179–81, 182, 184, 189–91; author's struggle with, 189–91; and getting lost, 77; and slowing down, 37, 48, 127
aparigraha (non-attachment), 182
apocalypse, 84, 90
Argentina, 106, 107
artists, 141, 152, 153
asanas (yoga poses), 46
assumptions, challenging, x, 20, 72
attachment, 181–83
automation, 120, 124, 138, 145, 160–61
autonomy, 126
awakening *(satori)*, 60

Bali, 77
banks, 94, 106
bardo, 84, 90
being more human, 6, 17, 18 Table 2, 21, 27, 29, **160–176**; and consciousness, 172–74; exercises, 171, 175–76, 210; imbalance within, 167–70; and suffering, 164–66; and technology, 160–64, 170–72; and trust, 98–99
bento box metaphor, 17, 148
Bhat, Nilima, *Shakti Leadership*, 170
Bhutanese culture, 133–34
bildung (Nordic system), 85–86
BlaBlaCar (ride-sharing platform), 106
#BlackLivesMatter, 67
Black representation, 67
boards of directors, 82, 102
Bolivia, 77
Botsman, Rachel, *Who Do You Trust?* 94
brahmacharya (non-excess), 131
Brand, Stewart, 50
breathing practice, 43, 45–46

Brewer, Judson, 192
Brown, Binta, 139
Brown, Brené, 172
Buddhism, 37–38, 60, 84
Burnout Generation, 35
Butler, Octavia, 193
Butterfield, George, 53

Campbell, Ailish, 160
capitalism, 59, 104, 124–26
career planning, x, 13 Table 1, 22, 142–46. *See also* portfolio careers
Cavenaugh, Kevin, "How Much Is Enough?," 122, 123
CEOs, 68, 93, 101, 102–3, 104, 110, 121
cernere (to discern), 87
chakras (energy centers), 105
change: acceptance of, 187–88, 191; as an opportunity, x, 12, 13 Table 1, 17; compass for, 16; cultural views on, 87–89; and disorientation, ix, 16; and enoughness, 118; inevitability and universality of, ix, 11, 29, 184; internal relationship to, 27–28; Japanese embrace of, 85–86; pace of, ix, 3, 29, 160–6; types of, 4–5, 25; vocabulary for, 29, 204. *See also* Flux Mindset; Flux Superpowers
Chase, Robin, 139
children, 27, 93, 100, 202–3
China, 37–38, 60, 83, 160, 167
Chinook Jargon language, 131
Chödrön, Pema, ix
choice, 4–5, 62–63, 100, 115, 181
chokkshay ("the knowledge of enough"), 133–34
citizenship role, 34, 64–67, 71, 104, 108, 200
clarity, x, 13, 15, 24, 128
climate change, 2, 9, 24–25
coddiwompling, 89–90, 91
cognitive behavioral therapy (CBT), 48
Cohen, Josh, 36
Cohen, Leonard, 112
Cole, Alex, 139
collaboration, 11, 61, 167, 170, 201
collectivist societies, 24, 60–61
college graduates, 144, 154
colonialism, 102, 104
community, 11, 103–4, 203–5

compass, 16, 26, 77, 153
compassion, 53, 129
compensation (salary): economic
    inequality, 101, 102–3, 104, 109,
    121, 200; gender inequality, 168; and
    motivation, 127
complexity theory, 22
confidence, x, 94–95
consciousness, 173–74
consumerism, 39, 40–41; *versus* citizenship,
    64–67, 200; and "enoughness," 115,
    116–17, 124, 125; and trust, 104, 108
consummare (used up), 65
contentment, 133–34. *See also* enoughness
contentus (to contain), 133
control, 179, 181–83, 186–88
cor (heart), 172
coronavirus pandemic, 2, 10, 68, 138, 145,
    161, 165
corporations: and the economics of more,
    124–26; flux in, 200–202; new shifts in,
    145; resilience and stability in, 102; trust
    in, 93, 102–3, 104, 108–9, 200
courage, 172–73
creating portfolio careers. *See* portfolio
    careers
crisis, 83–85
cultural diversity, 11–12; learning about,
    23; in orientation, 15–16, 83–86; and
    trust, 93
curiosity, 13 Table 1, 17, 72; about the
    future, 191–93; and getting lost, 77; and
    trust, 98, 100

death, 26, 84
Denmark, 85
Design from Trust, 108
digital intelligence (DQ), 170–72
Digital Intelligence Institute, 171
disorientation / orientation, 9, 15–16, 91.
    See also getting lost
distractions, 35, 42
diversity, 11, 67-69, 82. *See also* cultural
    diversity
diversity, equity, and inclusion (DEI), 11,
    67–69, 121, 200
doma india (horse gentling), 106, 107
Doughnut Economics, 126
Doyle, Glennon, "Lessons from the Mental
    Hospital", 134
DQ (digital intelligence), 170–72
drishti (focused gaze), 16, 26

*Drive: The Surprising Truth About What
    Motivates Us* (Pink), 126
Dweck, Carol, 12

economy: derivation of the word, 124; and
    enoughness, 122–26; gig economy, 149;
    global, 10, 103, 125; on-demand, 35;
    South African, 55–56
ecosystems, 24
education, 94, 100, 138, 154,186
efficiency, 41, 79, 145, 161–62
egalitarianism, 168–70
ego, 164
Emerson, Ralph Waldo, 163
emotions, 26; *chakras* in charge of, 105;
    emotional intelligence (EQ), 170–72; to
    getting lost, 90–91; identifying reactions,
    14; and technology, 186. *See also* fear;
    grief
employment: future directions, 137–38,
    154–56; policies, 120–21, 124–26,
    137–38, 168; recent trends, 144; and
    trust, 93, 102, 109
enenkein ("to carry"), 116, 133
enoughness, 17, 18 Table 2, 21, **113–36**; and
    author's childhood, 113–14; derivation
    of word, 116, 133; economics of more,
    124–26; exercises, 119, 122, 128, 136,
    209; and leadership, 121–24; new script
    for, 128–36; and privilege, 118–19;
    psychological view on, 126–28; and
    striving, 116–18
Enspiral Network, 157
Essentialism (McKeown), 52
executives, 68, 93, 101, 102–3, 104, 110,
    121; female, 167–68; and portfolio
    theory, 141, 153
expectations, 184, 193
expectations, challenging, x, 12, 13 Table
    1, 47
eye-movement desensitization and
    reprocessing (EMDR), 48

faith, 11, 27
families, 2, 9, 202–3
fear, 11, 17, 26, 42; ancient wisdom on,
    199; of the future, 179–81, 189–91; and
    getting lost, 79, 88–89; of slowing down,
    47, 50–52; and trust, 95; of the unknown,
    163–64
financial advisors, 141
Financial Independence, Retire Early
    (FIRE), 132

First Nations peoples, 131
"flight, flight, or freeze" response, 9
flow, state of, 38, 193
flower metaphor, 148
Flux Mindset: baseline, 14, 197, 201, 207;
defined, 3–4, 29; diagram, 19; elements
of, 13 Table 1; exercises, 3, 14–15; and
nature, 198–200; new script for, 8,
20–26; opening up to, 8, 11–16, 196, 197;
practicing, 195–96; roadmap to, 27–29;
Theory of Flux, 5–8, 19–20, 204
Flux Superpowers. combining, 196; in
families, 202–3; and Flux Mindset,
relationship to, 18–19, 22; identifying,
14; and nature, 198–200; in
organizational culture, 200–202, 210–11;
unlocking, 8, 16–20, 18 Table 2, 196, 197.
See also being more human; enoughness;
getting lost; letting go (of the future);
portfolio careers; running slower; seeing
what's invisible; trust.
FOBO (Fear of Better Options), 50–51, 52
FODA (Fear of Doing Anything), 51–52
foglio (sheet of paper), 141
FOMO (Fear of Missing Out), 50–51, 52
forest bathing (*shinrin-yoku*), 44
Four Agreements, The (Ruiz), 105
Francis, Pope, 172
freelancers, 138, 144
Friedman, Milton, 122
future. *See* letting go (of the future)

Garcia, Jerry, 137, 149
GDP (gross domestic product), 64, 65–66,
204
Generation Flux, 158
Generation Z, 144
generosity, 15, 130–32, 136, 165
getting lost, 17, 18 Table 2, 21, **74–92**;
author's experience with, 26, 74–76,
77, 81–82; coddiwompling, 89–90, 91;
cultural difference and views in, 15–16,
82–86; in diverse domains, 86–88;
exercises, 79, 83, 90–91, 208; experiences
of, 78–79; and scarcity thinking, 80–81
Ghosh, Amitav, 87–88
gig economy, 149
Gilbert, Dan, 175
Give and Take (Grant), 130
global economy, 10, 103, 125
global trust crisis, 93–94, 102–4
goals, 7, 12, 13 Table 1, 34
Goethe, Johann Wolfgang von, 99

Goodall, Jane, 72
government, 86, 93, 120, 139
GPS, 74, 88, 91
Grant, Adam, *Give and Take,* 130
grasping, 47, 193
Greece, 83, 84
greed, 122, 123
grief, 1–2, 22–26; author's struggles with,
189; and humanity, 165–66; and slowing
down, 38
grounding, 12–16, 27, 80–83
guilds, twenty-first century, 157–58

harmony (*yin* and *yang*), 167–70
Harvard Business School, 50, 67
"heads-down society," 160
health, 44–46
Hemingway, Ernest, 93
Heraclitus, 195, 198
hierarchical structures, 168–70
Himba people (Namibia), 58
hope, 11, 13 Table 1, 17, 94–95
Housel, Morgan, 127
"How Much Is Enough?" (Cavenaugh), 122
HR (human resources) departments, 107,
141, 198
Huang, Laura, 67, 68
hub-and-spoke metaphor, 18–19
humanity, embracing. *See* being more
human
100 Best Business Books of All Time, The
(Sattersten and Covert), 67

identity: personal, 11, 15, 152; professional,
120, 141–42, 146–47, 159
ikigai (life purpose), 148–49, 150, 153
impermanence, ix, 84, 88
independent workers, 138, 144, 145, 154–56
India, 84, 105
indigenous wisdom, 103–4, 131, 133,
198–99, 204
individualist societies, 60–61
Industrial Revolution, 85–86
inequality, 9, 11, 67–69; and enoughness,
122, 125, 129, 200; and mistrust, 98, 102,
121
inner wisdom, 7, 173–74, 199
innovation, 79, 100, 201
intention, 71–73, 95, 97–99
interdependence, 202
investment and investors, 50, 101, 141, 153
invisible, seeing the. *See* seeing what's
invisible

IQ, 170–72
"ironic mental processing," 182
Iroquois tribes, 58–59

Japan, 44, 60, 84–85, 148
Jha, Amishi, 179
jiu-jitsu (martial art), 148
job interviews, 59
journaling, 26, 37
Joy of Missing Out (JOMO), 52–53
judgment, delaying, 48–50, 72

Kahneman, Daniel, *Thinking Fast and Slow*, 49
Kasser, Tim, 41
kenshō ("seeing into one's true nature"), 60
Kibera, Nairobi, 107
kindheartedness, 53
kintsugi ("golden joinery"), 85
knowing you "enough." *See* enoughness
krisis (act of judgment), 83
kumbhaka (breathing practice), 43

Lao Tzu, 135, 177, 182
Latinx representation, 67
layoffs, 31–32
leadership: anxiety in, 9–10, 48; assessment of, 25; diversity in, 67–69; and enoughness, 121–24, 130; Flux Mindset in, 11, 13 Table 1, 200–202, 210–11; legacy of, 121, 122; new script for, 24, 34, 67, 170; and trust, 108–11; women in, 167–70
Leaders on Purpose, 24
legal system, 94, 100–101
"Lessons from the Mental Hospital" (Doyle), 134
letting go (of the future), 17, 18 Table 2, 20, 21, 22, 96, **177–94**; and anxiety, 189–91; author's experience with, 25–26, 177; and control, 179, 181–83, 186–88; exercises, 185, 193–94, 210; and fear, 179–81; new shifts for, 183–86; scenario mapping, 185, 194
life purpose *(ikigai)*, 148–49, 150, 153
life scripts. *See* scripts, life
Little, Tias, 47
losing one's way. *See* getting lost
loss, 80, 165–66

Maciunas, George, 202
managers, 141, 153, 168
Masahide, Mizuta, 85
mass marketing, 64, 101, 104, 109, 124, 186

May, Rollo, 31
MBA curricula, 67, 68–69
McGinnis, Patrick, 50–52
McGowan, Heather, 145, 156
McKeown, Greg, *Essentialism*, 52
meditation, 37, 46
mental health, 21. *See also* anxiety
#MeToo movement, 67
Michalski, Jerry, 65, 108
microfinance, 55, 106
micro-sabbaticals, 43–44
Millennials, 35–36, 144, 154
mindfulness, 192
mistrust, 100–103, 108–11, 121. *See also* trust
mobile devices, 35, 68, 160
Mother Nature, 6–7
Mulcahy, Diane, 139
multitasking, 51

Nairobi, 107
Nakama, Mari, 139
Namibia, 58
nature: and flux, 198–200; human relationship with, 103–4; *orenda* (invisible power), 58–59; *shinrin-yoku* (nature bathing), 44
Navy Seal adage, 48
negativity bias, 180
nervous system, 9
Netflix, 106, 107–8
Netherlands, *niksen* in, 37
networks and networking, 24, 86, 157
neuroscience, 9, 87, 173, 179
niksen (to do nothing), 37
1980s, economic shift in, 124–25
niyamas (ethical restraints), 105
nomadic cultures, 88–89
non-attachment (*aparigraha*), 182
Norway, 85

Observe-Orient-Decide-Act (OODA) loop, 50
oikonomia (abundance), 124
oikos (household), 124
open-source initiatives, 107–8
optionality, 4–5, 62–63, 100, 115, 181
orenda (invisible power), 58–59
organizations: challenges in, 59; flux in, 200–202, 210–11; trust in, 93–94, 96, 102–3, 104, 108–9
orientation / disorientation, 9, 15–16, 91. *See also* getting lost

pandemic, coronavirus, 2, 10, 68, 138, 145, 161, 165
parasympathetic nervous system, 9
parental leave policies, 168
Partnoy, Frank, *Wait: The Art and Science of Delay*, 49
passion, 150
Patanjali, attrib., *Yoga Sutras*, 105
patience practice, 43
patriarchies, 168–69
peers, 13 Table 1
perfectionism, 134–35
peripheral vision, 68, 69–71
personal identity, 11, 15, 152
Pink, Daniel, *Drive: The Surprising Truth About What Motivates Us*, 126
planning, 184, 199
portare (to carry), 141
portfolio careers, 15, 17, 18 Table 2, 21, 26–27, **137–59**; building, 147–52; curating, 139–40, 152–54; defined, 140–142; exercises, 147–48, 153, 159, 211; and guild concepts, 157–58; and lifelong learning, 154–56
potlatch system, 131–32
power, 13 Table 1, 163, 167–70
prana (breath), 46
predictions, 183–84, 199
presence, 41–44, 179–80, 182, 188, 192
privilege, 7, 62–64, 73, 118–19, 181, 202, 203
problem-solving, 187–88
productivity, 35, 39–41
professional identity, 120, 141–42, 146–47, 159
profits, 101, 102, 122, 123, 124, 145
Proust, Marcel, 55
psychology: of consciousness, 173–74; of more, 126–28
public health, 2, 56
purpose: and enoughness, 126, 132; in the Flux Baseline, 207; and getting lost, 89; and letting go, 179; and portfolio building, 138, 141; and slowing down, 32, 33, 37, 48

racial diversity, 67–69
Raggi-Moore, Judy, and family, 173
relationships: building, x, 21, 157–58; in collectivist societies, 60–61; and emotional intelligence, 171; and enoughness, 123–24; and running slower, 34; and trust, 95, 103–4, 111

reminiscing, 179–80
remote work, 138
resilience, 102
résumés. *See* portfolio careers
retirement, 132
ride-sharing, 106, 107, 126
Rinne, April: and anxiety, 177, 189–91; and getting lost, 74–76, 77; personal journey, 1–2, 22–27, 165–66; regaining trust, 95–96; slowing down, 38, 39–40
risk management, 24, 148
Romania, 74–76
Ruiz, Miguel, *The Four Agreements*, 105
Rumi, 200
running slower, x, 3, 17, 18 Table 2, 19–20, 21, **31–53**; exercises, 34, 43–44, 46, 54, 208; and FOMO, 50–53; and health, 44–46; and judgment, 48–50; and not-doing, 37–38; and presence, 41–44; and productivity, 39–41

sabbaticals, 43–44
Sala, Enric, 139
Satir, Virginia, 5
satori (awakening), 60
Sattersten, Todd, 67
satya (truthfulness), 105
sawubona (Zulu greeting), 55–56
scarcity thinking, 80–81, 128, 135
scenario mapping, 185, 194
screen time usage, 160, 161, 172
scripts, life, 6–8; rewriting, 13 Table 1, 20–26, 28, 197; and running slower, 41–44; and social norms, 56–64
seeing what's invisible, 15, 16, 17, 18 Table 2, 21, **55–73**; and consumerism, 64–67, 71; and diversity, 67–69; and enoughness, 135; exercises, 59, 63, 65, 71–72, 73, 208; and nature, 199–200; and peripheral vision, 68, 69–71; and privilege, 62–64, 73; and social norms, 56–61
self-interest, 95
self-worth, 35, 65, 118, 119, 136
Senge, Peter, 5
Sensory Awareness Training (SAT), 46
Seventh Generation Principle, 199
Shabbat, technology, 44
Shakti Leadership (Bhat), 170
shikoba (Zulu response), 56
shinrin-yoku (forest bathing), 44
silence practice, 43
simplifying, 129–30

skills: digital, 170–72; and portfolio building, 147–52

slowing down. *See* running slower

social norms, 5–8, 56–61, 62–64

software, open-source, 107–8

Solnit, Rebecca, 74

somatic tools, 45–46

South Africa, 55–56

Southern Cross, 15

speed, optimizing for, 41

Spiegelman, Marti, 163–64, 173–74

stability, 13, 15

starting with trust. *See* trust

status, 11, 47, 81, 127

stillness practice, 43

success: ancient wisdom on, 199; and anxiety, 10, 182–83; measurement of, 13 Table 1; and motivation, 127

suffering, 164–66

"superhero capes," 134–35

surveillance capitalism, 104

sustainability, 41, 102

svadhisthana (sacral chakra), 105

Sweden, 85, 120

sympathetic nervous system, 9

systemic injustices and inequalities, 67

Taoism, 37–38

technology: and anxiety, 9; digital intelligence (DQ), 170–72; disconnecting from, 44; and employment trends, 145, 157–58; and FOMO, 50–53; human relationship with, 160–64; new, 7, 21; and productivity, 39

Thinking Fast and Slow (Kahneman), 49

Thunberg, Greta, 24

Tibet, 84

time management, 50

Toba Beta, 113, 122

to-do lists, 37–38

Toltecs, 105

trade-offs, 80–81

travel, 23, 26, 40, 74–77, 81–82, 90

trust, 6, 15, 17, 18 Table 2, 21, 78, **93–113**; and ancient wisdom, 103–7; author's experience with, 26, 95–96; breaches of, 100–103; defined, 94; and enoughness, 135, 200; exercises, 99, 110, 112, 209; global crisis in, 93–94; and intention, 97–99; leading with, 106, 108–11; and vulnerability, 110

truthfulness, 105

"tunnel vision," 70

24/7 lifestyles, 35

uncertainty: about the future, 191–94; attitudes on, x, 4, 11, 179; derivation of word, 87; and getting lost, 86–89; and trust, 94, 111

unemployment, 138, 145

values, 11, 14, 22, 27, 128

Vedas (ancient text), 105

venture capitalists, 50, 126, 141

vision, 13 Table 1, 15, 24, 68–71. *See also* seeing what's invisible

VUCA (Volatile, Uncertain, Complex, and Ambiguous), 169–70

vulnerability, 6, 59, 110, 163, 172–73

wabi sabi (imperfection and transience), 85

Wait: The Art and Science of Delay (Partnoy), 49

walking, 46

Watts, Alan, 204

wealth, 127, 131–32

wēijī (危机) (crisis), 83–84

Who Do You Trust? (Botsman), 94

Wikipedia, 106

Winnie the Pooh, 37

wisdom, ancient and indigenous, 7, 103–4, 107, 131, 133, 173–74, 198–99, 204

wisdom, inner, 7, 173–74, 199

women, 67–69, 167–69, 170

Woolf, Virginia, 203

work-life balance, 144

worldview. *See* scripts, life

wu wei (lack of exertion), 37–38

X, Malcolm, 166

yamas (ethical restraints), 105

yin-yang balance, 167–70, 175

yoga, 16, 45–46, 131, 204

Yoga Sutras (attrib. Patanjali), 105

young adults, 160, 161, 202–3

Zen Buddhism, 60

Zulu greeting / response (*sawubona / shikoba*), 55–56

ABOUT THE AUTHOR

APRIL RINNE has been weaving a story about how to navigate change, personally and professionally, for as long as she can remember. *Flux: 8 Superpowers for Thriving in Constant Change* is the container to express this story and cast a broader vision for humanity as a whole.

Her perspective is best understood through three lenses on change: as a futurist and trusted adviser; as a global citizen, adventurer, and cultural connector; and as an orphan and lifelong student of anxiety.

April spent the first half of her career focused on global development and financial inclusion, and the latter half on the "new" digital economy and the future of work. Over more than two decades, she has seen emerging trends early, understands their potential, and helps others do the same.

For example, April was in the vanguard of microfinance, impact investing, the sharing economy, remote work, and portfolio careers—all of which were largely "invisible" until they whipsawed the world and changed for good how we live, work, purchase, travel, invest, and think about what's next.

Today, April is an acclaimed futurist, sought-after speaker, and trusted adviser, especially known for her role as a bridge: between start-ups and governments, between executives and customers, between financial and social returns, between for-profit and for-benefit business models, between developed and developing countries, and between those excited about change and those resistant to it. She walks the talk: bucking conventionality, seeing differently, and constantly seeking to level up her ability to help others reshape their relationship to change.

April's work and travels in more than one hundred countries have offered her a front-row seat to change at both local and global levels. This includes the better part of four years spent solo without a permanent address and with a backpack and an insatiable desire to better understand how the rest of the world lives. Change is universal; how we deal with it is not.

From relatively small instances of flux, like not knowing where she'd sleep that night in Indonesia or being held up at gunpoint in Bolivia, to much bigger (and often borderless) issues, such as how climate change affects megacities in Africa or whether mobile banking helps reduce inequality in Latin America, April has seen firsthand how different places and cultures grapple with change. She is as comfortable at Davos as she is talking with microfinance borrowers in an urban slum. She constantly Gets Lost (intentionally or not!), Starts with Trust as often as she can, and Knows Her "Enough" in part thanks to observing how other cultures live more sustainably.

However, experiences *not* on April's CV have had the most profound impact on her quest to understand the landscape of change. When April was twenty years old, both of her parents died in a car accident, which threw her into a world of flux. She put her expectations on hold to deal with the aftermath, ultimately letting go of how she thought her own future might unfold. She'd struggled with depression already, but now her anxiety went into hyperdrive. Her desire to rebuild family, coupled with her hope to live a life of meaning and her hunger to make sense of it all, made April a lifelong advocate for mental health and humanity. *Flux* is peppered with her personal stories, insights, and observations that underscore the fundamentally human nature of change . . . and that the best way we get through all this change is together.

April holds a JD from Harvard Law School, an MA in International Business and Finance from the Fletcher School at Tufts University, and a BA in International Studies and Italian summa cum laude from Emory University. She is a Fulbright Scholar and studied at Oxford University, the Harvard Kennedy School of Government, and the European University Institute. She is one of the fifty leading female futurists in the world, one of the earliest Estonian e-Residents, and—for balance—a certified yoga teacher. In 2011, the World Economic Forum named her a Young Global Leader. For more details and inspiration, including handstands from around the world, head to **aprilrinne.com** and **fluxmindset.com**.

Dear reader,

Thank you for picking up this book and welcome to the worldwide BK community! You're joining a special group of people who have come together to create positive change in their lives, organizations, and communities.

What's BK all about?

Our mission is to connect people and ideas to create a world that works for all.

Why? Our communities, organizations, and lives get bogged down by old paradigms of self-interest, exclusion, hierarchy, and privilege. But we believe that can change. That's why we seek the leading experts on these challenges—and share their actionable ideas with you.

A welcome gift

To help you get started, we'd like to offer you a **free copy** of one of our bestselling ebooks:

www.bkconnection.com/welcome

When you claim your **free ebook**, you'll also be subscribed to our blog.

Our freshest insights

Access the best new tools and ideas for leaders at all levels on our blog at ideas.bkconnection.com.

Sincerely,

Your friends at Berrett-Koehler

Smouldering Fire

by

D·E· STEVENSON

HOLT, RINEHART AND WINSTON

New York . Chicago . San Francisco

First published in 1938

New Edition 1972

ISBN: 0-03-001311-9
Library of Congress Catalog Card Number: 72-78109

Printed in the United States of America

CONTENTS

AUTHOR'S FOREWORD   **7**

ARDFALLOCH IN MAY

I.	Donald	9
II.	Janet	17
III.	Margaret	29

LONDON INTERLUDE

IV.	Mr. and Mrs. Hetherington Smith	44
V.	Linda	54

ARDFALLOCH IN AUGUST

VI.	Ardfalloch House	69
VII.	The Fairy Woman	82
VIII.	Morag's Story	93
IX.	Ardfalloch Inn	102
X.	The Storm	109
XI.	The Twelfth	131
XII.	Margaret	148
XIII.	The Picnic	155
XIV.	Linda	170
XV.	Unexpected Visitors	178
XVI.	The Dinner Party at Cluan	186
XVII.	The Ball at Ardfalloch House	194
XVIII.	The Emerald Bracelet	209
XIX.	The Interview	229
XX.	Oatcakes	239

Contents

ARDFALLOCH IN SEPTEMBER

xxi.	Facing the Future	250
xxii.	The Inspector's Visit	268
xxiii.	Iain and Linda	278

ARDFALLOCH IN NOVEMBER

xxiv.	Ardfalloch House	293
xxv.	Donald and Morag	304

AUTHOR'S FOREWORD

ARDFALLOCH is not a real place in the geo-
graphical sense of the word. There is no metal-
led road that leads to Ardfalloch—the best road
to take is an easy-chair before the fire on a wet
afternoon. Somewhere in Scotland there is a
sea-loch (ringed by purple mountains and dark
green forests) where the brown seaweed is
buoyed by millions of tiny bladders, and the
storms come suddenly from the west and drive
the still water into giant waves: but there is no
island, with a ruined castle upon it, in the
middle of this loch, and no salmon river flows
turbulently into its clear depths. Somewhere
in Scotland there is a square solid house with
high windows and slender pillars at the door:
but it boasts no wide domains, and the name
of its owner is not MacAslan. So, in one sense,
Ardfalloch is not real, and it is the same with
the people who live in the glen; but you will
find Janets and Donalds galore in the Lowlands
and Highlands of Scotland, and there are
MacAslans, too, who live on their estates, fishing and shooting, trying to improve the conditions of their people, trying to make ends
meet and seldom succeeding.

CHAPTER I

Donald

IAIN MACASLAN pulled slowly across the loch. The sun had set, but a bright glow lingered in the gap between the mountains; and the single planet, at the edge of an indigo cloud, was nothing but a silver pin's point in the sky. The mountains to westward were dark—outlined against the glow—and the loch was dark save for a bright patch near the island which reflected the sky's grandeur in bold streaks.

The small boat cut a silver streak in the dark waters—a bamboo rod was fixed to the thwarts close beside Iain's hand, and the line sweeping through the water made a silver ripple. The surface of the loch was leaden-grey, but when Iain leaned over the side of the boat and looked down into its still depths it was green—dark and mysterious.

After a little while Iain rested on his oars and pulled in the line. He had had no luck to-night, the mackerel were not taking. He pulled up the line, disentangled the spinners and unshipped the rod, laying it carefully in the bottom of the boat. It was no use to try any longer. As a matter of fact, Iain had not come out to fish—the fishing was merely an excuse. He had felt too restless and disturbed to remain indoors—the May night had called him, had drawn him forth as a magnet draws iron. But the May night had not soothed his restlessness, nor stilled the disturbance in his soul.

9

Iain raised his eyes and looked at the mountains . . . and the loch . . . and the smoky darkness of the forests. His eyes were fiery and yet sombre, they burned with passion . . .

It was all his:—the loch, the mountains bare and rocky, the little island which lay like a dark cushion upon the smooth surface of the water—that most of all perhaps—all his. It was his land, the cradle of his race.

The tiny boat rocked gently as he moved back to his seat and a few silvery ripples spread outwards. They died away and everything was still, quiet, peaceful. Iain was part of the stillness, his restlessness was within.

Suddenly his body came to life, he threw up his head and listened. There was a faint 'chug-chug' in the distance and presently he saw the glimmer of a light over towards Balnafin, and a small shabby motor-launch came crawling across the loch like a water-beetle. Iain did not move, even when the launch turned out of its course to approach him. He waited quietly until the launch was within a few yards and the engine had stopped.

The launch rocked on the water and the small lamp sent an unsteady glimmer upon its leaden surface.

'Good evening, Donald,' he said at last.

'Good evening to you, MacAslan,' was the soft reply. 'An d'fhuair sibh iasg?'

'No fish, Donald.'

The two boats rocked gently on the water which had been disturbed by the launch. It was darker now, only a pale primrose glow remained in the sky, fading into violet towards the meridian. The man called Donald peered anxiously through the gloom at the occupant of the little boat. When you have known a man since childhood, have grown up with him, shoulder to shoulder; when you have spent long days with him on loch and river, have followed him over moor and mountain, and crawled beside him on your belly through heather and bog, you know a man well, you know a man inside out. And, if you know a man inside out, it is not difficult to tell when there is something wrong. These were Donald's thoughts as he peered through the gloom. He hesitated a few moments with that innate delicacy of feeling which marks his race, and at last he said:

' I wass thinking you might like the evening paper, Mac-Aslan. It wass Miss Finlay came back from Glasgow by the train and she gave it to me . . .'

Iain smiled in the darkness. He had no desire to see a Glasgow evening paper, but he would not say so. He was too mindful of Donald's feelings to refuse the gift. He knew that Donald had sensed his discomfort and had offered the paper as a soothing balm, and as a soothing balm it must be accepted. The paper, tied in the middle with a piece of tarred twine, flew through the air and landed in the coble at Iain's feet. He picked it up and smoothed it out carefully. It had come a long journey. It was queer, when you thought of it, how far the paper had come—it had been printed in Glasgow at noon, sold to Margaret in the street, had accompanied her in the train all the way to Balnafin, had been given by her to Donald, and now by Donald to himself. How far it had flown! And the other papers that had been printed with it—where had they flown? . . . So Margaret Finlay had come back from America! He wondered whether, if he had known she was back, he would have hesitated longer this afternoon. Would he have waited and talked it over with Margaret and her father before doing what he had done? But this was futile—he had done the thing now and he could not draw back.

Donald's great hands were cupped skilfully about a match, for there was a slight breeze wandering upon the loch—a breeze as fitful as a lost soul—gusts of flame and smoke poured from Donald's pipe as the tobacco caught, and the red glare illuminated his strong rugged features.

Ardfalloch in May

'So Miss Finlay is back!' Iain said slowly.

'She is back,' said Donald. 'Mr. Finlay is coming back to-morrow. I wass to tell MacAslan they will be expecting him at Cluan.'

'Ah!'

There was a little silence. The water lapped gently against the sides of the boat. Donald wondered if it was any use to wait. Did MacAslan want him or did he not? Sometimes when people were troubled they liked to be alone . . . Donald had been up at five that morning and had done his day's work before going to Balnafin with the eggs. He had met some friends at the inn and had had a few drinks—not many, for Donald was a temperate man, but just a few friendly drinks—he had done some shopping for Morag, visited the station to see the arrival of the train (a social occasion this, at Balnafin), had done some business with a man he knew, business connected with rabbit wire for his little garden, and had come back all the way down the loch in his old launch. It was near midnight now and Donald was used to early hours—he was tired, and Morag would be waiting. All this counted for naught if MacAslan wanted him, but did MacAslan want him? He glanced again at the still figure in the little boat. Only the outline of the figure was visible in the darkness—a hunched outline. MacAslan has forgotten me, said Donald to himself, his soul is not here any longer.

He leaned forward to start his engine.

'Donald!'

The stretched-out hand was arrested in mid-air.

'Donald, I've done—I've done something rather serious to-day. Already I am regretting it, but there was no other way—I want you to help me, Donald.'

MacAslan was speaking in the Gaelic now, and Donald was glad. It was their custom to speak to each other in both languages—sometimes in English and sometimes in the

Gaelic. For ordinary everyday affairs connected with the estate, MacAslan used English; but when they spoke together heart to heart of the things that mattered, or when MacAslan was happy and at peace with the world, or unhappy and in need of sympathy, it was always the Gaelic. Donald was glad when he heard the Gaelic from MacAslan's lips, because MacAslan had asked for his help. It was foolishness, of course, MacAslan had no need to *ask*. Did MacAslan doubt him that he should ask his help? Did he not know that Donald would lay down his life in the service of MacAslan? What could this thing be—this thing that MacAslan had done and already regretted?

'And who else would help you, MacAslan?' he said quietly.

'People must not know—not yet. It must be known later, but I do not want a lot of talk—I must get away from here before it is known—and yet how can I leave Ardfalloch?'

It was a killing, then, Donald thought. 'I will hide you,' he said; 'Morag and I. They will not find you. There is a place I know—a deep cave amongst the heather. There is no need for MacAslan to be leaving his own land——'

He was startled by a low chuckle from the other boat. 'Oh, Donald—and if it were for murder I was wanted, you would hide me.'

'That is true indeed.'

'But it is not murder, Donald.'

'What is it, then?'

'I have let Ardfalloch for the season.'

There was silence for a few moments, and then the voice continued in a low tone full of bitterness. 'You think it worse than murder, Donald? A betrayal of Ardfalloch—but what was I to do? I have tried to think of other ways. I went to Balnafin this morning and I saw Mr. Simpson. He had a letter from a London gentleman who wanted to rent the MacLaggan's place at Athnabeg, and the place was

taken already. " Offer him Ardfalloch for three months,"
said Mr. Simpson. " You need the money." I told him I
did not want to let Ardfalloch. " You will sell a farm then,"
he told me. " Something you must do, MacAslan." He
showed me figures in a book, Donald, and I saw, then, that
it was true.'

Donald was silent, he was not listening now, he was too
overwhelmed. His thoughts were chaotic—MacAslan was
in trouble, but it was no trouble that *he* could help. He
could be of no assistance at all. Money! In his own life he
knew what it was to lack money, to pinch and scrape and
make do with uncomfortable substitutes for the necessities
of life, but that MacAslan should lack money was incredible, unthinkable—it was all wrong, thought Donald dazedly.
If Ben Falloch had moved he would have been less surprised, less helpless. Ardfalloch to be let—let to strangers!
A London gentleman fishing on MacAslan's water, shooting MacAslan's birds—and his deer!

Other big landowners had done it, of course—Donald
knew that. Only this afternoon there had been talk at the
inn about Athnabeg and the people who had taken it for the
season. It was a London gentleman who had taken Athnabeg—Lord Somebody—Donald could not remember the
name, he had not paid much attention to the name. The
same people had come last year, and MacFarlane—the
head keeper—had told Donald about the way these people
had carried on at the Big House. Well, let them—Donald
had thought—that is what is to be expected if a place is let
to strangers. And then, suddenly, he remembered that
MacAslan had asked for his help, and he was filled with
pride that it was to him that MacAslan had come—to him
and no other. But how could he help?

' Are you listening, Donald?'

' I wass not,' he owned humbly. ' I wass thinking.'

' What were you thinking?'

14

Donald

' I was thinking of many things, MacAslan. One of the things I was thinking was this—the London gentleman— you will have given him the forest and the moor——'

' Yes, I have given it all.'

The forest too—and the moor! ' If it were the only way——' Donald said in a low voice.

' Would I have done it otherwise?'

Donald was silent. There was another way that Mac-Aslan might have taken—he knew that. All the glen knew it. Not a creature in Ardfalloch but knew that MacAslan might have Miss Margaret Finlay for the asking—and all her money too. And Miss Margaret was a nice lady—' Tha i cho math's a tha i cho breagha '—(She is as good as she is pretty) they would say in the village when they spoke of her, and was that not high praise? She had lived amongst them all her life; she was almost one of themselves; almost good enough for MacAslan. But, if MacAslan said there was no other way, it was not for Donald to question his decision, not for Donald to make any suggestion.

' It was the only way,' Iain repeated. ' There was nothing else to be done—yet, even so, I am regretting it—wondering what I shall do, wondering how I am to tell my mother——'

There was silence on that word. An owl cried eerily from the small rocky island where the old castle of the MacAslans was crumbling into ruins.

' That is almost the worst, Donald,' the low voice continued. It was easy to talk like this in the darkness—you could say things that you could never have said in the light of day. Already Iain had told more—much more—than he had intended. Donald's dark bulk in the motor-launch was an easy thing to talk to. ' It is almost the worst, Donald. Will it kill her?'

' It will not kill her,' replied Donald with convincing readiness. ' There is a strength about her——'

'She must go to Edinburgh,' Iain said. 'She will be near my uncle and aunt, and Janet shall go with her.'

'And what will you do, MacAslan?'

Iain flung out his hand with a movement that set the boat rocking. 'I shall remain,' he said firmly. 'I have said to myself a dozen times that I must leave the glen, but I know I cannot. I cannot leave the glen, Donald——'

'There is no need for that—we will think of a way——'

'I have thought of a way. I shall stay in the old cottage down by the loch.'

Donald drew in his breath quickly—MacAslan in the old cottage, and strangers in the Big House! He said quietly, 'The roof is not sound—it is a damp cold place——'

'Have the roof patched,' Iain told him. 'But go about it quietly. Nobody must know——'

'If I could be telling Morag,' Donald said slowly. 'She is handy—she could be helping with one thing and another——'

Iain laughed lightly. 'Oh, Morag!' he said. 'You must tell Morag, of course. I will not burden you with a secret to keep from Morag.'

'You are before her,' Donald replied. He, too, was finding the darkness a safe curtain for speech—and it is easier for the thoughts of the heart to find expression in the Gaelic tongue. 'You come first, MacAslan.'

'I am fortunate,' said Iain in a low voice, and then he added in a different tone: 'It is the question of ghillies that is troubling me, Donald. We do not want a strange keeper here, one who would not care for the forest—and the moor.'

'God forbid!'

'If you would stay—if you would do it, Donald—and look after things for me.'

There was a little silence, and then out of the darkness the voice came—'I will do it for you, MacAslan.'

CHAPTER II

Janet

IAIN waited until the sound of the motor-launch had died away, and then he sighed heavily, and, taking up his oars, rowed slowly towards the shore. A small pier, or jetty, of rocks and stones, roughly plastered together, made a harbourage for his motor-launch and the fishing coble. There they lay all summer side by side, protected from storms by the jetty on the east, and, on the west, by a promontory of rock welded together by the roots of fir-trees. In the winter the boats were dragged up on rollers and stowed in the boat-house—a ramshackle building on the southern shore. To-night the loch was so calm that it was difficult to believe in storm, difficult to believe that the loch, lashed to fury by an easterly gale, should break upon the pier with a sound like thunder. It was impossible to visualise storm to-night— flying spray and fir-trees bent like live rods before the gale's force—impossible to visualise . . .

To-night the water was like green glass. The seaweed floated upon the surface of the water, buoyed by its thousands of tiny brown bladders. The tide was out, and the bare rocks rose from the tangle of weed like weird black monsters of the deep. Iain made the boat fast and climbed out. He was tired now—deadly tired—and his feet and hands were stiff with cold. For a moment he was tempted to sleep in the launch. There was a bunk in the tiny cabin, with a brown army blanket and a horse-hair pillow which he used occasionally when he was fishing at night. It would be pleasant to crawl into that bunk and sleep there, rocked by the incoming tide. But he must not do that, he had been out all day and Janet would be anxious if he were not in his bed when she went to call him in the morning. It was even possible that Janet was waiting up for him, he hoped not, because he did not feel equal to a talk with Janet to-night; he felt utterly worn out, and his nerves were on edge. A sleep would make a difference. He would feel stronger in the morning, more able to battle with the problems which beset him.

Iain threw his mackintosh over his shoulder and went up through the dark trees. There was now a faint lightness in the sky, dawn was not far off, the short night was almost past. But, beneath the trees, it was still very dark, and if Iain's feet had not known every inch of the stony path, and every pine root that straggled across it, he would have had some difficulty in picking his way.

The house of Ardfalloch stood in a small strath—all about it were woods, mostly of pine, and thickly carpeted with brown needles. In front of the house ran Ardfalloch burn, dropping from pool to pool with a pleasant splashing. Iain stood for a few minutes on the little bridge that crossed the burn and looked at the house—he felt that he had betrayed it. No people save his own had ever lived in the house, and now he had sold it into slavery. For three months it would shelter strangers beneath its roof. Iain loved every part of his home—the loch, the moors, the forest. The house was the core of his home, the hub of the wheel round which everything revolved. The house lay before his eyes in the grey light of dawn, it was large and square with high windows and a close-fitting roof. Perhaps Ardfalloch House was not strictly beautiful, but its proportions were good and it was thoroughly sound and thoroughly fitted to its surroundings. There was no nonsense about Ardfalloch House, no useless ornamentations, no excrescences. It had been built for comfort, and it was warm in winter and cool in summer. Iain had been born in the house, and his father had been born in it; his father's father had been born in the old castle in the middle of the loch. It was when Iain's grandfather was a child that *his* father had built the house and moved his family into more comfortable and convenient quarters. The house was large, comfortable, airy. It was too large for Iain and his mother and their small staff, so part of it was shut—the drawing-room and some of the bedrooms had been shut for years, the furniture swathed in dust sheets. Every now and then Janet would enter these quiet rooms like a tornado, with brooms and pails and dusters—the windows would be thrown wide open, and fires lighted to dry the air.

The house slept before Iain's eyes, the high windows were shuttered. It was all dark save for one room on the second floor—here a light burned and the curtains were looped back from the open window. Janet is awake, thought Iain. He gave a soft call, and, in a moment, the head and shoulders of a woman were silhouetted against the light.

'These are strange hours to keep!' said a low-pitched voice. 'These are strange hours, MacAslan.'

He signalled to her to come down, and crossed the gravel sweep to the side door. He had not long to wait. The door opened quietly and Janet stood in the lintel, candle in hand. Iain went in, and, together, in silence, they chained the door.

Like Donald, Janet sensed at once that something was the matter. (She, too, had known Iain all his life.) Unlike Donald, she approached the matter squarely.

'What's wrong, MacAslan?' she demanded.

He did not answer at once, the dull weariness that lay upon his spirit made words difficult.

'Come away into the morning-room,' Janet said. 'The fire's not oot yet—you're starved with the cold.'

Iain followed her across the square hall into the morning-

19

room. She set the candle on the table and moved over to the fire of peats that smouldered on the hearth. She was an elderly woman, but she moved well and easily, with a straight back and lithe hips. She sank on to her knees by the fire, took the poker in her hand, and lifting one corner of the smouldering turf, blew it into flames.

Iain cast himself into a shabby leather chair and watched the trickle of flame curl upwards through the rent in the turf. The fibres caught—the firelight flowed out over the floor; Janet's kneeling figure was bathed in a red glow; her strong-featured face with its high cheek-bones, firm mouth and broad brow was accentuated by the ruddy light; her shadow filled the room from ceiling to floor.

She sat back on her heels and looked at him. 'What's wrang, MacAslan?' she said again.

Iain moistened his lips, it was no use to beat about the bush with Janet—besides, she had to know sometime.

'I've let Ardfalloch for the season,' he said.

Janet did not speak for a moment, she watched him quietly. His face was in shadow, but in the red glow of the fire she could see the tension of his thin nervous hands.

'I'm hoping you've got a guid price for it, then,' she said in a firm tone.

He laughed involuntarily. 'Oh, Janet!' he said. 'Here have I been grieving over it the whole day, making a tragedy of the thing, and you bring it all down to a matter of pounds, shillings and pence.'

Janet glanced at him sideways—the hands had relaxed a little. 'And what else is it, pray?' she enquired tartly. 'It's for the money you're daeing it, I'm thinking.'

Iain laughed again. They understood each other well, these two; there was deep affection between them, though they seldom, if ever, showed it. Iain's way of showing his affection was to speak to Janet in her own idiom; he knew that nothing gave her more pleasure than to hear the broad vowels of her Lowland tongue from his lips. He had learnt it from her as a child and he used his facility to coax or tease her as occasion demanded. It was easy for Iain to please, he had a natural charm of manner and he enjoyed exercising this charm. He drew people to him by his personal magnetism. He was interested in people and he let them see that he was interested—it was very simple. He had a careless, almost regal, grace of manner combined with a boyish joy of living. It was the kind of charm that had conquered Scotland in the person of Prince Charlie—the Stuart charm of manner—but in Iain MacAslan it was allied to a sense of responsibility, to an unselfish desire for the welfare and happiness of others, and especially for the welfare and happiness of his own people. Iain was a king in his own domain. His power was absolute within the boundaries of his small kingdom. His word was law in a literal sense. He ruled by right of his ancestry, by right of possession, and by right of the affection which he inspired in the hearts of his people. In the old days the chiefs of Ardfalloch ruled by the first two rights, but conditions were changing now, and, without the affection of his people, Iain would not have found his kingdom so easy to rule.

Iain laughed at Janet's downright words. He knew it was not lack of sympathy that prompted them. 'Yes,' he said, 'I'm doing it for the money, Janet, because I must.'

'Was there nae ither way?' she asked him.

Their eyes met gravely. He knew quite well what she meant. She meant that he might have married Margaret Finlay. He had thought of that way, of course; he believed that Meg would have married him, and he liked Meg. He was very fond of her.

'There was no other way, Janet,' he said firmly.

Janet drew in her breath and turned her face to the fire. She could not look at him and say what she had in her mind.

'MacAslan, pride is a good thing, but dinna let pride be

21

your master. The lassie loves you. Can you not put pride away, and be happy?'

' I might put pride away,' he said, gazing at the fire, and speaking as if he were communing with his own thoughts, ' if that were all. But you see, Janet, there's something else. You would say I was mad to let it stand in the way—there's no reason—it's just a feeling——'

' Anither lassie!' she whispered.

' I only saw her once,' Iain continued in the same low tone. ' Just once, for a few minutes. But, somehow, I knew that she was everything that I wanted—had always wanted. I don't even know her name. I don't know anything about her except that she is beautiful and good. It seemed to me that I had always known her. When I looked at her I felt I knew her all through—knew exactly what she was like. I've never forgotten her. Perhaps I never shall. If I could think I was mistaken—that she was not really as I imagined her——'

Janet was silent. This explained many things that she had not been able to understand. The thing was madness, of course. It was utterly crazy to her matter-of-fact mind, but she knew Iain well, and understood him. It was just like MacAslan to fall in love with a vision, an insubstantial dream, and to let the dream govern his life and wreck him.

Iain was watching Janet's face. He laughed quietly. ' Perhaps she was a fairy, Janet,' he said in a lighter tone.

' Hoots!' Janet cried angrily. ' Are you a bairn, Mac-Aslan, to blether of fairies? You ken as weel as I dae there's no such thing—*fairies* indeed!'

He smiled. It always amused him to rouse Janet, and it was an easy thing to rouse her when you knew the way. Janet was always impatient of anything supernatural. You had only to mention fairies, or kelpies, or witches, or enchantments and she was up in arms at once, with all the strength of her Free Kirk training to back her up. Was there ever such a sensible, downright, practical creature as

Janet condemned to live her days amongst a pack of superstitious Highlanders!

' It fits the case, Janet,' he continued with feigned gravity. ' If she was a fairy woman and stole my heart; stole the substance of me so that nothing but the husk is left. . . . Fairies can look like mortals, you know, Janet; they move noiselessly, and the wind blows them where they will. You know the story of the man who had a fairy sweetheart—they were very happy together, they met in the woods and loved each other . . . then the fairy grew tired of the man—he was only a mortal after all—and she left him. He pined for her for years, and then, at last, he was able to forget her, and he took another woman—a mortal like himself. You know what happened then, Janet. The fairy woman was jealous: she came back and killed him—perhaps that is what I am afraid of——'

' Och, away with you!' Janet cried. ' Bairns' tales, the whole of it. You dinna believe in it yoursel'. Get you a wife, MacAslan, and hae done with such-like noansense.'

There was a little silence after Janet's outburst, and Iain's mood changed again.

' Perhaps . . . some day . . .' he said at last in a serious voice. ' But not yet, Janet. It would not be fair to . . . to any woman, to ask her to marry me, when another woman's picture is in my heart—you see that? So there was no other way at all but the way I have taken. Something had to be done. We live very simply, but we're spending more than what is coming in (and there are repairs that must be attended to)—that can't go on for long.'

She said quickly, ' You're welcome to what I've got, MacAslan, if it's any use—you ken that.'

Iain was too moved to reply, there was a lump in his throat. He had had a wearing day—things had piled up on him until they were almost unbearable.

' Bide here by the fire,' Janet said. ' I'll away to the

kitchen and make you a bowl of gruel.' She heaped a few small logs on the glowing peat and hurried away. The man's fair dommered, she told herself—no supper most likely, and less tea. It's little wonder he canna thole the idea of letting Ardfalloch . . .

She busied herself in the kitchen, coaxing the fire into a blaze, warming milk to prepare the gruel, and, while her hands were busy with these well-accustomed tasks, her mind was free to wander where it would. It would be a strange thing to leave Ardfalloch, Janet thought, after all these years. She remembered the day she had come to Ardfalloch for the first time. She was young then, young and bonny. She had come to wait on Iain's grandmother who was a Lowland woman like herself, and who preferred a Lowland girl as her personal attendant. Janet had been unhappy at first—the place was so strange, the people were foreign; their speech, their clothes, their way of thinking were strange, foreign, incomprehensible. Janet pined for her own land and her own people. Only the old lady was Lowland like herself, and, because of the old lady, Janet stayed on. She thought now of the old lady—Iain's grandmother—*there* was a woman after Janet's own heart, straightforward, uncompromising, direct in speech. There was no nonsense about old Mrs. MacAslan. Her son, Iain's father, was different altogether. He was Highland to the core, a proud man and not easy to understand. Janet remembered the night that he had brought his bride home to Ardfalloch. She was a dark-haired girl from the Western Isles, with a pedigree as long as MacAslan's. There had been something strange about her, even then, something out of the ordinary. She looked as if she did not belong to the workaday world, as if her footing in the world were insecure. . . .

How long ago it all seemed, and yet how clear! I'm getting old, Janet thought, it's old people who see long-ago things so clear. The big kitchen was full of shadows as the grey light of dawn crept in at the window, and the flame of the candle she had lighted leapt and flared in the draught of her movements. Janet straightened her back and gazed before her. In imagination she could see the hall of Ardfalloch, crowded with ladies and gentlemen waiting for the bridal couple to arrive. She could hear the buzz of conversation, the ripple of laughter. The doors were flung open, there was a cheer from the tenants waiting outside, and the big carriage with its pair of well-matched horses rolled up to the steps. Janet saw again the tall, burly figure of Iain's father in its swinging kilt—he caught his bride in his arms, sprang up the steps and set her down in the midst of the company. She stood there, half dazed by the noise and the lights and the spate of good wishes and congratulations. That was Janet's first sight of the new Mrs. MacAslan (a dwaibly body, she had said to herself half in pity and half in scorn). It was as clear in her mind as if it had happened yesterday.

The next thing of importance in Janet's life had been the arrival of the baby. Old Mrs. MacAslan had insisted that Janet should have charge of the baby, and had released her from her other duties for that purpose. Old Mrs. MacAslan's word was law—it was wise law in this case, at least —her own son had been born and brought up amongst Highlanders, her grandson should have the benefit of another view of life. He should experience contact with a matter-of-fact personality, it would enlarge his outlook and minimise the danger of his being spoiled as the head of his house, the little chief. Janet would give him discipline. Old Mrs. MacAslan saw all this quite clearly, but she did not put it into words. She merely said that Janet was trustworthy and was to look after the baby—nobody dreamed of questioning her decision, least of all her daughter-in-law.

Ardfalloch in May

Janet devoted herself to the baby. It became her very life. She watched the tiny puling thing grow into a thin wiry boy, and from a thin wiry boy into a graceful man. Old Mrs. MacAslan died when Iain was fifteen; she died full of years. There was no tragedy in her death, it was just a passing on. Janet missed the old lady (she had been a good friend and a wise mistress) but she realised that it was inevitable for old people to die. Old Mrs. MacAslan would not have wished to live on and lose her grip on life gradually, she could not have borne to become a useless burden on her friends. No, there was no tragedy in that death, just a sadness and an emptiness in the house. It was very different when MacAslan died (Iain's father). The man was in his prime—in full health and strength when he was snatched away. Janet could not think of it now without a shudder of horror. His young wife had been there when the accident happened . . . she had seen him fall . . . the shock was too much for her brain. . . .

So MacAslan had died and the responsibilities connected with his position had passed to Iain—Janet's beloved boy. He was eighteen, and the burden had been a heavy one for his shoulders. Times were difficult and money was scarce. Janet's heart was sore for her boy, but she hid her sympathy and gave him a dry bracing companionship, full of common sense and free from sentiment. She gave him a strong shoulder to lean on, and he leant on it more than he knew.

All these things passed through Janet's mind as she made the gruel and laced it with whisky. As she fetched the biscuits from the cupboard, and a spoon, and the salt-cellar and laid them neatly on the tray, her life at Ardfalloch passed through her mind in swift review. Her own personal life had been uneventful. No man had sought her in marriage, she was too forthright, too matter-of-fact for the imaginative people amongst whom she dwelt. They laughed at her behind her back; she despised them.

Janet

The tray was ready now. Janet took it up and carried it along the draughty, flagged passage and across the hall to the morning-room where Iain was waiting beside the fire. It was broad daylight now, and, in that clear cold light, his face looked pinched and wan. He had not moved since she left him, but when he heard her coming he looked up and smiled. She put the tray on the table beside him, and stood and looked at him with her hands on her hips.

'Drink it up noo, and away to your bed,' she said sternly. 'You're gey and shilpit looking, and it's small wonder—trapesing off without a bite of supper and coming hame at these unairthly hours——'

Iain sipped the gruel, it was warm and comforting. 'Sit down, Janet,' he said. 'I want to talk to you.'

'Can you not talk to me standing?'

Iain smiled. 'No, I can't. You're like a giant in the room. It's an uncomfortable thing to talk to a giant.'

'Hoots!—you and your giants!' Janet said; but she complied with his request, drawing a little stool before the fire and seating herself upon it.

'It's about—about my mother——' Iain said in a difficult voice, and, again, at the word there was a little silence. Janet looked at the fire—the logs on the top of the peat were blazing merrily, the small flames were leaping up the wide chimney.

'Aye,' she said, after a little, 'and what were you thinking of, MacAslan?'

He understood all that was implied in the simple question, and answered it in a word which was in itself another question.

'Edinburgh?' he suggested tentatively.

Janet nodded. 'I was thinking the same, masel'. A wee flat maybe—just for the three of us. We'll not need a gurrl. I can manage easy enough. I'm thinking she will like it fine when she once settles——'

'There will just be two of you, Janet. I'm staying here.'

'Staying here!'

'In the old cottage by the loch-side.'

'You'll no can stay your lane!' Janet cried, her Doric gaining in strength with the violence of her emotions. 'Why, you'd be just meeserable—with strangers in the hoose, and all——' Her breast rose and fell stormily beneath her grey gown with its white, starched ruffles—*and me not here to see to him,* she thought!

'Well, we'll see,' Iain said. His mind was made up, but it was no use fighting with Janet to-night. There was time yet before the question need arise—three months of peace before he need hand over his home to the London man with the money—three months.

Janet left the subject, too, with much the same thoughts at the back of her mind. When the time came he would find it impossible to stay here alone and he would come with them to Edinburgh. She would have him with her in Edinburgh—the three of them together in a wee flat. It would be kind of cosy, Janet thought, a holiday from the struggle of running the big house with insufficient means.

Iain had been watching her face. 'I believe you are looking forward to it, Janet,' he said with a little sigh. 'I don't blame you—it must be dull for you here.'

She turned towards him quickly and put her hand on his knee—it was a large-boned hand, roughened by hard work in his service, but well-shaped and flexible still. 'I'm wae for ye, MacAslan,' she said softly.

CHAPTER III

Margaret

IAIN allowed several days to elapse before taking advantage of the Finlays' invitation. He was not looking forward to telling them that he had let Ardfalloch, and he could not go over and see them without telling them his news. He had a suspicion that they would think it foolish and unnecessary. He and Meg had so often fulminated together upon the folly of landowners who let their places for the season and loosed a horde of ignorant Sasunnachs upon the innocent country-side. And now he had done this very thing himself.

At last he felt that he could put it off no longer. He had no excuse for putting it off. It was a beautiful afternoon, sunny and bright, with a fresh breeze. He walked down to the little harbour through the woods. There was a pair of cuckoos in the woods somewhere above the house, they had been calling to each other all the morning and they were still at it. ' Cuckoo, cuckoo,' said one, and a moment later came the reply—if such it could be called—' Cuckoo.' Then came the first one again, ' Cuckoo, cuckoo.' It went on and on interminably, it rasped his nerves, it was a weariness of the flesh. Even so must the psalmist have found the grasshopper a burden. . . .

Donald was mending the roof of the boat-house, perched on a high ladder, struggling with a piece of tarpaulin that flapped and wriggled like a live thing in the wind.

' Hallo, Donald!' said Iain.

'The roof is bad, MacAslan,' Donald told him gravely, looking down from his perch. 'It is very bad indeed. I am thinking it will not be lasting us another winter.'

'We'll get a new roof,' replied Iain cheerfully. 'I shall have lots of money to spend on repairs——'

'And the harbour,' added Donald, pointing with his hammer. 'Could we be digging out the harbour a wee bit, do you think? It's an ill thing if you are wanting the motor-boat and the tide at ebb.'

Iain was well aware of that. There was a submerged sandbank at the entrance of the little harbour which masked it completely. The motor-launch drew a good deal of water, and, when the tide was out, there was not enough water to float her over the bank. So there was a period at every low tide when the launch could not be taken out, or, if she were out, could not be brought in. The period varied according to the wind and the state of the tides.

'I'm afraid that would be a big job!' said Iain doubt-fully.

'Och, well, we do very well as we are,' replied the philo-sophical Donald. 'It will be a fine thing to be getting a new roof to the boat-house, and a wire fence——'

'What's the tide like at present?' Iain enquired. 'Can I take her out just now?'

'You can take her out fine. It is two hours past the ebb,' replied Donald promptly. Like every sea-fisherman he had the state of the tides at his finger-ends.

'Good, I'm going over to Cluan. You had better come with me, Donald.'

Donald climbed down the ladder with alacrity. He was tired of wrestling with the tarpaulin, and a trip to Cluan was after his own heart. Besides, it would not be the thing at all for MacAslan to go over to Cluan alone. He had very strict ideas of what was correct for MacAslan, and it was certainly not correct for the chief to go and visit Cluan

—or any other place—unattended. If Iain had allowed it he would have constituted himself a bodyguard on every occasion. Unfortunately, Iain had different ideas—new-fangled ideas in Donald's opinion—he went about alone, driving his own boat, and often even rowing himself upon the loch if there happened to be none of his men at hand when the spirit moved him to go. The old chief would as soon have thought of making his own bed as rowing his own boat. There was no motor-boat in his day, of course—none at Ardfalloch anyway—but Donald was pretty sure that, even if there had been, the old chief would still have taken a couple of men with him when he went out in it to visit his friends.

Donald said something of this in his own quiet tactful way. He was sitting at Iain's feet with his eye on the engine as they sped across the loch. Iain tucked the tiller under one arm and stooped down to light his pipe in the lee of the cabin.

'It's interesting that,' he said. 'I hadn't thought about it really, but of course what you say is true; my father never went anywhere without a couple of men. It's an old custom dating from the days when it wasn't safe for the chief to go alone and unattended, and, like many old customs, it persisted when the need was gone.'

'It is more dignified for MacAslan to have a servant with him,' said Donald obstinately.

Iain sighed. 'Dignity is a fine word, Donald.'

'It is a fine thing.'

'But it is not for me. I had to swallow my dignity when I let Ardfalloch.'

'MacAslan is still MacAslan.'

They said no more. The breeze blew stiffly from the east; they got the full force of it on their starboard beam as they sped across the loch. Small waves slapped the sides of the launch and broke in fine spray. Iain laughed aloud, he could never be depressed for long, his nature was too sunny, too buoyant. The wind and the waves were vitalising. He loved the spray in his face; he loved the feeling of the launch cutting through the water, lifting to the waves, rolling a little as the wind struck her broadside on. The sun had warmth in it to-day, it was bright and golden. The sky was blue and flecked with racing clouds. In the dark woods patches of bright green showed where the larches grew; they had put on their summer finery. There was pale-green bracken on the lower slopes of the hills, and, round about the small crofts, patches of different tones of green—tiny fields of sprouting oats, or potatoes, or hay.

As they neared the pier at Cluan, Iain brought the launch round in a big sweep. The engine ceased throbbing and the launch bumped gently against the mats. The two white motor-launches were both at home. They were fine boats, no bigger than Iain's own, but smarter and faster and better found. Donald looked at them enviously—' You would not be thinking of getting a new boat, MacAslan?' he suggested hopefully. 'A boat like Mr. Finlay's, maybe.'

'I would not,' replied Iain, smiling. 'There are dozens of more important things to think of.'

He jumped lightly onto the pier and walked over the hill to the house.

Cluan Lodge was almost forty years old. It was a large white building with a grey slate roof. It lay, sheltered from the winds, in a meadow behind the promontory of rock. The meadow had been turned into a garden, formal and tidy. It was not Iain's idea of what a garden should be—he preferred the natural wildness of his own place—; but the garden at Cluan was beautiful in its own way, full of colour and scent, and the hum of innumerable bees. Here, sheltered from the wind which swept the loch, it was warm —a different climate altogether. There was nothing wild here, even the wild wind was excluded.

Margaret

Cluan belonged to the people who had built it, but Mr. Finlay had been here so long (renting it from the owners on long leases) that everybody in the countryside looked upon Cluan as belonging to the Finlays. Mr. Finlay had built garages and green-houses, had made the garden and improved the pier. He was fond of Cluan, and he had plenty of money, so there was no reason why he should not do as he wished. If other people thought it foolish to spend money on somebody else's property, it did not affect Mr. Finlay.

Margaret Finlay was some years younger than Iain, they had known each other since they were children and had always been friends. When her mother died, Margaret took over the housekeeping and did it admirably; she was a capable creature, sensible, honest, friendly. She and her father lived together, for the most part at Cluan, but, once a year, they went to America for a few months so that Mr. Finlay could keep an eye on the business and on the stock market. He was a wise speculator, and money seemed to pour into his lap without much effort on his part. People said he was lucky, both in his business and in his domestic life, and this was true. He and Margaret were very comfortable together, they got on splendidly, they were the greatest of friends. They were rather like each other in a way—though it was difficult to say exactly *how* they were like each other. Mr. Finlay was plump and round in figure, he had a round rosy face and was very bald, and Margaret was a good-looking girl with a nice figure—slightly inclined to plumpness, perhaps, but none the worse for that—and a great deal of pretty light-brown hair. Yet, when you saw them together, it was easy to see that they were father and daughter. Perhaps it was because they were exactly the same height—five feet six to be exact—or perhaps it was the frank, cheerful, kindly expression which illuminated their two faces, or it may have been because their eyes were the same dark shade of brown. Whatever it was, Margaret was quite used (and almost resigned) to being informed by strangers that she was "exactly like" her father, and to looking at the little man—whom she dearly loved—and enquiring rather pathetically of herself—'Am I as bald as an egg? Have I a bow window? Is my face the colour of a nicely baked brick?'

This extraordinarily unfilial daughter observed Iain's arrival from the window of her bedroom, and hastened to arrange her hair and powder her nose before running downstairs to meet him at the door.

'Here you are at last!' she exclaimed. 'Didn't you get my message from Donald? What have you been doing?'

They were shaking hands, and Iain was in the middle of explaining how busy he had been all the week, when the door of the library opened and Mr. Finlay emerged, beaming.

Meg can say what she likes, they *are* alike! Iain thought amusedly, as he greeted Mr. Finlay and made the usual polite enquiries.

'You'll stay to dinner, of course,' Mr. Finlay said. 'There's a fine salmon to eat if Meg's cook doesn't ruin it. I caught it yesterday, myself, and fine sport it gave me, I can tell you.'

'Ruin it!' cried Margaret indignantly. 'When have you ever known Jean ruin a fish? Don't listen to him, Iain, he's just full of himself because he has made a lot more money in America——'

'There's nothing like a salmon for sport,' continued Mr. Finlay, ignoring his daughter's protest completely. 'Come over one day, Iain, and we'll have a day on the river. The water is perfect.'

'Thank you. I'd like nothing better,' Iain said.

'Good, we'll fix a day. I'll see you at dinner?'

34

'Yes, I'd like to stay. I've got Donald with me. He'll go home and come back for me——'

'He'll do no such thing!' exclaimed Mr. Finlay. 'Tell Donald to come up to the house for his meal. I suppose there's sufficient food in the house to give Donald a meal of some sort?'

'Don't try to be funny,' Margaret adjured him sternly. 'It doesn't suit your particular style of beauty at all.'

He snorted with sudden laughter. 'She keeps the old chap in order,' he said to Iain in a stage-whisper. 'Can't call my soul my own. Not even allowed to be funny in my own house. What a life! Well, I've got some work to do—see you at dinner, Iain.' He shut the door of the library and left them standing in the hall.

They looked at each other and laughed.

'He's in splendid form!' Iain said.

'Yes, isn't he?' agreed Margaret. 'He gets younger every year.'

They went out into the garden together and walked about. It was very pleasant to be with Meg again. Iain would have enjoyed it more if he had not been obsessed with the feeling that he must tell Meg about the letting of Ardfalloch. He tried to tell her several times, but the words stuck in his throat. He did not know how she would receive the news and he was afraid to put it to the test. They talked about their neighbours. Margaret wanted to hear all the news, she plied him with questions:—had a certain engagement which had been in the air materialised yet? How was So-and-So's baby? Were Mr. and Mrs. Something Else really going to separate? Iain answered some of the questions seriously, and others with deplorable facetiousness. They laughed and teased each other. The sun shone and the bees hummed in the mignonette. Iain forgot his troubles for the time being and was happy—he was nearly always happy with Meg.

Ardfalloch in May

It was not until after dinner, when Margaret had retired to the drawing-room and left the two men to their port, that Iain found the courage and the opportunity he had been seeking.

'I've let Ardfalloch, sir,' he said baldly.

Mr. Finlay put down his port untasted, and looked at Iain in amazement.

'*You've let Ardfalloch!*'

'I've let it for the season to a London stockbroker—a Mr. Hetherington Smith,' said Iain quietly. It was quite easy now that the first admission had been made.

'Why the devil have you done that?' enquired his host.

'I need the money,' replied Iain simply.

Mr. Finlay's face became even redder than usual with indignation. He gasped twice. 'What the devil d'you need money for?'

Iain laughed. It was a comical question from a man who had as much money as Mr. Finlay.

'I need money for the estate,' he replied. 'Every penny I get goes into the estate—I don't live riotously at Ardfalloch—but unfortunately there aren't enough pennies. Some of the farms need new byres or barns—one of them needs a new roof. The house needs repairs, the boat-house is tumbling down. I'm sick of pinching and scraping——'

'Pinching and scraping's no use to anybody,' said Mr. Finlay. 'It's anti-social, uneconomic. What a man should do is make money and spend it lavishly—circulate the stuff. That's what's the matter with this country: we've got too many pinchers and scrapers. Why the devil couldn't you come to me about it?'

'Come to you, sir!' exclaimed Iain, flushing to the roots of his hair with outraged pride—did the man think he was a beggar?

'Come to me,' nodded Mr. Finlay. 'I could have put you in the way of making a nice little pile—made a nice

36

little pile myself as a matter of fact. Why didn't you trust me, Iain? I wouldn't have let you down.'

'You've got to have money to be able to make it, sir.'

'Not very much if you start in a small way—say a couple of thousand—if you've got a couple of thousand handy I'll tell you what to do with it——'

'If I could lay my hands on a couple of hundred I should consider myself lucky,' said Iain a trifle bitterly.

Mr. Finlay was dumb with surprise. He poured out another glass of port and drank it without the appreciation it most certainly deserved. He thought: This is frightful. I suppose the boy would have a fit if I offered him the two thousand to play about with—these proud Highlanders that stick in their glens and never set foot in the world—you get that nonsense knocked out of you when you begin to move about. Good God, I don't know what to suggest! I suppose he'd have another fit if I suggested he should sell a farm—they don't like parting with land—like cutting off their fingers or their toes. Bah, what nonsense it all is! Don't suppose he *could* sell a farm for anything worth having unless I bought it myself, and he'd twig that at once. He could mortgage, of course, but perhaps he's mortgaged already—better not suggest that either. Why the devil doesn't he marry Meg? She's eating her heart out for him—perhaps it's the money again—*Pride*—the devil's in this Highland pride! It gets them every way, binds their hands—ugh, blast it all, it's upset me!

He said at last, 'Well, you've surprised me. I'd no idea —oughtn't the estate to be self-supporting?'

'How could it be self-supporting?' Iain replied with some heat, for the subject was a sore one. 'The land is so poor. The soil is wretched. There's scarcely a decent field on the whole estate, and the grazing is not much better. I've let them burn a lot of heather—my father would turn in his grave if he knew how much—but even so there's not grazing for more than a score of sheep to each croft. How can I wring money out of my tenants? I go round and see them, and look at the hole in the roof of the byre and the stones in their fields——'

' And you let them off their quarter's rent,' put in Mr. Finlay.

' Sometimes,' Iain admitted, smiling rather sadly.

' But the government doesn't let you off your taxes?'

' No. So you see I felt the only thing to do was to let; to make the forest and the moor pay for the farms. What else was I to do?'

' Meg will be sorry,' Mr. Finlay said thoughtfully. ' Meg was looking forward to seeing something of you this summer——'

' I'm afraid Meg will think it foolish of me, but you see how it is, don't you? You understand the situation. I thought perhaps—I thought—I wondered if you would tell Meg about it, sir—explain it to her, I mean.'

' Wouldn't it be better to tell her yourself?'

' I'd rather you told her.'

' I suppose you think she will be angry with you.'

' I think she might be—rather,' Iain said, smiling a little at the thought. ' We have often said it was foolish of people to let their places to strangers—it might be difficult to explain the necessity——'

' You have known each other a long time,' said Mr. Finlay gravely. ' I think you should know Meg better than to doubt her sympathy——'

' Oh, I don't,' Iain cried. ' How could I?'

' How could you, indeed! Meg doesn't wear her heart on her sleeve, but you must surely know that she is very fond of you, Iain.'

' I'm very fond of Meg,' said Iain truthfully.

' You've seen a lot of each other,' Mr. Finlay continued, choosing his words carefully. ' That's the modern way, and

38

it has its advantages. When I was young, things were very different. Young women were surrounded by a sort of hedge. You couldn't dance with a woman more than twice without rousing comment. All that has changed now—and rightly—but sometimes I wonder if we haven't gone to the other extreme. Young people go about together all over the place nowadays, and nobody bothers. Nobody knows what they are up to—not even themselves——'

Iain had listened to all this with growing alarm; he broke in desperately:

'Meg is like a sister to me,' he said.

'Eh? Like a sister, is she? I don't think there's much sister about it if you ask me,' said Mr. Finlay with an attempt at jocularity. 'Meg doesn't feel like a sister to you —if either of you had a sister you would realise the difference much more readily. We preferred other fellows' sisters when we were young. But to return to what I was saying before you interrupted me with this talk of sisters— nobody knows what young people want, it's this shilly-shallying that I don't understand——'

Iain's anger rose—how dare the old fool talk like that about him and Meg? What did he think he was doing? Iain sprang to his feet. 'Sir,' he said, in a queer stilted voice, 'are you—are you accusing me of tampering with Meg's affections?'

It was exactly what Mr. Finlay was trying to do, but he knew that he must deny it to his last breath—*what have I done?* he thought—*Meg would skin me—this is frightful . . .*

'Good God, no—of course not,' he cried; and again, 'Good God, no. Nothing of the sort. Meg can look after herself. Keep Meg out of it—it's my own idea—mine. Here's the truth, Iain. I'm an old-fashioned sort of buffer and I'm fond of you, Iain, very fond of you. Sometimes I've hoped that you and Meg—well, I'd like to see the child

39

settled with a man I could trust. I shan't live for ever, and
Meg will have a lot of money—I don't want somebody to
marry her for that. You're the man I'd like to have as a
son-in-law. There, you've had it now. I've come clean, as
they say. But you young people—it's in your hands entirely
—yours and Meg's. Sit down for God's sake——'

Iain sat down. He had gone as white as a sheet, and his
hand trembled as he moved his glass on the polished table.
'Thank you, sir,' he said. 'You have paid me a great
compliment—I am proud of your—of your regard—but I
feel sure that Meg—that Meg feels as I do. I admire her
more than I can say—she is a splendid friend—loyal—and
—straight——' His voice died away.

'Well, that's that,' said Mr. Finlay with a forced laugh.
He thought—poor Meg, I've done what I could. I've been
clumsy perhaps, but I don't think I've done any harm. It's
not pride that's kept him away—not pride and poverty—
that's certain at any rate. It may be that he has seen too
much of her, knows her too well. He may really feel that
she is like a sister to him. This modern idea of letting young
people see as much as they like of each other seems to cut
both ways—they have more opportunities of getting to
know each other, but they lose the glamour—in my day
every woman had glamour, even the ugly ones. Poor
Meg isn't ugly by a long way, but she hasn't much glamour.
Good God, what a fool the man is! Meg's white all
through. There may be hope yet, of course, unless there's
another woman—I've put it into his head, anyway . . .

'We had better go in,' he said at last. 'Meg will be
wondering——'

They went into the drawing-room. Margaret was sitting
by the fire with her toes on the fender, smoking a cigarette.
She was surrounded by a cloud of blue smoke—it was one
of Margaret's peculiarities that she managed to make more
smoke with one cigarette than most people make with half a

dozen. Iain had often teased her about this, and called her the smoke stack.

'What ages you've been!' she said, smiling up at them. 'Has Father been telling you the latest naughty stories from America?'

'We were discussing business matters,' Mr. Finlay replied.

'How dull!' exclaimed Margaret.

Neither of the men replied to this. Their conversation could hardly be described as *dull*. Iain felt utterly exhausted after the strain, his collar was clinging to his neck, his knees felt weak . . .

'Poor Iain,' Margaret continued. 'Was it frightfully dull —all about stocks and shares and floating capital?'

'No, it wasn't dull,' replied Iain in a strained voice.

Margaret looked at him swiftly, and then at her father. She thought: What have they been talking about? They both look odd. They both look uncomfortable . . .

'What about a game of piquet?' she said aloud.

Iain agreed with alacrity. It would be much easier to play piquet than to keep up a three-cornered conversation with Margaret and her father. He fetched the card table and set it up near Margaret's chair.

'How nice it is to have somebody to do things for one!' she said, lying back with an elaborate pretence of laziness. 'Yes, the cards are in the usual drawer—got the markers?'

'We all know how lazy you are!' Iain told her, trying to speak lightly.

'I suppose that means I *am* lazy.'

'It means you're not lazy,' replied Iain, shutting the drawer with a snap. 'It means that your activity—or whatever the opposite of laziness may be—is practically a vice. You will never allow anybody to do anything for you if you can do it yourself——'

' Because I can always do it better myself,' retorted Meg.

This was unanswerable, because it was true. Meg was an extraordinarily capable person; she always knew what to do in an emergency and did it without fuss.

Iain sat down on a pouffe, and soon they were deep in their game. Mr. Finlay watched them over the top of his newspaper. He thought: The man really is a fool; Meg is exactly right for him and he for her. Friendship is a good foundation for marriage, better really than love—though you'll never get young people to believe that. How I should hate it if Meg were to marry! What the devil should I do without her? It's rather mad to work and hope for something to happen when you know all the time you'll hate it like poison if it *does* happen. But after I'm gone—and I can't live for ever—seventy-five now, though I don't feel it—I can't have many more years to look forward to, and what about Meg? I'd like to see Meg happy—I'd like her to have children. She's cut out for that . . .

' Point of six,' Iain said.

' Oh, you wretch!'

' That means " good," I suppose?"

' Yes, it does. I was a fool——'

' Quarte major.'

' No good.' Meg was bubbling with laughter.

' Oh, Meg! And I have a tierce as well!'

' Go on,' she giggled. ' There's worse to come.'

' Trio of aces.'

' No good.'

' No good!' he echoed incredulously.

' I've got a quatorze of tens.'

' Of tens? You *are* a cad—really, Meg, I wouldn't have thought it of you!'

She was lying back amongst the cushions, laughing, her face was a little flushed, her light-brown hair a little rumpled; the excitement of seeing Iain again had made her almost beautiful. Mr. Finlay watched them both and thought: They are children. When I was that age I was a staid respectable business man with a wife and family; but they're just children. Perhaps they'll grow up—perhaps they'll never grow up. Iain was thinking: Meg's sweet, Meg's a darling! Why can't I marry her and be happy?

CHAPTER IV

Mr. and Mrs. Hetherington Smith

MRS. HETHERINGTON SMITH was waiting for her husband in the lounge of the De Luxe Restaurant. He was late, but she was not impatient. She had ' got over ' being impatient long ago; she had attained a philosophical attitude of mind in a life of worries and ups and downs. Most people have ups and downs in their lives, but Mrs. Hetherington Smith had had more than her share of uneven fortune. She had started life fairly low in the social scale, and had married Arthur Smith (as he was then) when she was eighteen years old. Arthur Smith was only a broker's clerk, but he had a genius for finance and ambitions far above his station. He started climbing. Once or twice his foot slipped on the ladder of success and down he went to the bottom again, taking his wife with him. Mrs. Hetherington Smith, who had just been getting used to a certain degree of comfort and affluence, would suddenly find herself plain Mrs. Smith once more, back in a small dark kitchenette cooking Arthur's dinner and washing up the greasy plates with her own hands. The strange thing was that she didn't mind—she settled down quite contentedly and made the best of it. There were compensations in poverty—so she discovered. You could talk to your neighbours and take part in their lives, and she found them more interesting than the people she met in the upper circles of society. They were real, and

44

you were real. You could lend a hand when they were in trouble. . . . Another great advantage of being poor was that you had no servant worries, there was no need to bother your head about what the servants would think. If you took a fancy to tripe and onions for supper you could have it; you could have a kipper for tea, and go to the pictures if you felt inclined; or you could take off your corsets and slop about comfortably in an old dressing-gown and a pair of bedroom slippers. But the chief advantage of poverty lay in the fact that your husband was your own. You cooked his food as you knew he liked it cooked, and you mended his clothes, and, at night, you lay in his arms, and he was yours.

Mrs. Hetherington Smith thought of all this rather sadly as she waited for Arthur to come. Arthur was not really hers now. She had no female rival in his affections— Arthur was not that kind—but, since they had risen to their present high estate, the highest they had yet attained, she had lost Arthur—they had drifted apart. It was Business that had come between them—Business and the pursuit of pleasure—the making money and the spending. You never had a moment quietly, at home, by yourselves. You went out to parties or you had people in—it was good for Business. (*Business!* Mrs. Hetherington Smith was sick of the word.)

She sighed and her gaze wandered round the elaborately decorated room. People were going in to dinner now, but there were more arrivals every few minutes to take their places—a steady stream of fashionably attired people flowing in through the swing doors, delaying a little, as if the lounge were a whirlpool in the stream, and passing on——

She watched a party gathering round one of the little tables; the women were pale, with bright eyes and painted mouths, the men sleek in evening dress. They were all

chattering with unnatural gaiety, sipping sherry or cock-
tails, and nibbling biscuits or olives, or salted almonds.
They were typical of this kind of life, thought Mrs. Hetherington Smith, this life that Arthur liked. He was prospering
now and she was glad for his sake (of course she was glad,
she told herself firmly). Her shoes pinched, and a bone
was running into her side. She moved a little, easing her
constricted body in the soft chair, and smoothing out the
folds of her black charmeuse frock—black was slimming—
it was a new frock from Gaston's; the price of it would
have kept them for about two months in their poverty-
stricken days. It seemed a pity, somehow, Mrs. Hetherington Smith thought vaguely. It was so hot and stuffy, and
the noise was so monotonous that her thoughts became
vague and disjointed, they ran into each other and got
mixed. She thought: I wonder what's keeping Arthur—I
wonder whether that girl in green is engaged to that young
man—she's letting him hold her hand, but you never can
tell nowadays. If Effie had lived she would have been
rather like that girl—nineteen she would have been. Perhaps it's just as well, she might have *minded*. It's funny
how I don't mind. I'm better at the other kind of life, it
seems more real—less bother. It's dressing up bothers me,
and the servants, of course, but I'm quite good at it. I see
things quicker than Arthur—I can do both kinds of lives—
I wonder if anyone else has had such funny experiences—
I must be a funny kind of person. If Arthur came to me
to-morrow and said, 'We've lost everything,' I believe I'd
be glad. Sorry for him, of course, because it would mean
he had failed, and he hates failure—but glad for me. At any
rate, it wouldn't *worry* me. I wonder why Arthur doesn't
come.

The party she had been watching moved off slowly into
the restaurant to dine, and Mrs. Hetherington Smith was
revealed to herself in the large gilt mirror which hung on

the opposite wall. She saw a big blonde woman in a black frock with diamonds, and smiled at the reflection. My hair's nice to-night, she thought—that new man has done a softer wave—and I always had a nice skin—I'm glad Arthur needn't be ashamed of me, anyhow. . . .

Something made her turn her head and she saw Arthur coming towards her. He was smiling, and his somewhat heavy face was temporarily lightened. He was almost handsome. He had iron-grey hair, smoothly brushed, and a neat grey moustache; his evening clothes were immaculate. Mrs. Hetherington Smith rose to meet him; she thought suddenly: *We're like actors . . .*

' Sorry to keep you waiting,' he said; ' I've had a long day.'

' You look tired! '

' I am tired.'

' Let's go home after dinner,' she suggested. ' I'm not very keen on this play—— If you're tired——'

' Oh, I want to see Beldale—he said he might be going to *White Nights.* I want to have a word with him.'

' Business, I suppose?' enquired Mrs. Hetherington Smith with a little sigh.

Arthur did not reply—there was no need; of course it was business. He sat down and ordered a cocktail.

' I've had a good day,' he told her. ' Satisfactory all round. I've taken a place up north for the shooting.'

Her eyes widened—' In the north?'

' In Scotland,' he said with studied carelessness. ' They all do it. It's the right thing to do. Lord Beldale always takes a place in Scotland. We'll shut up the house and take the servants north with us. That's how it's done—you'll have to find out the details.'

She nodded. It wasn't the first time she had had to find out the way things were done—she remembered the worry she had had over their first dinner-party.

'Have you taken the house without seeing it?' she asked after a moment's thought.

'How could I see it? As a matter of fact, it isn't the place I wanted—somebody else got in before me—but it doesn't really matter as long as there's shooting.'

'Partridge shooting?' enquired Mrs. Hetherington Smith.

'No, grouse and deer.'

Mrs. Hetherington Smith was surprised—shooting deer! The only deer she had seen were those in the King's Park at Windsor. She wondered how you would shoot deer—it seemed cruel to shoot tame pretty creatures like that. Would they be all round the house, she wondered. Fortunately Mrs. Hetherington Smith had learned to be silent when she did not understand. Things cleared up by themselves, she found. She was silent now.

'How do you like the idea?' asked Mr. Hetherington Smith with a shade of anxiety in his manner.

She thought: It's not much good asking me that now, when he's taken the place, but she was too wise to say so.

'It'll be a change,' she said cautiously.

He nodded. 'You'll like it, Mary. You like the country, don't you? I've taken it for three months, and I'm paying a pretty penny for it, I can tell you.'

'Are *you* going to shoot deer?' she asked.

'I don't think so. It's too difficult. But I shall shoot the grouse, of course. I'll have to learn,' he said, bending forward and speaking in a low tone. 'There are places where you can learn. I don't want to make a fool of myself.'

'You won't do that,' said Mrs. Hetherington Smith comfortably. 'I should start with the deer, though. You're much more likely to hit a deer than a bird——' She stopped suddenly. I'd better shut up, she thought; I don't know a thing about it . . .

Mr. Hetherington Smith had not been listening. 'I shall

have to make time somehow,' he said in a worried voice. 'I shall have to have at least a dozen lessons, I suppose. It would spoil everything if I were to make a fool of myself before the others——'

'What others?' she enquired quickly.

'The house-party, of course. We must have a house-party—ask people to come and stay with us and shoot.'

'Goodness!' exclaimed Mrs. Hetherington Smith.

'It will be all right,' he said irritably. 'You must get books and learn the right words. It's got a special jargon the same as hunting—I shall have to learn it, too.'

She nodded thoughtfully.

He leaned forward still farther. 'It's Stacey I want,' he said softly. 'Mr. Grant Stacey. It's him I'm doing it for. I must have him. They say he'll go anywhere if you offer him shooting——'

She nodded again, her brow smoothed. She understood now what it was all about—it was Business.

Mr. Hetherington Smith finished his cocktail and they went in to dinner. The restaurant was packed with the fashionable London crowd. It was hot and scented, and the brilliant colours of the women's gowns gave it the appearance of an exotic flower-garden. The band was playing a modern composition, full of unresolved chords. It was struggling to make itself heard above the bubble of talk and the ripple of artificial laughter.

A table was found for the Hetherington Smiths in a corner some distance from the band. Mr. Hetherington Smith was well known to the head waiter—his tips were munificent. In a moment the table was ready and the Hetherington Smiths were seated.

Mrs. Hetherington Smith watched her husband ordering their dinner, and thought: He does it well, now. He takes longer to learn things than I do, but somehow he's part of it all when he *has* learnt—not outside like me. It's acting to

49

me all the time, but he's really living it—at least I think so, you never can tell for certain with Arthur. Perhaps it's because he enjoys it and I don't.

She put her jet-encrusted pochette on the table beside her and her thoughts veered. It cost a lot, but it's just right with my dress, she mused. Then she lifted her head and looked round the room to find the green girl who was like what Effie might have been, if Effie hadn't died of croup in those dreadful lodgings in Frick Street. It was fourteen years ago and the Hetherington Smiths had experienced several fluctuations of fortune since those days; but Mrs. Hetherington Smith could still see the pattern of the red and green repp cloth on the table in the sitting-room when she shut her eyes, and the yellow china vases on the mantelpiece with bunches of daisies painted on the sides, and the picture that hung over the sideboard of Highland cattle in green glen with a waterfall. These things were indelibly painted on her mind. She remembered, also, the empty feeling when they had taken the limp body of her child out of her arms . . .

Her thoughts shied away. I suppose there will be Highland cattle *there*, she reminded herself as she sought for her fish-knife and fork amongst the cutlery beside her plate —Highland cattle and waterfalls—and, of course, deer. . . .

The head waiter appeared with a gold-necked bottle wrapped in a napkin. *Fizz*! thought Mrs. Hetherington Smith; how nice of Arthur! It's to celebrate this new venture—I hope to goodness it will be a success. If he told me more I could help him better, but he thinks I'm a fool. He's excited about it or he wouldn't have said ' It's him I'm doing it for '—Arthur doesn't often make mistakes like that nowadays.

Arthur was raising his glass and saying, ' To Ardfalloch! That's the name of the place, Mary—*Ardfalloch*.'

' Ardfalloch!' she repeated, smiling at him and drinking

the toast. 'It's a nice name, anyhow. Who does it belong to?'

" A Mr. MacAslan,' Arthur told her. ' Very old family, they are. Never let the place before, but he needs the money, apparently. Five hundred a month, I'm giving him.'

Her eyes went round, and the well-marked eyebrows, which she had the sense not to pluck, rose a little at the corners. ' One thousand, five hundred pounds!' she said, in an awed voice. ' Will it be worth all that, Arthur?'

' If *he* comes it will,' replied Mr. Hetherington Smith significantly.

There was silence between them for a few minutes and the light roar of conversation filled Mrs. Hetherington Smith's ears. She said at last, ' I suppose we shall be asking other people besides this Mr. Stacey?'

' Of course we shall,' replied Arthur. ' I don't want him to think—I mean it's got to be quite casual. I just meet him at the club and say, " I wonder if you'd care to come up to Scotland—I've taken a place up there for the season " —something like that.'

' But supposing he doesn't come?' she said, appalled at the thought of that fifteen hundred pounds spent for nothing.

' He'll come,' Arthur said, trying to convince himself. ' He'll come because of the shooting. It's supposed to be one of the best places in Scotland. He'll come all right—you'll see.'

' I wonder if Mrs. Bastable would come?'

' Come! Of course she'll come if you ask her,' he cried. ' It's the thing to do. Anybody you ask will come.' He calmed down a little and added, ' I think you *might* have Mrs. Bastable. She's smart, and she knows everybody— you might do worse——'

Mrs. Hetherington Smith nodded. I suppose I had better

ask her, she thought; Greta Bastable would be a help. She knows the ropes. Yes, I had better ask her. I wish I could have Mrs. Hogg and the children—what a holiday it would be for them! But it's quite impossible, of course, so it's no use thinking about it. (The Hoggs belonged to the lowest strata that the Smiths had plumbed and they would certainly not meet with Arthur's approval as prospective guests.) But I might send them ten pounds, thought Mrs. Hetherington Smith—no, fifteen—and they could have a nice holiday at Brighton, or Southend. She smiled tenderly at the thought of the children's delight at seeing the sea, and then sighed at the thought that she would not be there to watch them wading. She had liked the young Hoggs, and the youngest—who had been born when they lived on the same stair—was her godchild, and had been named Mary, after herself. Mary would be five now.

The smile and the sigh and the remembering look which accompanied these reflections were lost on Arthur (he was busy peeling an apple and was intent upon his task), but a tall military-looking gentleman with an eye-glass who had just come in at the door and was looking round the room for an empty table caught sight of Mrs. Hetherington Smith's face and was interested.

He turned to his companion. ' Who's that damn' fine-looking woman dining with old Hetherington Smith?' he enquired. ' No, over there by the window—in black with diamonds——'

' God knows!' replied his companion irritably. ' Who's Hetherington Smith, anyhow? And why do we come to this hellish place for a meal, when we could eat in comfort at the club?'

The first speaker did not reply; he crossed the room with some difficulty and procured an introduction to the woman whose face had intrigued him. He was surprised to find that she was Hetherington Smith's wife. Hetherington

Mr. and Mrs. Hetherington Smith

Smith was rather a dry old stick—clever as a monkey, of course, but not very interesting—this woman had personal attraction. He sat down and talked to the Hetherington Smiths while they had their coffee.

Colonel White was the first guest to receive an invitation to spend a fortnight at Ardfalloch—for the shooting—he accepted without a moment's hesitation.

CHAPTER V

Linda

GRETA BASTABLE received her invitation to Ardfalloch the following afternoon. She met Mrs. Hetherington Smith at ' Gaston's ' private mannequin parade. This was not such a coincidence as it might appear, for Greta had introduced Mrs. Hetherington Smith to ' Gaston's ' and had, thereby, gained the privilege of choosing a frock for herself from his latest models. M. Gaston and Greta understood each other very well. There was no ugly talk about commission, but, when Greta introduced a really good client to the establishment, M. Gaston felt grateful and showed his gratitude in a becoming manner.

Greta Bastable was a widow with a little money and expensive tastes. She had a passion for Society. Nobody knew much about her except that she was smart and amusing and went everywhere—or nearly everywhere. She lived in a small but very modern flat on the right side of the Park, and she gave parties occasionally—rather noisy parties that went on until the early hours of the morning.

Greta was talking to M. Gaston about the new models. She said, ' That petunia model wants a touch of colour. Perhaps a rose pink spray—or orchids.' It amused her to find fault with M. Gaston's models, and she was nearly always right in her criticisms, for her taste in clothes was impeccable. She wrote the fashion column for a big daily paper, and the Society News for a weekly, to augment her income, but not even her most intimate friends were aware of this. Greta found it gave her a freer hand to be strictly anonymous—especially for the Society News.

M. Gaston hurried off to try the effect of the spray, and Greta made her way over to the small gold sofa where Mrs. Hetherington Smith was ensconced.

'What luck meeting you here!' exclaimed Mrs. Hetherington Smith, who was now an adept at the patter of Society, and had long ago given up the middle-class habit of saying how do you do to her acquaintances.

'I was thinking the same thing,' Greta said, smiling and sitting down on the sofa beside her. 'I was just wondering how on earth I could cadge a lift home, and there you were—an answer to my prayers.'

Mrs. Hetherington Smith smiled. Greta's frankness amused her. 'But I'm not,' she said. 'I sent the car away. I'm going to walk home across the Park.'

'Good God!'

'I don't get enough exercise,' explained Mrs. Hetherington Smith apologetically. 'I don't dance, you see——'

She broke off and her gaze wandered vaguely round the room. She wanted an afternoon frock, but these were all too flamboyant for her proportions. Greta looked at her and thought: I wonder who she is—and what she is. She looks as if she had a history—an interesting face, and yet she never says anything interesting. Is she full of secrets, or empty? I don't think she's empty, somehow. I wonder where they have come from—nobody seems to know. It might be interesting to find out—and lucrative . . .

Mrs. Hetherington Smith was thinking, Now is the time to ask her, but the thing is to do it casually. I wonder why I'm nervous about it. She said, 'I want an afternoon frock—that grey one is pretty, but grey doesn't suit me.'

'No, it wouldn't,' agreed her companion. 'But you might have something the same in navy blue. Gaston doesn't copy his models, but he could design you something on the same lines.'

' I might ask him, mightn't I?' said Mrs. Hetherington Smith. ' I want something simple—for Scotland. We've taken a place there for the season. I wondered if you could fit in a couple of weeks with us——'

' How sweet of you!' Greta exclaimed. ' I adore Scotland. Is it a big party?'

' Oh, no!' replied her prospective hostess. ' It's quite a small place—only fourteen bedrooms, and Arthur wants most of them for his men friends. He took it because the shooting is excellent. It's called Ardfalloch, and it's miles from everywhere—no electric light or gas—I don't know what the servants will say.'

Mrs. Hetherington Smith was rather proud of this speech. It was in the right tradition, she felt; she waited for Greta's reaction to it with interest.

' I adore candlelight!' cried Greta enthusiastically.

She stayed with Mrs. Hetherington Smith long enough to clinch the matter, and then wandered off to find somebody less mad on the subject of exercise to give her a lift home.

Mrs. Hetherington Smith continued to sit on the sofa; she watched the mannequins and thought her own thoughts about them. What were they like *really,* she wondered, when they were clad in their everyday garments. What sort of homes did they go back to?

Suddenly a soft voice said, ' Do you mind if I sit here?'

' No, of course I don't mind,' replied Mrs. Hetherington Smith quickly. ' I may be big, but I don't need a whole sofa to myself.' She ended with a chuckle, and then thought: I shouldn't have said that; she took me by surprise. It certainly was a trifle out of keeping with her part. It was the sort of thing Mrs. Smith might have said, and the chuckle was pure Mrs. Smith. I'll have to look out, she thought. I'll have to be more careful. . . .

Linda

The girl—or woman—who had spoken sat down on the sofa beside her, and they looked at each other. Mrs. Hetherington Smith saw a pale face, rather small featured, and dark blue eyes beneath the drooping brim of a fashionable hat. The girl—or woman—saw Mrs. Hetherington Smith. She had heard Mrs. Smith speak, but it was Mrs. Hetherington Smith that she saw—it was rather intriguing.

'I get so tired,' she said.

'Standing about is tiring,' agreed Mrs. Hetherington Smith. 'I like walking, it is not nearly so tiring.'

'No,' said the girl. 'I like walking, too—in the country, of course.'

'Yes, of course.'

Mrs. Hetherington Smith thought: I'd like to talk to this girl *properly*. I oughtn't to, of course, it's not the thing, but I don't care. There's something interesting about her. She's *real*. She's been through things. What a sad face she has got!

'Do you live in the country?' Mrs. Hetherington Smith enquired.

'No. I wish I did.'

'Perhaps you lived in the country when you were a child——'

'I never lived in town until I was married,' replied the girl. 'I liked it at first, and then I hated it.'

She's married, thought Mrs. Hetherington Smith, I wonder how old she is. She looks about twenty-eight or thirty, but she said she was tired, so perhaps she's younger than she looks. She hasn't had her eyebrows plucked—they don't need it—I like the colour of them—sort of chocolate colour. She's got a lovely clear skin and her mouth is pretty—touched up a little, but not too much. I wonder if she minds me talking to her—she doesn't seem to. I shall go on talking to her; if she doesn't like it she can snub me.

'That pink frock would suit you,' she said.

'I don't feel like pink just now,' replied her companion, a trifle bitterly.

'You might feel like it if you wore it,' said Mrs. Hetherington Smith. 'It's funny how different frocks can make you *feel* different. I nearly always wear black, because I'm big, you see; but I often wish I could wear pink—it's cheery.' There now, she thought, I've done it again. This girl *is* having a funny effect on me. She makes me feel real.

'But have you ever felt that you had no clothes on at all?' enquired the girl. 'Have you ever felt that you wanted to muffle yourself up in a fur coat and crawl into a dark corner?'

'Yes,' replied Mrs. Hetherington Smith simply. She had felt exactly like that at her first dinner-party, her bare shoulders had cried aloud to Heaven for a covering. But this girl couldn't have felt *that*. This girl had been *born* to bare shoulders if Mrs. Hetherington Smith knew anything about it. She couldn't have meant *that*—what did she mean then?

'Well, if you've felt it——' the girl said, as if that were all there was to be said on the subject.

'But you're not big like me,' Mrs. Hetherington Smith pointed out. '*You* don't need to worry.'

The girl had turned away. She's disappointed in me, thought Mrs. Hetherington Smith distractedly. I've said the wrong thing and she knows I haven't understood. She'll go away in a minute and I'll never see her again. She spoke to me like that because she was desperate. It must be some other kind of nakedness she's felt—not bodily nakedness. Oh dear, why wasn't I born with brains?

She said quietly, 'I'm not clever, you know; but if you would tell me about it I think I could understand.'

The girl turned her head and looked at Mrs. Hetherington Smith for a minute. It was a kind face, not very clever perhaps, but full of intelligence; it was very kind, and eager, and friendly.

'Well,' she said hesitatingly, 'but not here——'

'No, of course not *here*,' agreed Mrs. Hetherington Smith, rising and gathering up her bag and her sable stole.

They went out together. It was not until she got outside that Mrs. Hetherington Smith remembered she had sent her car away. She told the commissionaire to hail a taxi. They got in and drove home to the Hetherington Smith mansion in Berkeley Square.

Tea was ready in the Hetherington Smith drawing-room —a low table, glittering with silver and china, stood before the fire. Linda Medworth drew off her gloves and sat down in the comfortable arm-chair selected for her. *Am I mad?* she thought. *Perhaps the strain and worry have affected my brain—I don't even know the woman's name.* The drawing-room was just right, neither too modern, nor too old-fashioned—it was almost too right, if anything, Linda thought, and everything was rather too new. She had a moment of sheer panic, and visions of crooks and the white slave traffic swept through her mind. Had the woman picked her up—like that—on purpose? (There was that queer tale of Stevenson's in which somebody had furnished a whole house for one night as a net to catch some people he wanted—she could not remember the whole story, but the furnishing of the house for one night had stuck in her mind, and the coming of the pantechnicons at dawn to take the furniture away.) Her eyes returned to her hostess's face and the panic fled—it was a good face, kind and interested.

'Milk or lemon?' enquired Mrs. Hetherington Smith.

'Lemon, please.'

'You ought to take milk. You could do with a little more flesh on your bones. Now, I take lemon because I'm big enough. I'm too greedy to diet properly, but I don't mind lemon in my tea.' She thought: I'm babbling—that's not the way to make her feel at home with me, or is it? I'm sure I don't know.

Linda Medworth held out her hand for the cup, and smiled at her hostess. 'Do you often do this?' she enquired.

'Do what?'

'Pick up perfect strangers and bring them home to tea with you.'

'Just as often as you allow yourself to be picked up by a perfect stranger and whisked off in a taxi to a strange house.'

'How do you know I don't often do it?'

'Well, do you?' retorted Mrs. Hetherington Smith. "The truth is we trusted each other and here we are.'

'Tell me why you did it,' Linda said.

Mrs. Hetherington Smith frowned thoughtfully. It was difficult to explain why she had done it. The girl had looked as if she needed a friend, or at least somebody that she could use as a friend—an ear to which she could pour her troubles—and Mrs. Hetherington Smith was tired of being useless and ornamental and artificial. *Here's somebody I can help,* she had said to herself, and she had hailed the girl off in a taxi. There were so few ways of helping people when you were rich (except of course by giving them money, which was a dull way). When you were poor it was so much easier to be useful to your neighbours—you could go in and give a hand when a new baby arrived, or when people were ill. You could be useful. Mrs. Hetherington Smith liked that. She had thought it would be easy, the girl needed a friend and *she* would supply the need. But it wasn't so easy, somehow; there was a sort of undercurrent of bitterness and defiance in the girl. She couldn't quite understand it. Perhaps the girl was regretting her impulse —perhaps she felt trapped. Mrs. Hetherington Smith retrieved a dish of crumpets from a silver stand beside the fire, and offered it to her guest. ' You were going to tell me something,' she said, a trifle shyly, ' and I want to hear, of course. But if you've changed your mind about telling me, it doesn't matter. People often change their minds—I mean, don't think that you've got to tell me because you've come. It's nice for me to have you to tea like this——'

' You don't know who I am?'

' No, ought I to know?'

' I'm Linda Medworth.'

Mrs. Hetherington Smith's face was blank. ' Well, I suppose I ought to know—but I'm afraid I don't,' she said slowly. ' You'll have to tell me whether you've flown to Australia or written a novel that everyone's talking about ——'

Linda put back her head and laughed. She had pretty white teeth and her eyes crinkled up at the corners. She looked years younger when she laughed.

' Why, you're quite a child!' exclaimed Mrs. Hetherington Smith in surprise.

' I'm twenty-six,' replied Linda, sobering down rapidly. ' And just at the moment I feel double that age—but never mind that. I've made up my mind to tell you everything —if you really want to hear—if you can be bothered with my troubles.'

' Of course I want to hear.'

' It's quite long.'

' Never mind that, my dear,' said Mrs. Hetherington Smith.

Linda's story took a long time to tell. She found it difficult at first, for she had never told it all before—not in this kind of way. It took longer because she missed out bits of it thinking—no, I won't tell her that—and then found that she had to tell her *that* because the story didn't hang together properly without. And they got tangled up because

Mrs. Hetherington Smith asked such a lot of questions and put Linda out of her stride. Linda realised before she had gone far that her new friend might not be exactly *clever* in the usually accepted sense of the word, but she was full of common sense, and she was comfortable—like an easy chair is comfortable—and as placid as a Gloucestershire mere on an August afternoon.

Mrs. Hetherington Smith accepted everything she was told with perfect calm. She digested the most hair-raising statements without blinking an eyelid. At first, in the bitterness of her pain, Linda tried deliberately to shock her new friend. If she wants to hear my story, she shall hear it, she told herself. But Mrs. Hetherington Smith was quite unshockable. She had lived for four years in a tenement in a street off the Edgware Road and she had taken an active part in the lives of her neighbours. A good many queer things had happened to her during those four years. She had helped to separate drunken husbands and wives, and to bind up their wounds, and had made them a cup of tea afterwards and stayed to share it. She had seen a man die of carbolic acid poisoning. She had helped to deliver a baby. All these things had seemed real to Mrs. Smith and quite natural—it was not likely that anything Linda told her could shock her.

'Tell me first of all why I ought to know your name,' Mrs. Hetherington Smith had said. It was evident to her that her guest was searching for a way to begin, and Mrs. Hetherington Smith always read the last few pages of a novel before she started on the story. She liked to know where she was, and whether to be prepared for a tragic *dénouement* or happiness all round.

'Oh, that!' Linda said. 'I thought everybody knew who I was—that's why I told you I felt naked. It's all been in the papers—Medworth *v.* Medworth and Stacker—photographs and paragraphs and more photographs until

I thought every errand boy in London must know my face——'

'I don't read the papers for days, sometimes,' Mrs. Hetherington Smith explained apologetically.

'I never knew it would be like that,' Linda continued. ' If I had known how awful it would be I would have hesitated before I decided to divorce Jack. I did hesitate, of course, because you don't divorce your husband without hesitating——'

'No, of course not,' agreed her friend.

'The lawyers never warned me that the publicity would be so—so appalling.'

'Perhaps if they had, you wouldn't have done it at all,' suggested Mrs. Hetherington Smith. I suppose I shall find out in time what it's all about, she thought.

'But I had to do it,' Linda said earnestly. 'I had to do it because of Richard.'

Richard, thought Mrs. Hetherington Smith—now who is Richard, I wonder. She divorced Jack because of Richard. I'm sure I got that right.

'Well, you're free now,' said Mrs. Hetherington Smith comfortably.

'Yes, I'm free. I can't help thinking about that man in the Bible who said, " At a great price obtained I this freedom." I'm free but I'm dirty. I've been mauled over with words till I hate myself and everybody else.'

'Why don't you go away for a bit?' suggested Mrs. Hetherington Smith sensibly.

Linda threw up her head. ' I'll face it out,' she said. ' I've done nothing to be ashamed of. People would think I was running away. I've been foolish and stubborn, of course, but I haven't done anything *wrong*. So I'm not going to run away. I was foolish to marry Jack,' she continued. ' Foolish and stubborn; I wouldn't take advice, I wouldn't be warned. Lots of people tried to warn me about

Jack before I married him, but I was young and foolish—
my head was turned. I thought I could keep him—I
thought I could keep him straight—I couldn't do either. I
was nineteen when I met Jack and married him. He
appealed to me because he was different from other men.
He was bold and reckless and amusing; he swept me off my
feet. I wouldn't listen to anything against Jack. It was just
jealousy, I thought, jealousy because he loved me. Even
then he had a stream of women after him—we laughed at
them together——'

'Jack Medworth!' exclaimed Mrs. Hetherington Smith
suddenly. 'Why, of course—he races cars, doesn't he?
Everybody knows about *him*. He won the Paris Grand
Prix, didn't he?'

Linda nodded. 'It was his racing that fascinated me—I
was a fool, of course, but only one amongst many. That
was why there was so much publicity over the divorce, you
see. Because Jack is so well known. As I said before he
always has a stream of women following him about, asking
for his autograph or if they may take a photograph of him
—just as if he were a film star.'

'It must have been very bad for him,' said Mrs. Hetherington Smith thoughtfully.

'It ruined him,' Linda agreed. 'Women flattered him
and he liked it. But when I married him—at first I mean—
we were happy. Not for long, because I soon found out
what he was like, but just at first. Then, of course, Richard
was born——'

'Richard was born,' nodded Mrs. Hetherington Smith.
She had placed Richard satisfactorily, that was something.

'I couldn't go about with Jack for a bit, so he went alone
to race at different places, and the women started pursuing
him again. He liked it.'

'He was hard to please.'

'Oh, I don't know. There are different varieties of people

—he wasn't the right kind of person for me; I wasn't right for him. We only had one thing in common and he spoilt that. After that was gone we had no common ground. He thought me a prig. He didn't even bother to hide his affairs from me—after we had quarrelled once or twice. He didn't mind being found out—he rather enjoyed it; he enjoyed shocking me. He found me dull—perhaps he would have found any one woman dull—he likes variety in women. Are you awfully bored with all this?'

'Not bored at all,' replied Mrs. Hetherington Smith. 'I'm beginning to understand now. How unhappy you must have been!'

Linda did not answer; her face was tragic in its sorrow.

'It's a good thing you've got Richard,' said Mrs. Hetherington Smith with a little sigh.

Linda noticed the sigh. 'Have you—have you got children?' she asked a trifle diffidently.

'Not now,' replied Mrs. Hetherington Smith.

'Oh—I'm sorry,' Linda said. 'I might have known you had had troubles of your own—you wouldn't be so kind and understanding——'

'Yes, I've had troubles in my time. But never mind that now—tell me about Richard.'

Linda was silent for a moment, and then she said, 'Richard—that was the worst part. It was because of Richard that I *had* to—to take steps. Jack frightened Richard—he didn't understand him. He thought Richard was a coward because he was frightened of loud angry voices. He took Richard out in his racing car and Richard was terrified—Jack was furious. He came home and said that Richard was a coward. He wanted to thrash Richard. He shouted and stormed and said that no son of his should grow up a coward, he would rather see the boy in his grave—it was all my fault for coddling the boy——'

'How old is Richard?' enquired Mrs. Hetherington Smith.

'Six,' replied his mother. 'And he's not a coward—he's a sensitive child, nervous and sensitive. I wasn't going to allow Jack to thrash him—it would have made him a thousand times more nervous. There was a frightful scene over that. I seized Jack's arm and told him he could thrash *me* if he liked, but he wasn't to lay a hand on Richard. I managed to stop him that time, but I realised that something would have to be done—we couldn't go on like that. I decided to divorce Jack. It was quite easy to get the necessary evidence—he has women everywhere. I thought he wouldn't bother to defend the action and it would just pass through the court in the ordinary way—my solicitor thought so, too. When Jack was over in Ireland I left the flat—taking Richard with me, of course—and we went into rooms. I wrote to Jack and told him what I proposed—my solicitor helped me to write the letter. I thought it would all be quite easy. Then Jack came back from Ireland—he hadn't done well there and he was angry. He said my letter had upset him; he said he was going to defend the action.'

'I wonder why.'

'Because of Richard,' Linda said. 'That was why. He said to me, "You can go to hell, for all I care, I want my son, and I'm damn' well going to have him." Only he didn't say damn'.'

'I don't suppose he would,' agreed Mrs. Hetherington Smith comfortably.

Linda looked at her in surprise.

'Go on, my dear,' urged her hostess. 'He said he wanted to knock the boy into shape, didn't he?'

'Yes, he did—how on earth did you know?'

'I just knew.'

'You seem to know a good deal!'

'Well, I've seen a good many different kinds of people.'

Linda

She thought: This Medworth man is like the drunken bruiser who lived on the third floor—I remember the night he half killed his wife—funny how much alike people are under their skins—quite different on top, but just the same underneath. Aloud, she continued, 'Well, anyhow, my dear, you've got rid of him, I suppose—and that's a mercy —and you've got Richard, which is the main thing.'

Linda nodded. 'I hope I've got rid of him,' she said. 'But I'm still frightened—a little. He's gone to America to race, so we're safe—Richard and I—till he comes back. We're safe until August.'

'What are you afraid of?'

Linda raised her hands a trifle helplessly. 'I don't know —exactly,' she said. 'I can't explain. I have a feeling that he hasn't given up the struggle. I shan't feel safe until the decree is made absolute—then of course I shall be really free.'

Mrs. Hetherington Smith did not understand. But it doesn't matter, she thought, I'll find out what it all means— Arthur will know. Meanwhile, of course, it was obvious what was to be done. 'You and Richard must come to Ardfalloch,' she said confidently.

'To Ardfalloch!' exclaimed Linda in amazement.

'Yes, we've taken a place called Ardfallŏch for the summer—a place in the Highlands. You and Richard must come there. It is a splendid plan. It fits in beautifully.'

'But, my dear Mrs. ——'

'Hetherington Smith,' suggested that lady with a smile.

'Mrs. Hetherington Smith,' repeated Linda obediently. 'You can't mean it——'

'Of course I mean it—why not? I shall love to have you—and Richard, of course—it will be lovely. I'm looking forward to it already. You'll be quite safe at Ardfalloch— it's miles from everywhere. You can shoot deer if you like —or grouse—and Richard can play in the garden. It will be a nice little change for him—Scotch air is so bracing, isn't it?' added Mrs. Hetherington Smith benevolently.

Linda gazed at her—the woman really meant it. She was extraordinarily kind, and Linda was extraordinarily grateful. Even if she did not accept the invitation, it was a nice comforting thing to have been asked. But what a queer mixture she is, Linda thought, I can't place her at all, because every time I place her she says something quite out of keeping with the label I have given her. I thought she was a little common at first—and then I was sure she wasn't, and I've gone on pasting her with labels and tearing them off all the time I've been talking to her. Who is she and what is she? She's frightfully kind, anyhow, and isn't that enough? Lots of people know nothing about Scotland—I don't know much about it myself for that matter—yes, thought Linda, but that really isn't the point. I don't know much about Scotland, but I do know something about the conditions—I know the jargon, so to speak. And how do I know it? Simply by mixing with people of my own class. This woman would know it, too, if she were really what she seems, if she had mixed with my kind of people all her life. How snobbish this seems! Linda thought; and yet I must be careful for Richard's sake if not for my own. I know nothing about this woman—nothing. And then she looked at the woman again and her doubts were extinguished. She's kind, Linda thought, most awfully kind—and sensible. And it really would be a good solution. The whole thing comes to this—can I trust her? Or rather can I trust my own instinct, for of course I *do* trust her. . . .

CHAPTER VI

Ardfalloch House

IAIN MACASLAN stood on the steps of his house and watched the car lurch off down the rutty drive and disappear into the shadow of the trees. His mother and Janet were going to Edinburgh and he was remaining as he had arranged. His mother had been excited like a child over their departure, and Janet was looking forward to ' seeing life '—so they were both pleased. But, just at the last, Janet's heart had failed her. She had turned to him with eyes suddenly wet, and had said in a queer husky voice, ' Eh, MacAslan, I'm sweir to leave Ardfalloch!'

It had brought them very close together, that impulsive cry. Ardfalloch was hard to leave. He thought that Ardfalloch was particularly beautiful to-day. The sky was pale blue, not a cloud marred its brightness. The atmosphere was clear and crisp, the line of hills clear cut against the blue vault of the heavens. Beneath the dark trees were cool shadows. A film of dew hung upon every leaf and masked the verdant green of the grass, but the sun was gaining strength every moment and sucking up the moisture in a dazzling golden mist. Soon, now, the moisture would be gone—it was going to be very hot to-day.

Iain was alone in the house. He wanted to go through the house, through every room, quietly, by himself, before the tenants arrived. For three months he would not have

the right to set foot in his own house—he had sold the
right.

Iain sighed. He saw quite clearly that he was going to
hate being here in the glen, with strangers in his house. He
was putting himself in an invidious position by staying.
There was no actual law against a landlord remaining on his
land when he had let the place to tenants, but the thing was
not done. The Finlays had been horrified at the idea. They
had tried to persuade him to stay at Cluan, and, when they
had failed in that, had besought him to go away. He
realised that they were right, but he couldn't go. Something
bound him here, something stronger than his pride. He
could not leave his home.

As far as the tenants were concerned there was no need
for Iain to go. It would make no difference to them whether
he were here or not. They would never know, because
nobody in the glen would tell them. Donald had let it be
known that MacAslan was staying on, but the London
people were not to know. That was all that was necessary.
Not a creature in the glen would breathe a word on the
subject. There was no difficulty about that. No, the only
difficulty was Iain's own pride—that he should be staying
here—practically in hiding—while strangers lived in his
house.

But Iain had gone over all that before and had told himself that he must be sensible, and had reminded himself of
the money that he was getting, and of all the improvements
that he was going to carry out . . .

He started off on his tour of the house, opening every
door and taking a farewell glance at every room. The
rooms were all ready now, of course, the furniture was
uncovered and the windows were flung wide to admit the
sunshine and the sweet morning air. It was delightful to
see all the rooms open again—all the old, well-remembered
furniture and pictures. He lingered for a little in his

mother's room, opening and shutting the drawers in the big old-fashioned wardrobe where she kept her small stock of jewellery and the little treasures which meant so much to her. He had seen her sitting here so often with a drawer open, fingering a pretty scarf or a string of coloured beads. They were all gone now, these treasures, Janet had seen to that—the drawers were empty and freshly papered. Iain went out of the room and along the passage to the gallery which ran round the top part of the house. There was a railing of fumed oak round the gallery and you could look down into the big square hall below. The sunlight streamed through the staircase window, showing up the worn places on the carpet, gilding the tarnished frames of the pictures, shining on the polished horns of the royal stag that Iain had shot when he was seventeen. It was his first stag. He remembered the day very well—he would never forget that day. It was a day of sunshine, with sudden misty clouds that appeared from nowhere, and clung to the mountains for a little while until they were swept away by a fitful breeze. He and Donald had gone out together—the two of them. He could see them climbing up the bare face of Ben Falloch, striking off across his jutting shoulder, crawling down the narrow corrie on the farther side. What a stalk it was—the blazing sun, and then, all at once, the cloud, wet and misty all about them so that they could scarcely see three yards before them. They had lain by a rock and waited until it should clear—there was nothing else to be done, and then, just as suddenly, it had cleared, and there was the stag—a sixteen pointer—the very one that they had pursued all day, standing in all his pride and glory within easy range. It was an ineffable moment. He could scarcely believe his eyes. He remembered how his hands had trembled as he moved his rifle very carefully to take a sight, and how Donald had whispered, 'Do not be hurrying yourself—there is time and to spare.' He remembered the deaf-

71

ening report—the fear that he had missed, and how the proud creature had bounded high into the air and fallen dead in a crumpled heap. He remembered Donald's wild shout of triumph as he rushed down the hillside to gralloch the kill. *Those were the days,* thought Iain with a little sigh—all the happiness of Ardfalloch and none of its responsibilities, all the joy and none of the pain.

He went slowly down the stairs and across the polished floor of the hall, and opened the drawing-room door. He had left the drawing-room to the last. The long, beautifully-proportioned room was full of sunshine, the furniture shone. The china in the cabinets glistened in the bright light. A fire of peats flickered on the hearth. The little boudoir off the drawing-room had been his grandmother's room. It was full of her presence. The bureau where she wrote long letters to her southern relations in a thin flowing hand, the chair by the fire where she sat and read or knitted —her old-fashioned work-table with its little drawers, these things all spoke to Iain of his grandmother and spoke with no uncertain voice. There was a picture of her hanging on the wall, a picture of her as a young woman with a child— Iain's father—standing at her knee. Iain had never known her as a young woman, but she had not changed fundamentally—the contours of her face had remained the same to the day of her death, and the eyes . . .

Iain looked at the calm face with its wide-set eyes and high cheek-bones and large, firm, well-shaped mouth and he thought: *She* would understand and approve of what I am doing—none of the others would understand—my father would have gone on until everything crashed about his ears. I suppose I must have a little of grandmother in me—I wish I had more.

His reflections were interrupted by a sound of footsteps in the quiet house, and, turning quickly, he found Donald at the door.

' I was saying good-bye to my grandmother,' Iain told him. This was one of the things that could be said to Donald—but not to Janet.

' She wass a great lady,' Donald said gravely. ' Sometimes I think there is much of her in MacAslan, and sometimes I think there is not any of her at all.'

' I've been thinking the same thing,' Iain said.

There was a little silence, and together they looked at the picture of old Mrs. MacAslan, resurrecting her in their thoughts.

' Did you want me for something?' Iain asked at last.

' What time would you be expecting the London people to come?' Donald enquired, answering Iain's question with one of his own.

' About three, I suppose. They were staying the night at Fort William. I'm waiting to hand over the house.'

' I wass wondering—could I not be doing that? Morag is getting your dinner at the cottage——'

' Morag shouldn't have bothered.'

' Och, it wass no bother at all. It wass Morag thought maybe I would do to be here for the London people when they arrive.'

They looked at each other gravely. Iain saw that there was more in this than met the eye.

' Tell me what you are thinking, Donald,' he said.

' It wass Morag,' Donald said, looking down at the pattern on the carpet. ' Morag wass saying this—if MacAslan does not want the London people to be knowing he is in the glen, it would be better for them not to be seeing MacAslan when they come. For then they would not know it wass MacAslan, if they would be seeing him in the glen.'

Iain considered this, and he saw that there was a good deal in it. If his tenants did not know him by sight he would be free to come and go about the place as he chose—not to come near the house, of course, that was far from his mind

—but to move about the moors, or visit the village. If he were seen, his tenants would merely think he was one of the men on the estate. He would not have to hide. . . .

'Morag's right,' he said at last.

The big man chuckled.

Iain walked down to the cottage by the loch, carrying a small suitcase containing a few odds and ends that he had collected in his last tour of the house. As he got near he saw a thin spiral of smoke rising from the chimney. The door opened directly into the living-room; it was a good-sized room. The floor was stained with dark varnish and a couple of old blue mats had been laid upon it, the walls were distempered in cream. There were a few odd pieces of furniture which Janet had retrieved from the attics of the big house—an old sofa, a couple of comfortable but exceedingly shabby basket chairs, a book-case, a solid table with a blue-checked cloth and a cupboard of fumed oak—rather roughly finished—with a vase of roses on the top of it. Iain put his suitcase on the floor and looked round. It was a comfortable room now, marvellously transformed from a dull frowsty apartment into a home. Janet and Morag had done it between them. They had become almost friendly over the shared task. ' Yon Morag's got some sense in her heid,' Janet said, qualifying the praise with the grudging addenda, ' for a Heiland body, I mean.' Morag was less open in her speech, and Iain had no means of knowing what Morag thought of Janet, save by an occasional ghost of a smile that lingered round her lips when the older woman was more than usually trying and dictatorial. Iain had watched the transformation of the cottage with something very like awe. He had bought nothing save an oil cooking-stove for the kitchen and a few kitchen utensils. Everything else that was needful for his comfort had been ' found ' in some marvellous manner by his helpers. The little house had been scrubbed and polished till it shone

74

with cleanliness. Donald had mended the roof, and knocked up cupboards and shelves, and distempered the walls.

Iain crossed the room and smelt the roses in the vase—they were out of Donald's garden, he knew. How good to him they all were! He could hear Morag moving about in the tiny kitchen, humming a little song to herself. There was a savoury smell in the air. He took his suitcase and went up the steep narrow stair. There were three bedrooms upstairs; Iain had chosen the one overlooking the loch. It was very small, but it was clean and fresh and airy. There was a camp-bed in it, with brown blankets, and a dressing-chest with a mirror on the top; a press in the wall contained his clothes—what more could a man want?

He opened the casement window and looked out over the loch—it was queer to see it so near him, and the mountains looked different from this angle. The sun was high overhead and a small breeze from the south-west ruffled the surface of the loch into silver ripples. Iain leaned his elbows on the window-sill—above him and below was the roof—sloping down to the flat eaves. The ground—from where it came within the angle of his view—sloped gently to the loch's edge. It was composed of grass and heather, green and purple in the bright afternoon sun. A sheep and a lamb —black-faced and nimble—were eating the grass between the patches of heather with amazing industry. It was all very peaceful.

Morag was still busy in the kitchen when he went downstairs. He looked in to let her know he had come.

' It is good that MacAslan has come,' she said, smiling at him shyly. ' Dinner is ready—I will bring it through.'

He went into the living-room and sat down at the table—there were things he must say to Morag, and it was a good opportunity to say them now with Donald firmly tethered at the house waiting the arrival of his tenants.

Morag brought in his dinner and stood looking at him

while he helped himself—what was he but a bairn? Morag thought; all men were just big bairns, helpless and simple and easily pleased and—but this was not so fortunate—easily put out about small matters.

'What are you thinking about, Morag?' he asked, looking up and seeing the ghost of a smile on her pretty fresh face.

'I was hoping MacAslan was enjoying his dinner,' she replied demurely.

'I should be an ungrateful wretch if I were not enjoying it. But, Morag, *this can't go on.* You're not to come here again and cook my dinner.'

'And I was hoping MacAslan was liking it!' she cried with assumed dismay.

'It is not fair to Donald,' continued Iain gravely, ignoring her protest completely. 'Nor to you either. You have your own work to do. I did not come here to be a trouble to my friends.'

'And who will cook MacAslan's dinner and make his bed for him?'

'MacAslan will do it himself,' replied Iain, smiling. 'I suppose you think I couldn't do it properly.'

Morag smiled, too. 'I do not think that,' she said. 'I think MacAslan could do it very well when he felt inclined. But if he were to be out in the boat, or walking on the hills, he would not be inclined—and there would be no dinner at all—and that would be a pity.'

'It would be his own fault,' Iain pointed out.

'Yes, it would be his own fault,' she agreed. 'But it would be no comfort to Donald to be thinking it was Mac-Aslan's own fault that he was not having any dinner. Donald would not be eating his own dinner if he thought maybe MacAslan was having none.'

'Well,' said Iain in perplexity—for he was beginning to visualise the difficulties more clearly now that he was actually confronting them. 'Well, Morag, perhaps you're right. You had better arrange for a woman to come in daily, a woman from the village.'

'Och, and that would not do at all!' she cried in real dismay. 'Is there one I could find who would make Mac-Aslan's dinner properly and keep the pans clean? Is there one I could be trusting to turn over the *mattress* every day?'

'Am I an infant in arms?' demanded Iain.

'Och, well—I wouldn't go so far—but a woman from the village—— Och, no, that would not do at all—and me promised to Miss Walker on the Holy Name to see to MacAslan myself——'

'Janet had no business to ask you,' Iain told her. He was beginning to feel quite angry. It was all very well for people to be fond of you, but these women were smothering him with their solicitude.

'I would have done it myself without Miss Walker,' Morag said, her eyes flashing fire at the thought of her enemy. 'Miss Walker is no more anxious for MacAslan than his own people. I was after saying that same thing to Miss Walker herself,' she continued, tossing her head as the recollection of the verbal battle passed through her mind, ' and Miss Walker said, " Then it'll not hurt you to swear," and I swore by the Holy Name that I would care for Mac-Aslan like my own son——'

Iain roared with laughter. 'Oh, Morag!' he cried, 'you'll kill me!'

Morag's anger subsided as suddenly as it had arisen, her eyes twinkled. 'And that would be a pity,' she said demurely. She took his plate away and put out a dish of oatcakes, and a piece of cheese, and a plate of radishes nestling among crisp lettuce.

Iain helped himself. 'I don't know what we're going to do,' he said.

'If MacAslan would be listening,' she said coaxingly, ' it

is all quite easy; I will come in the morning and make the dinner and tidy the cottage, and MacAslan will make the supper and the breakfast. It is all quite easy. Then, when Donald will be wondering what MacAslan is having for his dinner, I will be able to tell him.' She smiled at him—a whole real smile—with a flash of white teeth.

Iain rose and found his pipe on the mantelpiece. 'Well,' he said, 'it will be splendid for me, of course. Nothing could be better—I didn't want to be a bother, you know.'

'I know,' she said, nodding gravely. 'But it will be no bother. It will be easy and nice, and everybody will be pleased.' She thought again—men are just big bairns—easily enough managed if you have the way of it.

Iain spent the afternoon working at his boat. It was a very old boat (he had left his good one at the boat-house for the tenants, and the launch also). He fixed a couple of laths on the bottom and nailed them into place, but he was not pleased with the job. Donald appeared while he was still wondering how to improve it.

'Well, Donald?'

'The London people have come,' Donald said. 'There is a lady, and a gentleman, and a young lady, and a wee boy—a wee boy with a white face and dark hair—and there are seven servants——'

'What is Mr. Hetherington Smith like?' enquired the landlord with some anxiety.

'Cha'n eil ann ach Sasunnach,' said Donald helplessly. 'He is chust an Englishman, MacAslan.'

'I knew that,' Iain retorted irritably. 'Can't you tell me anything more about the people than that?'

'Well, now,' said Donald, taking off his cap and scratching his head in his perplexity. 'Well, now, let me be thinking a moment, MacAslan. The London gentleman is big and grey, his hair is grey and his moustache also. And the lady, she is big, too, and nice-looking, but not very young. And the young lady has dark brown hair and a pale face— she is very pretty, the young lady is. And they talk in a funny way—but you will be knowing the way that London people talk, MacAslan?'

'Yes,' said Iain. 'Did they seem pleased with everything?'

'Pleased? And why would they not be pleased?'

'What did they say?' Iain cried. 'Can't you tell me what they said when they saw the house?'

'Och, now, what did they say? The gentleman said, "Has Mister MacAslan never thought of making electric light out of the stream?"'

Iain laughed at Donald's mimicry of Mr. Hetherington Smith, but the laughter did not ring true. It was horrible to feel that these strangers were in his house prying out the poverty of the land.

'I did be taking them round the house,' Donald continued, warming up to his task. 'They liked the portrait of old Mistress MacAslan. The gentleman said it was worth a lot of money, for the artist who painted it was a great man, and he is dead.'

'I know,' said Iain.

'And the big lady said, "What a Scotch face!" and the young lady said she was thinking it was a beautiful face, full of character.'

'What did you show them next?' enquired Iain, whose pride was such that he could not bear to hear of his grandmother being discussed by a set of complete strangers.

'I showed them the gun-room,' Donald said. 'They are having a lot of gentlemen for the twelfth—a big party. The gentleman spoke to me about it. I think he does not know very much about shooting at all. He said to me, "Will you arrange it all, then? And can I hire beaters and dogs?" And then he said, "I suppose you know where the butts

are?" So then I said, " I am MacAslan's head keeper and
I will be arranging all those things for you, Mr. Hetherington Smith. The ghillies have dogs and there are plenty of
beaters to be had in the village. There is no need for you to
be troubling yourself about those things. You have only to
tell me the number of guns." And he looked at me and
said, " I have two guns, but one of the gentlemen who is
coming is a three-gun man." What do you make of that,
MacAslan?'

Iain sat down on the boat and laughed heartily at Donald's face. ' This is what I make of it, Donald,' he said as
soon as he could speak. ' This is what I make of it—you
had better see to it that you are close behind Mr. Hetherington Smith when he lets off his guns. I should carry them
myself if I were you.'

' That is what I made of it, too,' said Donald solemnly.

Morag and Donald stayed and had their supper at the
cottage that evening. It was the easiest way for everyone.
After Iain had finished his simple meal he went upstairs to
his bedroom to finish his unpacking. He could hear the two
of them talking beneath his window, for Morag was in the
little scullery washing up the dishes and Donald was sitting
on the back-door-step smoking his pipe.

' Yes, indeed, there are seven of them,' Donald's deep
voice was saying. ' A butler and six maids—ignorant, helpless creatures, every one of them. The butler is a stout man
with whiskers on his cheeks—he does not know his place,
that one. Strutting about as though the Big House belonged
to him and asking for this and that and the other—Tha
niseachd searb sgìth dhimbh!'

There was a ripple of laughter from Morag.

' And the maids,' Donald continued disgustedly.
There was no end to the things they were asking—' How
ar is it to the nearest town, Mister MacNeil? Is there a

80

bus service? Is there a picture house in the village?'—
and they not half an hour in the house! The cook is a foolish woman; she has no sense at all. " How shall I boil my
kettle with no gas and no electric light?" she asked me.
" Och, you will boil it on the fire like other people, I suppose," I told her. And the housemaid was at me wanting
some electric contrivance for sweeping the rooms—as
though a broom were not good enough for a woman to
sweep with!'

Iain could not help listening. He chuckled quietly to
himself at the way Donald took off the various members of
Mrs. Hetherington Smith's staff. Donald was a born
mimic, but it was very seldom that he would display his
talent before MacAslan. He was too shy. To-night, with
only Morag for audience, he was in great form.

Iain could not hear what Morag said next, but after a
few moments Donald answered, ' Cha n'eil fios agam co
iad ' (I do not know who they are), and then he added, still
speaking in his own tongue: ' But I am telling you, Morag,
the servants know nothing except that they are rich—they
know nothing but that, and they care nothing so long as the
money is good and their stomachs are filled. It is nothing
to them whom they serve.'

Morag had finished her task now; she came out onto the
step and leaned against the lintel of the door. ' But it is
strange, that,' she said slowly. ' They do not know that the
people they serve are any better than themselves? And
what of you, Donald? You will not care to be serving these
people of whom nothing is known?'

' I am MacAslan's man,' replied Donald quietly. ' It is
MacAslan I serve.'

CHAPTER VII

The Fairy Woman

SOME DAYS PASSED. Iain settled down in the small cottage. He saw nothing of his tenants, but he heard of their activities from Donald. Mr. Hetherington Smith had been out with one of his guns, shooting rabbits for practice.

'The gentleman is not a bad shot,' Donald said reflectively, pushing tobacco into the bowl of his big black pipe with a gnarled finger. 'He is slow, and a wee thing stiff— he is not friends with his gun, if you will be knowing what I mean; but he is not a bad shot at all at all, and he is a nice enough gentleman in his way. He said to me, "You tell me what I do wrong, MacNeil," he said—he is not wanting to shame himself in front of his guests, you see—and again he said, "Am I doing all right, MacNeil?" "You are doing fine, Mr. Hetherington Smith," I said to him. "It is chust practice you are wanting, chust practice, and to be knowing your gun—to be knowing the feel of it. Carry it about with you," I said to him. I did not tell him to take it to bed with him, but that is what I would have liked to be telling him.'

"I believe you like Mr. Hetherington Smith," said Iain, smiling at the description.

Donald did not answer. He thought about it seriously. It is true, Donald mused, there is a fondness in me for the man—but he did not say so to MacAslan.

'I wish you would have a look at this boat, Donald,' said Iain at last—he was still tinkering with the wretched thing.

'Look here. If I nail a strip of wood on in one place the old wood crumbles away——'

Donald bent his mind to the problem. 'Och, it is rotten, MacAslan! Why not take my boat if you are wanting a boat at all? The only thing you can be doing with this is to be stretching a piece of canvas across the bad places with strips over it and tar on the top.'

'Yes, I see,' said Iain.

'It will not be a safe boat,' Donald warned him.

'No—but it will do for messing about on a calm day.'

Donald went away after that. He had an appointment with Mr. Hetherington Smith to shoot rabbits. In the afternoon Iain set to work on the old boat in real earnest— he had found a piece of canvas in the wood-shed. He stretched the canvas over the bad places and began to nail it down.

'Do you mind me watching you?' said a small voice suddenly.

Iain looked up and saw a boy in a grey flannel suit—it was not one of the boys from the village. Who could it be? Hadn't Donald said something about a small boy arriving with the Hetherington Smiths?

'Hallo!' said Iain.

'Hallo—you don't mind me watching, do you?'

Iain looked at him more closely. He had a pale face, delicately boned, and large dark eyes. His bare legs were thin and very white.

'Do you like watching people?' Iain asked.

'I like helping better,' the boy replied. 'I suppose—I suppose you don't want anybody to help you, do you? To hold things for you or—or anything——'

'You would get dirty,' objected Iain. 'It's a dirty job, mending boats.'

'I wouldn't mind that a bit!'

Iain said no more; he was immersed in the task he had

83

undertaken. It was not an easy matter to stretch canvas and hold it in position and nail it down . . .

The boy had approached nearer and was watching intently. 'Look!' he said. 'I could hold it down while you nail it—see?' Two small thin hands, very white but amazingly capable, appeared at the edge of the canvas and tugged it into place. Iain nailed it down securely. They worked away together after that—it was certainly much easier. . . .

'There!' said Iain at last. 'That will have to do in the meantime—it's too hot to do any more.' He straightened his back and wiped his forehead. 'You've helped a lot,' he added.

The boy blushed with pleasure. 'It's really a job for two,' he suggested. 'I could come back to-morrow—easily.'

Iain looked at him—there were little beads of moisture below his eyes, and his cheek had a smear of tar across it.

'I hope you haven't got tar on your clothes,' said Iain.

'No, only on my hands '—he showed his hands to Iain. 'Aren't they dirty?' he added proudly.

'You better come into the cottage and wash,' Iain told him.

They went into the cottage and cleaned the tar off with butter, and washed, and dried their hands on the kitchen towel. Iain had never seen a child he liked so much. He was frank and natural, and friendly and amusing without being the least bit cheeky or precocious. I wonder who he thinks I am, Iain reflected, or doesn't he think about it, at all?

'What's your name?' Iain enquired.

'Richard Medworth.'

'Well, Richard, you've got some tar on your face.'

The child held up his face for Iain to clean it off. Iain dipped a cloth in the butter and cleaned it carefully. It was a trustful little face, delicate and childish. Something caught at Iain's heart. 'There, that's better,' he said gruffly.

They left everything in a mess and went into the living-room.

'I must be going now, I s'pose,' Richard said.

'Stay and have tea with me,' suggested Iain. 'You've earned it, you know.'

'I'd like to stay.'

'That's right—I hope you like ginger-nuts.'

Richard said he did. He helped his host to lay the table and followed him into the kitchen to boil the kettle.

'I like being here,' Richard said. 'I suppose you live here always. I live in London, you know. Is there lots of snow here in the winter?—Ellen says there is. Ellen is Mrs. Hevverington Smith's maid, and puts me to bed. Ellen doesn't like it here, she says it's too quiet—she says it gives her the jim-jams. Is there lots of snow, Boatmender?'

Iain was amused at the name, but he answered seriously about the snow, and told Richard how the glen was some-times snowbound for days at a time, and described the deep drifts and the icicles in the burn.

'You can hardly believe it *now*,' Richard said. 'I mean it's so hot now, isn't it? But of course I *do* believe it,' he added quickly, in case the boatmender should think he doubted his word. 'I'd like to be here in the winter. I think it would be lovely——' He prattled on.

Iain found himself listening to the clear childish voice with a strange pleasure. Richard spoke well, but, now and then, a word was deliciously mispronounced. Iain found himself watching for these words. 'I found the matches on the mankle-piece,' Richard announced proudly; and when the tray was ready to carry into the other room he said, 'I'll open the door for you. You can't turn a door-hangle when you're carrying a tray.'

Soon they were seated at the table drinking their tea and eating ginger-nuts out of the tin.

'This is fun,' Richard said with a sigh of pleasure. 'A kind of picnic—isn't it? Mrs. Hevverington Smith's teas are very proper. Thin bread and butter—*you* know."

'Do you like picnics—real picnics?' Iain asked him.

'*Yes.*'

'I like them, too. Sometimes I go for picnics by myself—would you like to come?'

'*Yes,*' he said again. His eyes shone.

'The best place of all for a picnic is an island,' Iain continued. It was a fascinating thing to play on this sensitive instrument—to watch the glow on the little face, the sparkle in the eyes.

'An island!' Richard exclaimed.

'The island in the middle of the loch.'

'Would we—would we be allowed?'

'The island belongs to me,' Iain told him, ' so we can go when we like. There's an old castle on the island; it belonged to my great-great-grandfather and *his* father before him——'

'Is the castle a ruin?' Richard asked. He was more interested in the castle than its owners.

'Yes, it's a ruin,' Iain replied; 'but one of the rooms in the tower is still standing—still fairly watertight. I've got a cupboard there to keep things in—picnic things—just a candle and a kettle and a tin of biscuits——'

'Oh, I *would* like to go!' Richard cried eagerly. 'Would you really take me some day—when the boat is mended?'

Iain smiled at him. 'When the boat is mended,' he agreed.

'What else is there?' Richard wanted to know.

'Not much else, I'm afraid,' said Iain. 'I made the cupboard myself when I was a boy—older than you, of course

—and I made a table and a settle (a sort of wooden sofa with a high back). Donald helped me—you know Donald MacNeil, don't you?'

'Yes. Did you play there—when you were a boy—did you play at shipwrecks and things?'

'Yes, we used to play all sorts of games. Brigands and pirates and things like that. The castle made a splendid brigands' lair.'

They had finished tea by this time and Iain lighted his pipe. Richard watched him with interest.

'D'you like pipes best?' he enquired. 'Mr. Hevvering-ton Smith smokes cigars.'

'I like a pipe best,' Iain told him. 'And it's just as well. I couldn't afford cigars if I *did* like them.'

'We're poor, too,' Richard said thoughtfully, 'Mummy and me. When I'm grown up I'm going to make lots and lots of money for Mummy.' He was silent for a moment, and then he said, 'I s'pose I'd better be going now, Boat-mender. They might be wondering. P'r'aps I'd better go, if you don't mind.'

'Perhaps you should,' Iain agreed. He did not want a search-party from Ardfalloch House invading his privacy.

'Can I come back to-morrow and help you with the boat?' Richard enquired a trifle anxiously.

'Yes, if you like.'

Richard slipped down off his chair and held out his hand gravely. 'Good-bye,' he said.

The house felt very empty when he had gone.

The next morning Iain had started work upon his boat when he heard a shrill 'Coo-ee,' and, looking up, he saw Richard coming down the path out of the woods. There was a lady with him, a slim figure in well-fitting tweeds. . . .

Iain put down his tools and swore softly. I ought to have foreseen this, he thought.

'Mummy's come to see you, Boatmender!' cried Richard, pulling the lady along with one hand.

She said, 'I wanted to thank you for being kind to Richard.'

Iain did not raise his eyes. He stood there in silence, a frown creasing his brows. He was angry, angry and ashamed. He felt it a kind of insult that he should thus be taken at a disadvantage. How dared she invade his solitude, discover him in such an invidious position—dirty and untidy, a pariah on his own land?

She said a trifle diffidently, 'I hope—I hope Richard wasn't a nuisance——'

Iain looked at the boy. The eagerness had faded from his face, he felt that something was wrong. The boatmender was different to-day—he wasn't pleased.

'Richard was very useful,' said Iain quickly. He was not going to hurt the child.

Linda Medworth looked at the boatmender in surprise. He was not in the least like her preconceived idea of the man. Richard had prattled of the boatmender without ceasing, but this man was no boatmender—except, of course, that he was engaged in mending a boat—this man was a gentleman; he spoke like a gentleman, as far as she could judge by the one curt sentence he had uttered, and he was amazingly good-looking. He was rather dirty and untidy, but there was something about him—— The extraordinary idea visited her that he was a prince in disguise, that she had seen him before—somewhere—in different circumstances. It was an absurd notion, it flashed through her mind and was gone.

Iain's anger subsided a little. He realised that he was being foolish. It was his fault that he was in an invidious position—not theirs. He raised his eyes and looked at Richard's mother . . .

It was the lady of his dreams . . . it was the girl . . . the fairy woman who had stolen his heart. He stood there staring at her as if he had been turned to stone.

She was older, of course, and the dark blue eyes were a little shadowed as if troubles had visited her and left their mark. She was beautiful—more beautiful, even, than he had remembered. There was a sort of radiance in her face, and her skin had the same transparent whiteness as Richard's skin. He gazed at her—he could not speak. Did she remember him, he wondered.

Richard had run across the soft turf to the boat. He was looking at it carefully, examining the work that had been done that morning.

'Come on, Boatmender,' he cried impatiently. 'Come and hammer in the nails. Mummy can't wait—can you?' he added, anxious for her to be gone so that the work could start.

Linda smiled at his impatience. 'Can you really put up with him?' she said to Iain. 'I am going for a little walk and I could call for him on my way home.'

'He can stay,' said Iain ungraciously.

She looked at him doubtfully, wondering what to do. The man didn't seem very keen for Richard to stay, and she was too anxious for her child's welfare to leave him if the man were not going to be 'nice.'

Why am I so stupid? he thought; but he could not speak naturally. He was too upset, too overwhelmed by the sudden meeting; and the dregs of his anger were still there, embittering him. He had remembered her so long, and she had forgotten him. He would have chosen to appear before her in his proper guise as the proud Highland gentleman that he really was, and, instead of this, she had come upon him when he was engaged upon a menial task, clad in his oldest and most disreputable garments.

Iain could not trust himself to speak. He turned away from her to the boat and seized the hammer. The work began vigorously. . . .

Linda watched them for a few moments, and then she went away—somewhat reluctantly.

The work went on. Iain was hammering away his anger; he had been ungracious, he had been boorish, stupid. The nails were being driven into himself. There, he thought as he drove them in—there, take that, you fool, and that, and that—she won't ever want to speak to you again—that's certain. I suppose you're pleased with what you've done. She thinks you're a peasant, of course—only no peasant would have behaved as rudely. Donald would have asked her into his house and offered her a glass of milk—any of them would. It was left to MacAslan to behave like a lout —like a boor—like a savage from the wilds.

The heat was intense, not a breath of wind stirred the leaves of the surrounding trees. Iain brushed the sweat from his brow, and worked on more fiercely than before.

Suddenly the small hands, which had been tugging at the canvas and handing the nails, faltered in their task. Richard gave a little sigh and collapsed in a limp heap at his feet.

Iain dropped the hammer with a clatter. 'My God!' he said aloud, 'the child has fainted.' He was appalled when he saw the white still face bedewed with perspiration— appalled by what he had done. For a horrible moment he thought the child was dead.

He lifted the small light body in his arms and carried it into the house.

'Morag!' he called. 'Look what I've done—Morag!'

She came running in from the kitchen. 'Och!' she cried in dismay. 'It is the little lad—what is it that is on him? See, MacAslan, lay him here on the sofa——'

'Bring brandy, Morag,' Iain told her.

'Cold water is best,' she cried.

They put him down on the sofa and Morag fetched cold water and bathed his head. Iain watched her, almost beside himself with anxiety and remorse.

'It was my fault,' he kept saying. 'I kept the child out there in the boiling sun—it was my fault.'

'Do not be troubling too much,' Morag whispered. 'See, the little lad is better.'

He opened his eyes and smiled at Iain rather wanly.

'Hallo, old chap!' Iain said.

'Hallo, Boatmender—I've—I've been—asleep,' Richard said faintly.

'I know. It was very hot—much too hot to work.'

'I feel—funny——'

'You're all right, old chap,' Iain told him, trying to believe it was true.

Morag poured some brandy into a small glass and held it to his lips.

'Is it medsun?' he asked anxiously.

'Yes,' nodded Iain. 'Drink it up quickly like a good boy.'

'The wee lamb,' soothed Morag. 'It will make you better, little son.'

He drank it obediently, coughing and spluttering as the fiery liquid caught his throat, but a tinge of colour came back to the pinched face and the lips lost their blue pallor.

'He is better,' Morag whispered. 'MacAslan need not be worrying himself too much——'

'Worrying!' whispered Iain fiercely. 'I'm a fool and a villain combined to keep him out there in the sun—working him to death, and all because I was angry with myself——'

'Cha n'eil a ro thìnn,' comforted Morag. 'He is fine now. Lie quiet on the couch, little lamb, and you will be fine. See, his colour has come back. Chaidh e ann an laigse —he is fine now.'

She brought a blanket and tucked it round him and arranged the cushion more comfortably behind his head.

'The medsun made me better,' Richard said.

' That's splendid! ' Iain told him. ' Just lie quiet for a bit—it was too hot, you know.'

Richard beckoned to him to come closer and whispered, What's her name, Boatmender? Is she your cook?'

' Her name is Morag,' replied Iain softly. ' And she is Donald MacNeil's wife. She comes in and cooks my dinner for me.'

Richard nodded. It was always satisfactory to have your questions answered sensibly. He said, ' I like her. She's pretty and nice. She can stay with me while you finish the boat.'

' I'll stay with you,' Iain said.

' No, you must finish the boat—d'you think you can manage by yourself? You see we must get it finished soon because of the picnic.'

Iain did not want to leave him, but he saw that the child was worrying. It was better to do as he wanted.

CHAPTER VIII

Morag's Story

Morag busied herself putting the room to rights. She was aware of bright eyes following her as she moved about. Presently she came over to the sofa and stood there, looking down at him. Her heart turned over in her breast—how pretty he was, she thought. She would like a little son—a little son with dark hair—not red, like her own fiery mop, but dark and smooth—a little son with a pale face and dark eyes.

'Talk to me, Morag,' he said. 'At least if you're not too busy.'

'I am not busy,' Morag said. 'MacAslan's dinner is on. There is little for me to do.'

He made room for her on the sofa, and she sat down on the edge of it, settling the rug about his slim body.

'Tell me a story,' said Richard.

'Och, now—and what would I be telling you about?'

'Anything,' he said, looking at her eagerly. He knew from her face that she was thinking of something to tell him, and only wanted a little persuasion. 'Do tell me a story, Morag. I don't mind what it's about. I like *all* kinds of stories."

Like most of her race she was a born story-teller, and she was quite willing to be persuaded. 'Well now,' she said. 'Well now, perhaps I might be telling you about my uncle—would that do?'

Richard nodded, his eyes intent on her face.

Morag clasped her hands round her knees and leaned back a little; she shook her hair back from her face and began:

' Well, you must know that my uncle lived in a wee bothy, close by a fairies' hill. You will have seen the fairies' hill on the other side of the Big House—it is a green round hill —round like a bee-skep. Well then, the fairies' hill where my uncle was living was like that one, so you will be knowing what it was like. My uncle was knowing it was a fairies' hill and he was careful not to offend the Little People. He was putting out milk for them at night, and a handful of meal when he could be sparing it, and he did not gather his kindling in the woods close by, but took care to gather it where he would not be troubling the Little People. Och, he was very careful at first! But, as time went by, my uncle was not so careful. He had lived beside the Little People for so long and they had not harmed him—he was beginning to think there was no harm in them at all. So one day, when he was tired with working and the kindling had run short for his fire, he went into the woods on the hill and gathered some sticks. The Little People might not have been minding so much for the one time, but my uncle went again. The Little People had not harmed him the first time, so he went a second time and a third time—and the Little People were angry.'

' Is it true, Morag?' asked Richard excitedly. ' Are there really fairies living in the round green hill?'

' Och, no, it is not true,' Morag said. If she had really believed in it herself she would not have told him. She was of the transition generation, the generation which neither believes nor disbelieves. Her parents believed in the legends and superstitions of the countryside with implicit faith—her children, if she had any, would be complete sceptics.

' But if it was your uncle it must be true,' Richard urged

her eagerly. 'If it was your very own uncle it happened
to——'

'It is true for me,' she said thoughtfully. 'But it is not
true for you, Richard. For you it is chust a story that Morag
is telling you—chust that and no more.'

'But if it is true it must be true for everybody.'

She shook her head. 'No, it is not, then,' she told him.
'It is true for me, for it was my uncle. For you it is chust a
story.'

'Well, go on,' he said. 'What happened when the Little
People were angry?'

'They came out at night from their little houses inside
the hill,' Morag said, 'and they came down to the bothy
where my uncle was sleeping, and they took away the good
that was in everything. And then it was a bad way my
uncle was in, for the walls of the bothy did not be keeping
out the wind and the rain any more—the wind and the rain
did be blowing through the little house, and the——'

'But how?' Richard said, interrupting the tale again.
'How could it, Morag?'

'Well,' she said, 'and it is quite simple, then. The wee
house was there, and it was looking chust the same as ever,
and the walls were there to feel with your hands, but there
was no goodness in the walls any more, to keep out the rain
and the wind, and the rain and the wind were blowing
through the little house the same as if it was blowing across
the moor.'

'Did you see it?' Richard enquired.

'No, I did not see it, but my father saw it, and he would
be telling us about it when we were children. Often and
often he would be telling us. But that was not the only
thing that happened. The Little People took away the good
that was in the meal, so that the meal had no goodness in it
at all, and they took away the goodness that was in the
cow, so that there was no goodness in the milk. Well, my

uncle he got thin and pale, and there was Fear in his eyes
(for he did be knowing what the meaning of it was), so that
when his friends went to see him they could not talk to him
in comfort. They would sit with him in his little house,
talking of this and that—but never talking of the Little
People or what was happening to my uncle, for that would
not be lucky at all—they would sit there with the collars of
their coats about their ears for the wind that was blowing
through the walls. And when they would be coming away
they would be whispering to one another, and crossing their
breasts for the Fear that was in that place. Well, one day
when they went to see my uncle he was not there, and there
was no sign of him in the little field, nor in the byre. Only
the cow was in the byre, lowing with pain, for she had not
been milked that day, and her bag was full. And everybody
knew that the Little People had come at last and taken my
uncle away to be their servant to them in their houses; to
tend their cattle and to draw water and hew wood. A year
and a day passed, and my uncle came back, but there was
nothing in him at all when he came back; no memory of
what had happened to him, and no sense, no sense at all. He
came to my home to live, for he could not be taking care of
himself any more.'

'But they were bad fairies, then!' Richard cried.

'I think they are neither bad nor good—or perhaps they
would be both,' Morag said in a puzzled manner. 'For
there are good things they are doing as well as bad things
when they do be liking people.'

'I thought fairies were good,' said Richard. 'I thought
they were good and pretty and flew about with wings——'

'Och, no!' Morag replied. 'Those are not real fairies
at all—those are chust bairns' tales. The Little People do
not be having wings. They are like us, only not so big.
Down below in their hills they have their homes, and their
homes are like our homes. They have fires and beds, and the

women cook and spin, and the men take care of the beasts chust like we do. They have no need of wings, the Little People, for they can fly on the wind; and they move about without noise so we cannot be hearing them—and we cannot be seeing them——'

Morag stopped and glanced nervously over her shoulder. She was moved to sudden terror by her own tale.

'Then it's *true*,' Richard said, his eyes shining with excitement. 'It's true—it must be true if it happened to your uncle and you saw him——'

'Och, no—it's chust nonsense! You must not be believing it at all, Richard. It is chust Morag's story to pass the time away.'

She was half sorry, now, that she had told the story, and more than half afraid. It was not lucky to speak of the Little People—they do not like to be spoken of—and Morag had spoken of them to this child who was not of her own people.

She had started to tell the story in a spirit of disbelief, to while away the time for a sick child—but the story had gripped her in the telling of it, and she believed it now, just as she had believed it when she was a child and the old crazy man had come to live with them in their house. She could see, again, his vacant, staring eyes, and the queer, vague movements of his wrinkled hands, and she felt again the strange cold shudder of fear creeping up her back.

'Och, now, look at the time!' she exclaimed, jumping up and trying to shake off the discomfort that had invaded her being. 'I must be putting on the potatoes for MacAslan's dinner——'

When Linda returned from her walk she found Iain working at the boat. He looked up and saw her coming—he had been watching for her for the last half-hour, with only one eye upon his work. He had thought of all that he would

say to her, but, now that she was here, the carefully prepared phrases left him, and there seemed to be nothing he
could say. How could he excuse his behaviour? She would
be angry with him and justly angry—the child had been
left in his care. He put down his hammer and went to
meet her.

'Has Richard gone home?' she asked.

His pulses fluttered again at the sound of her voice—how
was he to tell her? He must not frighten her, must not
make too much of Richard's collapse. He fixed his eyes on
her shoes—neat brown brogues, they were, and the feet
inside them were narrow and well-shaped, with arching
insteps.

'Where is Richard?' she said again.

'In my house,' Iain replied, finding his voice with some
difficulty. 'The sun was very hot—I should have seen it
was too hot for him——'

'Do you mean he's ill?' she enquired, her voice sharp-
ened by anxiety.

'He *was* ill,' said Iain. 'He seems all right now. It was
just the heat, I think. He never told me it was too much for
him. He is such a plucky little fellow——'

She was hurrying up the path, but, at his last words, she
turned and faced him. 'You really think that?' she asked
breathlessly.

'What?'

'That he is plucky.'

'Of course. Most children would have given in. Richard
went on until he collapsed.'

'Collapsed!' she echoed, with returning anxiety.

'He fainted,' Iain told her, speaking in a low voice, for
they were near the door now and he did not want Richard to
hear them discussing him. 'He fainted. It was the heat. I
can't tell you how sorry I am—it was all my fault—I should
have seen—I carried him into the house and he was all right

98

in a few minutes, but we made him keep quiet.' Iain opened the door as he spoke and showed her into his house.

Richard was sitting on the edge of the sofa. He was carrying on a conversation with Morag who was in the kitchen. Iain was thankful to see that he looked quite himself again.

'Can I get up?' Richard said, smiling at his mother. 'Can I get up now? I promised Morag I wouldn't get up till the boatmender said I could—so can I now?'

His mother nodded.

He ran across the room and jumped into her arms. 'Did you have a nice walk?' he asked her with his arms round her neck.

'A lovely walk.'

Iain watched the little scene with a strange pain. They were so much to each other—these two—so alike in their slim grace, so near to each other. Was there room for another in their hearts? Iain felt left out of it, he felt like an intruder in his own house—it was absurd to feel that, but he couldn't help it. Perhaps her husband is alive, he thought, and yet, somehow, I feel she is free. How am I to find out?

He pulled a chair forward for her, and she sat down with the boy on her knee.

'I hope he'll be all right,' Iain said anxiously.

'I'm fine,' said Richard, smiling. 'That's what Morag says—I'm fine. Morag is Mr. MacNeil's wife and she cooks the boatmender's dinner for him. She's nice and pretty and I like her——'

Morag came in and overheard the last words. She blushed and smiled attractively. She certainly was pretty, Linda thought. What was she doing here?—besides cooking the boatmender's dinner—it seemed queer. Morag was carrying a tray with tea and a glass of milk and some ginger-nuts.

'Oh, I couldn't!' Linda exclaimed. 'It's almost lunch-time——'

'But you must,' Iain told her seriously. 'Morag knows that you can't go into a Highlander's house without partaking of his hospitality.'

'That is so,' said Morag, smiling. 'It would not be the right thing at all——'

They had tea together and Richard drank some milk. Iain was more comfortable with her now—now that she was actually in his house, partaking of his food, she was no longer a dream. He watched her white teeth crunching the hard biscuit, and he watched the lovely line of her neck as she turned her head, and the softness of her eyes as she spoke to her boy. He told himself she was all he had thought—and more. She was perfect; she was his; she must be his—nothing could stand in the way.

At last she stood up and said they must go.

'Come, Richard—are you feeling all right?' she said. 'Well enough to walk home?'

'But he must have a horse,' Iain cried.

'A horse?' queried Richard. 'Have you got a horse? Where's the horse, Boatmender?'

'Here,' said Iain. He stooped down and made a back for the boy.

'Hurrah!' cried Richard, jumping onto the boatmender's back. 'Hurrah, I've got a horse!'

Iain pranced round the room like a very high-spirited horse indeed—it was great fun.

'Well,' said Linda doubtfully, 'are you sure he won't be too heavy for you?'

They went out together and struck up towards the trees. The child was light and he clung with his knees. Iain felt he could have walked miles with Richard on his back, he liked the feel of the soft arms round his neck. He felt nearer to the mother through the child's nearness.

100

Linda went ahead up the rough path through the woods. She stepped, surefootedly, from root to root, raising herself lightly on the ball of each foot; springing over the moist patches like a deer. That was how a woman should walk, Iain thought; and her ankles were right, too—strong and fine (but not too fine) as ankles should be.

'How quiet it is!' Linda said, pausing for a moment on the top of the hill before the path dropped down to Ardfalloch jetty. 'How quiet and—and golden!'

It was very hot and still. The skies seemed to press down upon the glen. Across the loch came the sound of a cart rumbling over a stony road. They heard the lurch and rattle as the heavy wheels rocked to and fro, the squeak of the axle.

Iain stood still beside her.

'Are those pigeons?' Linda asked in a low voice.

'Yes,' he said. 'Listen.'

They listened.

'I like it,' Richard said softly. 'It's a sad kind of song—but *nicely* sad, don't you think?'

They went on together. There was a bond between them now—a bond between the three of them. There was no need to talk, the woods spoke to them, and the golden sunshine bathed them all in one radiant bath. Iain thought: If the place were mine—if I had not let it—if I could say to her 'This is mine,' and take her, and show it to her . . . but if I had not let it she would not be here. . . .

CHAPTER IX

Ardfalloch Inn

For the remainder of the day Iain could think of nothing but her face—pale and fine-drawn beneath the brim of her shady hat—of the way she moved, the buoyancy of her step as she breasted the hill; he could hear nothing but her soft laugh, and the notes of her voice. He tried to interest himself in his boat, and, when that failed, in a book that had just come from the library—it was no use.

He went to bed and slept fitfully, dreaming that he had lost her again, that she had gone from the glen and he could not find her. . . . He rose early and made his breakfast, then he took his field-glasses and went up on to the hill. The pull that drew him to her was like the pull of a magnet, it was irresistible. He thought: If I could just see her, even in the distance, so that I would know she was still here. . . . Perhaps she would come. Perhaps Richard would come and she with him.

The day moved on and the sun rose higher; it was not so hot to-day, for there was a breeze, and white clouds moving slowly across the blue sky. He finished tarring his boat that afternoon and left it to dry. By that time he was dirty, and hot in spite of the breeze, and, when he had cleaned most of the tar off his person, he caught up his towel and went down to bathe. The tide was coming in, creeping up the rocks, oozing between the stones, trickling gently between the half-dry seaweed. The water near the shore was quite warm, but, as he waded in, it grew colder . . . he struck out boldly, the small waves flipping him in the face.

When he came out of the water he was tingling all over. He felt refreshed in mind and body, some of his impatience had been washed away. He decided to walk over the hill to Ardfalloch Village and hear what was going on. It would be a change.

Ardfalloch Village was a small place—just a double row of cottages, a post office and a shop. The inn was kept by a big burly man called MacTaggart—it was a comfortable place, clean, and well run, and the village took full advantage of its amenities. There were four or five men in the bar-parlour when Iain walked in and asked for a drink. They greeted him with the respectful familiarity of their breed; one of them offered him an evening paper. They were talking about some sheep-dog trials which had taken place that afternoon, and, after a few minutes' general conversation, they returned to the subject.

Iain felt happy and peaceful. The bathe and the walk had eased the fever in his blood. He drank his beer and glanced through the paper and listened with one ear to the conversation. He was at home with these men, and they with him. He understood them. They were staunch and brave, with a kind of childish simplicity of heart; they were also deep and secret as their own mountain lochs; they respected themselves and each other. There were black sheep among them, of course, as there are amongst any community, but, for the most part, they were good-living men with high ideals. It was a fine breed.

You could tell their professions by looking at them—even if you did not know them. Alec Finlay could be nothing else but a shepherd. He had a weatherbeaten face with high cheek-bones, and sunken chaps, and pale-blue eyes that could see far on the hills, with deep brown creases at the corners. Nobody except a shepherd could have such patient eyes, and his hands were patient, too. Iain had seen them tending a sick sheep and knew how gentle those great gnarled hands could be. Beside Finlay, MacTaggart was commonplace. His work was different: he was indoors most of the day, but his face was not exactly an 'indoor' face, it was round and smooth and rosy. He wore a white apron tied tightly across his broad stomach. The other men were farmers—two of them from Balnafin way, and the third from Auchencraigs, one of Iain's own farms—Auchencraigs was the smallest croft on Iain's estate and the poorest. Iain always felt sorry for Alec MacNeil—(he was one of Donald's numerous cousins)—the man looked overworked and underfed, and, most probably, was both. That man is a real hero, Iain thought; it's a lone fight against poverty and the elements. This land is not intended for farming, and Nature seems inimical to farmers. I must do something for Alec MacNeil when I get the money from Hetherington Smith. What would he like, I wonder?

Iain caught the man's eyes and leaned forward. 'How are things, Alec?' he enquired with his interested smile.

'Things are not so bad at all, MacAslan,' replied the man. 'The London shentleman is wanting ghillies and the children are to be beating. It is Donal' that has been arranging it all—Och, we will be doing not so bad.'

'Perhaps I could build you a few pigsties,' suggested Iain.

Alec's eyes brightened. 'Och, and that would be grand!' he said. 'We could be doing nicely with some pigs— Och, it would be grand—if it would not be troubling MacAslan——'

'That's settled then,' Iain said. 'But don't say too much about it, Alec, or everybody in the glen will be wanting pigsties.'

Alec laughed. 'And that is true,' he said. 'I will keep my mouth shut, MacAslan.'

'That's right—keep your mouth shut and you shall have what you want,' Iain told him.

They were so intent upon their discussion that they did not notice the door open to admit a new-comer.

'Can I get a drink here?' he enquired, looking round the room.

Iain looked up and saw a tall, very broad-shouldered man in a brown check overcoat and a soft hat. He had a fair moustache—rather bushy—and his eyes were very bright and roving.

MacTaggart started to his feet. 'Indeed and you can, sir,' he said politely.

The new-comer leaned against the bar counter, and consumed his drink slowly, conversing with the landlord in a pleasant English voice. He asked questions about the fishing in the neighbourhood, and whether there was any likelihood of his being able to get a day on the river.

'The river is mostly Mr. Finlay's,' said MacTaggart; 'Mr. Finlay is the man—he might give you a day.'

'I'd like that,' said the stranger. 'I'm fond of fishing, but what I've really come for is to observe bird life in the district.' He was talking to the whole room now, leaning comfortably against the counter with the glass in his hand. 'I'm writing a treatise on the habits of birds.'

The company listened to him politely. If they thought it a queer occupation to observe the habits of birds they did not show it. A man could do what he liked—and, if he liked things that seemed odd to other people, that was his own affair.

'Can you give me a bed here?' enquired the stranger, turning towards the landlord.

'And why not?' replied MacTaggart hospitably.

The stranger looked a trifle puzzled at this truly Highland reply to his question.

'You can?' he enquired again.

'And why not, indeed—it will be a pleasure.'

'Good. That's settled. I don't know how long I shall be staying—it depends on the birds,'—he smiled in a queer way, Iain thought, and added, 'My name's Middleton—James Middleton.'

'And would the gentleman be having any luggage?' Mac-Taggaret asked anxiously.

'It's outside in the taxi,' Middleton said. 'I came over from a place called Balnafin in the oldest taxi I've ever seen —over the worst road. The fellow's waiting outside with my gear. Hi! give the fellow a drink,' he called after Mac-Taggart as that worthy waddled off to the door to arrange for his new guest's luggage to be brought in.

Mr. Middleton took off his hat and his overcoat and hung them on the rack behind the door. He smoothed his fair hair and took a seat near Iain.

'Nice place, this,' he said conversationally.

Iain was quite pleased to talk to the man, and he found him interesting. He had travelled a lot and he made his reminiscences amusing. Soon they were all listening to him. He told some funny stories rather well—they were not drawing-room stories, but this was not a drawing-room, and Iain, although he would not have cared to repeat them himself, was not such a fool as to take exception to them. He thought the man amusing—rather a good fellow in his way —not the sort of man one would choose for an intimate, but excellent company for an evening of this kind.

It was late when Iain rose to depart. Middleton rose, too, and offered to walk home with him, saying that he wanted a breath of fresh air before turning in.

'Can we see Ardfalloch—the house, I mean— from this path?' enquired Middleton as they walked along.

'No, it's farther down the loch,' Iain said. 'You could see it from the hill, of course.'

'Hetherington Smith has got it, hasn't he?'

'Yes, d'you know him?'

'I've met him,' Middleton said. 'Don't suppose for a moment he'd remember me. D'you know who he's got staying there?'

Iain smiled—it was easy to see through the man's elaborately casual questions. Quite obviously Middleton wanted to get a footing at Ardfalloch. It was *shooting* birds he was after, not observing their habits. Iain had noticed a gun-case amongst the other luggage that had been brought into the inn—rather a battered-looking gun-case with 'J.M.' in large letters on the side. He thought: Well, why shouldn't he shoot my grouse? I don't care. Why shouldn't he get a footing at Ardfalloch if that's what he wants?

'I don't know who's coming for the twelfth,' Iain said slowly. 'My keeper tells me he's got people coming. If you do meet the Hetherington Smiths I'd rather you didn't mention my name.'

'Of course not,' Middleton said. 'It's no business of mine—nor of theirs either as far as I can see.' He was silent for a moment and then he added, 'I thought the Hetherington Smiths had some people staying with them *now.*'

Iain felt a twinge of annoyance—he had not wanted to mention the Medworths to this man. But after all it was foolish not to—he could hear about them from anybody—and he had been quite decent.

'Yes,' he said, trying not to sound reluctant; 'there's a Mrs. Medworth staying there.'

'She has a boy, hasn't she?'

'Yes.'

'I've met her. Good-looking woman, isn't she?'

'Yes,' said Iain. He could not help sounding reluctant—he didn't like to think that this man had met her and admired her. This man wasn't the sort of man—quite a good fellow, of course, but . . .

' Have you got a boat on the loch?' Middleton enquired.

' Yes—such as it is. You can have it any time you like you get mackerel out there——'

' Thanks,' Middleton said. ' I'll take you at your word.'

' Do. Look me up some time and have a drink.'

They shook hands and parted; Iain went home to bed.

CHAPTER X

The Storm

THE day before the twelfth was a Sunday; Iain woke late. He had been dreaming all night—dreaming that he was at home in his own house—and, for a few moments, his sleep-dazed brain refused to adjust itself to its new conditions. Why was it that the window was in the wrong position—and so small? And the roof had been squeezed down over his head. . . . Gradually the realisation of where he was, and of all that had happened, came to Iain. He got out of bed and looked out of the window. The loch was very calm and dark, reflecting grey skies. The trees stood dejectedly, their leaves hung down—there was not a flutter amongst them. It was very quiet, even the birds seemed to have joined in the conspiracy of silence. It doesn't look too well, Iain thought.

He spent the morning wandering about rather aimlessly. Hoping that Richard might come—or Richard's mother. He was restless and unhappy. It seemed so strange that to-morrow was the twelfth and he would not be shooting. Perhaps it would be better to go to Edinburgh—to give up the whole thing—if it had not been for Mrs. Medworth he would have gone to Edinburgh. But I can't leave Ard-falloch while she's here, he thought—until I know whether she's free, until I know all about her.

To-day he felt depressed and wretched about everything. He felt certain that her husband was alive, that she was not for him—everything was hopeless and dark like the skies.

109

Ardfalloch in August

The skies seemed to press down upon the glen, the barometer was falling rapidly.

After tea, Iain took his field-glasses and seated himself at the edge of the loch. The loch was very still, it was a queer dull-grey colour—like lead—and there was no transparency in the water. The mountains were very clear, outlined harshly against the sky. The air was so heavy that the rare sounds in the glen were intensified—a dog barked twice. A flight of geese flapped heavily over his head and fled away inland.

There was a storm coming. Iain had felt it all day. It was the imminence of the storm that had depressed his spirits and crushed his optimism.

' I wish to God it would come, and be done with it!' he said aloud.

He looked over towards the island—was that a boat? None of the natives would be so foolish and misguided as to be caught in a storm on the loch—who could it be? He focused his glasses and saw that there were two people in the boat—a man and a woman. They were rowing towards Ardfalloch. Iain kept the glasses glued to the boat—in a few minutes he was practically certain that the woman was Mrs. Medworth.

He fetched his waterproof from the cottage and strode off rapidly in the direction of Ardfalloch jetty. The loch was unnaturally calm, not a ripple broke its leaden surface. He went quickly through the woods; there was a queer sighing sound in the trees now, and a few leaves, immaturely withered, fell about his ears.

Iain ran onto the narrow breakwater and shouted—the boat was about two hundred yards away. He shouted again and waved and beckoned. The man in the boat looked up and saw him. He waved again and yelled with all his might. He thought: Can't the damned fool understand? Can't he feel the tension in the air? Is the man crazy?

The Storm

The man evidently did understand at last: he bent to his oars, and the boat shot towards the pier. Iain saw that the second figure in the boat was indeed Mrs. Medworth. She was sitting quite still, with her hands folded in her lap. As the boat came nearer he could see her face—he thought it was paler than usual, but it was perfectly composed. They were only about fifty yards away. He thought: They will do it—but only just. . . .

They were twenty yards away . . . now ten . . . the trees were soughing. A shower of leaves flew past his head. The wind struck him full on the back—it was like a blow—Iain braced himself against its force. He saw the wind touch the surface of the loch beyond the boat, and the loch shiver like a mirror broken to pieces. . . . The boat was quite near now, and Iain was waiting. The full crash of the wind broke upon them as the boat touched the pier.

The man scrambled out with the painter; Iain caught him as he stumbled on the rocks and seized the rope from his hand—and then, suddenly, he saw the boat drifting away and realised that the rope was slipping through the ring on the boat.

There was no time to speak—no time even to think. Iain flung himself into the water and seized hold of the boat with both hands. The wind swept down out of the woods like a mad thing, bending the trees almost double with its force; it caught the boat and swept it out into the loch like a withered leaf. Iain clung to it with all his strength, he was breathless, half drowned with spray. He thought: I shall never be able to climb in—I must just hang on. His clothes were sodden now, heavy with water. The wind roared in his ears. . . .

Suddenly he felt a hand tugging at his collar and he looked up and saw her face. It was quite close to his face, for she was kneeling in the boat, and he had time to marvel that there was no fear in it, but only determination and urgency. She had one arm over the side of the boat and he saw what she meant him to do. He made a frightful effort and lifted one knee, she seized it and pulled it over the side. With an almost superhuman effort Iain raised his body—the boat heeled over dangerously; for one awful moment he thought it was going to capsize. The water rushed over the side like a torrent, carrying him with it—he rolled over into the bottom of the boat.

The wind was increasing in force every moment as they were swept farther out into the loch, farther from the shore. It was like a live force, malicious in its intensity. (Fortunately the boat was strong and seaworthy, and broad in the beam, or it would have been overturned.)

Iain scrambled up and seized the oars—they were almost wrenched out of his hands, but he clung to them stubbornly and tried to get the bows into the wind.

The wind was too strong, blowing down upon the loch, for the waves to rise; it shrieked and whistled past his head. The boat rocked and wallowed—the water which had come over the side was swishing about in the bottom. Iain shouted to his companion to bail and signalled to her that there was a tin under the seat. She could not hear a word he said, for the wind took the words out of his mouth and scattered them, but she realised what he meant her to do, and found the tin. She crouched in the bottom of the boat and tried to bail.

Every nerve and sinew in Iain was concentrated in fighting the wind. He saw that they were being blown straight onto the island—he tried to visualise what would happen when they struck. He knew the island as he knew the palm of his hand and he saw that their only chance was the little bay. If he could arrange for them to be blown into the bay between the two jutting rocks they would have a better chance. It was almost impossible to steer the water-logged boat, his whole energy was taken up in preventing it from being swamped. There was no rain yet, but the skies were dark and the air was full of spray, so that it was difficult to see where they were going.

They approached the island rapidly—the waves were breaking on the rocks and curling back, green and hungry— or leaping up like fountains. Iain saw that they were being driven straight onto the rocks; he dipped his oars and pulled with all his might. The boat was a little lightened now, and it answered feebly to his efforts—he pulled at the oars like a madman—his chest was almost bursting. A wave broke over the rock and curled back over the boat's gunwale; it swept them into the bay. He dropped the oars and seized her in his arms—the boat was sinking now—it sank under his feet. He flung himself forward out of the boat and his feet found the shingle—the backwash caught at his legs and the stones rattled down the slope, but the wind was behind him, pushing him on. He staggered for a moment and then stumbled forward up the slope.

The wind still shrieked and howled amongst the trees and tore at their hair and clothes, the spray was all about them like salt rain, but there was firm earth beneath them— they were safe. He put her on her feet and took her arm in a firm grip—it was impossible to speak, for the noise of the wind was appalling. The trees were bent before it like reeds, broken branches fell upon their heads as they staggered up the slope and through the trees to the entrance of the castle. The wide doorway gaped before them. He guided her inside. . . .

It was quite dark inside the hall, but they were in shelter, they were out of the wind. They could hear it shrieking outside like a beast deprived of its prey, but it could not reach them now—those battered walls had survived worse gales.

The sudden deliverance from the wind's fury was almost

uncanny. Their bodies, attuned to its buffetings, had suddenly found harbourage. Iain wondered what she was thinking—and feeling. He could not see her face. It had been a terrific experience for anybody to go through, and this was a delicately nurtured woman—a town-bred woman, or so he imagined. He said in a matter-of-fact voice: 'I hope you're not very wet.'

He was amazed to hear a low laugh in the darkness.

'Are you—are you laughing?' he said incredulously.

'I'm sorry—but it sounded so funny,' she said.

'What sounded funny?'

'I hope you're not very wet.'

He had to laugh, too, at her mimicry of his casual tone. 'Well, but I hope you aren't very wet,' he told her, 'because, you see, I haven't got anything else for you to wear —and we shall probably be here all night.'

'It seems to me we're very lucky to be here at all,' she said gravely. 'If it hadn't been for you I should have been at the bottom of the loch—and that would have been a good deal wetter.'

He couldn't deny this if he had wanted to—and he didn't want to. 'We must light a fire,' he said sensibly. 'That's the first thing to do. There's a part of the castle where the roof is still fairly sound. I have some things there. I'll lead you if you give me your hand—it's frightfully dark and the floor is full of holes.'

She put her hand into his with the confidence of a child— it was a slim hand, very cold and wet. He thought: Good God, she is cold—I must get her warmed or she will be ill. He moved off slowly in the darkness. 'This way,' he said, and then: 'Two steps up here.'

Linda thought: He knows this place, every stone of it— who is he? What is he? How strange that I don't feel frightened!

Suddenly the darkness was shattered by a blinding flash

of lightning which showed Linda massive ruined walls, hung with ivy. The crash which followed seemed to shake the very ground on which they stood—it echoed round the mountains like a salvo of guns.

'Are you frightened?' he asked, squeezing the cold hand reassuringly.

'Not very,' she replied, with a breathless laugh. 'But thunder is rather—rather horrible, isn't it?'

'Yes, horrible,' he agreed.

They moved on. They seemed to go a long way in the darkness. Presently he said, 'Stand still now, until I find a light.' He let go of her hand and moved away.

Linda stood still, scarcely breathing. She heard the scrape of a match, and saw him standing beside a rough wooden table, lighting a candle in an old-fashioned iron candlestick. The light showed up his face, dark and intent.

Linda saw that they were in a large circular chamber—part of one of the towers of the old castle. The walls were of bare grey stone, the floor was of large grey flagstones. There was a big open fireplace in the wall, with a fire laid ready for lighting, and, before the fireplace, was a roughly made wooden settle, very wide in the seat. The only other furniture in the chamber was the table and a cupboard. There were two small windows high up in the walls, barred with rusty iron bars.

Iain looked at her and smiled. 'Not much of a place to spend the night, I'm afraid,' he said apologetically, 'but it will look better when we get the fire going.' He took a black bottle out of the cupboard and poured it over the sticks. 'Paraffin,' he explained. 'The sticks get damp here, so I always keep a bottle of paraffin handy. There's a kettle here, too, so we can make something hot to drink—I hope you like cocoa.'

She said, ' I think you are a wizard.'

' If I were a wizard I would do better than this,' he told her. 'Dry clothes for us both—and ortolans in aspic.'

The flames were leaping amongst the sticks by this time. She crossed over to the fire and held out her hands to the blaze. Iain looked up at her and his thoughts were disturbed, scattered. Who was she? What was she? He wanted to know everything about her, every thought that had passed through her mind, every pain she had suffered, every joy she had tasted. He wanted to have been a child with her when she was a child, so that they could share the memories of childhood. It was so dreadful to love her like this and know nothing about her—nothing except that she was good and beautiful and brave. She could meet danger with a laugh—he knew *that* about her and it thrilled him. He loved her a thousand times more because of that. His heart thudded against the walls of his chest. She was brave, and—God, how beautiful she was! Her lashes were long and curved and dark against the pallor of her cheeks. Her hair was dusky, neither black nor brown, her eyebrows were arched in well-defined lines. They were the same colour as her hair, he noticed.

The fire leapt and crackled. There was warmth in it now —warmth and comfort and cheerfulness.

'Take off your shoes and stockings,' he said to her. 'They will dry if you put them near the fire.'

' I'm not really very wet,' said Linda. ' But you're soaking, of course. Haven't you got anything here to change?'

' Nothing but a bath towel,' replied Iain, smiling. ' But I'm used to being wet—it won't harm me. Will you be all right while I fill the kettle?'

' Of course.'

He took the kettle and went away. In a few minutes he was back, and the kettle was sitting on the fire. He saw that she had done as he suggested; her shoes and stockings were

116

spread out on the hearth, and she was warming her bare feet, curling her toes luxuriously in the glowing warmth.

Iain broke up some peat and stoked the fire scientifically, propping up the kettle between two small pine logs.

' It's a lovely fire!' Linda said. ' I see you understand peat. Mrs. Hetherington Smith's servants couldn't do anything with the fires at Ardfalloch—we had to get MacNeil to deal with them.'

' It takes a Highlander to deal with peat,' Iain replied. ' There's a special knack—we're rather like peat-fires ourselves, not easily understood by the Sasunnach. We smoulder away and look as if we were half dead, but it only needs a touch and a little draught to set us ablaze.'

' You understand the Highlander,' she said, probing for the secret in him.

' Yes,' he agreed. ' Sometimes I think I understand better because I'm a mixture myself.'

He rose and got a tin cup out of the cupboard, and a tin of cocoa and some biscuits. The biscuits were soft and limp, but they toasted them in front of the fire and found them eatable. They sat on the settle in front of the fire drinking cocoa. Linda felt as if she had known this man all her life, she felt safe with him—completely comfortable and happy. The wind shrieked outside, questing round the thick walls like a hungry beast, and, now and then, a flash of lightning flickered through the narrow windows and a crash of thunder shook the tower.

' You're a very mysterious person,' Linda said suddenly. ' I've been trying to think where I saw you before, and who you can be——'

' I don't want to be mysterious,' he said quickly. ' But well, you see I can't explain anything without explaining everything—and it would take a long time.'

Linda laughed. ' We've got the whole night before us.'

Iain looked at her sideways. She was leaning forward a

117

little with her eyes on the fire. It irradiated her pale face with glowing light. Her dark hair was damp and dis-ordered, a damp curl lay on the cheek nearest to him in a ring. He saw again the lovely line of her throat from chin to breast.

He thought: It's an invitation to tell her all about myself, and his heart sang. 'I'll tell you where you saw me,' he said. 'Do you remember in London, one night, at the theatre—after the play—you were waiting for somebody to fetch you? He had promised to meet you, and he didn't come.'

'Oh.' she cried. 'It was you. How stupid of me! You took me back to the hotel in a taxi. I knew I had seen you ——' She thought: What a fool I was, not to remember! And yet how could I? How could I connect the two men—the London dandy, so impeccably smart in his evening clothes and his opera-hat, and Richard's boatmender? But, of course, he is not a boatmender, I know that. She said aloud, 'That makes you even more mysterious.'

Iain laughed. 'I'll tell you a little story,' he said. 'There was once an impecunious Highlander with a big estate, and no money to run it with. So he let the estate to Mr. Hetherington Smith——'

'That explains it,' she said.

'And instead of taking himself off—as a well-brought-up landlord should have done—he remained in a little cottage by the side of the loch.'

'You couldn't leave it!' she exclaimed, turning and look-ing at him with glowing eyes. 'Oh, I can understand that! Even I—seeing it like this for a few short days—I love it already. I can feel the glamour of it and how the whole valley is full of history—it is calm and peaceful and sad and happy and—and exciting. How could you go away and leave it when it was at its most beautiful best? And you—you are part of it all. You are part of its history, part of the

118

actual soil, I feel *that*. I feel that you would only be half you—away from Ardfalloch.'

He was too moved to answer her outburst. He was filled with a strange excitement, an exhilaration. She was everything he had dreamed—she understood everything.

' And now it's your turn,' he said. ' I know nothing about you. Tell me your name.'

' Linda Medworth.'

' Linda,' he repeated. The name was like music in his heart.

She was silent for a few moments, battling with something in herself which urged her to tell him nothing further; and then she thought: He wants to know, and, after all, who has a better right to know all about me? He saved my life at the risk of his own. At last she said: ' If you want to know about me——'

' Yes,' he said eagerly. ' Yes, of course, I do.'

Linda told him. She found it much more difficult to tell her story to this man than it had been to tell Mrs. Hetherington Smith. She did not tell him all that she had told Mrs. Hetherington Smith, she softened it down for him, but, even so, she could feel the passion that she was arousing. Mrs. Hetherington Smith had received her story calmly—with sympathy, it is true, but with calm sympathy. This man received it with tense emotion which she only partly understood. He was so sensitive to her thoughts that he guessed the pieces of her story which she had left out to spare his feelings and her own. Guessed them and laid them bare, so that she could hide nothing from him. The very calmness with which she tried to tell the tale seemed to add to its tragedy. She felt at last that her very soul was naked, and she was ashamed.

When she had finished—and he had finished asking his searching questions—he jumped up and strode about the room. For the first time she was frightened of him. She thought: I ought not to have told him—how strange that he should be so upset—so angry—I ought not to have told him *now*. The room, which had seemed so safe and friendly, had become full of a tense atmosphere.

'But you're free,' he said at last, as if he were answering some unheard argument. 'But you're free *now*. That's what really matters. You must forget it all—you must never think of it again.'

'I'm not really free yet,' she reminded him. 'Not until October when the decree becomes absolute. And only then if—if——'

'If what?' he cried.

'If nothing happens.'

'What could happen?'

'I don't know,' she said slowly, and she didn't know. She had always suffered from a curious fear of what was going to happen round the next corner. Even when life went smoothly and nothing occurred to justify her vague apprehensions, they did not altogether disperse. She had tried to face these fears and conquer them, but she could never do so entirely, she could only strain forward into the darkness of the future, expecting and fearing the unknown. She was brave in the face of dangers she could see, but she could not arm herself against shadows. These fears were her weakness. They had probably arisen in some forgotten episode of her childhood, and the experiences she had undergone in her married life had intensified them a thousandfold.

'But what *could* happen?' Iain said again, pausing in his stride and looking at her anxiously.

'I feel somehow—I feel he won't give up Richard without a struggle,' she said, trying to catch her elusive fears and pin them down. 'You don't know him as I do. He—when he sets his mind on anything, he pursues it—with all his might. It's the same with everything—big or little—he

120

has to have it, and then, when he's got it, he doesn't want it any more——'

'But what could he do?'

'I don't know,' she said helplessly. 'He's clever, you know—in a way. Perhaps it's silly of me, but, when I think of him, I feel—I feel frightened.'

Iain came to the back of the settle and she felt his hands on her shoulders: they were firm hands, firm and reassuring.

'You mustn't be frightened,' he said quietly. 'You weren't frightened in the boat——'

'That was different,' said Linda. ' That was quite different. It's people who frighten me—people frighten me when they are cruel and deceitful—and he—was both.'

'The devil!' said Iain softly, but with concentrated rage.

They left the subject alone after that, and talked about other things. It was too dangerous a subject to discuss; it roused their emotions. They both, in their different ways, and from their different points of view, felt that the subject had better be avoided. They made more cocoa and finished the remainder of the biscuits, and smoked cigarettes out of Iain's case which was commendably watertight. Iain went out to look at the weather and returned to report that the wind had gone down a little and it had started to rain, but the waves had risen and were dashing over the rocks in an awe-inspiring manner.

'They will think we are drowned,' Linda said.

'No, they will know we are all right,' Iain told her. 'Donald will see the light in the window of the tower and he will know I am here. He'll come for us when the sea goes down—whenever it's safe. Are you worried about Richard?'

'Only a little,' said Linda. ' Mrs. Hetherington Smith is awfully kind and sensible, she understands Richard and he's

very fond of her. She won't let Richard be frightened about
me. The Hetherington Smiths have been very kind to us.
The time here has been quite perfect—so calm and peaceful.
It's a pity that it's over——'

'Over!' cried Iain in dismay.

Linda smiled. 'The house-party has arrived in full
strength,' she told him. 'Some yesterday, and some to-day.
It's a very funny house-party. Nobody seems to know anybody else—and they're all so different. I can't quite see
how it's going to work.'

'How d'you mean?'

'Well,' she said, 'you know how house-parties divide up
into groups of people who are the same kind—in this house-
party nobody is the same kind as anybody else. They seem
to have been chosen at random. The women consist of
Greta Bastable, Mrs. Hetherington Smith and me. I know
Greta, of course—everybody knows her—she's a smart
London sort of person. Mrs. Hetherington Smith is mysterious—I like her awfully, but—Oh, I don't know! I have
a feeling, sometimes, that she's acting a part, that she's not
really sincere; and yet I know she is sincere in her friendship for me—and for Richard. She loves Richard. It's
when she's talking to the others—to Greta Bastable, for
instance—that I feel she's acting. She's quite different then
—not like the woman I know—or think I know. Isn't it
queer?'

'Who else is there?' Iain asked. He had sat down on the
wide stone hearth at her feet—he could see her better like
that—and he wanted her to go on talking so that he could
watch her and see the swift expressions chase each other
across her face.

'Mr. Grant Stacey, for one,' she said. 'Have you heard
of him?'

'Who hasn't heard of him!' Iain said. 'He's come for
the shooting, of course.' It gave Iain a moment's pleasure to

think that this man—so well known in sporting circles—was going to shoot his birds.

'Yes, he's come for the shooting, and something else. I don't know what it is. Mrs. Hetherington Smith began to tell me and then stopped herself suddenly.'

'He's a big financier,' Iain told her. 'And I heard—or read—that he's floating a new company. I'm an ignoramus on these subjects——'

'That's what it will be,' said Linda. 'And then there's the foolish young man—Jim Wyllie his name is—and Desmond Cray. *He's* a sort of "man about town," rather a ladies' man. And there's a funny little man called Proudfoot, and Colonel White——'

'They *do* sound a mixed bag!'

'Yes, they are—and, lastly, Sir Julius Hastie.'

'Sir Julius Hastie!' Iain exclaimed. 'Do you mean the Harley Street doctor? He generally goes to Cluan. Why has he deserted Cluan, I wonder?'

'Well,' she said, smiling a little. 'I rather think he has come for me—likes shooting, too, of course——'

'He can have the shooting,' Iain said, in a voice grown suddenly gruff—'but he can't have you.'

'Perhaps not.'

He reached up and put a hand on her knee. 'You know why he can't have you,' he said, trying to speak lightly. 'He can't have you because you're mine.'

'But I don't know you,' said Linda, almost tearfully. 'I don't know you——'

'You can know everything,' he told her. 'I won't hurry you, my dear. Say what you want to know and I'll tell you.'

She did not speak nor move, she was too shaken, too utterly bewildered, not only at what he had said, but at her own reaction to his words. If she had been told that she would allow any man to go so far without turning upon him and destroying his mad delusion she would have laughed. But somehow she could not turn upon this man and destroy his delusion—and she liked—yes, she actually liked the feeling of his hand upon her knee.

After a few minutes Iain began to tell her about his life. He told her of his grandmother, and his parents, and about Janet, and Donald, and all about his childhood at Ardfalloch, and how he and Donald had grown up together and had run about the glen, bare-legged, fishing the burns and climbing the trees and bathing in the loch.

'Those were the days!' he said. 'Perhaps the happiest days of all. Donald and I were a couple of ragamuffins—our kilts were always in ribbons, but we didn't care for that. Then I went to school—it was pretty grim at first, for I was as proud as the devil and as wild as an unbroken colt. I settled down after a bit, of course, and bent my neck to the yoke.'

'What happened next?' she asked, for he had fallen silent as if that were all he was going to say.

'My father—died,' Iain said. 'My father's death was a tragedy—he was killed. My mother was there and saw it happen, she was devoted to him, bound up in him—there was nothing else in her life that mattered—so—part of her died then, too. She—she has never been—never been herself since then. It was rather a dreadful house to come back to. Everything was so different—so dreadful.'

'Yes,' she said softly. 'To come back and find it all so changed from what you were looking forward to——'

'Janet helped me,' he said. 'It was Janet who insisted that I should go to Oxford. My father had arranged it all before he died—that I was to go to Oxford. But afterwards I felt there was so much to do here—so many responsibilities, I didn't see how I could go. Janet made me. She said my father had wanted it, and, of course, that was true. Janet took it all on her own shoulders—she did everything. I couldn't have done it if it hadn't been for Janet.'

The Storm

' I should like to see Janet,' Linda said.

' You shall see Janet,' he replied, looking up at her and smiling.

' Perhaps——' said Linda softly.

' There's not much more to tell you. Since then I have lived here, looking after the place and trying to help my people—fishing and shooting, trying to improve things, trying to make ends meet and never succeeding—I'm a poor man, Linda.'

She said lightly, ' You must marry a rich wife.'

' Do you say that?' he asked her whimsically. ' But for you I should have done so long ago.'

' But for me——' she began in surprised tones.

' Listen,' he said. ' Five years ago a Highlander went to London and a fairy woman stole his heart. Wasn't that a queer thing to happen to a Highlander in London? They say London is a dangerous place for Highlanders. This one that I'm telling you about took good care of his sporran—but his heart was stolen. He never thought of taking care of his heart. He knew it must have been a fairy woman who stole it from him because she vanished—he couldn't find her anywhere. He went back to the hotel where he had taken her; he went back early the next morning—and she was gone. The foolish fellow had never asked her name; he knew nothing about her; he didn't know where she lived—she was gone, vanished into thin air. So then he knew that she must have gone back to her fairy hill and taken his heart with her. The Highlander went back to his glen and there he stayed. He had no——'

' It isn't true,' she whispered.

' It's true, Linda. The Highlander could not look at other women after that—they did not interest him. He hadn't any heart, poor devil, because the fairy woman had stolen it. The fairy woman was so beautiful, so good—nobody else was any use—he knew that she was good—he

125

only had to look at her and he knew what she was like all through. He thought of her and he dreamed of her, and when he saw her again, he knew that she was all he had thought—and more.'

Men had made love to Linda before—for she was a beautiful woman—but this was different—different from anything she had ever experienced or imagined. She had told herself that once she was free she would settle down somewhere in some quiet place with Richard—she would devote her whole life to Richard—they would be happy together—she had done with love. But now she realised that this was something quite different from love as she had known it, this was something quite new, and it was beautiful. She realised also—but only dimly and vaguely—that this man was making love seem beautiful to her because he was beautiful himself—inside as well as out. It was strange, Linda thought, that she had been treasured in his heart all these years and had never known it. Anything so strong and lasting should surely have made itself felt—should have bridged the gap between them and communicated itself to her. It was strange that she had felt nothing—nothing at all. She tried to find the difference that lay between this man's love, and love as she had known it. Did the difference lie entirely in the man himself? No, not entirely. He had endowed her in his own mind with all the things he wanted in a woman —with all the things he admired.

Linda felt her whole being rushing out towards him. She felt she wanted to give him everything—everything she had to offer. Had she enough in her to satisfy his needs? Had she all the things he wanted in a woman?

She said in a low voice, 'How do you know what I am like?'

'I don't know how I know,' he answered thoughtfully.

'Things aren't always what they seem. Sometimes you

126

see a peach—it looks perfect, smooth and rosy, but when you bite into the heart of it you find a maggot——'

He threw back his head and laughed. ' You can't frighten me,' he told her. ' Every word you say fits into the picture of you that is in my heart. It's like a jig-saw puzzle—you have the picture, and the little heap of pieces, and they all fit in. Oh, Linda, why isn't everybody in love with you?'

She smiled at his boyishness—it was so different from the sophistication of Jack Medworth. This man was the opposite of Medworth in everything. He was gentle and considerate, he approached her through her mind and heart—Jack had approached her through her senses. Jack's lovemaking had been passionate; he had swept her off her feet and kissed her into love—or what she had mistaken for love. No man would be able to do that again, he had made it all horrible. It was because Iain was so entirely different that he was able to touch her heart.

They talked all night, drinking cocoa at intervals and smoking cigarettes. They talked of everything that was in their hearts, everything except their feeling for each other (Iain was too wise and too considerate to press the advantage he had gained. He said to himself, ' She hasn't told me to go to hell, and that's something,'—it was a good deal if he had only known it). They talked about their childhood, and discussed abstract subjects—there was a resonance between their hearts. *Almost* he knew what she would say before she said it—almost, but not quite, for her flexible mind gave a quaint turn to her words that delighted him. He discovered—or confirmed—that she had humour and originality; she saw reason in views which she did not share —a rare virtue this! Their talk was more vital and friendly than any talk that either of them had had.

A pale-grey shadow began to lighten the windows—it was dawn. The wind had fallen considerably by now and it had stopped raining. Iain and Linda went out together, passing through the dark passages and the ruined hall. It was not so far as she had thought, but she marvelled afresh at his knowledge of the place which had led her so confidently in the darkness. They stood in the ruined arch which had been the entrance to the castle and watched the light creeping into the sky and the dark peaks take form against its grey pallor. Torn clouds, riven by the storm, were chasing each other across the fading stars. The light grew; one of the mountains was touched by a rosy finger—and then another. The dark loch became grey; the clouds had rosy edges. . . .

'Look, Linda!' Iain said.

She followed his pointing finger. At first her eyes could see nothing in the faint light, but, after a moment, she saw a boat putting off from Ardfalloch jetty. The distant sound of an engine came to her ears in the stillness of the dawn.

'It's Donald,' Iain said quietly.

They watched the boat draw near with mingled feelings —the night was over. They were both different, fundamentally different from their selves of yesterday.

Iain took Linda's hand and they went down to the little pier to await the arrival of the boat. It came nearer and nearer. Iain waved his handkerchief and the figure in the boat waved back. It was Donald, just as Iain had said.

The waves were still troublesome and it took some manœuvring to bring the launch in, but at last it was accomplished—a rope was thrown and made fast to a ring. Donald jumped out and seized Iain's hand.

'Och, MacAslan!' he cried in a shaking voice. 'Och, MacAslan, taing do Dhia! Taing do Dhia! God be praised. . . . When I saw the light,' he continued, still speaking in his own tongue. 'When I saw the light showing in the tower . . .' He broke off and turned away.

128

The Storm

Iain went after him and put a hand on his shoulder; they talked together for a few moments in low voices.

Linda was moved at the man's devotion. His face was haggard and drawn in the cold morning light. It must be wonderful, Linda thought, to have devotion of that nature poured out at your feet. Iain had told her about it in their long talk. He had said, lightly, 'Donald would die for me, of course, and I for Donald.' She saw that there was deep truth in the casual words.

Presently they came back to her, full of apologies for leaving her alone. 'Mistress Medworth will understand,' Donald said humbly. 'It has been a very bad night for me. When I wass seeing the light in the tower I wass hopeful that all wass well—but I could not be sure—no, I could not be sure. I wass telling Mr. Hetherington Smith that it wass all right—and he wass believing what I wass telling him, but I could not be believing myself so easily. Mistress Medworth will understand I could not be coming before to the island, for the tide wass out, and there wass no water to float the big boat even if it had been safe for the waves and the darkness——'

'The little boat is done for, I'm afraid,' said Iain rather sadly.

'Och, and what of that!' Donald cried. 'If MacAslan be safe—and Mistress Medworth.'

'Let's be off!' said Iain. 'I think some breakfast is the next thing—what do you think?'

'Morag is making ready at the cottage,' said Donald eagerly. 'The Big House will be asleep still—with those lazy London servants. I will go up to the Big House and leave a message that all is well——'

Iain looked at Linda enquiringly. She nodded. She was not going to spoil Donald's arrangements by suggesting anything different.

Iain stepped into the launch and Donald stood on the

pier. There was still a good deal of swell on, even on the lee shore of the island. They handed Linda from one to the other like a precious parcel. She felt the strength and gentleness of the two men—it was something she had never known before. Iain did not look so very strong, he was slim and lightly poised, but his muscles were like cords, and he was supremely fit. Donald's strength was more apparent. He was tall and broad-shouldered—largely made.

Linda sat in the stern with Iain beside her, steering, and Donald at their feet attending to the engine. The launch ran swiftly across the loch, bouncing over the waves. Linda was tired now, she leaned back against the shabby-cushioned seat and listened to Iain's account of their adventures. He was telling Donald all about it—in English, of course, for it would not have been polite to Linda to have spoken in the Gaelic. Until now she had thought that Donald Mac-Neil was a dour man—perhaps, even, rather stupid—but now she saw that he was neither. The dourness and the stupidity was a sort of mask, a protection against people that he did not know and did not understand. Iain, he knew and understood well—almost too well, Linda thought. She had the strange feeling that Donald knew all that had happened to them on the island; that he read between the lines of the bald tale and was aware just how far she and Iain had voyaged together.

CHAPTER XI

The Twelfth

THE news of the disaster had caused a good deal of anxiety at Ardfalloch House. Jim Wyllie had arrived, looking wild and dishevelled and announced that Mrs. Medworth had been swept out into the middle of the loch in a small boat. Everybody started talking at once, suggesting different courses of action, arguing, declaiming, asking questions and informing the company at large of occasions when similar —or somewhat similar—accidents had happened to themselves or their friends.

Mr. Hetherington Smith was aware that it was up to him to do something about it, but his knowledge of boats and lochs in general was so extremely vague that he had no idea at all what course of action was open to him. Donald Mac-Neil will know, he thought; the first thing to do is to get hold of him.

The storm was now at its height. Lightning was flashing, thunder was crashing, and rain had started to fall. The wind was still terrific, but Ardfalloch House was sheltered from the full force of the wind. Mr. Hetherington Smith went to the front door and looked out. By this time the rain was jumping up from the gravel in the drive. It was filling the holes and running down the ruts like miniature rivers. The clouds were very low and black, the hills had all disappeared, it was getting darker every minute. Lightning zigzagged eerily over the loch, thunder rumbled amongst the shrouded hills and the wind whistled mournfully amongst the trees—it was not the sort of night one would choose to be out on the loch in a small boat, even Mr. Hetherington Smith realised that. He was alarmed.

Mrs. Hetherington Smith was upstairs with Richard. She had watched him having his bath, and was now reading *Winnie-the-Pooh* to him while he took his supper of bread and milk. It was unfortunate, Mrs. Hetherington Smith thought, that they had just arrived at the part where Piglet is marooned by the rising flood. She tried to skip the more alarming pieces of description, but Richard knew the story by heart and insisted on hearing every word. Well, it can't be helped, she thought, and read on with a chill in her heart. She had managed to reassure Richard as to his mother's safety by comfortable placid lying. His mother was sheltering from the storm in the MacNeils' cottage and would be back soon, she told him. Richard must take his supper like a good boy, and go to bed.

Richard trusted Mrs. Hetherington Smith. She was large and calm and soothing. She helped him to feed the dilapidated Polar Bear which was the apple of his eye; listened to his prayers, and tucked him up securely.

'If Mummy comes back before I'm asleep tell her to come and see me,' Richard said, as he snuggled down comfortably between the sheets.

'Yes, of course,' agreed Mrs. Hetherington Smith. She lighted the night-light, turned down the lamp and went away. Richard was almost asleep already.

Mr. Hetherington Smith was waiting for her in her room.

'Well?' she said anxiously. 'Well, Arthur?'

'I've seen MacNeil,' Arthur told her. 'He's just left. He says she's on an island in the middle of the loch.'

'How does he know?'

'Because there's a light in the window of a house on the island.'

Mrs. Hetherington Smith digested this information.

'Why?' she said at last. 'Why should the light prove that Linda's there?'

'I asked him that, and he said that nobody lives there now, so if there is a light it must be them. I suppose the people who lived there found it inconvenient and came over to the mainland.'

'I see,' said Mrs. Hetherington Smith thoughtfully; then she added, 'Did MacNeil know who the man was—the man who went with her in the boat?'

'He said he knew the man well,' said Mr. Hetherington Smith. 'He's a sort of relation of MacNeil's as far as I could make out. But you know how vague these people are —they never seem to be able to answer a question directly. Sometimes I wonder how much they really understand. Even MacNeil, who speaks quite good English, seems so dense sometimes. I think he finds difficulty in putting his ideas into words. He's extraordinarily good in his own line, but, when you get him on to something else, he seems—dull. You can't make him understand what you want to know.'

Mrs. Hetherington Smith nodded. She had experienced the same difficulty herself. 'Is the man a sort of ghillie?' she enquired.

'I suppose so. MacNeil seems to have absolute confidence in him—said he was a "grand man with a boat" and that he knew the island well. Altogether he seemed certain that the man would look after Linda all right—I got that much out of him.'

'Well, that's a comfort, anyhow,' said Mrs. Hetherington Smith, 'and I suppose, now he knows where she is, he can take the motor-launch and fetch her home.'

'He says it's impossible. It would be dangerous to attempt it. Even if he got there he says he could never get back again. We shall have to wait until the storm is over——'

'D'you mean Linda will have to stay on the island all night?'

'It looks like it,' said Mr. Hetherington Smith with a sigh.

'That's *awful*! Can't we do anything?'

'Well, what can we do? I know so little about it. MacNeil says the thing's impossible—I've got to take his word for it. He says Linda is safer where she is, even if he could get there in the launch—which is doubtful. He knows the conditions and I don't. I really feel we must go by what he says, Mary.'

Dinner was an uncomfortable meal. Some of Mr. Hetherington Smith's guests thought that 'something should be done'; they did not specify what should be done, nor offer to take action themselves. Others—more conversant with the conditions—were aware that nothing could be done, until the storm was over, to rescue Mrs. Medworth. There were acrimonious passages between the two factions. The host and hostess were silent, occupied with their own thoughts. Mr. Wyllie was also silent. He felt guilty and ashamed, and, at the bottom of his heart, furiously angry with himself and everybody else.

The party broke up early and went to bed—if not to sleep. The wind had gone down a little by now and the actual storm was passing over. There was still an occasional growl of thunder from the distant hills. Mrs. Hetherington Smith went into her husband's room.

'I don't see why MacNeil can't go for her now,' she said. 'The storm is nearly over and the wind has gone down. I think we ought to try. It may be uncomfortable for her on that island—the beds are sure to be damp.'

'MacNeil will go directly it's safe,' Mr. Hetherington Smith assured her. 'He promised me he would, and he will. I can't do any more, Mary.'

Mary sighed. She didn't believe that Linda couldn't be

fetched, but she realised it was no use saying any more about it.

The news that Mrs. Medworth was safe and well was spread over the house by the bearers of morning tea. It was well received by all. Even those who had no special interest in Linda were delighted to hear of her safety, for, if 'anything had happened,' the shoot would have had to be postponed. Now, all was well. Mrs. Medworth was safe and the storm had blown itself out. Watery sunshine, growing stronger every moment, poured in at the eastern windows, rousing the sluggards. Birds were singing, the earth was wet and goodly smelling. There was also a comforting and delicious smell of fried bacon drifting up the stairs.

Linda arrived as the gong boomed loudly in the hall. She avoided the dining-room (she had breakfasted already) and ran up the stairs to Richard's room. Mrs. Hetherington Smith was there with him, helping him to part his hair—it was a task Linda always undertook herself. She lingered in the doorway, unperceived, amused at their efforts.

'That's too near the miggle, Mrs. Hevverington Smith,' Richard was saying. 'I think p'r'aps I'd better try myself. You see you're not really accusomed to boys' hair——' He turned round, and saw Linda, and, in a moment, he was in her arms.

When Mrs. Hetherington Smith went down to breakfast she found that the shooters had finished their meal and the hall was full of the bustle of their departure. It was full of men in nailed boots with guns and cartridge bags. The drive was cluttered with ghillies and dogs. Mr. Hetherington Smith was speaking to Donald on the steps—he wore a worried expression.

'But if we've got to ballot for places, how can you be

sure that Mr. Stacey will get a good place?' he enquired anxiously. 'Couldn't we just arrange who's to have which butt in every drive?'

'It would not be the thing at all, at all,' Donald assured him. 'The other gentlemen would not be liking that way. But if you would be leaving it to me, Mr. Hetherington Smith, then everything will be all right. You will see it will be all right, and there will be no difficulty at all.'

Mr. Hetherington Smith had no option but to leave it to Donald. He turned away with a sigh and found his wife at his elbow enquiring about lunch. When and where was it to be sent? Donald was called back to solve the problem. He solved it without any difficulty.

'It will be best to have lunch in the wee bothy on the moor,' he said gravely; 'the wee bothy at Ballochgorm. If you will be telling them to have it ready at midday or soon after.' He told the chauffeur how the bothy was to be reached, and went out to give some final directions to the ragged group of beaters.

A few minutes later the whole party moved off towards the first drive. The moors were so near the house that there was no need for cars. They walked through the woods and found themselves knee-deep in purple heather. Everything was astonishingly wet, and the heather was wettest of all. It was more like paddling than walking, Mr. Hetherington Smith decided. At every step the water was driven from the heather like spray. But, in spite of the discomfort, there was something rather pleasant about it—the sun was delightfully warm and there was a small fitful breeze. Mr. Hetherington Smith was enjoying himself until he suddenly found Mr. Stacey at his elbow.

'Your keeper says I have drawn Number Three in the first drive,' said Mr. Stacey. 'You're letting him arrange it?'

'Yes,' replied Mr. Hetherington Smith. 'At least there's

no arranging. We ballot for places—it's the fairest method, I always think.' He thought: I hope to Heaven Number Three is a good place. Why on earth don't I know more about it? I should have gone round with MacNeil and got him to explain, instead of pottering round shooting rabbits.

'Well, of course it's fair in one way,' Mr. Stacey replied. 'But I'm usually damned unlucky, *balloting*. Sometimes people like to put the best shot in the best butt for the sake of the bag——' He laughed a little to cover the flagrancy of the hint.

'One would like to do that, of course,' agreed the wretched host, with an equally forced laugh, 'but I find that leads to a good deal of trouble sometimes—a good deal of unpleasantness. Anyhow, you seem to have been pretty lucky *this* time. Number Three is an excellent position in this drive.' He thought: Now I've done it. Supposing it's an absolutely rotten place—behind a hill or something—but MacNeil *said* it would be all right.

They were approaching the butts for the first drive and taking up their positions. Donald had constituted himself loader to Mr. Hetherington Smith because he thought it as well to keep his eye on that gentleman. He was anxious for the gentleman not to make a fool of himself. In the excitement he might easily forget his careful instructions and loose off at the wrong moment. He might shoot a beater, or a dog. Donald felt confident that he could prevent these disasters if he were there, and he wanted to prevent them. He was fond of Mr. Hetherington Smith—increasingly fond of him. The gentleman was foolish in some ways—and lamentably ignorant—but there was something nice about him. His very helplessness and ignorance were endearing. Donald intended to see that the gentleman got a fair chance and his due share of birds.

Mr. Hetherington Smith found himself in Number One butt with Donald beside him and an astonishingly wet black dog between his legs. Sir Julius was in Number Two: Mr. Stacey in Number Three, and the others distributed down the line. Donald loaded the two guns and whispered some last-minute instructions. The birds would come over the shoulder of the hill, they would be flying low. Mr. Hetherington Smith was to wait until they were fairly near before firing, he was to choose a bird—one particular bird out of the covey—and swing well in front of it. Mr. Hetherington Smith nodded, he had heard all that before, the theory of grouse shooting was an open book to him. It was the practice he lacked. At the moment he was much more anxious as to whether or not Mr. Stacey was well placed. He enquired of Donald as to Mr. Stacey's position in the drive— was he in a really good butt?

' The gentleman has been very fortunate,' said Donald gravely. There was a ghost of a twinkle in his eye and the nearest approach to a smile that Mr. Hetherington Smith had yet seen on his rugged face.

Mr. Hetherington Smith sighed with relief and turned his attention to the birds. They began to come over quite soon—there was a ragged volley of shots down the line. A few stragglers came over Number One butt—Mr. Hetherington Smith shot at several and missed.

' If you would be waiting a wee bit longer——' Donald suggested.

A covey came over as he spoke. Mr. Hetherington Smith was flustered and shot wildly into the brown with both barrels. A dark brown body fell with a queer thump just in front of the butt, it fluttered feebly for a moment and was still. Mr. Hetherington Smith had killed his first bird. He was inordinately excited, and, but for Donald's restraining hand, he would have rushed out and retrieved it.

The next covey—a small one—turned when it reached the shoulder of the hill and flew down the line. It was flying low and Donald was just in time to prevent Mr. Hetherington Smith from shooting the occupant of the next butt. He knocked up the barrel of the gun and the charge exploded harmlessly in the air. It was unfortunate that the butt of the gun should hit its owner on the ear, but it was a glancing blow and did no serious damage. Mr. Hetherington Smith took the accident in good part, and accepted Donald's explanations and apologies very graciously.

'Good heavens, it would have been frightful if I had killed Sir Julius!' he exclaimed.

'Och, you would not have killed him!' said Donald comfortably. 'Gentlemen are not so easily killed, but you might have annoyed him a little—gentlemen do not like to be shot at when they are out shooting.'

The drive was now over. Donald collected the slain bird, and sent the black dog after a runner which really belonged to Sir Julius..

'Have I shot two—I mean a brace?' enquired Mr. Hetherington Smith eagerly, as they walked down the hill to the next butt.

Donald held up the two birds for him to see. There was no harm in claiming the runner, for Sir Julius had done quite well, and two birds were more than twice as good as one. Sir Julius was pleased with his own performance and displayed two and a half brace. Mr. Stacey in Number 3 had done terrific execution, there was a heap of brown feathers behind his butt and he was still urging his unpleasant bitch to locate another in the heather.

'Perhaps you just wounded it,' suggested Mr. Hetherington Smith helpfully.

Mr. Stacey turned and glared at him. 'I'm not in the habit of wounding birds,' he said.

'Good lord, no, of course not. It was only a joke,' his host assured him, trying to retrieve his ghastly blunder.

'H'm,' said Mr. Stacey. It was a peculiar sort of joke, he thought, but he had had excellent sport and was inclined to be magnanimous. No more was said and the three gentlemen with their loaders walked on down the hill.

The other members of the party had acquitted themselves according to their capabilities; everyone was pleased except Jim Wyllie, who thought he had been allotted the worst position in the drive—but Jim Wyllie didn't matter.

Donald dispatched the beaters to the next drive and led his flock over the hill. He was not worried about the beaters, for they were under the direction of one of his many cousins, a man who bore the same name as himself—Donald MacNeil. This man, to differentiate him from our Donald, was known to his intimates as Donald Dubh—or Black Donald—on account of his swarthy complexion. He was an excellent ghillie and absolutely reliable so long as there was no whisky about. It was unfortunate that Black Donald combined a fondness for whisky with the inability to stand it like a gentleman. One dram went straight to his head and made him belligerent—not to say dangerous—two drams laid him out. If Black Donald had one dram there was usually somebody willing—not to say eager—to stand him another. He was a powerful man. Donald was aware of his cousin's weakness, as indeed was everybody in the glen. They were all very sorry for him; it was generally agreed that Black Donald was much to be pitied.

The shooters walked over the shoulder of the hill. The heather here was not so high, but it was still troublesome to Mr. Hetherington Smith. The strong woody stems twined themselves round his ankles and impeded his progress. He fell into holes and stumbled into boggy patches which looked as if they would afford firm foothold, but were really a delusion. Donald pulled him out of several of these devilish snares and adjured him to ' be avoiding the sphagnum now.' It was all very difficult; he envied Donald's careless stride.

The sun was gaining strength, and sucking up the moisture from the heather; the cap of mist on Ben Falloch was thinning rapidly; a lark soared up from their feet and sang lustily in the blue sky. They skirted a sheep fank of unmortared stones and found their butts on the other side.

The second drive was much like the first except for the rearrangement of the shooters. Mr. Stacey was again fortunate in his position, he had Number Five. Mr. Hetherington Smith was in Number Three, with Mr. Proudfoot on one side of him and Colonel White on the other. He acquitted himself better this time, shooting when Donald told him to shoot, and withholding his fire when the birds passed between the butts.

After this they climbed higher, the ground became more rocky—a few gnarled pine-trees clung with bare distorted roots to the stony soil. The earth was shallow, the skin had split, as it were, and the bones were showing through. There was little heather here and Mr. Hetherington Smith was glad. They scrambled up a scree of gritty stones and found themselves on the flank of the hill. Mr. Hetherington Smith had drawn Number Eight; it was the highest of all, and was out of sight of the others, on account of an outcrop of boulderous rock. He scrambled into his butt and sat down. He was panting after his climb and perspiring freely. It was extremely hot and there was no shade of any description, the sun seemed to be straight over his head; it glared down, golden, baking, dazzling.

Mr. Hetherington Smith mopped his red face. 'You shoot this time,' he said to Donald.

'Well,' said Donald doubtfully. 'But you must not be telling the others. It is not the thing at all.'

'Nobody will know,' said Mr. Hetherington Smith, 'so if you would like to——'

'Och, I would be liking it fine—and it would be a help to our bag—so it would.'

Mr. Hetherington Smith didn't mind about their bag—he had not yet learned the importance of a good bag—he was merely tired and very hot, and disinclined for further slaughter.

Donald loaded the guns carefully, and took up his position—it was lucky that the butt was out of sight of the others. He handled the guns reverently—he had never seen such guns in his life. The birds were a long time in starting to come over—so long that Donald began to wonder, a little anxiously, whether his swarthy namesake had discovered any whisky. There was just a possibility that the beaters had met the lunch. However, they began to come over at last and they came quickly down-wind. Donald had a busy five minutes and trebled Mr. Hetherington Smith's bag. It was grand sport. They collected the slain and walked down the hill to meet the others. Mr. Stacey was in high good humour. Jim Wyllie was somewhat *distrait*; he confided to his host that Mr. Proudfoot had shot a bird directly over his head. 'The man's not safe,' he said earnestly. 'He ought not to be trusted with anything more lethal than a pop-gun. Look at him now!'

Mr. Hetherington Smith looked, but he could see nothing wrong with Mr. Proudfoot—'I see what you mean,' he said.

'You see,' said Jim Wyllie. 'The man's not safe to come out with a party like this. He might pepper anybody, I mean.'

'Yes,' agreed Mr. Hetherington Smith. 'Yes, of course.'

The shooters were all glad to hear the word 'lunch,' although Mr. Stacey remarked that lunch was a waste of time—the ideal thing was to have a couple of sandwiches in your pocket.

They put up a small covey as they neared the bothy. Mr. Stacey shot two with an admirable left and right, the remnant swung outwards past Sir Julius at about a hundred yards and were sped on their way with both barrels. Sir Julius never let a chance go by. He was not a bad shot, but he was a very inconsiderate one.

'Damn' fool!' said Grant Stacey under his breath.

Donald echoed the imprecation silently. He hated his birds to be wounded—a man should know what he could do, and do it, he should not attempt the impossible.

Lunch was all ready in the little bothy at the entrance to the green pass. Mrs. Hetherington Smith and Greta Bastable were there, so, also, the bewhiskered butler. The chauffeur had brought them to within a few hundred yards of their destination over the most appalling road he had ever seen. They had carried the baskets the rest of the way.

The shooters were exceedingly hungry and thirsty; they sat down and ate. There was shepherd's pie, deliciously hot in a Thermos dish, there was cold ham and cold beef and salad, and banana tartlets, crisp and short, with chocolate sauce. The beer had been iced, and there was hot coffee and a bottle of liqueur brandy, and whisky for the men. It was an excellent repast.

Greta sat between Grant Stacey and Desmond Cray. She enquired anxiously how they had got on and received their accounts of their prowess with well-feigned interest. Colonel White managed to obtain a seat near his hostess. He was still interested in her face, although, so far, he had not heard her make a remark worthy of attention. He set himself out to please her and draw her out, and after a few minutes he began to succeed. Mrs. Hetherington Smith was feeling very cheerful—it was a lovely day and she liked picnics. She thought Colonel White was a nice man, and his conversation interested her—he had travelled a great deal and knew how to talk. Very soon Mrs. Hetherington Smith was laughing heartily at his jokes and quite forgetting to be on her best behaviour. Her husband was not altogether pleased at her absorption in Colonel White; it

143

gave him a strange feeling of emptiness, he was used to having the whole of Mary's attention—when he wanted it —and he had to ask her three times to pass the salt before she heard him. He looked at her with new eyes—he had not really looked at her for years—and realised, almost with surprise, that Mary was still an exceedingly good-looking woman. When she laughed like that she looked quite young.

The men lunched outside. Donald kept an eye on his namesake and diverted the whisky when it came his way. Mr. Stacey's loader—who was also his valet—drank a good deal of whisky, but he seemed none the worse. He spoke to Donald and complimented him on the arrangements. ' We go about a lot,' he said. ' 'E's very partikler about 'ow things is done, an' 'e was sayin' jus' now 'e 'adn't never seen a better run show.'

Donald accepted the eulogy without enthusiasm. He didn't like the man any better than his master, and he had taken an unmitigated dislike to Mr. Stacey at first sight. He liked Colonel White's man better. The other gentlemen had not brought loaders and were provided with local men —most of whom were Donald's cousins or relations of some sort.

The day was very successful from Mr. Hetherington Smith's point of view—very successful indeed, but extraordinarily long and tiring. From the moment when he had emerged from Ardfalloch House, to look at the weather and discuss the prospects with Donald, until he sought his bed at midnight he had not had a moment's peace nor leisure. Everything had gone off well, thanks to Donald. The drives had been well timed, the birds had been plentiful, and he had been saved on several occasions from making a complete fool of himself. But the most important thing that Donald had done, and the thing for which Mr. Hetherington Smith was most grateful, was the manner in which

The Twelfth

Donald had carried out his instructions with regard to Mr. Stacey. Somehow or other—Mr. Hetherington Smith had no intention of enquiring how it had been arranged—somehow or other Grant Stacey had managed to draw the best butt—or nearly the best butt—in every drive. So it had been all right, just as Donald had assured him that it would be. Mr. Stacey had been so delighted with his day's sport, and with the number of birds that had fallen to his share, that he had asked to be allowed to remain longer than he had intended in this delectable spot; and it had been quite easy—in the library after the ladies had gone upstairs to bed—to hint, in the most vague and gentlemanly manner, that his host would not refuse a directorship in the new company which Mr. Stacey was forming. Indeed it had scarcely required a hint. Mr. Hetherington Smith had merely opened his mouth, and the directorship, ripe and juicy as a sun-warmed peach, had fallen in.

Mr. Hetherington Smith washed his teeth noisily and vigorously and thought about it all. He decided that life was easy to manage when you knew how to manage it. He was so pleased with himself at the way he had Managed Life, that he felt he would like to talk to somebody about it. Mary was the obvious person to talk to—indeed, the only possible person—he wondered if Mary were asleep. The thought of Colonel White strayed through his mind and made him vaguely uneasy. It was a long time since he had seen Mary so full of animation as to-day at lunch when she was talking to that man. *Well,* he thought, *that man can talk to Mary if he likes, but she's mine—she belongs to me.* Just to show the truth of this assertion he opened the door of her room and peeped in. She was not asleep; the lamp was burning on the table near the bed—she was reading.

' Hallo!' she said, smiling at him over her book. ' Did everything go off well, Arthur?'

' Splendidly. Grant Stacey is staying on another week.'

'That's good.'

'He's offered me a directorship in the new company.'

'That's very good,' said Mary. She thought—so that's what he wanted, how funny men are! I wonder why he wanted it so badly.

'Yes,' said Arthur. 'Yes, I think I shall accept it. There are big responsibilities attached to the post, but a man in my position must shoulder—are you laughing, Mary?'

She was laughing. She said, 'Oh, Arthur, you don't have to act to *me*. You know quite well that was why you took Ardfalloch.'

He looked rather taken aback for a moment, and then he chuckled. 'Well,' he said. 'Well—what if it was?'

'Nothing—except that I think it was rather clever of you,' Mary told him.

He chuckled again. It was pleasant to have his cleverness appreciated.

'Now tell me about your day,' said Mary. 'Tell me all about it.'

He sat down on the edge of the bed and told her about his day. She was wide awake and interested in everything. She wanted to know if the lunch was all right and whether he had shot many birds himself. He told her that the lunch was exactly right, and that his own performance, though capable of improvement, had been good enough to pass muster.

'The whole thing was a success,' he said complacently, 'and the whole success was entirely due to that man, Donald MacNeil. I'll have to give him a good tip when we leave here, Mary.'

'He's a nice man,' she agreed. 'But don't spoil him, Arthur.'

'I don't think you could spoil him,' said Arthur thoughtfully.

It was very pleasant talking together like this; the house

was very quiet—everybody else was asleep. The big room was full of shadows, Mary Hetherington Smith lay in bed with the soft lamplight shining on her; she was very good to look upon—fair and plump and comely—her complexion was milk and roses, her blue eyes were bright and kind. Arthur looked at his wife and he thought: *No wonder that old stick of a colonel admired her—but she's mine.* He said aloud, 'You're very pretty, Mary.'

Mary laughed delightedly. 'Go along with you!' she said. 'I'm too old for compliments.'

'And you're very clever, too,' he added. 'Fancy you guessing it was the directorship I wanted out of Stacey! We've come a long way, haven't we? And we've come all the way together. I couldn't have done it without you.'

Her eyes were suddenly wet. They had come a long way and it had been a weary road, but if Arthur was pleased, if Arthur appreciated her efforts to keep up with him it had been worth while.

'Yes,' he continued, nodding gravely, 'you're clever, Mary. Cleverer than I am in some ways. We're really rather an extraordinary pair.'

They looked at each other and smiled.

Arthur thought—she's a beautiful woman, and she's mine.

Mary thought—Arthur has come back to me.

CHAPTER XII

Margaret

SEVERAL days passed. Iain did not see Linda, but he heard from Donald that she was none the worse for her adventure. He was not unhappy, for he knew that she was here in the glen, and he felt that things would come right for him if he waited patiently. He practised his pipes and roamed about with his field-glasses, and sometimes he went out in the old boat and caught some mackerel for his breakfast.

One day when he was finishing his solitary dinner he heard the sound of a motor-launch approaching.

'It is Miss Finlay,' Morag said, putting her head in at the kitchen door. 'It is Miss Finlay and Calum in the Cluan motor-boat.'

Iain left his coffee and went out. He met Margaret coming up the path.

'Just in time for some coffee,' he said, smiling at her. 'Morag makes it very well now that I've persuaded her not to boil it.'

'So you're still alive!' Margaret exclaimed.

He wondered if she had heard of his adventure on the island with Linda and, if so, what garbled version she had heard.

'It's nice to see you, Meg,' he told her.

'You knew where to find me if you *wanted* to see me.'

'But I haven't got wings.'

'Oh!' she cried remorsefully. 'Oh, what a fool I am! Here have I been cursing you for not coming over, and you haven't a boat. You know, Iain, you really are a difficult person to get hold of. Why haven't you a telephone? I haven't been able to do a thing I wanted since the grouse-party arrived; it's been one thing after another. Father nearly demented because of people falling off at the last moment; Fergus in bed with lumbago—and you know how Father relies on Fergus for everything, he simply hates anybody else to load for him, poor dear—and my cook's uncle falling downstairs and insisting that nobody else can nurse him properly. Of course I had to let her go—I couldn't have her weeping into the soufflés——'

Iain put her into a chair, gave her some coffee, found a cigarette and lighted it for her.

' " Basingstoke, Margaret, Basingstoke ",' he said, smiling.

' I know,' she said, laughing a little, despite herself, ' I'm sort of worked up about everything. Oh, Iain, d'you remember that time in Edinburgh when we saw *Ruddigore*? —*How* I laughed!'

' Yes, it was fun,' he said. He thought: Poor lamb, she's worried and bothered—I feel exactly as if she were my sister in spite of what old Finlay said. The worst of it is I mustn't be too nice—how horrible!—*Ruddigore* was fun. I almost asked Meg to marry me that night—I wish I had *shared memories* with Linda.

Margaret was looking at him through the smoke of her cigarette—as usual she had managed to shroud herself in a smoke-screen in a few moments.

' What are you thinking about?' she asked.

He picked amongst his thoughts for a suitable offering. ' *Ruddigore*,' he said. ' It was fun. Tell me about your worries, Meg, but tell me slowly.'

' Oh, Iain, you *are* nice! But I don't want to bother you. I really came over to cheer you up, you know. Would it cheer you up to hear about my worries?'

He laughed. ' I'm not such a hard-hearted brute as all

that. But I don't really need much cheering. I'm all right.'

' Yes, you look quite cheerful,' she said, looking at him intently. ' I expected to find you a bit under the weather with the guns popping off all round you——'

' I'm all right,' he said again.

' Well, I wish I were. I told you about my cook. I've got a temporary with a foul temper who's upsetting the whole house and making everybody's life a burden. Father's annoyed because Sir Julius has deserted him at the last moment and gone to Ardfalloch. I can't say I'm sorry because I've no use at all for Sir Julius, but it's rather cool. What's the attraction at Ardfalloch?—Who *are* those people, Iain?'

' The Hetherington Smiths?—Oh, they're just London people—as Donald says—I don't know anything about them except that they have plenty of money.'

' They seem quite nice. I wondered if you knew anything about them. I called, you know—Father made me— and she was in. I rather liked the woman. She's plump and comfortable, and unshockable—I don't mean that I tried to shock the poor lady, but I felt she was unshockable—I felt she would have been perfectly calm if I had turned a somersault in the drawing-room or put my feet on the tea-table. It was *horrid* going to Ardfalloch and finding strangers there—simply horrid—— Oh, Iain, why did you do it?'

' I had to,' he said firmly.

She sighed. Then she continued : ' They're coming over to lunch at Cluan on Sunday—and they want to give a dance.'

' A dance!' he exclaimed.

' Yes. It's rather sporting of them, I think. Mrs. Hetherington Smith said the drawing-room would be perfect for a dance—of course it would be. I'm to ask anyone I like and as many as I like. She wants it to be a success.'

'A dance,' Iain said again—they were going to give a dance in his house! At first he was almost angry, and then he thought—how foolish I am! Of course they've a perfect right to give a dance at Ardfalloch, why shouldn't they? And then he thought—Linda will be there—*Linda.*

'I wondered about pipers,' Margaret was saying. 'Pipers for the reels. They're getting a band from Glasgow— money seems to be no object—but we must have pipers for the reels. What about Alec MacNeil?'

'Alec, of course,' agreed Iain; 'and Gregor Macpherson from Balnafin——'

'I thought of Black Donald,' Margaret said.

'No, not Black Donald,' said Iain, smiling. 'He's a very good piper, but somebody might give him whisky by mistake—on no account must you have Black Donald.'

'Well, what about Duncan?'

'He's very good,' Iain admitted; 'but Gregor is better for reels. Alec and Gregor are the two to get, Meg. Are you going to ask me to the dance?'

'You!' she exclaimed in amazement.

'Yes, I'd like to go,' he replied. He thought—I shall dance with Linda.

'Is it a joke, Iain?'

'No,' he said quietly.

'But, Iain, you don't want to go—you don't want to go to a dance—at Ardfalloch.'

'Yes, I think I do.'

'But, Iain—you can't mean it,' she said incredulously. 'My dear—you would hate it. You would be miserable.'

'I'd like it,' he said stubbornly. He thought—it will be heaven to dance with Linda—of course Meg thinks I'm mad. I can't help that. I must go. I wish I could tell her about Linda—it would be the best thing—but I can't do it.

'Well,' she said in a strained voice, 'well, that's settled then. You had better dine with us first. I'll send a boat for

151

you. The date isn't settled yet, but I'll let you know when it is——'

'Don't be cross with me, Meg.'

'Cross!' said Margaret almost tearfully. 'How can I help being cross? I don't understand—it's not like you, Iain. It's not *you*. It's all horrible, the whole thing. You living here in this *pigsty*—simply because you're too proud —too proud——'

'It's not pride, Meg.'

'Yes, it's pride. And then you say you want to go to this dance—to go to your own house as a guest—you of all people—to accept the hospitality of this London upstart who wouldn't know his own grandfather if he met him in the street—to go to your own house as this man's guest—it's not *you*, Iain.'

'Don't, Meg,' he said, holding out his hand and trying to stop the wild rush of words.

Meg took his hand and held it. She looked up at him, smiling shakily through her tears. 'Basingstoke again, I suppose,' she said.

'Basingstoke again,' he agreed, trying to speak lightly. He rose and walked across to the window and stood there, looking out. This is horrible, he thought—this is ghastly!

She was talking more calmly now. 'It's because I don't understand,' she explained. 'I thought I knew you so well. You see, when you know a person well—have known them for years and years—you know how they feel about things. You know how they'll act in given circumstances— and you—I thought it was the last thing on earth you would want to do. It isn't even as if you were mad about dancing. There must be something . . . something I don't know. . . .'

Her voice died away into silence.

'Yes,' he said at last. 'Yes, I suppose that's it.' He thought—she'll guess now. It was the only thing to do, but how I hate myself for hurting her! What a brute I am!

What a darling she is! I wonder if she could ever be friends with Linda, or is that too much to expect?

He heard her saying in a queer strained voice, 'Well, I must be going. Calum will be tired of waiting—I left him in the boat. It's such an inconvenient landing-place here. Come over and see us soon.—Oh, I forgot, you haven't a boat. I'll send one over for you.'

'Yes, I'd like to come—but there's no hurry, Meg.'

'I had better get back,' she said quickly, almost desperately. 'It might rain. I only came over for a few minutes. What an awful storm it was on Sunday night! The waves were enormous, breaking over the pier. Father said he had never seen a worse storm in summer—it came on so suddenly—you're sheltered here, of course——' She was gathering up her bag and searching for her gloves as she spoke.

Iain longed to comfort her, but he knew he mustn't. He dare not offer her sympathy. The only thing he could do for Meg was to help her to get away quickly. He found her other glove, which had fallen under the table, and followed her to the door.

As they went down to the boat together, through the summer afternoon sunshine, they heard a staccato volley of shots coming from the Ardfalloch moors, and a covey of grouse swooped over their heads, uttering terrified squawks, and fled away over the loch.

'I'm sorry for them,' said Margaret shakily. 'It must be horrible. If they were shot all the year round it wouldn't be so bad, but to be left in peace for months and months—and then—suddenly——'

'I know,' said Iain. 'I've been feeling the same thing all week. It's not logical, I suppose, because, if I were shooting them myself, I wouldn't think about it. But when you see them flying away like that—flying away from their homes where they have been so happy and peaceful—it makes you think.'

153

They had reached the boat. She pretended not to see Iain's hand and jumped in by herself. She was so shaken that she was afraid to take his hand.

' It will be all right about the dance,' she said, ' I'll let you know——'

Calum started the engine and let in the clutch, they sped away in a splurge of white foam. Iain watched the boat to see if she would look back and wave—but she did neither— he watched it out of sight and then went slowly home. He felt utterly exhausted and miserable. Far from cheering him up, Meg's visit had depressed him beyond words.

CHAPTER XIII

The Picnic

IT was a glorious afternoon of golden sunshine. The loch was very calm, the breeze was fitful; here and there a patch of ripples caught the rays of the sun and shimmered like burnished brass; here and there on the shore a wave plashed feebly, or ran along the side of a rock in a silver undulation, before it was drawn back into the calm bosom of the loch— for the tide was starting to ebb.

Linda and Richard and Iain were on their way to the island in the old patched boat. It was the long-promised expedition.—On the very first day that Richard had met the boatmender they had talked about the island, and the boat-mender had promised that some day they would go for a picnic there—some day when the boat was mended. The boat had been mended for days and days, and Richard had begun to think that ' some day ' would never come—and then, suddenly, it came. Richard shivered with happiness— it was quite perfect—there was nothing else that he wanted. He leaned over the side and dabbled one hand in the water. It was so clear, that, in the shallows, you could see the little shells at the bottom, and the seaweed moving gently with the ebbing tide—it was so green that you almost felt it would stain your hand green—but it didn't.

Linda was happy. It was a lovely day (the sort of day when it would have been a crime not to feel happy); if there were another reason for her happiness, she did not seek it.

Iain was happy. Of the three, he, alone, knew and appreciated to the full the happiness that possessed him and the reason for it. There was really only one reason for his happiness—*Linda*. He rowed with full strokes, bravely, confidently. The old boat clove through the water; the mainland receded; the cottage dwindled into a house for dolls. He beached the boat at the old landing-place on the north side of the island and helped his passengers to disembark. Then he lifted the tea-basket onto his shoulder and led the way up the grassy slope.

The turf was short and resilient; here and there were grey-green cushions of leaves from which sprung long wiry stems supporting the pink flowers of sea-thrift—round pink balls of stiff petals that looked as though they were made of paper. Richard ran ahead and began to pick them with cries of delight.

'How different it looks!' Linda exclaimed.

It was extraordinarily peaceful, the whole island seemed to dream in the warm sunshine. The castle, hoary with age, was slumbering, too—it was grey amongst its green surroundings, old and grey. Linda saw how completely ruined it was—the tumbled stones were covered with thick ivy, there was yellow lichen on the walls. Here and there, where soil had gathered amongst the rubble of fallen stones, there were cushions of purple thyme which gave off a thick sweet smell like honey. Graceful strands of 'Ladies' Bedstraw,' yellow as gold, lurked in sheltered corners. It was all so green and pretty, but, beneath the greenness and the prettiness, Linda saw the bones of the dead giant.

For a long time she did not speak, and then she said, 'I can't—I can't imagine it—as it was—people living here.'

'Have you been trying to imagine it?' he asked her.

'Yes, but somehow I can't—can you?'

'Sometimes I can,' he replied. 'But not to-day.

The present is enough for me to-day. I don't want the past.'

In the outer courtyard was the well. It was very deep. Linda looked down, and saw, far below, the glimmer of dark water. It looked like oil, Linda thought, there was a faint shine upon it like oil. The sides of the well were uneven and covered with brown fungus, and small pale green ferns.

Iain took her hand and they went inside the great hall of the castle. The roof gaped forlornly; two large oak trees overhung the roofless part and dimmed the light, the sun-shine fell in yellow splashes on the uneven floor. Here, in the great hall, it was almost as if they were standing at the bottom of a still pool, for the light that filtered through the leaves was pale green, and the shadows moved quietly and reluctantly like sea-weed in undulating water. The pale green blades of grass that had sprung up in the crevices between the tilted flags treasured a light of their own— they seemed dimly luminous as glow-worms are.

Iain and Linda walked through a crumbling doorway onto a little terrace bright with sun. Linda gazed round her, gazed at the ruined mullions, the ivied windows, the heaps of rubble spilled from the thickness of the ruined walls. At last she said:

' It is wonderful—all of it. Other ruins have histories, but these ruins are yours—your history. Your own people lived here—they lived their lives just like our lives— they were born here, and died. These stones sheltered them——'

She scarcely knew what she said, her thoughts were too evasive, too inconsequent to put into words. Iain watched the expressions chase each other across her face—he did not interrupt her thoughts. The castle meant a great deal to Iain, it was precious to him for many reasons. He was glad that Linda felt the strange appeal of the place, that she was moved by its pathos and its history.

'Do you ever wish you still lived here?' she said at last.

'Sometimes,' he admitted. He laughed a trifle ruefully, and added: 'The past must have been easier to live in.'

'Do you mean easier financially?'

'Partly, I suppose, but not altogether. My ancestors did not need much money—they lived on the produce of their land and took what they wanted.'

'What else did you mean?' Linda wanted to know. She sat down on a sun-warmed stone and looked up at him. The sun fell upon her small intent face; Iain saw that the white skin had warmed to a pale gold, and there were some tiny freckles on her nose, and beneath her eyes—Ardfalloch freckles, he thought, with a warming of his heart.

'What else did you mean?' she said again.

He pulled himself together to answer her question. 'Life is awfully complicated now,' he said, trying to express his thoughts; 'you have got to conform to laws that your instinct tells you are false laws—it makes me angry sometimes.'

'*They* must have had laws, too.'

'They had their own laws, of course,' Iain admitted. 'Natural laws, dictated to them by their own consciences, by their honour, by their own feeling of what was right for themselves. If the chief happened to be a bad chief—a few of them were bad—he made life a hell for everybody; but, if he had naturally fine instincts, the thing worked admirably. Everybody was happy and prosperous. Laws are made for bad people, really. They are made for people who have no decent instincts. My ideal state would have no laws.'

'But you would be king,' Linda said, laughing at him.

Iain laughed too. 'King!' he exclaimed. 'At present I

am king of a deserted island. But, yes, you are right. I envisaged myself as a benevolent autocrat—rather funny, isn't it?'

Linda did not think it funny, she thought it was natural. He was descended from a line of men who had been kings in their own small way, and even now, in the sight of his own people, he was a king. Their devotion and loyalty could not fail to influence him, he had been influenced by it from his cradle. Linda thought he was wonderfully humble and human considering the circumstances of his life. She had found no arrogance in him.

' Let's go and see the tower room,' Linda said at last.

' Yes, if you like,' Iain replied. ' It will be damp and gloomy to-day, but we will visit it for the sake of old times.'

He led her through the passages; they were quite light to-day, for the sunshine streamed in through the gaping holes in the walls and roof. The tower chamber was cold and damp and gloomy—just as Iain had said—there were evidences of their tenancy in the empty cocoa tin which stood on the table, and the grey ash of the dead fire in the hearth.

Linda shivered. ' I almost wish we hadn't come,' she said. ' It was so warm and cosy that night——'

' I must put it straight and refill my cupboard,' said Iain. ' Donald usually cleans it up, but he's too busy.'

' Perhaps we had better see what Richard's doing.'

They went back to where they had left Richard (the sunshine was warm and comforting after the damp chill of the ruins). He had not moved far from where they had left him. He had picked a big bunch of flowers, yellow and pink, they were lying beside him on the ground.

' Look at him!' Iain said softly. He put his hand upon Linda's arm with a restraining movement, and, together, they stood looking at Richard.

Ardfalloch in August

He was sitting in a little hollow of soft turf with his feet doubled back at either side of him, the sun shone on his dark hair giving it the greeny blue sheen of a raven's wing, his small pale face was serious and preoccupied. Before him on the short turf were some pebbles, and one or two shells that he had found on the tiny strand. Richard took the pebbles in his hand, one by one, and looked at them and put them down again, he was singing a little tune to himself the while, a little crooning song with no beginning and no end. Now he bent forward over his treasures, now he leaned back and looked at them sideways. He was entranced by his occupation, caught up into a world of his own—a little friendly world, a little sheltered place in the big unknown world. These things were fragments of his child's world—a piece of broken china, a few rounded pebbles, two shells—they were sharp, or smooth, hollow or rounded, they were different in shape, in colour, in texture.

Another thought flitted through his mind in a shadowy way—they were his because he had found them himself, and they were precious—*his treasures*. In a little while Richard's standard would change, but these treasures were the beginning of his education in values—they had set him a standard of what was worth while. Values are only arbitrary after all. Why should a golden pebble be of more value than a stone one? The world has decreed that it shall be so. Richard's values were his own, he knew nothing of the world's standard of values—that would come when the savage became civilized. He treasured this pebble for its strange shape, that one for the vein of quartz that ran through it like sugar; the piece of china was pretty, he had found it when he was picking flowers amongst the debris of the ruins, it was part of an old cup—there were pink roses on it and a band of gold. The jagged fragment of china belonged to the past, but it was not for its associations that

Richard valued it; he valued it because it was pretty—the past was nothing to him. For Richard the world started afresh each day when he awoke, and was rounded off by bed-time.

'He is making a little garden,' Linda whispered.

Iain shook his head. 'No,' he said. 'It's something much more—fundamental. Don't let's disturb him.'

They retreated and sat down a little way off, on a heap of fallen masonry.

'What is he doing? What do you mean?' Linda asked. She felt a strange sense of annoyance, a shadow of anger: Richard was hers, why should Iain think he knew what the child was doing better than she did?

Iain handed her his field-glasses and, after a moment or two, she got them focused upon the small intent figure in the hollow. She saw that Richard was not making a garden —he was not *making* anything.

'What *is* he doing?' she said again, but this time the note of irritation was absent from her voice, it was a question pure and simple.

'He is discovering—Life,' Iain said, trying to explain.

'I don't understand.'

'The world is so big—so strange and complicated. Have you ever thought what a queer thing it must be for a child to be pitchforked into Life—into this big strange terrifying world that it knows nothing about? It doesn't happen quite like that, of course, because the unconsciousness of a child protects it, and only lets a little bit of the world through at a time. The child's consciousness grows, gradually it can take in more and more of the world, but the world is not *real*. And then there comes a time—there must come a moment when things become real—it happens suddenly. I think Richard is realising the reality of things—it is difficult to explain, but I feel sure I am right. If he had lived in the country it would have come before—less dramatically, because he would have been younger, and his consciousness would have been less developed——'

With a sudden return of her anger Linda said, 'Why should you understand Richard better than I?'

Iain laughed. 'Darling, you're not jealous!'

Linda considered this carefully and then she smiled. 'I believe I am a little,' she admitted. 'You see Richard has been all mine——'

'And now I want a bit of him,' Iain said gravely.

'Oh, Iain, I am a fool! It is good for Richard to be with a man—with you. I have always wanted it for him——'

'You have done splendidly,' Iain told her. 'Richard is perfect—not spoiled at all—but he is getting older. In a little while he will need a man—and I shall be here to help you with him.'

'You are very sure!' she exclaimed, withdrawing a little.

'I am very sure,' he replied. He was sure. He knew quite well that unless Linda had loved him she would not have allowed him to go so far; she would not have allowed him to say what he had said without making it plain that there was no hope for him. He was quite sure that the only barrier between them was the fact that she was not yet free. She would not let him approach any closer until she was free, and he loved her all the more for her scruples.

After a little, Richard tired of his treasures; he looked up, like a person waking from sleep, and saw Iain and Linda, and waved. Then he came towards them, running up the slope.

'Look what I've found,' he said eagerly, anxiously.

Linda said nothing. She did not really understand, and she was afraid of saying the wrong thing. She watched while the two dirty little hands unfolded to display their treasures.

Iain was grave. He took the pebbles and examined them carefully; then he looked at the piece of china——

' Do you know,' he said, ' that piece of china is a piece of a cup which belonged to my great-grandmother? She used to live here when these ruins were a castle. There are still two cups and saucers belonging to the set.'

' I've seen them,' Richard said breathlessly. ' They're in the cabinet in the drawing-room.'

Linda took the fragment. She held it in her hand and thought—I wonder how it was broken—was she sorry? China was very valuable in those days—and tea was a luxury. Perhaps somebody brought her these pretty cups and she valued them—life must have been rough and bare here—and the cups were pretty and fragile. How sad she must have been when one got broken!

' I'll show you something funny about your pebbles,' Iain was saying. He had unscrewed one of the lenses of his field-glasses and was holding it near his eye. Richard leaned against his knee. ' This is a magnifying glass—it makes things look bigger. Look at your pebble—can you see it, Richard?'

' No,' said Richard, screwing up his eyes. ' Oh, yes—no —oh yes, I can. Oh, Boatmender, how queer! It's all made up of little bits.'

Linda watched them and her heart enveloped them both. There was no shadow of jealousy left. She thought—he is perfect with Richard. She listened to the careful, simple description of how rocks were made, and pebbles, and gravel, and sand. Richard's eyes were bright, he was listening eagerly, asking the meaning of words that were unfamiliar to him. She thought—I am not enough for Richard —not enough. There was pain in the thought, but there was happiness too. A strange new beautiful happiness was flooding her life. It had started that night on the island and she had fought against it. She had told herself over and over again that she would have nothing to do with love, she had finished with men—and marriage—all that was over and done with. Good heavens, hadn't she suffered enough! She was free now, and she would remain free, she would devote the rest of her life to Richard.

She had told herself all this again and again with quite unnecessary vehemence, unnecessary since there was nobody to argue with her. She could have disposed of Iain MacAslan in a few words, but she didn't. She argued with herself instead. And the queerest thing was, that, despite all her arguments and brave decisions, the tide of happiness rose. . . .

The gates opened, Linda saw a glimpse of that possible future—future with Iain. It was very beautiful, and warm and safe. She and Iain and Richard together—Iain protecting them with his strength and his gentleness, loving them. She saw a future in which days like this would be frequent; days of sunshine and leisure in the glorious surroundings of Ardfalloch. She saw long evenings before the fire—she and Iain reading and talking, with Richard safely in bed upstairs. She saw—with surprise—that there was nothing to prevent these dreams from becoming realities. They loved each other, what could part them? Once she was really free, free to acknowledge her love for Iain, free to give him what he wanted and make him happy, there would be nothing between them—there could be nothing—ever again. . . .

And then, quite suddenly, the gates closed; the shadow of her fears returned; the future was dark again, she could see no happiness there, no safety.

Linda struggled against the impending sense of doom— how foolish it was to be afraid of shadows! They loved each other; what could happen? She did not know the answer now, she only knew that she was frightened. The golden sunshine was a mockery. She rose and went over to the place where Iain had left the hamper and began to unpack it and set out the tea. She was too restless to sit still, and the peace and quietness of the afternoon had become oppressive. As she unpacked the cups and spread the white cloth upon the grass she looked up and saw that Iain and Richard were still examining the pebbles, still discussing them. The two heads were very close together, bent over the magnifying glass. Two heads, both dark and smooth—they might have been father and son if fate had been kinder.

They sat on the short resilient turf and had tea. Richard was in the highest spirits; he chattered continuously about all he saw, or had seen. It was just as well, for his innocent chatter eased the tension. Iain felt the shadow that had fallen upon Linda's soul; it showed in her eyes. He wondered what it was; perhaps she did not know herself. If they had been alone he would have tried to find out what the shadow was, but they were not alone. He thought—she has suffered a great deal. I shall have to be patient and very gentle—it will all come right—it must come right.

Presently Richard, too, fell silent; he was replete and contented. The sun was warm, but there was a small cool breeze off the water, it came to them in little whiffs scented with seaweed from the rocks which had been bared by the receding tide. A rabbit came out of its hole and looked at them, it came quite near and sat erect with pricked ears, gazing at them in surprise. They all kept very still.

'Why is it so tame, Boatmender?' Richard whispered.

'Because the island is so quiet—so deserted,' Iain told him. 'Nobody comes here for months at a time, so the rabbits forget that they ought to be frightened.'

Richard threw a small piece of scone at the rabbit—it was gone in a flash, bounding away with a whisk of its white scut.

'Oh!' said Richard in a disappointed tone. 'I thought it would like something to eat——'

'You frightened it, Richard,' Linda said. 'Rabbits don't like scones—they eat grass and lettuce.'

'Silly old rabbit!' said Richard crossly.

'It is you who are silly,' Linda told him, with rare and inexplicable irritation.

'I'm not,' he said. 'Rabbits are silly not to eat scones—aren't they, Boatmender?'

Iain looked at him gravely, there was a smile lurking in the corners of his mouth, but he kept it carefully in check. 'Mummy's right,' he said. 'Rabbits know what's good for them. It was because you didn't know what was good for it that you offered it a scone.'

Richard considered the matter, frowning thoughtfully.

'You see,' Iain continued, 'I might offer you something that wouldn't be good for you—a glass of whisky, perhaps —well, if you refused it you would be wise. I should be silly for offering it to you.'

Richard laughed. 'The rabbit was me and I was you,' he said. 'I was silly to offer it a scone—I was silly, not the rabbit. If I had offered it whisky would it have drunk it, Boatmender?'

'I'm sure it wouldn't.'

'Why?'

'Because rabbits don't drink anything. They couldn't live here on this island if they needed water to drink. The only water here is in the well, far too deep for any rabbit to get near. There are casual pools amongst the rocks when it rains, but they are always a little brackish——'

'What's brackish?'

'Salty,' said Iain, smiling.

'D'you mean rabbits never drink *anything*?' Richard asked incredulously.

'They drink the dew, I suppose, and they get moisture from the grass and the sap that is in all growing plants.'

'I didn't know that either,' Linda said, 'about rabbits

not needing water. It's interesting. I'm afraid I don't know much about the real country.'

'You'll soon learn,' Iain said with a significant look.

Linda blushed, and her eyes fell, but she did not contradict his assertion.

It's all right, Iain thought, it really is all right. His heart sang within him, and, all at once, the sunshine seemed more golden and the loch more blue.

After tea Richard collected sticks and they made a fire— a little picnic fire amongst the rocks near the shore to keep the midges at bay. There was driftwood amongst the rocks (some of it from Iain's boat which had been dashed to pieces the night of the storm) and pine branches full of resin which caught the flame and roared themselves into fine grey ash. Richard's face as he watched and tended the fire was solemn—almost awed with happiness.

'It's lovely,' he kept saying. 'It's lovely—it's a *real* fire, Boatmender.'

'I think he ought to call you—something else,' Linda whispered. 'It seems——'

'No,' said Iain quickly. 'Leave it just now—I like the name. It's Richard's own name for me. Later perhaps——'

Richard sighed. 'I wish we could stay here always and always,' he said gravely.

They lingered over the fire, talking intermittently until it was time to go, then they embarked in the little boat and rowed back to the old cottage.

'When am I going to see you again?' Iain asked anxiously.

'Soon,' Linda replied. 'I can't promise anything definite—it's so difficult with the house full of people, and Mrs. Hetherington Smith really needs me.'

'I'm coming to the dance. Are you glad, Linda?'

'Yes, of course,' she said simply. 'But—but you won't like it, Iain——'

'I'm coming to dance with you,' he told her.

'You must come and see me in bed, Boatmender,' Richard said. 'I won't be asleep—I'll stay awake specially. You *will* come, won't you?'

'If Mummy lets me,' Iain promised, smiling.

It never occurred to Richard to be surprised at the news that his friend the boatmender was coming to the dance at Ardfalloch House. Social distinctions mattered nothing to Richard, his world was divided sharply into two classes: those who liked him and whom he liked, and those who took no notice of him and of whom he took no notice. There were one or two exceptions to the rule, but that was all.

Richard jumped out of the boat as it touched the shore and pulled at the rope with energy and determination. Iain and Linda got out more slowly—it had been a happy time and they were disinclined to end it and say 'goodbye.' They got out slowly and the boat was made fast; they walked up slowly to the little house.

'We must hurry,' Linda said. 'It is past Richard's bed-time—no, don't walk back with us, Iain, it will be better—not to.'

They stood still for a few moments, looking at the loch, at the sun that had begun to descend towards the western hills, at the reflections of the tall trees in the water.

'I shall be late for dinner,' Linda said. She found it difficult to go, difficult to leave him. She wanted to stay; she was safe with Iain. She loved him.

Richard ran on up the path.

'I *must* go,' Linda said, almost desperately. She let her hand rest in Iain's hand for a few moments, and then she withdrew it. 'Good-bye,' she said.

'Au revoir, Linda.'

'Yes, au revoir.'

She turned quickly and followed Richard up the path

that led through the woods to Ardfalloch House—the steep path with the tree roots that held it together—at the top of the slope she stopped and looked back—he was still there, standing just where she had left him; they waved to each other.

CHAPTER XIV

Linda

IT was very quiet in the little cottage, a fire burned slowly on the hearth, for the evenings are often chilly in Ard-falloch, and, besides, Iain liked a fire—it was company. Iain was busy at the table working out the accounts for the estate. He had not seen Linda for two days, but he was not really impatient—he was sure of her now.

The table was covered with books and papers and bills. Iain was trying to decide how much money he would have in hand for improvements and renovations, and to decide what was necessary and what was not. The repairs to the boat-house were absolutely necessary, he must get an estimate from Fraser for that, and Donald's cottage must have a new roof unless the old roof could be satisfactorily repaired. He owed it to Donald and Morag to do what he could for them—they were doing so much for him and they would not accept payment in the ordinary sense. And he had promised Alec MacNeil that he would build him some pigsties—that was a promise. He would have to see what all this was going to cost before he could think of deepening the harbour, or putting wire along the road to Balnafin, or doing a hundred and one things that he wanted in the house itself. Simpson wanted some of the money put aside for the land taxes, and the overdraft at the bank must be paid off.

Iain sighed. The money had seemed so large at first, but now he began to think it would not go very far. He wondered how other landowners managed; how did people make money—Mr. Finlay, for instance. Supposing he asked Mr. Finlay for a stock exchange tip and put the thousand into that—it might double itself, and then he would not have to let Ardfalloch next year. Iain lay back and thought about it—had he the right to risk it? There was very little risk really. Mr. Finlay knew what he was doing. It wasn't like gambling on horses—that was a mug's game, if you like! Iain thought—other men make money, but I can't do that, partly because I haven't been trained to make money, and partly because I haven't time. If I had a factor—but what factor could run Ardfalloch as I can?

He was still thinking about it, trying to find some way out of the difficulties of his position, when he heard light steps on the path and somebody knocked at the door.

Iain went to open the door. It was quite dark outside, dark and cloudy, a slight figure was standing on the step.

'Linda!' he exclaimed in amazement.

'Let me come in, Iain,' she said breathlessly.

He took her hand and led her into the little sitting-room. The hand was cold, it trembled in his.

'I had to come,' she said, still in that breathless voice. 'I ran—nearly all the way——'

'My dear—what is the matter?'

She sat down and loosened the silk scarf which was tied round her head; he saw that she was in evening dress beneath her fur coat—a little string of brilliants was clasped round her bare throat, they rose and fell in time with her hurried breathing.

'I was mad to come—like this,' she said, raising her eyes and looking at him. 'But I had to see you, Iain—I had to see you——'

'Of course,' he said incoherently. 'Why shouldn't you —it's all right, Linda, why shouldn't you come?' He

171

thought—how lovely she is! How lovely—and dear—something has frightened her and she came to me. He was very gentle with her.

'Tell me what is the matter,' he said, taking her hand again.

Linda let her hand lie in his—how kind and comforting he was! She was glad now she had come, glad that she had given way to that wild impulse to see him.

'I'll tell you what happened,' she said in a calmer voice. 'Perhaps you'll think I'm mad to make such a fuss. It was Richard—he was out in the woods—he often plays alone in the woods near the house—he's quite sensible really, he doesn't go far. He was playing in the woods after tea, and all of a sudden he came running back, terrified, simply terrified—I couldn't find out at first what had frightened him, he just clung to me and shook all over. Mrs. Hetherington Smith told me to give him a hot bath and put him to bed—she is such a sensible, practical woman, so kind, and—and calm. I got him into bed and he lay there holding my hand, and at last I got it out of him—he had seen Jack——'

'You mean—Medworth?' Iain said.

She nodded with her eyes on his face.

'But that is—that is awful,' Iain said. 'Awful that the boy would be so frightened of—of him.'

'It wasn't just seeing him,' said Linda slowly. 'There was more in it than that. It was something he said that frightened Richard so. I couldn't find out exactly what he *did* say—Richard wouldn't tell me—couldn't tell me. He just clung to my hand and said, " I don't want to go away " —he said it over and over again. He was frantic.'

'Are you sure it really was Medworth?'

'That's what Mrs. Hetherington Smith said. She thinks it was a tramp or something—*tinkers,* there were some tinkers camping in the quarry—of course Richard hasn't seen Jack for months, so he might have been mistaken, I suppose. I couldn't question Richard much, he was so frantic.'

' It can't have been Medworth.'

' I feel it *was*,' she said desperately. ' I *feel* it was Jack. He's followed us here—I'm frightened, Iain.'

' There's no need to be frightened, darling,' Iain said quietly. ' He can't do anything to harm you, even if it *was* Medworth; but really and truly it isn't likely that it was Medworth, is it?'

' No,' she said doubtfully. ' And yet——'

' It isn't likely that Medworth would follow you here, and skulk in the woods just to frighten Richard—there's no sense in it, is there?'

' Not just for that,' she admitted. ' There must be some other reason—he must have some plan——'

' If it really were he,' said Iain again. He saw that his doubts were beginning to affect her.

' Mrs. Hetherington Smith thinks the same as you,' Linda said. ' She thinks it couldn't have been Jack. She thinks it was a tinker—a sort of gipsy—and that he said to Richard, " Wouldn't you like to come with me," or something like that, as a kind of joke, and that Richard thought he really meant it and connected it with Jack. Jack used to say things like that and Richard was always frightened; he used to say, " I'll take you away from your mother and make a man of you ".'

What a beast! Iain thought—what an unutterable swine! He stifled his rage and said aloud—' Well, you see how easily the mistake might have occurred—especially as Richard hasn't seen Medworth for such ages.'

' Richard is so terrified of anyone taking him away,' said Linda thoughtfully, ' it's a sort of obsession——'

' That's because he was frightened when he was very small,' explained Iain gently. ' Medworth frightened him and made such a tremendous impression upon him that the fear was created in the child's mind. I think it will pass away in time—Richard is a plucky little boy really.'

'You said that before—the first day.'

'It's true. He is plucky. But he is highly strung, and that particular fear—the fear of being " taken away " has been planted in his mind.'

They were silent for a little, thinking their own thoughts. Iain was sitting on the arm of the big chair with Linda's hand in his.

She said at last, ' I'm frightened, too.'

'What are you frightened of, Linda?' Iain said quietly. ' Even if it were Medworth—I don't see how it could have been, but even if it *were,* what possible harm could he do? You're not—you're not afraid of physical violence from him, are you?'

' No. Oh no, Jack wouldn't do anything like that,' she replied confidently. ' He's too—too civilised—too afraid of the law—of putting himself in the wrong. He's reckless when he's driving a car, horribly reckless, but—oh, I can't explain it, but I just know that he wouldn't.'

Iain thought about this. He wondered whether Medworth had any idea of kidnapping Richard, but he wasn't going to put that thought into Linda's head.

' He's afraid of the law?' Iain said doubtfully.

' Yes, he is afraid of the whole big machine of the law,' Linda told him. ' From the judge who tried our case down to the traffic policeman at the corner. Jack wouldn't do anything that would put him on the wrong side of the law.'

' Well, what could he do, then?'

' I don't know,' Linda said. ' I don't know—that's just the horrible part.'

There was silence again, and suddenly Iain heard a slight noise—it was so slight that he could not tell what it was, but the night was very still and the room was very quiet.

' Hush,' he said, raising his head.

'What is it, Iain?'

'I thought I heard something——'

They waited in silence, not a sound broke the stillness save the rapid whisper of Linda's breathing and the beating of his own heart.

'Oh, Iain, what was it?' she said again.

'Wait here,' said Iain. 'I'll go and have a look round—it may not have been anything at all——'

He took his electric torch out of the cupboard and went outside; it was still very cloudy and very dark. The moon was hidden behind the clouds, it made a luminous patch in the sky but gave little light. He stood in the doorway for a few moments until his eyes became used to the darkness, and then he began his tour of the house. He looked in the little wood-shed, flashing his torch into the dark corners; he looked behind the water-butt. He went down to where the boat was drawn up on the shingle, and looked about carefully amongst the bushes—there was nothing to be seen. He stood still for a minute, considering—the noise might have been made by some night creature of the woods—only night creatures don't make any noise as a rule. He tried to think what *kind* of a noise it was, but the more he thought about it the less clear it became—it was like trying to recapture a dream. He thought—was it a human noise, a step on the path or the snapping of a dry twig? I can't pin it down as being anything. Supposing it was somebody prowling about—the tinker who frightened Richard—or was it really Medworth who frightened Richard, and is it Medworth—but no, that's absurd—absolutely ridiculous. I'm being infected with Linda's fears. All the same she had better go home.

Linda was waiting for him; she had not moved. She looked up at him when he came in and her eyes met his. He saw that all her fears had returned.

'There was nobody and nothing,' he said lightly.

'Are you sure?' she asked in a low voice.

'Quite sure. I've looked everywhere—perhaps it was a mouse.' He laughed and added, 'Fancy a mouse frightening us like that! Perhaps you are frightened of mice.'

'No,' she replied, trying to smile. 'I'm not frightened of mice—women are supposed to be terrified of mice, but I'm not. It's funny, isn't it?' She added in a different tone, 'I keep my fears for—for other things.'

He looked at her gravely, he could see by her eyes that she was frightened, but she had her fear under control.

'You had better go home now,' he said gently.

'Yes, I must,' she agreed, standing up and tying the scarf round her hair. 'You will walk back with me, won't you, Iain?'

'My dear,' he said, taking her hand, 'did you think I would let you walk back alone—did you think it for a moment?'

'Then—there was someone——' she whispered.

'There was nobody. I wouldn't deceive you, Linda. If I had seen anybody, or any trace of anybody, I would have told you. But the woods are dark, and—I should like to walk back with you, my dear. D'you think this is easy for me?' he added desperately. 'D'you think it's easy for me to let you go?'

'I shouldn't have come,' she said. 'It wasn't fair, really——'

'No, don't say that. I'm glad you came—proud. Always come to me, Linda. I'm not impatient, I can wait. I've waited five years—I can go on waiting——'

'Wait,' she said softly. 'When I am free—if everything is all right——'

He was satisfied with that. He drew her arm through his and they went out into the night. Iain locked the door behind him and put the key in his pocket. They walked up through the woods together.

Linda

It was very dark. Iain's torch made a spot of yellow light on the ground before them as they went; it showed the roots of the trees, and the stones in the path. They went slowly because Linda was tired—he felt her lean on his arm—she was tired out with fears and anxieties.

CHAPTER XV

Unexpected Visitors

A FEW days later Linda and Richard were having tea with Iain in the cottage. The Ardfalloch house-party was shooting the West Moors, so Linda was free. She and Richard had spent a quiet day together, and, in the afternoon, they had walked down to the cottage and had been invited to stay to tea. It was a happy meal. They had scones, made by Morag, and oatcakes and honey, and, of course, ginger-nuts.

'I had tea with Morag yesterday,' Richard said. 'I like Morag's cottage. She lets me help her with things.'

'Do you think it bothers Morag?' Linda enquired anxiously. 'Richard is always running down to the Mac-Neils' cottage——'

'I'm sure Morag likes it,' replied Iain. 'She is very fond of children. Richard will take no harm there.'

'Yes, she likes me,' Richard said confidently.

Linda and Iain looked at each other and smiled.

They talked about various things, Linda had some comical little stories about the house-party, about Mr. Stacey's conceit and the calm way that Mrs. Hetherington Smith smoothed out the tangles that arose, and how amusing it was to see Desmond Cray pursuing Greta Bastable.

'And what about Sir Julius?' Iain wanted to know. He had not forgotten what Linda had told him of Sir Julius Hastie's admiration for herself.

Linda frowned. 'He's rather a nuisance, sometimes,' she

said. ' So frightfully pleased with himself that he is difficult
to snub. He turns every topic until it reflects himself——'

' Yes, I know,' Iain said. ' I've met him at Cluan and
I always thought he was objectionable and conceited.' He
was glad that Linda had seen through the man—lots of
people didn't.

When tea was over, Richard and Iain retired to the
kitchen to wash up. Linda had offered to perform this
essentially woman's job, but she was told, kindly but firmly,
that her services were not required.

' There's no room for three,' Richard explained. ' And
the boatmender and I know where things are.'

' Very well,' said Linda meekly. She sat down on the
old wicker chair and looked about her. She had been here
before, of course, but she had never had the time nor the
opportunity to see the little room at her leisure. Everything here was very personal to Iain. There were one or
two pictures on the wall which he had brought with him
from Ardfalloch House, his pipe was on the mantelpiece,
and there were a few books on the table beside the fireplace.
Everything in the room was shabby, but it was all clean and
tidy, and, somehow, homey. It was the room of a man who
was fastidious about his surroundings.

From the little kitchen came sounds of clattering dishes
and babbling talk. Richard was happy—he had got over
his fright. Linda thought it was strange how quickly he
had recovered from his fright. Somehow or other the re-
membrance of it had passed from his mind. She could not
understand it. She thought—how strange it is that I cannot
see what is in Richard's mind!

Linda was still meditating rather sadly upon the hidden
secrets of the human heart when the door of the cottage
opened, and a figure stood on the threshold, outlined against
the brightness of the afternoon sunshine. There was something strange and dreamlike about her sudden appearance;

Linda had heard no sound of a step on the path, nor creak of the door opening—one moment the door was shut and there was nobody there, and the next moment the door was open and the figure was outlined in its frame.

The figure was that of a lady, small and slight, and dressed in a dark grey coat with a fur collar and a small black hat. Her hair was pure silvery white, her eyes were very dark, and her face was pale, but, as she stood there, gazing at Linda, a sudden wild-rose colour flooded her cheeks.

It was difficult to struggle back to the everyday world. Linda had been deep in thought, and the suddenness and unexpectedness of the stranger's appearance was almost uncanny. Uncanny, too, the way she hesitated in the door-way looking back over her shoulder with a kind of timidity. She had the timidity of a wild creature of the woods.

They gazed at each other in silence. Linda was recovering from her surprise, but she felt that if she moved or spoke the woman would be gone, would take fright and vanish like the small red fawn that she and Richard had seen one day when they were walking in the woods above Ardfalloch House.

After a moment or two the stranger came farther into the room and looked round, vaguely and timidly. Linda's impression that there was something strange about this woman was confirmed—she could not have said what it was that was strange about her, only that she was not like other people. Linda thought—*this is absurd, I must speak to her and ask her what she wants*—but she was inhibited by the feeling that, if she spoke, the woman would disappear. She was still wondering what to do—held in a kind of dream—when another figure appeared in the doorway—a tall angular woman dressed in black, carrying a suitcase in either hand. This woman was a different person altogether, she was flesh and blood, capable and practical. She marched straight in and set the suitcases down on the floor with a dunt as if she were glad to be rid of them. Then she raised her eyes and saw Linda.

There was a moment's silence. Linda thought—*she is annoyed at finding me here. I wonder why.* She said with sudden shyness, 'Are you looking for—for MacAslan?'

'He's here, is he not?' enquired the second woman in a downright manner.

'He's in the kitchen,' Linda said. 'I'll tell him.'

She rose quickly and went to tell Iain that two visitors had arrived to see him.

'Visitors!' Iain said, frowning with annoyance as he dried his hands on the cloth behind the kitchen door. 'It must be Meg—nobody else knows I'm here. What a bore!'

'You had better go quickly,' Linda told him. 'I'll finish up here.'

'What a bore!' he said again. 'I'll get rid of them——'

He went into the sitting-room and found his visitors standing near the door, silent and troubled—they were his mother and Janet.

'Mother!' he cried. 'Janet! What's happened? Where have you dropped from?'

'Edinburgh,' said Janet grimly. 'But we can gang back there by the next train if we're no wantit.'

Iain kissed his mother tenderly and drew up a chair for her to sit in. 'You never told me you were coming—sit here and tell me all about it. You must be tired after the journey——'

'You've got a veesitor, MacAslan,' Janet said, not moving from her position by the door. 'You'll not be wanting us, I doubt.' She was obsessed by the picture of Linda which had revealed itself to her astonished eyes—of Linda sitting in the old basket chair, looking—thought Janet—as if the whole place belonged to her. Who was she? What was she? Why was she here in MacAslan's house?

181

Iain met her troubled eyes and smiled inwardly. He knew exactly what was worrying Janet, it would have been fun to tease Janet a little, but he must not do that. The situation was delicate and must be cleared up at once. It was so important that Janet and Linda should like each other.

'Yes,' he said lightly. 'I was having a tea-party. Mrs. Medworth and her little boy have been having tea with me. I wasn't expecting you or I would have met you at the station. Why didn't you send me a line?'

'It never crossed my mind,' said Janet simply.

'Well, it doesn't matter—you're here anyway, safe and sound. I suppose—I suppose you're staying,' he added, glancing at the suitcases.

'Aye, we were meaning to,' Janet said. 'The heavy luggage is coming on.'

'Wasn't Edinburgh a success?'

'It was not.'

'I see,' nodded Iain. 'Well, we must get the rooms prepared——'

'I'll sort them,' Janet told him. 'I'll sort them if we're tae bide. If you're not wanting us here, MacAslan, we can——'

'Don't be ridiculous, of course you must stay,' said Iain.

He went to the kitchen door and called Linda and Richard. There was no time to explain anything, he must just trust to Linda's innate good sense to deal with the situation.

'Mother, this is Mrs. Medworth,' he said, 'and Richard. Linda, this is Janet. You said you wanted to see Janet.'

He was pleased at the natural way in which Linda received these unexpected and somewhat startling introductions. There was dignity and kindness in her smile as she took his mother's hand, and unaffected friendliness in the hand she tendered to Janet. He saw that she was making a good impression, and he was glad, for it was an important moment. Richard, also, was adequate, he shook hands gravely and held his tongue.

There was an awkward pause when the greetings had been said. Linda plunged into it with questions about their journey and small anecdotes about her own journey over the same route. She spoke to Janet, including Mrs. MacAslan in her remarks with an occasional smile. Iain looked on and thought—it's wonderful, how does she know? (His mother was frightened of strangers, she hated contact with people she did not know well. If a stranger spoke to her she was dumb like a shy child, her whole being seemed to shrivel at a touch like a sea anemone.) Linda did not know all this, of course, but her perceptions were delicate and she felt that Mrs. MacAslan was better left alone. Iain had told her that his mother was not like other people, and she had realised that it was true. She must go slowly and win her confidence before there could be any *rapprochement* between them.

So Linda spoke to Janet—it was uphill work at first, for Janet was inclined to be ' stand offish,' keeping very carefully in her place and putting Mistress Medworth in hers. Janet was on the defensive—who was Mistress Medworth, anyway? A London lady, somebody who had ' got round ' MacAslan. What was she doing in the cottage? What was she up to?—*No good*, thought Janet grimly. But, after a few minutes' conversation, Janet began to thaw, she could not help it. She found herself discussing the journey from Edinburgh with its changes and the long waits at wayside stations, she found herself fulminating on the delays and discomforts of Highland travel. From thence to the discomforts of the Highlands in general, and the stupidities of the natives, was an easy step. Iain smiled to himself as he beheld Janet mounting her favourite hobby-horse; he caught a glimpse of a twinkle in Linda's eye and blessed her for her grave face.

Linda waited (talking and listening with friendly interest)

183

just long enough to make it clear that her departure was not due to the arrival of the unexpected visitors, and then she went away, saying that the hour of Richard's bed-time was approaching. Iain followed her out of the cottage.

'Don't come,' Linda said. 'Your mother will want you.'

'I can't think what has brought them back,' Iain said, frowning.

Linda smiled. 'Go back and hear all about it,' she said. 'If you stay out here any longer, you'll undo all the good——'

So she knew what she had done—thought Iain—and of course it was true, he must go back.

'I shall see you at the dance,' Linda added.

He nodded and waved, and ran back to the cottage.

It was not until they had eaten their simple supper, and his mother had gone to bed that Iain learned the reason for their unexpected return. He was sitting before the fire in the sitting-room, Janet was washing up the supper dishes. He called to her, and she came in, drying her hands.

'I'm through now,' she said. 'Were you wanting something, MacAslan?'

'I'm wanting to know all about it,' Iain said, smiling.

'Mphm,' she said. 'Well, there's no much tae tell. It was just impossible, the hale thing—just impossible.'

'She wasn't happy?'

'Happy! She was that meeserable and restless there was no daeing anything with her. It was "Ardfalloch, Ardfalloch" all day long! I was almost deived with it. Twice I missed her frae the flat an' found her wandering aboot the Waverley speirin' aboot trains tae Ardfalloch. It was just as weel that naebody in the hale place kenned the way tae Ardfalloch. Hoo should they ken, seein' that nae trains gang tae Ardfalloch? They were tryin' tae persuade the creature it was Ardnamurchan she was wantin'——'

' Goodness!' Iain exclaimed. ' She might have got lost.'

' That's so,' agreed Janet. ' I was near demented when I missed her.'

Iain looked at Janet and saw that she was tired, and there were lines in her face that had not been there before. His heart smote him—Janet was not young, and he had bound too heavy a burden upon her willing back.

' Was that *all,* Janet?' he said anxiously. ' I mean there was nothing else—worrying—that happened.'

' Mphm—she was just restless,' Janet said—and that's all you'll get out of me, she thought, you've enough troubles on your shoulders already without me burdening you with all the palaver I went through with the puir creature in Edinburgh. . . .

CHAPTER XVI

The Dinner Party at Cluan

IAIN came out of the cottage and stood for a few minutes in the doorway, smoking a cigarette; he was dressed for the ball at Ardfalloch. Never before in his life had he dressed so carefully, nor taken so much trouble over the hang of his kilt, and the immaculacy of his lace falls, never in his life had he spent so much time over the set of his hair. He was to see Linda to-night, and Linda was to see him for the first time dressed as a Highland gentleman should be dressed. Janet had helped over his toilet. She had heated the water for his bath, had laid out his kilt and brushed his black doublet and polished the silver buttons till they shone. She had cleaned his shoes, and had mended the tiny rent in the frail lace of his falls; but, all the time, he had sensed her disapproval of the whole affair. She was surprised, disappointed, puzzled. Iain knew it. He knew the depths of her disapproval by the very fact that she did not put it into words. The downright Janet usually said what she thought in no uncertain terms. To-night she had said nothing, she had merely pursed her lips and withdrawn from him.

Only Donald had understood and approved of his intention to attend the ball—or at least he had seemed to understand. Did he really understand, Iain wondered, or was it just, that, in Donald's eyes, MacAslan could do no wrong?

Janet came out onto the step beside him. 'You'll need your big coat for the boat,' she told him. 'See and keep warm now.'

' It's not cold,' Iain said. ' It's a lovely night, Janet.'

' It'll be cauld later,' she warned. ' You'll be late back, I doubt. I'll not snib the door, and I'll leave a tray in the sitting-room. See and take something warm before you gang tae your bed.'

' Go off to bed early,' Iain advised her.

' I will that.'

' Take care of yourselves.'

' We'll need tae, I doubt—there's nae other body tae dae it.'

They heard the sound of the motor-launch approaching—the Cluan boat which was to take Iain across the loch to the Finlay's dinner: Iain still lingered. He wanted to ' be friends ' with Janet before he left. He was half amused at himself for the childish feeling—Janet had made him feel like a small boy.

' Weel,' she said, ' there's the boat. You'll best be away. It's to be hoped you'll enjoy yoursel', anyway.'

' I'd enjoy it more if you were nice to me,' he said coaxingly.

' Och, you and your havers!' she cried, not ill pleased at the implied compliment. ' What dae you care for an auld wumman's tantrums! Away wi' you and see and enjoy yoursel'—you're a sicht for sore e'en the nicht, an' ye ken it weel. The lassies will be efter you like bees efter honey.'

He knew he was forgiven—Janet could never be angry with him for long. He went down to the boat with a stride that set his kilt a-swing.

It was a beautiful night; the sun was westering beyond the hills; the sky was clear and pale; a few white clouds lingered near the sun, their edges faintly tinged with rose. It was still almost full daylight, but to westward the hills were dark, outlined delicately against the sky, while those to eastward were lighted by the sun's rays. Here and there, upon the hills, lights peeped out showing the situation of the scattered crofts. Ahead lay the jutting promontory which sheltered Cluan Lodge.

Iain sat in the bows of the launch, the faint breeze of their passage ruffled his hair. His thoughts were shadowy and inconsequent, but Linda ran through them all like a thread through beads. He thought of Linda's visit to him —of her fear of Medworth. (It could not have been Medworth that Richard had seen, for a week had passed and no more had been heard of the man.) Her fear of Medworth was unreasonably great—what could the man do? He thought of the ball, and wondered who would be there, and how often he would be able to dance with Linda. He thought of Janet and Margaret—the dour disapproval of the one, and the grief of the other—they couldn't understand him because they didn't know about Linda. He was ringed about with women—he thought—women who wanted to shape his life, to mould him into their own moulds, but they couldn't do it because he had poured himself out at Linda's feet. I wish she were here—he thought. Where is she now? She is in my house—that is something —but I don't even know which room they have given her. The blue room, perhaps, with the view across the loch—I hope they have given her the blue room. Perhaps she is dressing now, for the ball, sitting before the mirror winding her soft dusky hair into the knot that lies on the nape of her white neck . . .

A vast tenderness for Linda flooded his whole being, and an almost unbearable longing for her bodily presence. How was he going to bear the hours that must pass before he saw her? It was as if his very soul were straining out towards her.

The launch ran into the shadow of the promontory. She circled slowly and drifted with a barely perceptible bump against Cluan pier. Iain threw a lavish tip to the boatman and sprang out of the launch. He hurried through the gardens towards the brilliantly lighted house.

Cluan Lodge was lighted by electric light, made from a convenient burn. To Iain's unaccustomed eyes it was almost blinding. The drawing-room was full of people— he knew most of them well, they were people who had neighboured him all his life. The MacKenzies from Ardna-foil, the MacArbins from Dalnahuilish, the Buchanans from Balnafin. The people that he did not know were strangers to the district, people who had taken shootings for the season, and their guests. Mr. Finlay had a strange craving to know everybody. He entertained a great deal at Cluan and enjoyed it. The role of host suited Mr. Finlay down to the ground; he was never happier than when the house was full, when he could look down his table, elong-ated to its fullest extent, and see it filled with people, eating his food.

Iain pushed through the crowded drawing-room, laugh-ing, and acknowledging greetings and parrying questions as to where he had been all this time. He wanted to speak to his hostess, and his hostess was over by the window. Mar-garet saw him coming and her breathing almost ceased, she felt as if she were suffocating—he was so beautiful, there was a sort of radiance about him to-night. Everybody else in the room faded out. He alone was vital, glorious as a young god.

She took his hand and said, ' No, you're not really late, and, even if you are, it's my fault for not sending the boat earlier.'

' I kept it waiting a minute or two whilst I argued with Janet,' he replied. ' So you see it really is my fault—and I'm very sorry, Meg.'

The room was beginning to empty, as couples moved slowly towards the dining-room. Margaret wished she had arranged for Iain to be her partner, but she had not done so, and it was impossible to alter it now. And it's just as well you can't alter it, she told herself, because it would look most peculiar. You've got to have Lord Beldale and make the best of him.

'I've given you Sheila,' Margaret said aloud. 'Sheila MacArbin. She's frightfully shy, and it's her first ball. I knew you would be nice to her.'

'Sheila!' Iain said. 'I thought Sheila was about twelve ——'

'She's grown up,' said Margaret hurriedly, for she saw her dinner-partner approaching. 'There she is—in pink— over near the piano.'

Iain found Sheila without any difficulty, she had not changed much since he had last seen her, riding a very small pony in the juvenile section of the Inverness Show. She still had fair fluffy hair and long thin arms. Iain thought she looked rather like a little girl who was dressed up in her mother's clothes for fun. The pink frock was the only ' grown up ' thing about her—Iain thought—he was amused to notice that her nose was pink too.

They went in together and found their places at the long table—there were pink roses in crystal vases, and tall candles with pink shades. The silver and glass gleamed softly on the dark polished wood.

'So you're grown up,' Iain said gravely.

'Yes.'

'What does it feel like?'

Sheila looked at him to see if he were teasing, but he was perfectly serious; he might have been a doctor enquiring about some symptom of an obscure complaint.

'Well,' she said thoughtfully, ' it doesn't feel any different. I mean I'm still me, and exactly the same as before; but I've got to—well, to *behave* differently.'

'I don't believe you really *are* grown up,' he said.

'Oh, yes, I am—I'm eighteen.'

190

'Fancy that!'

'M'm,' she said, biting the crust of her roll with sharp teeth. 'I'm eighteen and two months.'

'Are you enjoying this?' Iain enquired.

'Not awfully,' admitted Sheila frankly. 'You have to get used to things before you enjoy them, haven't you?'

'I believe that's true,' Iain said thoughtfully.

'I hated school for ages, and then, of course, I adored it.'

'I hope you aren't *hating* this!'

'Well, I am really,' she replied with a little sigh. 'Only don't tell Margaret, will you, because it was awfully decent of her to have me.'

'I won't tell Margaret,' he promised.

'I'm glad I've got you as a partner,' she continued seriously. 'It would have been far worse with anybody else.'

Iain laughed. 'Do you always say exactly what you think?'

'Practically always,' Sheila admitted. 'I know you shouldn't, of course, but if I didn't say what I thought I wouldn't have anything to say. And you *must* say something, mustn't you? I mean it would be so dull not to say anything at all.'

Iain agreed that it would—he was finding her rather amusing.

'I can't do Conversation at all,' she confided. 'Mummy says she learnt the Art of Conversation at school, and Deportment—but they don't teach you those things nowadays.'

'I'm glad they don't,' Iain told her.

'Why?'

'Because your own ideas are much more interesting than Conversation taught at school.'

Sheila looked down at her plate, and her nose grew a little pinker.

She's rather a dear, Iain thought. What a good thing she doesn't powder her nose! It's so intriguing to see it react to her emotions.

The dinner was excellent, as Margaret's dinners always were. The temporary cook must have put her best foot foremost—Iain thought. He glanced at Meg down the long table and saw her doing her duty by Lord Beldale. His glance drew hers, and for a moment their eyes met and she smiled at him. Then his right-hand neighbour claimed his attention—a dark girl with odd eyes which he found strangely embarrassing. She had just returned from a fortnight in Germany, and seemed anxious to tell him all about it. Iain found her inordinate admiration for everything Teutonic slightly boring—with every moment Linda came nearer.

The ladies withdrew, and the men moved up the table to be nearer their host. A tall man, whom Iain had never seen before, sat down beside him, and discoursed bitterly on the subject of dances in general and the dance at Ardfalloch House in particular. 'Puts your eye out,' he complained. 'What people want to go and dance for, I can't imagine. We shall dance all night, I suppose, and I shan't see a bird to-morrow—not a bird. That's the effect it has on me— perfectly sickening! If you want to dance, go and dance in town—go to a night-club and stay there if that's your line. But here, in Scotland, shooting's the game. The Scotch aren't dancers, they're shooters. Scotland isn't the place to dance——'

Iain hardly heard the man, he let him twaddle on, his eyes were fixed on the clock—it wouldn't be long now, if he knew anything about Meg.

It wasn't long. The dining-room door opened, and the ladies appeared, wrapped up to the eyes, swathed in fur, swaddled in rainbow-coloured scarves.

'It's half-past nine,' one of them cried.

192

'We ought to be going, Father!' said Margaret.

'All right, my dear,' agreed Mr. Finlay. 'We're just coming——'

They finished their port—or brandy—hastily, flung their cigarettes in the fire and swarmed out into the hall to find their coats.

CHAPTER XVII

The Ball at Ardfalloch House

THE night was still and beautifully clear, the sky was brilliant with stars. A wisp of mist was flung about the top of Ben Falloch like a scarf of filmy tulle. Iain followed the chattering throng through the gardens and down to the pier. There were half a dozen motor-launches in the little harbour belonging to the Finlays' guests. Most people in the neighbourhood found them more useful than cars, for the roads were bad and less direct than the loch.

The boats swept across the loch, the waves from those in front tossed them hither and thither, spray flew in their faces. Some of the boats were racing each other—there was laughter and gaiety in the air.

There was some delay in disembarking, for the Ardfalloch harbour was too small to allow more than two boats in at a time. They lay off, waiting their turn. Presently they were walking up to the house through the trees. Iain found Margaret at his side; she looked at him sideways, and he knew she was wondering what he was feeling.

She said, 'Am I to introduce you as MacAslan?'

'Yes, please,' he replied. 'I don't suppose they'll hear, or if they do hear they won't realise who I am—it doesn't matter if they do——'

'What does matter, Iain?' she asked, a trifle bitterly.

He took her hand and said, 'Friendship matters,' and then, in a lighter tone, he added, 'May I have the first reel, Meg?'

'Yes,' she said quietly. She thought: *Friendship,* he

means to make it clear that he has nothing but friendship to offer me. Why haven't I more pride? It's dreadful to love a man who only wants friendship. And then she thought: I wonder if *she* will be here to-night—but of course she will be here. That's why he has come to-night—so as to meet her. Who can she be? I shall know when I see him dancing with her. I shall know at once.

Meg had left her hand in his, she did not withdraw it, his kindness was something to be grateful for. It was not what she wanted, but it was better than nothing—she could not bear to lose him. If she lost Iain there would be nothing to live for—nothing. She thought suddenly: Oh God, what shall I do if she takes him away from me—altogether?

Iain almost turned and fled when he found himself in the hall. He heard himself talking to people he knew and exchanging the usual badinage. It was difficult to remember that these people were not his guests, and that the disposition of the coats and hats was no concern of his. There was a certain rueful satisfaction in the thought that he would not have to pay for the candles—there seemed to be hundreds of candles. . . .

Margaret collected her flock in the hall, they were ushered into the drawing-room. The butler with the side whiskers was finding a good deal of difficulty with the names of his master's guests. He mumbled them feebly. Iain found himself shaking hands with his host and hostess— they had no idea who he was.

'So nice of you to come,' murmured Mrs. Hetherington Smith. She was in black as usual, a black lace gown with diamond ornaments which showed off the dazzling whiteness of her neck and arms. Iain looked at her with interest. He liked her at once. Perhaps he was not unprejudiced, for he knew that she had been a good friend to Linda. He thought: Her eyes are kind. He lingered at the door to chat with her.

Iain's interest was reciprocated. Mrs. Hetherington Smith looked at him and thought: Who is he? Frame is such a fool with names. He looks like a prince—beautiful and romantic.

'I'm afraid I don't dance,' she said. 'May I introduce you to Mrs. Bastable?'

Iain bowed gravely to Mrs. Bastable, he could think of nothing to say. His eyes roved the room in search of Linda —where was she? Greta Bastable was determined to keep him beside her. He was the best-looking man she had seen to-night—extraordinarily decorative. He should stay beside her and talk to her, and, afterwards, she would dance with him. Greta had plenty of social experience; she produced all her charms for Iain's benefit. Suddenly, with a murmured apology, he left her—left her in the middle of a sentence and strode across the room . . . he had seen Linda.

Linda was in pale grey with a spray of salmon-pink roses at her waist. Iain thought she was like a young birch-tree, like a fairy, straight from the woods. The music started as he reached her side; she looked up and saw him.

'Iain!' she said.

For a moment their eyes met, and a swift colour rose into her cheeks. He swung his sporran over his hip, put his arm round her and drew her into the waltz.

'Iain!' she exclaimed. 'I was engaged for this dance.'

He laughed softly—what did it matter? Nothing mattered except that at last he had found Linda and was dancing with her—it was like dancing with a moonbeam, he thought.

Their steps matched perfectly, they had the floor to themselves (for the others were still chattering by the door and finding partners), but they did not realise that they were the only couple dancing, they were unconscious of everything save each other and the music. They were oblivious of the interest they were arousing.

The Ball at Ardfalloch House

Margaret saw them and thought: *That is the woman.* For a moment she thought she was going to faint—but that was ridiculous, of course; she had never fainted in her life and she was not going to start now—she made a tremendous effort and steadied herself. When the mist cleared she saw them dancing together—slowly, gravely, decorously. She thought: Why am I so sure it is she? But she was sure. They went round the room, turning this way and that with dignified precision. They were unconscious of everything except each other, there was something almost pathetic about their absorption. They were not speaking to each other, they were simply moving in perfect accord. Margaret felt that it was almost a sacrilege to watch them—and yet what was there to see?—Two people dancing together gravely, smoothly, perfectly; two people alone with each other in a crowded room; two people who loved each other.

Linda's feet in their pink shoes moved in and out between Iain's, her long silver-grey chiffon gown moulded her graceful figure, or swept out as they turned; she held herself straight, and her dark-brown head was a little above his shoulder. She is beautiful, Margaret thought, beautiful and dignified—if she is as lovely as that all through no wonder he loves her. She is younger than I am, but not just a girl. She has known sorrow—there is a strength about her —and a softness. Who is she?

Greta Bastable saw them and thought—so that's it— Linda Medworth. Where did she meet him? Greta was angry at the cavalier way Iain had left her, and Greta angry was unpleasant and sometimes dangerous. She seized Mrs. Hetherington Smith by the arm and said, ' Who's that man dancing with Linda?'

' I don't know,' replied Mrs. Hetherington Smith. ' Frame is hopeless with names, and I must say the names to-night have been rather difficult—don't they make a lovely couple?'

' H'm,' said Greta ambiguously.

' I seem to know the man's face,' continued Mrs. Hetherington Smith vaguely. ' And yet, if I had met him before, I wouldn't be likely to forget him. He's not the sort of man you *could* forget. Perhaps I've just seen him somewhere— in church, or in the village or something—and yet I don't know—I don't feel it's that, either——'

Sir Julius Hastie saw them—he could hardly fail to see them, since he had been about to dance with Linda himself. He thought: My God, these fellows have the cheek of the devil—who on earth *is* he? Why, bless me, it's Mac-Aslan himself! Strange his appearing here to-night, very strange. I suppose he's staying with the Finlays. He watched them for a few moments longer, and then crossed the room and asked Greta Bastable to dance with him.

By this time the floor was filling up with revolving couples, the candles flared and flickered in the draught. Mrs. Hetherington Smith and Margaret were busy introducing those who had been slow off the mark and had found themselves left without partners.

The music stopped, and went on again after a volley of clapping—finally it stopped altogether. There was a buzz of talk and laughter, and the crowd moved slowly out of the room to find seats in the hall or outside on the terrace.

Iain and Linda sat on the stairs. They had not spoken a word all the time they were dancing, and, even now, there was silence between them. How could they speak to each other amongst this noise of chatter and laughter? The feeling between them was too deep. Linda felt a little shy of Iain. He was so different to-night from Richard's boat-mender. She had known before that Iain was a personage in his own land, but she had not realised it fully until now. To-night she saw that he was not only the best-looking man in the room, but the most distinguished—he would have shone in any gathering.

Linda had seen Iain in various guises; she had seen him in his oldest clothes; she had seen him covered with tar, and dripping wet from immersion in the loch—to-night he was dressed like a prince.

'Will Richard be asleep?' Iain asked.

'I don't know,' she said. 'Would you like to go up and see him? Richard would scarcely know his boatmender to-night——'

Iain looked down at himself and smiled. 'It is rather a metamorphosis,' he said; 'but Richard doesn't attach much importance to clothes—he will know his boatmender.'

They went quietly up the stairs together; it was dark on the upper landing.

Linda gave a little laugh. 'We always seem to be wandering about in the dark together,' she said.

'We should have brought a candle——'

'It's all right, I know the way—there is a night-light in Richard's room.'

They groped their way down the passage that led to the bedrooms—far away in the distance (or so it seemed) they heard the music starting, and the laughter and buzz of conversation, here it was dark and quiet. They spoke in whispers.

'This is Richard's room,' Linda told him. 'Mine is next door. Mr. and Mrs. Hetherington Smith have the suite at the end of the passage.'

It was just as Iain had thought; the Hetherington Smiths had his mother's suite and Linda was in the blue room—he was glad of that. Linda had opened the door of Richard's room—it was full of soft yellow light and dark shadows, the window was wide open—a square of dark blue, flecked with stars.

Richard was asleep. He was lying on his side with one hand beneath his cheek, his dark hair was ruffled and there was a faint rosy flush on his face. His breath came and went easily and lightly—it was the only sound in the quiet room.

Iain leant over the bed—how lovely he was, and how helpless! His heart went out to the child in a wave of tenderness. He was part of Linda—bone of her bone—and, as such, precious beyond words, but even if he had not been Linda's he would still have been precious.

He said suddenly in a low voice, ' I love Richard.'

' I know,' whispered Linda. She tried to tell him how glad she was, but she could not put her feelings into words.

He made a sudden movement towards her. ' Do you know that I have never kissed you?' he said.

' Not yet,' she whispered, raising her hands and putting them against his breast to hold him away from her. ' Please not, Iain. Perhaps it's silly, but I don't want that—I don't want anything definite until—until I'm free. It's a sort of superstitious feeling—as if it wouldn't be lucky——'

He looked down at her gravely; his feeling was the opposite—he felt that if he once held her in his arms and kissed her she would be his for ever. It would be a bond between them that nothing could break—nothing. In a way he was sure of Linda now, for he knew she loved him and would not change, and he was determined that nothing should keep them apart when once she was free; but, beneath that warm certainty, there was a vague fear, a shadowy premonition of trouble and disaster. He was no seer, but he had felt before, on several occasions, a vague fear, an indescribable spiritual discomfort, and always something had happened—the feeling had presaged death or disaster. To-night he felt it strongly, a heaviness upon his spirits for which nothing that he knew of could account.

They stood quite still for a moment or two. Iain thought: If I could kiss her—just once——

' We must go back,' Linda said softly.

The moment was over and he had not kissed her—he was half glad and half sorry. They crept softly out of the door and shut it behind them—once more they were in black darkness. There was black darkness all around them, but, at the end of the passage where it opened on to the gallery, there was a dim reflection—the reflection of the light from the hall. Suddenly a shadow moved between them and the light. Iain saw it, and he knew that Linda had seen it too, for she clung to his arm with sudden alarm. Iain did not move, he was concentrated upon what he had seen. Was it a man or a woman, or was it some manifestation from another plane? It was coming towards them, slowly and noiselessly. Now it was no longer between them and the light, and was therefore invisible in the darkness of the passage, but it was still evident to some sense that was neither sight nor hearing. It went past them softly, soundlessly. It almost brushed against them as it passed.

Linda leaned upon his arm, he could hear the quick beating of her heart.

'What was it?' she breathed.

Now that it had passed the spell broke—Iain could not understand why he had allowed the shadow to pass unchallenged. Why hadn't he seized hold of it—or spoken? He turned from Linda and began to follow it down the dark passage.

'Don't leave me,' Linda cried.

'We must see who it was,' said Iain. 'Get a candle from Richard's room.' He was angry now—angry with himself and with the shadow—whoever it was. Some idiot playing a practical joke, he supposed.

They found a candle and explored the passage, and the rooms at the end of the passage—there was nobody to be seen.

'Whoever it was must know the house well,' Iain said. 'They must have gone down the back staircase—I think it was a woman, don't you?' He had an idea of a veil of some sort of filmy material brushing his hand as it passed. The idea was too vague to put into words, he scarcely knew whether he had really felt it or merely imagined it.

Linda didn't answer. She was sure it was not a man—but perhaps it was not a woman either.

They went down the stairs together as casually as they could, and joined the throng, pushing towards the drawing-room door. There was a skirl of pipes heralding a reel. Iain found himself wondering how many dances they had missed—it seemed to him as if they had been away for hours. The lights and the heat and the perfume, and the chatter and laughter of the dancers, struck upon his senses like a blow.

He had asked Margaret for the first reel—he saw her standing by the small raised dais speaking to Alec and Gregor. He crossed the room to her side, trying to smile naturally and to look as if he were perfectly at ease; trying to erase the troubling experience from his mind. He felt as if only a part of him had returned to the ball-room. The real Iain was still wandering about in the dark passage, looking for a shadow that had passed by.

Alec and Gregor were dazed and anxious, they had been looking forward to playing the reels for the Ardfalloch Ball. It would be fine fun, they had thought, to see all the grand people amusing themselves—they felt it a compliment to have been chosen to play—and the money would be useful. They had boasted about their distinction in the village, and had been envied by their less fortunate brethren. But, now that the long-looked-for moment had arrived, they were not so sure of their good fortune. The scene was so different from anything they had expected or imagined: the lights, the colour, the gay chatter, the incredible bareness of the women's shoulders and their painted faces, had demoralised them completely. They gazed round the crowded room with stricken faces, and fingered their chanters with trembling hands. Margaret had seen their distress and had flown to the rescue; she was trying to raise their morale with a little friendly conversation and a few well-timed jokes. Iain joined her and helped on the good work with his usual tact.

' We will be watching you, MacAslan,' Gregor said, with more confidence.

' That's right,' said Iain. ' We'll show these Sassunachs how a reel should be danced—are you coming, Meg?'

She put her hand into his, and he led her onto the floor. They were absorbed into a set with two subalterns from Inverness, and Kenneth and Sheila MacArbin.

Sets were forming all over the floor. The Hetherington Smiths and their English guests had taken up positions on sofas and chairs round the room. Their faces wore expressions of boredom or expectancy, according to their experience—or non-experience—of the proceedings. Mrs. Hetherington Smith looked pleased and excited, she had never seen a reel before, and the preliminary skirl of the pipes had stirred her blood. She was like a small child waiting for the curtain to go up at the pantomime.

Greta Bastable sat on the arm of her chair—her expression was amused and disdainful. She thought: *savages, boors, barbarians*. Time had not softened her rage against Iain at the way he had treated her, but there was a weapon in her hand, now, which she would use when opportunity occurred. She had seen Iain and Linda vanish up the stairs, and had timed their absence from the ball-room. She had seen them return and marked the strangeness of their looks. The weapon might be very useful if it were put into the right hands. She blew a very creditable smoke ring and watched it tremble upwards in the overheated air.

Sir Julius, who had seen—and heard—reels before, had dropped into a chair near Linda and was trying, somewhat vainly, to gain her attention.

'It was unkind to cut my dance,' he told her.

'Oh—yes, I'm sorry,' said Linda vaguely. 'It was a mistake.'

'I'll forgive you this time,' he said slyly. He was obliged to forgive her because he had an uncomfortable suspicion that she didn't care whether he forgave her or not. 'Have you ever seen this barbarous rite before?' he continued, after waiting vainly for Linda's reaction to his magnanimity.

'No,' she replied, without turning her head. She was watching the sets forming and had picked out Iain and his partner at the other side of the room.

'It's frightfully noisy,' Sir Julius warned her. 'Let's go and find a quiet seat somewhere——'

'No,' she said again. 'I want to see it—but don't wait if you would rather not.'

She wanted to see Iain dancing his own dance. She wanted to see what it was like. . . .

Suddenly the pipes started with a blare of sound—Linda was stunned by the noise, almost frightened. The whole room leapt into motion. The figures leapt and twirled and yelled; the floor rocked under her feet, the candles flared in the draught. At first the whole effect was one of mad confusion; it seemed to Linda that there was no method in it— no sense. They leapt, and shrieked, and whirled, and stamped, and the wind of their passing stirred her hair. It was frenzy, she thought, the whole room had gone mad. . . . And then, gradually, a sort of pattern emerged, a rhythm, a kind of wild beauty. She saw that each dancer knew what to do and did it in perfect time. They were weaving intricate patterns with certainty and confidence. The men's feet twinkled in their laced shoes; neatly and lightly they sprang into the air or beat the time upon the shining boards of the floor, their bare knees rose and fell, their kilts swung out from their hips. The women were less whole-hearted about the steps, but there was dignity in their deportment as they wove their way through the mazes of the dance. She thought: It is beautiful and exciting—just as Ardfalloch itself is beautiful and exciting. It is right for them—no wonder they love it. This dance is helping me to understand what they are—and the meaning of this place—and the history that lies behind them. They ought to be dancing it in the castle on the island—they belong to this land and the dance belongs to them.

It was difficult to think consecutively because of the noise, but the whole effect made a tremendous impression upon her—the more so because her mind was in a peculiarly receptive condition. She had just gone through a strange and somewhat alarming experience, and she was deeply in love. She was in love, not only with Iain MacAslan, but with Ardfalloch also—they were really one in her thoughts—and this dance was the expression of something that lay beneath the calm surface of both.

After it was over she went out into the hall with Sir Julius. He found her a seat and fetched her some coffee. The refreshment-room was full of people who had been dancing the reel, they were clamouring for lemonade and hock-cup. Linda saw that they were flushed and happy— the bonds of convention had been loosened and the bonds of friendship tightened. She had a glimpe of the freemasonry that bound these people together, and she wondered, a trifle wistfully, if this freemasonry would ever include her in its scope.

Mr. Hetherington Smith came and spoke to them. He, too, had been overwhelmed by the exhibition they had just witnessed. Linda had never seen him so natural, nor heard him talk so much.

' It gives you a kind of clue,' he said, trying to express his feelings and becoming somewhat incoherent in the attempt. ' A kind of clue—if you know what I mean—I found the

whole thing rather terrifying. They're so smooth and quiet
—and underneath the smoothness there's this fire——'

' There isn't really,' Sir Julius said. He was standing in a
favourite position with his legs rather wide apart and one
hand beneath his coat-tails. 'There's no fire left in them.
It's all spoof. They're decadent—the whole race is decadent. This exhibition is a kind of hysteria—that's all.
They're looking backwards instead of forwards. No nation's
any good that looks backwards. They've too much tradition; they live in their past glories; they've too much pride
—and all their pride lies in the past. There's no push in
them. They've got a sort of cheek if you like—a sort of
damned self-confidence begotten of their pride, but that
doesn't take them far.'

' I don't see them like that,' said Mr. Hetherington Smith
mildly.

Sir Julius laughed. 'You don't know them,' he said.
' They've taken you in with their spoof. There's nothing
in them—nothing at all——'

' I can't help feeling——'

' Hysteria,' said Sir Julius loudly and dogmatically.
' That's my diagnosis—and I've seen enough hysteria in my
time to diagnose it fairly easily, hysteria and paranœa——'

Linda said nothing. It didn't matter what Sir Julius
thought—or Mr. Hetherington Smith either, for that matter.
Their ideas could not affect her own secret convictions.

Presently Iain came out of the dining-room with Margaret. She thought: We mustn't dance together again yet
—we mustn't. Even if he asks me I must refuse. She saw
his eyes rove round the hall . . . he had seen her . . . he was
coming towards her. . . .

' Mine, I think,' he said, smiling.

Linda rose and put her hand on his arm. The music
started, and, the next moment, they had swung out onto the
floor.

The Ball at Ardfalloch House

The evening sped on. Iain danced with Linda, and with Margaret, and with Sheila, and with Linda again. They danced until the grey dawn came in at the tall windows and put the guttering candles to shame. At last it was time to go. There was beer and bones in the dining-room, and hot soup and sausage-rolls to speed the parting guests.

Mrs. Hetherington Smith moved about from table to table, urging people to eat, and reminding them that they had a long way to go home. The party had been a success; she knew it, and she was pleased and excited, and not in the least tired. These people were nice, she thought, they were friendly and natural. They didn't say so much as London Society people, but they meant a lot more, and they were actually grateful to her for the trouble she had taken to provide an evening's enjoyment for them. This seemed strange to Mrs. Hetherington Smith—in London it was the hostess who was grateful to her guests for bothering to come.

' I *do* think it was good of you to have a dance,' they said with sincere conviction; or, ' Thank you so much, I *have* enjoyed it. It's been a lovely dance.'

Mrs. Hetherington Smith beamed upon them all. ' I've enjoyed it, too,' she said. ' I think your reels are wonderful. We'll have another dance next year if we're lucky enough to get Ardfalloch again.'

Iain overheard this and his heart sank a little. Next year —it seemed so far off. Would he have to let Ardfalloch again? Perhaps by next year he would have Linda—it wouldn't matter quite so much then. They would let Ardfalloch and go away somewhere together.

The guests finished their hybrid meal, and surged into the hall to find their coats and wraps and to say good-bye. They were still laughing and chattering, but the gaiety was a little forced now. Everybody was weary, and longing for bed, and bed—in most cases—was still far away. Iain found himself standing next to Margaret in the queue wait-ing to say good-bye. He thought she looked tired and unhappy and he was passionately sorry for her. She was such a good friend, so loyal and staunch; they had known each other all their lives and had had such good times together. Now she was hurt and miserable, and it was because of him—he was hurting her. He could not help it, could not do anything to ease the hurt except pretend that he knew nothing about it.

Margaret's head barely reached his shoulder, she looked up at him, and smiled bravely.

' You enjoyed it, Iain,' she said.

' Yes.'

' She is very pretty,' Margaret added, pressing his arm.

He was very much moved by her generosity. There was a choky feeling in his throat.

' Dear Meg,' he said.

' Is it going to be all right?' she asked him.

' I hope so—I think so,' he replied. ' It's a little—a little complicated. I can't tell you about it here.'

' If I can do anything——' she said.

' I'll remember, Meg.'

It was too early to ask her to be Linda's friend. He had no right to ask that, and, even if he had, it would be unwise. That would come in time—Meg and Linda would be friends (he was sure of it), and Meg would be happy again —they would all be happy. He was so happy himself to-night—the shadows had disappeared—that he felt virtue flow out of him. Because he loved Linda, he loved every-body, and everybody must love Linda.

CHAPTER XVIII

The Emerald Bracelet

IAIN walked back to the cottage alone. It was very early and the air smelt sweet and fresh after the hot, perfumed atmosphere of the ball-room. There was dew on the grass, and on every leaf—tiny, glittering beads of dew shining like diamonds in the early sunshine. Iain seemed to see everything more clearly, more sharply defined than he had ever seen it before. As he went through the pine-woods the smell caught his breath, it was sweet and clean and resinous; the straight trunks of the trees were like the copper pillars of a great hall, and, high above his head, the layers were like a roof—dark green, almost black against the pale-blue sky. The dun-coloured carpet of fallen needles was as soft as velvet beneath his feet.

He let himself into the cottage very quietly, and went up the narrow stairs as noiselessly as possible, but, when he reached the top, his mother called to him—she had been lying awake and listening for his step. Iain went into her room and found her sitting up in bed. Her face was flushed, like the face of a young girl, and her soft white hair lay in curling rings upon her forehead. *How pretty she is!* he thought tenderly.

She beckoned to him to come closer and held up her arm. 'Look, Iain!' she said. 'Look how it sparkles!'

Iain saw that she had a bracelet on her arm, a bracelet of flashing green stones set in platinum. It was a beautiful thing—it looked costly—Iain had never seen it before. He sat down on the bed and turned her arm this way and that, watching the stones flash in the sunlight that poured through the open window.

'What a lovely thing!' he said. 'I didn't know you had a bracelet of emeralds.'

'I didn't know I had it either,' she told him, smiling with pleasure like a child with a new toy. 'I found it in my treasure drawer.'

'In your treasure drawer?' said Iain in surprise.

She nodded, and her eyes sparkled with delight. 'It was such a surprise, Iain,' she told him; 'such a lovely surprise. There were lots of pretty things in the drawer, but this was much the prettiest.'

'Do you mean you found it here?' Iain asked, pointing to the small chest of drawers that stood in the corner by the window.

She shook her head. 'Oh, no,' she said; 'not here.'

'Where did you find it, then?'

'I found it in my own treasure drawer in my own room.'

Iain's heart almost stopped beating, but he tried to speak calmly. It was no use frightening her.

'Were you up at the house?' he asked.

'I must have been,' she said. 'I know I found it in my treasure drawer——'

'Oh, Mother!' he cried. 'You know I told you not to go there.'

Her eyes filled with sudden tears. 'I don't know,' she said incoherently. 'I can't remember—I only know I found it in my own drawer.'

'But I told you there were people in the house and you mustn't go there——'

'They didn't see me,' she said earnestly. 'They didn't see me, Iain. I crept upstairs so quietly. I didn't bother the people. There were bright lights in the house, and music—I think they must have been having a party—so I crept up the stairs very quietly. They couldn't mind me going to my own room——'

'It isn't your room now,' said Iain—he was too upset and horrified at what had occurred to consider her feelings, or be wise with her any more.

'It's always been my room,' she said—her lip trembled and the tears rolled down her cheeks. 'It's always been my room—I don't understand things very well, now, but I know my own room—my own room——'

Iain pulled himself up—it was no use scolding her, she couldn't understand; it wasn't her fault.

'Never mind,' he said, patting her shoulder. 'It doesn't matter, darling, it's all right. See, I'm not angry with you at all—but you must give me the bracelet to take back, because, you see, it doesn't belong to you——'

'Oh, no,' she said, clinging to the bracelet firmly. 'Oh, no—it's mine, Iain. It was in my drawer, so it must be mine. I had forgotten about it—you know how I forget things——'

'Please, darling,' Iain said gently. 'Please give it to me. You know it isn't yours.'

She shook the tears from her eyes and hid the wrist with the bracelet on it beneath the bedclothes. Her face hardened before his eyes in a queer way. 'No, you can't have it,' she said. 'You can't have it—I want it, and it's mine.'

Iain saw that he could not get it from her without a scene. She would forget about it soon, and they could take it away while she was asleep. That was the better way. In any case nothing could be done about restoring the bracelet to its rightful owner until later in the day. She might just as well keep it for a few hours and have the pleasure of it—his heart ached over her.

'All right, you keep it,' he said gently. 'But you must cuddle down in bed and let me tuck you up or you will catch cold, darling. There now, is that cosy?'

She lay down obediently, still clutching the bracelet tightly against her breast. Her long dusty eyelashes flickered over her dark eyes—she would sleep now—Iain knew that—sleep for hours perhaps. He went away and left her. Quite suddenly he was tired—so tired that his brain refused to deal with this new problem. He dropped his finery on the floor, crept into his narrow camp-bed, and, in a few moments he, too, was fast asleep.

When Iain woke it was midday. He opened his eyes and saw Janet standing beside his bed with a tray in her hands.

' It's time you were waking, MacAslan,' she said quietly.

Iain lay still and looked at her for a few moments. His brain was clouded with sleep, but he had a feeling that something was wrong—what was it? Janet's face was grave and stern—almost wooden—only her eyes were alive with expression, they were full of misery.

' There's something the matter, Janet,' he said, struggling to remember what it was.

' Aye,' she said, ' there's something the matter right enough. I doubt you'll be vexed with me, MacAslan.'

' Vexed with you?'

' I've betrayed ma trust,' she said solemnly. She put the tray down on the chest of drawers, and took the emerald bracelet out of her apron pocket, and showed it to him. ' See that, MacAslan,' she added. ' You'll never guess hoo that came here.'

' I don't need to guess. I know.'

' Och, for any sake!' cried Janet in horror-stricken tones. ' You're niver telling me you saw her at the hoose! She said naebody saw her—you're niver telling me she went intae the room——'

' Nobody saw her—that I know of,' he said quickly. ' It was when I came in. She called me into her bedroom and showed it to me.'

' Thank the Lord naebody saw her,' said Janet. She stood there for a moment in silence, looking at the glittering jewel that lay coiled up in her work-worn hand. ' Thank the Lord,' she said again, and then she added in a different tone: ' If you're sairtain of that, MacAslan, we can get it pit back where it came frae and nae hairm done.'

Iain lay still and thought about it—he was fully awake now—he was wondering if it was his mother who had passed when Linda and he were standing in the dark passage together—he was almost sure that it was she. That was the way she moved, lightly and noiselessly as one of the Little People themselves. If he had spoken to her then, or touched her, he could have prevented this thing from happening. He didn't know—he couldn't think—what strange inhibition had prevented him.

' It was my blame,' Janet was saying, her Doric very much in evidence as it always was when she was moved or upset. ' There's nae ither body tae blame but masel'. I was tired, MacAslan, an' I went airly tae ma bed. She must ha' creepit oota the hoose when I was sleeping. I kenned naething of it till I went in this morning, an' *there* she was happed up in her bed playing wi' the thing. It was my blame——'

' No,' said Iain firmly. ' You couldn't help it, Janet. How could you know she would take a thing that didn't belong to her.'

' I micht have kenned,' said Janet miserably. ' She's nae idea of what belongs tae her an' what doesna'. She did the same thing in Edinburgh in the shops. I had tae keep an eye on her there.'

' You never told me.'

' An' what was the use? You had eneuch trouble tae bear —an' there was naething much tae tell. It was just if she took a liking tae a thing——'

' You should have told me,' Iain said, sighing.

'An' she was all for gaeing up tae the hoose when we were oot in the morning,' Janet continued. 'It was all I could dae tae thwart her. I should niver have brought her back frae Edinburgh—and that's all aboot it. Here,' she added in a different voice, 'you'd best tak' your braikfast before it's cauld, an' the tea stewed,' and she took up the tray and set it firmly on his knees.

Iain could not help smiling in the midst of his anxiety. The skies might fall, but Janet would still insist, in her sensible downright manner, upon people taking their food before it grew cold. He sat up obediently and arranged his pillow behind his back.

Janet settled the tray comfortably. 'There now,' she said. 'Tak' your braikfast and then we'll conseeder what's tae be done. It's an ungoadly hour tae be taking braikfast, but I wasna' going tae waken you before noon. I've been stravaigling up an' doon the stair the hale morning watching for you tae waken—an' no a thing done in the hoose——'

'Poor Janet!' he said, half smiling at the picture evoked.

'Puir Janet indeed!' she echoed indignantly. 'I've been biting my thumb at masel'. It would be a kind of comfort if you'd be a wee thing vexed at me, MacAslan.'

Iain laughed outright at that. It was so typical of Janet— she set herself, and others, the highest standard of efficiency and was annoyed when human nature fell short of her ideal.

'You couldn't help it,' he said again. 'You can't be with her night and day——'

'An' that's jist it,' cried Janet. 'That's jist the verra thing folks will be saying if they hear aboot it. They ought to have her *watched,* folks will say, or, of they canna watch her properly, they ought tae pit her away——' The last words were almost a whisper, she did not dare to look at Iain as she said them. 'And you ken yoursel' there's nae-thing wrang wi' the puir soul but just a kind of vagueness, whiles. But if she was tae be watched an' thwarted there's

214

no saying where it would lead. You ken yoursel' she hates the verra idea of folks interfering wi' her. It would drive her clean demented—or intae her grave——'

'I know,' said Iain wretchedly.

'There's nae need tae be unco fashed aboot it,' Janet continued. 'She'll be fine when we get hame tae oor ain hoose. It's jist she's restless here and she doesna' understand why she's no getting hame tae Ardfalloch. She's for ever wandering—she's wanting back tae her ain hame that's a'.'

Iain nodded. He knew what people said about his mother —he knew it all. He could read their thoughts in their faces—or thought he could. But she was all right in her own home, just as Janet said. She could wander about the place at will, and there was nothing to hurt her. The people on the estate watched over her unobtrusively, they were fond of her, and they respected her strangeness; it was a distinction in their eyes to be different from other people. She wandered about Ardfalloch like a little ghost, and she was—in her own way—happy.

He thought of all this, and then he said, 'It's my fault, really, Janet—not yours. I had a feeling that it would upset her—the change. I should never have let Ardfalloch.'

'Och—away wi' you!' she said. 'What else were you tae dae? You didna' let Ardfalloch for the pleesure of the thing. Dinna fash yoursel', MacAslan, there's some way oot o' this coil—an' I'll tak' guid care it doesna' happen again.'

'Some way out of it,' echoed Iain thoughtfully.

Janet nodded. 'We'll get the thing pit back,' she said. 'If naebody saw her, naebody's tae ken who took it.'

'And who's going to put it back?'

'Donald will,' said Janet firmly. 'He's waiting on you the noo—doon the stair——'

It was afternoon. Iain was walking up to Ardfalloch House

with the emerald bracelet in his pocket. He had thought of every other way out of the mess, and none of them satisfied him—there was only one thing to do and Iain was on his way to do it, he was going to see Mrs. Hetherington Smith and tell her exactly what had happened. It would not be pleasant to lay bare the secret of his mother's weakness (he hated the thought of it. He never spoke of the subject if he could avoid it, he shied from speaking of it even with Janet, and now he was on his way to expose his secret to a stranger). Iain had thought of every other way first. He had considered Janet's suggestion that the bracelet should be restored to the drawer as surreptitiously as it had been taken, and Donald's suggestion that it should be dropped somewhere in the house where it would be found and restored to its owner. Donald and Janet had combined— for once—in trying to dissuade him from the course he was taking; Donald, because he felt the honour of the house was at stake, and Janet because she feared that if Mrs. Mac-Aslan's condition should become known she would be removed from her care; and both of them because they loved MacAslan and were anxious to spare him the ordeal of returning the bracelet, and explaining the circumstances of its removal to Mrs. Hetherington Smith.

Iain had listened to them both and considered their suggestions, but he knew that neither way would do. Somebody might get into trouble over the thing, somebody might be accused of theft. It would not do to shirk the issue, he must bear his mother's weakness on his own shoulders, it was his burden.

He rang the bell and waited quietly on his own doorstep for the butler to come. He found himself hoping that Mrs. Hetherington Smith would be out—but that was foolishness. If she were out he would merely have to sit and wait until she returned—what good would that be?

Mrs. Hetherington Smith was at home. Iain was ushered

into the big airy drawing-room and left there. He looked round with interest and some pain. Last night the room had been a ball-room—any ball-room—this afternoon it was once more a drawing-room—his own drawing-room. Queerly enough, the room seemed almost more strange to him than a totally strange room would have been—the furniture was disposed differently, and there were strange objects amongst the familiar ones. He thought there was a strange atmosphere in the room—it was probably imagination—the room did not seem to welcome him, it smelt different, somehow.

He was still trying to chase his elusive impressions when Mrs. Hetherington Smith came in. She was dressed in grey tweeds, very correctly and suitably for a Highland afternoon.

'How nice of you to come!' she said, giving him her hand and smiling at him. 'You're our landlord, aren't you?'

'Yes,' said Iain.

She thought: Goodness, the man's in trouble! He's nervous and miserable—what on earth's the matter with him, I wonder. 'You came to the dance with the Finlays,' she said aloud. 'I didn't know who you were when you spoke to me—our butler's stupid at names—but the funny thing was that I was sure I knew your face.'

'I don't think we had met before.'

'You hadn't met me, but I had met you,' said Mrs. Hetherington Smith, smiling. She made a little movement with her hand. 'The *pictures*,' she explained. 'You are awfully like the pictures of your ancestors, you know, especially the one in the library. I've been longing to see you and ask you about everything—who was he?'

'He was my great-great-grandfather,' replied Iain. 'A bit of a brigand in his day, I'm afraid.'

Mrs. Hetherington Smith nodded. 'He looks like that,'

217

she said. 'Now don't go and think I mean you look like a brigand.'

'It certainly sounds like it,' Iain said, half smiling.

It was on the tip of her tongue to tell him that he looked like a prince—she had thought so last night—but perhaps he wouldn't like it, and, now that she came to look at him again, he didn't look so like a prince as she had imagined. He was dressed differently, of course, but it wasn't only the clothes—there was something different about the man himself. The glory of him had vanished, the brilliance of him was dimmed; to-day he was just an ordinary young man—very handsome, of course, with those dark eyes of his, and the tanned skin, and the clear-cut line of nose and chin, but definitely not a prince.

Mrs. Hetherington Smith laughed. 'Well, you don't look fierce enough for a brigand,' she said.

Iain thought: This is awful. How am I going to tell her? It's far more difficult than I thought it would be. She is nice, of course. He looked at her with a sort of desperation.

'You've come about something, perhaps,' suggested Mrs. Hetherington Smith. 'Something about the house—is it? We love it, you know. It's so—so different from other houses. I'll tell you rather a queer thing about this place—it makes me feel *real*.'

'Real?' he echoed.

She thought: What a fool I was to think he would understand! Nobody could, unless they knew what my life had been, and I'm not going to start telling the Story of my Life to a perfectly strange young man on an afternoon call. She said aloud, 'Yes, real. London life is so artificial.' That'll put him off, she thought.

Iain said thoughtfully: 'People are usually real when they're in their own niche. I'm real when I'm here. If I go away from here I'm not myself—I haven't explained it well

—what I mean is this: if I go to London and meet people there, I'm a Highland gentleman in London—an actor on a stage—but when I am here in my own place I am Mac-Aslan.'

He *is* like a prince, she thought, and he does understand. If I don't want him to understand too much I shall have to be careful. 'It can't be that with me, can it?' she said lightly.

'It might be,' he replied thoughtfully. 'If you haven't found your own niche in London.'

This was all very well, but he was no nearer telling her about the bracelet than he had been at the beginning. How on earth shall I tell her? he thought, battling desperately with himself—I *can't* tell her. The thing's impossible.

Mrs. Hetherington Smith had been watching him. She said at last, 'You've come to see me about something, haven't you?' She thought: The poor soul had better get it off his chest, whatever it is. Perhaps he wants the money in advance, or something. Arthur will have to give it to him! I'll make Arthur do it.

'Yes, I've come to see you about this,' said Iain. He took the bracelet out of his pocket and laid it down on the table.

Mrs. Hetherington Smith took it up and looked at it. 'Fancy that, now!' she said calmly. 'Aren't I lucky to get it back?'

'You recognise it, of course,' Iain said.

'Oh, yes, it's mine all right. Arthur gave it to me for Christmas. I didn't say anything to Arthur about losing it. He gets so upset, and I hoped it might turn up. I'm rather apt to be careless about things.'

Iain said: 'You didn't lose it, Mrs. Hetherington Smith. It was—it was taken out of your drawer.'

She nodded. 'I know,' she said. 'I remembered I had left it lying loose in the drawer—I ought to have locked the drawer, but I was in a hurry, so I just popped it in. It was last night when I was dressing for the dance, I took it out, thinking I'd wear it, and then I thought I'd stick to diamonds. You can't ever go wrong with diamonds——'

Iain scarcely heard what she was saying. He was waiting for her to stop talking so that he could explain what had happened, but she went on and on—he had to interrupt her at last.

' I want to apologise,' he said. ' I want to explain. It was my mother who took it out of your drawer. My mother is not—not normal. She had a great shock, and, since then, her brain has been—her brain has been affected. She came up here last night when her maid was asleep. She—she came into the house and found her way to her own room. She found the bracelet in the drawer where she keeps her own little treasures—and she took it. She didn't know—she didn't mean any harm—she doesn't understand—she doesn't mean any harm——'

' Oh, poor soul!' exclaimed Mrs. Hetherington Smith.

' I can't tell you how sorry I am that this should have happened,' continued Iain wretchedly. ' It's—I can't tell you—her maid was asleep, you see——'

' How dreadfully sad!' said Mrs. Hetherington Smith. ' Of course it's quite easy to understand. She found it in her own drawer—and she thought it was pretty——'

' Yes,' agreed Iain. It seemed queer that Mrs. Hetherington Smith was not more horrified. She was a kind woman, of course—he had known that before—but even a kind woman might well be annoyed and upset at having a valuable bracelet stolen out of her drawer by her landlord's mother. He had expected her to be angry—she had a right to be angry—he had expected her to suggest that a woman with kleptomania ought to be locked up, or at least kept under proper control; but Mrs. Hetherington Smith said none of these obvious things.

The Emerald Bracelet

Iain waited patiently for the storm to break. He was quite prepared to abase himself, to accept all the blame. It was even possible that she might call in the police—possible but not probable.

'Poor soul!' said Mrs. Hetherington Smith again. She turned the bracelet over in her hand and looked at it thoughtfully. 'I wonder, now,' she said. 'D'you think the poor soul would like to keep it? It seems such a shame to take it away from her, doesn't it?'

Iain gazed at her in amazement. He said at last: 'You can't be serious, Mrs. Hetherington Smith—this is no joke to me.'

'No, of course it's not a joke to you—nor to me either—it must be dreadfully sad for you—dreadfully sad. I feel so sorry,' she said, raising her eyes from the bracelet and looking at him kindly. 'It was because I felt so sorry that I felt I would like to give it to her.'

'Thank you,' he said in a strained voice. 'But I couldn't take it, you know.'

'Well, perhaps not,' she replied doubtfully. 'But it seems a pity, because I would like to give it to her—and I expect she would like to have it.'

'I think you are a most extraordinary woman!' Iain exclaimed, and then quite suddenly he began to laugh. It was partly the reaction from strain—the relief of getting the dreadful thing told—and partly because he suddenly saw the humour of it. He tried to stifle his laughter, but it was no use. It rose like a tide, and overwhelmed him, he laughed and laughed. Mrs. Hetherington Smith laughed too.

At last Iain managed to control himself. 'I'm sorry,' he said shakily, 'but it *is* funny, you know. I've been worrying so awfully about what you would say——'

'What *could* I have said?' asked his hostess, wiping her eyes.

Iain did not answer that; he merely said, 'You are a most extraordinary woman.'

'Perhaps I am,' she agreed. 'I've had a funny kind of life, you know. But, of course, you don't know, and I'm not going to tell you,' she added hastily.

'Why should you?' Iain said, slightly at a loss.

She smiled at him in her kind way. 'Now we're friends,' she said, 'don't you think you might let me give your mother the bracelet?'

'I'm afraid not.'

'It's your pride,' she told him rather sadly. 'Sir Julius says that you Highlanders are as proud as the devil—and I'm afraid he's right.'

'It's not only my own pride,' Iain said. 'It's a sort of hereditary obligation—rather a burden in these difficult times.'

'I see what you mean—in a way,' said Mrs. Hetherington Smith. 'I see you've got something to live up to. That great-great-grandfather who was a brigand—though why he should stand in the way of me giving your mother a little present—but I do see what you mean——'

'I'm glad you see.'

'It must be rather nice,' continued Mrs. Hetherington Smith, pursuing her own line of thought. 'It must be rather nice to have lots of ancestors. Perhaps, if I had a picture of a great-great-grandfather who was a brigand, it would make me feel more real. I might feel I had a place of my own in the world instead of being outside things—neither one thing nor the other.'

Iain said nothing. He realised that she was not really speaking to him, she was merely uttering her own thoughts aloud.

She said at last. 'Well, now we know where we are. You'll stay and have tea with me, won't you?—Just to show there's no ill feeling.'

222

'Ill feeling!' exclaimed Iain. 'I don't know how to thank you—I can't ever thank you properly for your kindness. It's beyond words, beyond anything I could have imagined.'

'Then you'll stay to tea,' she said prosaically, getting up and ringing the bell. 'The men won't be back—they're shooting with Lord Beldale to-day—and Greta has gone out with a Mr. Middleton. I don't know who he is, but she seems to know him. To tell you the truth I'm thankful she has found a friend; there isn't much for Greta to do here. Sometimes I've felt rather sorry I asked her to come. Linda and I would have been much happier by ourselves. Greta has to be doing things all the time or she gets into mischief—so if she takes up with this Middleton man it will be all to the good and she won't want to go out with the guns. Sometimes it's a little awkward, you know.'

'Yes,' said Iain. He knew these women who were always wanting to go out with the guns.

'Do you know this man Middleton?' enquired his hostess.

'I've met him,' Iain told her. 'He's staying at the local inn.'

'What is he like?'

'Tall and fair and broad-shouldered——'

'But what is he like *inside*?'

Iain laughed. 'That's more difficult,' he said. 'He's rather amusing in a way—full of his own importance—rather bold——'

Mrs. Hetherington Smith nodded. That the kind of man Greta likes,' she said. 'I asked you about him because there was a kind of mystery—the man won't come to lunch; he wouldn't come to the dance; he won't shoot—queer, isn't it?'

'Very,' said Iain. 'I thought he wanted shooting.'

'Well, he doesn't. Greta says she has known him for

years, but she said it funnily—if you know what I mean—
either it wasn't true, or else there's something fishy about
him. What should you think?'

'I couldn't possibly tell you—I don't know anything
about him,' said Iain helplessly. He didn't really care
whether or not there was a secret understanding between
one of Mrs. Hetherington Smith's guests and James Middleton.

'Here's tea!' said Mrs. Hetherington Smith. 'Put the
table over near the window please, Frame.'

They sat down and had tea together. Mrs. Hetherington
Smith wanted to know all sorts of things about Ardfalloch.
Iain found himself talking eagerly, telling her about the
history of the place and about the old castle on the island.
She was an excellent listener. The afternoon sunshine
streamed in through the open window and showed up the
shabbiness of the carpet and the faded cretonnes. Iain
noticed it and sighed, the walls needed re-papering too.

'I love this room,' said Mrs. Hetherington Smith, following his eyes.

'I was thinking how shabby it was,' Iain told her ruefully.

'I like this kind of shabbiness—everything has faded
together—like people growing old together. You would
spoil it if you tried to alter it. I think a room like this is very
restful. Our house is all too new (I don't mean it's modern,
I hate that modern furniture made of steel tubes and things,
it reminds me of a dentist's chair. I don't know why it does,
because dentists' chairs are not a bit like that really). Our
furniture is very nice, but I think I shall feel happier when
it has got a little shabby, if you know what I mean!'

'Yes,' said Iain vaguely, and then he plucked up courage
and added, 'I wonder if Linda—if Mrs. Medworth is in.'

Mrs. Hetherington Smith smiled benignly. 'Linda has
gone down to the boat-house with Richard,' she told him.

'They were going to have a picnic in the woods. You're sure to meet them if you walk down towards the boat-house —why don't you?'

'Perhaps I will,' said Iain, with assumed carelessness.

'I think you should,' his hostess told him, and then she laughed. 'You needn't pretend to me,' she said, shaking her head at him. 'I could see last night that there was something in the wind—I'm not so blind as all that—and Sir Julius saw it too—he was furious——'

Iain blushed. 'Linda and I——' he said confusedly.

'It's all right,' said Mrs. Hetherington Smith. 'It's quite all right and natural. I thought when I saw you dancing together it was beautifully right. Linda is lovely, inside and out—she'll be free soon——'

'I know,' said Iain. He got up and stood there looking down at her—she really was a dear, so kind and comfortable.

'Sir Julius is old,' continued Mrs. Hetherington Smith ruthlessly, 'old and—and dull. He wouldn't have had a chance, anyhow. Don't worry about Sir Julius.'

'I'm not worrying about him.'

'What are you worrying about, then?'

'Linda is—afraid,' said Iain slowly. 'She's afraid of Medworth—afraid something will go wrong. And I—I'm afraid of shadows. It would be too wonderful, you see, too good to be true.'

She looked up at him and thought: He *is* nice—almost good enough for Linda. No man could be quite good enough. It's nice to feel they wouldn't have met if it hadn't been for me. How lovely it will be for Linda living here in this beautiful place—she'll be happy here. What a good thing he has fallen in love with the right one—men are so silly sometimes. 'You shouldn't be afraid,' she said aloud. 'Everything will come right. Ardfalloch is a lucky place— it's brought *me* luck anyhow.' It was Arthur she was thinking of—Ardfalloch had brought Arthur back to her arms; had weaned him from Business—that *exigent* mistress of his. He might return to his mistress when they returned to London—that was possible, of course—but, meanwhile, Arthur was her very own, and, even if he was only temporarily hers, it was something. It showed that his heart, which she had feared was dead, was still alive and warm and beating. 'Yes,' she said, 'Ardfalloch has brought me luck and I'm sure it will bring Linda luck too.'

'I should like to think so,' said Iain gravely.

Mrs. Hetherington Smith's mind travelled back to the first time she had met Linda at M. Gaston's mannequin parade. We've come a long way since then, she thought. Fancy, if I hadn't had the courage to speak to her! None of this would have happened; Linda wouldn't have come here, and I would never have seen Richard—the darling thing—and this young man would never have met her—how queer it is! She said aloud, 'Off you go, Mr. MacAslan—I know you're longing to find her. I won't ring the bell for you to be shown out, because it would be silly when it's your own house—and we're friends, now, aren't we?'

'I should think we *are* friends,' he said fervently.

Iain left her and went out to find Linda. The day had clouded over and dark clouds were gathering over the hills. He could smell rain coming and he was not altogether sorry, for the country needed rain; but Linda and Richard would have to hurry home, or they would get wet.

He had not gone far when he saw Linda. She was standing near the boat-house talking to a boy with red hair—one of Alec MacNeil's brood by the look of him. Linda looked up and saw Iain coming and came to meet him. He saw that she had a piece of paper in her hand. He saw, too, as he hurried to meet her, that she looked ghastly—her face was as white as a sheet, her hands were shaking.

'Linda!' he exclaimed. 'My dear, what is the matter?

226

Where's Richard?' It's Richard, he thought, something frightful has happened to the child.

'Richard is down at the boat-house,' she said tonelessly.

'Are you—are you ill, Linda?' he asked her.

She put the piece of paper into his hand. 'Read it,' she said. 'That boy has just brought it—just given it to me.'

Iain took the crumpled paper and smoothed it out. He read.

DEAR LINDA,—

I must see you. I have something to say to you. It is to your own interest to hear what I have to say. You'll regret it if you refuse. Tell the red-haired boy when and where I can see you. JACK

Iain read it twice and then he looked at Linda. 'Medworth!' he exclaimed. 'So it was he——'

'Oh, Iain, what am I to do?'

'You had better let me see him for you,' Iain said, trying to speak calmly.

'No,' she said. 'No, I must see him myself—there's something—I must see what he wants—what he means to do. Anything is better than this ghastly uncertainty.'

'What can he have to say to you?'

'I don't know,' she said, still in that queer expressionless voice. 'I don't know—but I feel—I feel it's something horrible.'

Iain felt the same—the tone of the letter was threatening —but it was no use tormenting themselves with vain speculations. The only thing to be done was to see Medworth, and if Linda felt she must see him herself she must do so.

'You had better arrange to meet him at my cottage,' Iain said. 'We can be undisturbed there—if you really feel you must see him yourself——'

'I must,' she said firmly. 'Yes, your cottage will be the

best place. Oh, Iain, I am sorry I have brought all this trouble upon you!'

Iain paid no attention to her outburst—the only way to help her was to be strictly businesslike. He made her write on the back of the note that she would see Medworth at the cottage at three o'clock the following afternoon. Then he folded the note and gave it to the red-haired boy.

'Where is the gentleman living?' Iain asked.

'He is living at MacTaggart's,' the boy replied. 'He did be giving me a sixpence to be taking the letter to the lady.'

'Here is another sixpence for you,' Iain said. 'Take the answer straight back to the gentleman.'

The boy thanked him and ran off, well pleased with his afternoon's work.

CHAPTER XIX

The Interview

EVERYTHING was prepared for Linda's interview with Medworth. Mrs. MacAslan and Janet had been sent out to have a picnic in the woods. Iain was hanging about, waiting for Linda to arrive. He had gone to the door for the fourth time to peer up the path, when he heard steps coming from the opposite direction, and saw James Middleton coming towards him through the trees. Iain was annoyed, he did not want strangers prowling round while the interview was taking place.

'Hallo!' he said, not very cordially. 'Do you want the boat?'

'Not to-day, thank you.'

'I'm sorry I can't ask you in,' said Iain frankly. 'I'm expecting some people on business——'

'You're expecting me,' Middleton replied.

The two men looked at each other for a few moments in silence.

'So you're Medworth!' Iain said at last. He thought—I might have guessed—and yet how could I?

They were still standing there, when Linda emerged from the woods and came quickly down the slope. She was dressed in a grey Shetland cardigan and skirt, and a small red hat. Iain glanced at her anxiously; she was even paler than usual, but she seemed quite calm and composed. They all went into the sitting-room.

'You're looking rather pale, Linda,' said Medworth, with

mock solicitude. 'Haven't you been enjoying your holiday?'

Linda sat down by the table and drew off her gloves. She said quietly, 'You didn't ask me here to discuss my looks.'

'Not altogether,' Medworth replied. 'But your looks are your strong point, you know, and I haven't seen you for a long time.' He sat down at the table opposite to her and stared at her impudently.

Iain lingered near the window, he would have liked to strangle the man, but he knew that he must not interfere. Linda had agreed to his being present at the interview, but had impressed upon him that she was to be allowed to manage it in her own way.

'Come to business, please, Jack,' Linda said. 'If you have anything to say——'

'I've got a lot to say,' replied the man with a breezy laugh.

Linda waited quietly—she was rather wonderful, Iain thought; there was something almost frightening about her. He had never seen her like this before—cold as ice—an ice maiden. He saw that she was undermining the man's confidence by her silence and composure.

'Well, it's like this,' Medworth began in a blustering voice, 'I want my son, and I'm damn' well going to have him. The judge gave him to you—I know that, so you needn't stuff that down my throat. He gave you the child because he thought you were a fit person to have him—but are you? That's what I want to know.'

He waited for Linda's reply, but none came. She was still waiting, looking at him with a kind of cold disdain, waiting for him to state his case.

'Supposing we had another little party at the Divorce Court,' continued Medworth. 'How would you like that, eh? You might not come out of it so well this time.'

'I don't know what you mean,' Linda said.

'You know quite well what I mean, but I'll put it baldly

if that's what you want. You're supposed to behave yourself for six months after your divorce, or you don't get your
decree absolute. Well, you haven't been behaving yourself.
You've taken a lover, haven't you——'

Iain started up—he would have to interfere—he would
have to speak. He was silenced by a look from Linda.

'You are wrong,' she said to Medworth. 'I haven't
taken a lover.'

Medworth laughed in a sneering way. 'So you say—
you *would* say that, of course, but you can't kid me. You
had plenty of opportunities. If you didn't take them you're
more of a fool than I thought.'

'You judge other people by yourself,' Linda said. 'Other
people——'

'See here, Linda,' he interrupted. 'I don't care whether
you went all the way or not; I've got enough evidence to
convince any ordinary-minded man that you and MacAslan
are lovers—that's all I want.'

'Evidence!' exclaimed Linda.

'Evidence,' he repeated. 'I've found out a good deal
about your goings on in spite of the way MacAslan has
bribed the villagers not to give you away——'

'Bribed the villagers!' Iain exclaimed in amazement.

Medworth turned his head and looked at Iain. 'Yes,
bribed the villagers,' he said in a sneering voice. 'I suppose you thought I wouldn't find out the way you had
bribed them. Why, the very first moment I set foot in the
village you were at your little game.'

Iain gazed at him, thoroughly bewildered.

'Oh, you're clever enough,' Medworth allowed, 'but
that innocent expression won't wash in a Court of Law.
When I came into MacTaggart's that first day you were
bribing Alec MacNeil—it was the first thing I heard you
say—"Keep your mouth shut and you'll get what you
want" you said to him. Those were your very words. I

thought there was something pretty fishy about it and I wasn't far wrong. I soon found that everybody in the place is bribed to keep their mouths shut. I've only got to mention your name and they shut up like clams.'

Iain said, ' My God! So that's how evidence is made.'

' But it doesn't matter a damn,' continued Medworth. ' That's the beauty of it—I don't need the villagers' evidence. I've got enough evidence without them.'

' You can't have evidence of something that doesn't exist,' said Linda with a touch of spirit.

' I *have* got evidence,' Medworth replied loudly, ' quite enough to make the King's Proctor sit up and take notice. What about that night on the island—the night of the eleventh August. You spent the whole night alone with MacAslan on the island.'

' We were wrecked,' said Linda. She was beginning to lose her ice-cold composure under the strain.

' That was very unfortunate for you,' Medworth said mockingly. ' Very unfortunate indeed. I wonder how you spent the night.'

' I will tell you how we spent the night,' cried Iain, goaded beyond endurance. ' We sat on a bench in front of the fire and talked all night—you are not likely to believe that, I suppose.'

' You are perfectly right,' agreed Medworth, smiling at Iain. ' I am not likely to believe that—nor the judge either. We will now pass on to the next piece of evidence,' he continued, putting on a mock-lawyer manner that was indescribably galling to his hearers. ' On the night of the nineteenth August the defendant visited the co-defendant's house at ten-thirty p.m. and stayed there with him alone in the house for about an hour. They came out of the house together about eleven-thirty p.m. (she clinging lovingly to his arm) and walked back very slowly and reluctantly to Ardfalloch House.'

'My God!' Iain cried, taking a step towards him. 'So it was you prowling about the place that night—it was you——'

'It certainly was,' laughed Medworth. 'We had a little game of hide-and-seek together, hadn't we? Rather tactless of me to butt in like that and interrupt you, I'm afraid.'

'There was nothing——' Iain cried hotly.

'Please be quiet,' Linda said, stopping him with a movement of her hand. 'Iain, please be quiet. You're doing no good. Can't you see how hopeless it is to make him understand?' She turned back to Medworth. 'Go on,' she said. 'Is this all the "evidence" you have managed to collect?'

'No,' he said, 'that's not all. The other night at the ball you were upstairs together for three-quarters of an hour. Greta Bastable saw you disappear and she saw you return looking half dazed. Greta is quite prepared to tell her little story if necessary, and I think the King's Proctor might find it interesting. It was strange behaviour in the middle of a ball, wasn't it?'

'We went up to see Richard,' said Linda.

'Really? And was Richard awake at that hour? No? Dear me, you sat and doted on the sleeping Richard for three-quarters of an hour—what a charming picture!'

'You swine!' said Iain softly. 'If Linda were not here ——'

Linda stopped him again with the same quieting movement of her hand. She raised her eyes and looked Medworth full in the face. 'What do you want?' she asked. 'What are you doing it for? What are you going to get out of it for yourself?'

'I am going to get Richard,' replied Medworth firmly.

There was a little silence in the room. Linda's breast rose and fell hurriedly; for the first time during the interview she was frightened.

'I want Richard,' Medworth continued. 'And I'm going

to have him. There are two ways. Either you can give him up to me voluntarily and we'll say no more about it, or else I shall drag you through the courts—as you dragged me. In either case I shall get Richard.'

'But you don't *like* Richard,' Linda said, striving to steady her voice. 'You aren't fond of him, Jack.'

'He's my son,' Medworth replied sullenly. 'He's my son and I want him. I want him brought up properly. I don't want my son to grow up a namby-pamby nincompoop. He bears my name and he's part of me. Surely the child must have some guts somewhere in him.'

'But Jack—I don't understand you. Why do you want to be bothered with him? Who would look after him when you were away?'

'Never you mind,' he replied. 'I'll put him to school— he'll be well looked after, you may be sure. I'll give him the chance of growing up into a man——'

'You don't understand Richard,' Linda said, struggling to control her tears.

'Nonsense, of course I understand him. I'll soon lick the little rabbit into shape when I get him to myself——'

'Look here, Medworth,' Iain said, coming over to the table and trying to speak calmly and sensibly. 'The whole thing is a mistake—a misunderstanding. Can't we come to an arrangement? I'll do anything you say. You can't take the boy away from Linda. The whole thing is a mistake. Linda and I . . . there's been nothing between us. I've never even kissed her. . . . I'll swear it if you like——'

'I don't care a damn,' cried Medworth, striking the table with his clenched fist. 'I don't care a damn what there is between you—or isn't between you. You can both go to hell for all I care—get that. I'm through with Linda— *through*—you can take her if you like icebergs. Personally I like something a bit more human. I don't pretend to be a saint and I don't expect other people to be saints. What I

234

want is my son, and I'm going to have him. All I want to
know is this—will you give him up, or must I drag you
through the Law Courts to get him?'

'I won't give him up,' said Linda brokenly. 'I can't
believe—there must be some justice—I haven't done anything—anything wrong. Justice—there must be justice.'

'You realise, of course,' Medworth said. 'You realise
that if I win my case you will still be my wife. It's nothing
to me—I don't care a rap whether you are or not—I'm
merely pointing it out to you in case you hadn't realised it.
I can go my own way and I haven't the slightest desire to
marry again—marriage is a mug's game—so it doesn't
affect me. All I want is the custody of my own son—and
I'll have him either way. You shan't stand between us like
you did before.'

'I can't give him up,' said Linda again.

'Well, that's that,' Medworth said. 'I'm off to London
to-morrow morning. You'll hear of this in due course.' He
rose and walked to the door. 'If you change your mind
before to-morrow morning you'll find me at MacTaggart's.
I advise you to think it over—you'll gain nothing by stick-
ing out against me, and lose everything.'

'Jack!' cried Linda. 'Oh, Jack, won't you change your
mind—won't anything I can say—or do——?'

'No, nothing,' Medworth said. 'You needn't try to get
round me, it's no use. I'm determined to have Richard.
Give him up and we'll say no more. It will come to the
same thing in the end, and save a lot of bother and unpleasantness.'

The next moment he was gone.

'Iain,' cried Linda. 'Oh, Iain—what have I done? It's
all my fault. I ought to have known better. . . .'

Iain came over to the table and stood looking down at her.
Now that the strain was over she had broken down completely, the tears were rolling unheeded down her cheeks.

She said, 'Richard . . . I've failed Richard . . . I've failed him. . . .'

'Don't cry,' Iain said. 'There is still a way to save Richard.'

'What do you mean?'

'Leave it to me, Linda.'

Something in his tone frightened her. She seized his arm. 'You must tell me what you're going to do,' she said urgently. 'I must know.'

'I shall have to kill Medworth,' said Iain quietly.

'Iain, you are mad!'

'It's the only thing to do.'

'You can't do that . . . Iain . . . promise me that you won't do anything so mad . . . so crazy . . .'

'It's not crazy,' he said. 'Let me go, Linda; let go of my arm.'

Linda clung to him more tightly than ever, clung to him so that he could not disengage himself without actual violence. 'Iain, listen to me for God's sake—you don't know what you are doing——'

'I'm quite calm,' he replied. 'I see clearly—it's the only thing to do.'

He *was* quite calm—that was the extraordinary part of it to Linda—the terrifying part. He was perfectly calm and reasonable about the whole thing.

'It's murder,' she said. 'Don't you understand? They would hang you——'

'Yes, if they found out about it,' he replied. 'But they might not find out—and, anyway, it's the only thing to do. I'm not thinking of us, at all. We can bear it if we have to. I'm thinking of Richard, who can't. I'm thinking of Richard in that man's power——'

She said, 'I know—but you mustn't do it.'

'It's our fault,' he continued in the same quiet, reasonable tone. 'You said you had failed Richard—we both failed him. We haven't done anything wrong but we have been—careless—stupid. We've got to do the best we can for Richard—and this is the only thing that is going to be any good. In this world people are punished for stupidity just as surely as for wrong-doing—more so, perhaps—and the same applies to Nature. It is the law of the jungle—if you know what I mean—a rabbit is doing no harm when it runs into a noose, but it is caught all the same.'

' Don't talk like that, I can't bear it,' she said. ' I simply can't bear it. Murder is wrong—it's unthinkable—it's the most dreadful wickedness. Promise me, promise me faithfully that you won't think of it any more.'

' It's the only way, Linda. I don't think of it as wickedness—the man is bad all through, you know it as well as I do——'

' I know, but you mustn't,' she cried. ' You can't take the law into your own hands like that. You can't kill a man, even if he is bad—it's murder.'

' It would be worse than murder to let him have Richard. Think of it——'

' I have thought,' she cried. ' Do you think I don't see how frightful it would be? I see it more clearly than you——'

' He's a bad man,' Iain urged. ' A dangerous man—a man without any decent instincts.'

' There must be some other way,' she said. ' There *must* be. The judge must be made to see the truth. Truth is strong, Iain, stronger than lies——'

' The evidence against us is very strong,' Iain said gravely. ' You must face that, Linda.'

' I know. We've been incredibly foolish. . . . I have been incredibly foolish . . . that night when I came here. . . . Oh, Iain, what a fool I was! . . . But I can't believe that God would let evil triumph—I can't believe it—we must trust God. Promise me that you won't do it . . . promise me.'

She wouldn't let him go until he had promised, she held him with all her strength, and, at last, she wrung the promise from him, the promise that he would take no action against Medworth's life. She let him go then, and sank back into the chair, exhausted with the strain.

He said, 'What then? What can I do for you, my dear? —What else is there?'

'There is nothing you can do,' she replied faintly.

CHAPTER XX

Oatcakes

RICHARD was in the MacNeils' cottage, sitting on the creepy-stool by the fire talking to Morag. He liked talking to Morag, and he liked watching her at work—sometimes she let him help her. On this particular afternoon she was busy making oatcakes. Donald was fond of oatcakes and there had to be a good supply always ready.

Richard thought the little cottage was a fascinating place. He liked the whitewashed walls, and he liked the way the beams bulged behind the flaking plaster. There were beams in the roof too, high up amongst the shadows—dark cobwebby-looking beams that supported the sagging roof. Darkness up above and brightness down below, thought Richard. The little stove gleamed brightly, the fire glowed red, it winked and twinkled in the brass lids that hung on the wall, and the pewter jugs on the dresser, and the handle of the door that led into the tiny bedroom. Over the stove there hung a text in a carved wooden frame, ' Is e Dia mo Bhuachaill.' Morag had told him how to say it, and what it meant in English. ' The Lord is my Shepherd,' Richard said it over to himself softly, it gave him a nice safe feeling. . . .

It was beginning to get a little dark inside the cottage, for the day was clouding over; the window was small, and two big trees near the door helped to obscure the light.

' It's cosy, isn't it?' Richard said. ' I like it when it just begins to get dark, don't you, Morag? Bright things look brighter, and dark things look darker—why do they?'

239

Ardfalloch in August

' I could not be telling you that, Richard,' Morag replied
thoughtfully. She was busy with her oatcake mixture, oatcakes are tricky things to make. Unless the proportions are
just right they are apt to be too brittle, or too soft. Morag
made them constantly, but they always worried her a little.
Richard's eyes dwelt upon her, he liked being with Morag.
There were no children at Ardfalloch for him to play with,
and Morag was the nearest approach to a child that he had
found. She was personally interested in all he said, and
personal interest turns an adult into a companion. He did
not realise this consciously, of course, he only knew that
he liked talking to Morag; they talked together frankly and
seriously as contemporaries talk; they had fun together,
and Morag enjoyed the fun as much as Richard. She did
not try to amuse him or entertain him, she became a child
with him. Another good thing about Morag was her stories
—other people could sometimes be induced to tell stories, or
read them out of books, but Morag's stories were true.
Morag believed in fairies—she said she didn't, but she did
really—Richard believed in fairies too. How could you not
believe in fairies when they were all around you? Richard
knew that there were fairies at Ardfalloch; he had not
actually seen them, yet, but he had felt their presence, had
felt, when he went through the woods by himself, that the
fairies were there, all round him, peeping at him. He was
quite sure when he came to a little clearing in the woods and
found it empty of life but very still, very full of sunlight, he
was quite sure that a moment ago there had been fairies
here—or Little People, as Morag called them—they had
heard him coming and they had vanished.

Richard was not frightened of them—not a bit frightened
—in fact, he felt their presence was a sort of protection. It
was loud things that frightened Richard—loud noises and
angry voices and big rough men with strong hands. Above
all, one big, cruel, loud-voiced man. Richard trembled a

little as he thought of that man—the thought of that man had come upon him unawares. He shut his eyes and squeezed the thought of that man out of his mind—he would not think about that man—*he would not*. If you didn't think of things they didn't exist—that man didn't exist. Already Richard had discovered the way to lock things out of his mind—or rather he thought he had. He thought he was locking that man out of his mind, but really and truly he was locking up the little cupboard in his mind where that man lived. Richard turned the key in the lock with an effort that left him quite weak and faint, and opened his eyes. The kitchen was full of soft cosy firelight, Morag was busy kneading her dough, everything was warm, and safe, and comfortable, and very quiet—nobody could come here except nice people. . . .

' Are your oatcakes coming out well?' Richard enquired politely—he was aware of the thrawn nature of oatcakes, it was one of the many things he had learnt from Morag.

' The mixture is a wee thing wet,' said Morag.

Richard rose at once and went to the cupboard where the big barrel of oatmeal was kept. He put in his hand and took out a handful of meal and brought it to her. Morag smiled down at him, he was so sweet, so serious, so anxious to be helpful.

' Tapadh leat! a laochain,' she said, in her soft clear voice.

' What does that mean, Morag?'

' It means, thank you, my wee laddie.'

' I think it sounds nicer in your language,' said Richard thoughtfully.

' Och, and so it does,' agreed Morag. ' It is a fine language, the Gaelic, when the heart is speaking.'

This was a little beyond Richard's comprehension, so he did not reply. He sprinkled the meal over the mixture and watched with interest while Morag mixed it in and kneaded it—what a fascinating thing it was, so doughy and cloggy. It assumed queer shapes under Morag's pummelling, it clung stickily to her fingers.

'Look now, Richard,' Morag said, 'I will give you a little piece and you can be making an oatcake yourself.'

'Oh, Morag!' he said eagerly. 'May I really?'

She fetched another board, and floured it and divided off a piece of the dough for him. Meanwhile Richard rolled up the sleeves of his jersey and got himself an oblong wooden stool to stand on. He had helped Morag before, helped to stir puddings, and, once, to decorate a pie, but he had never helped to make oatcakes before—oatcakes were difficult. His small face was quite pink with excitement as he started to knead. The dough was plastic under his fingers, he rolled it out and smoothed it, and then squeezed it up again.

'Look, Morag!' he said. 'I've made a rabbit—see its long ears.'

'It is very good,' said Morag gravely. 'It is very like a rabbit. We will bake it now.'

'Oh, Morag, can you have oatcake rabbits?'

She laughed. 'I have never seen one before,' she admitted. 'But there is no reason at all why we should not have one. We must squash it flat or it will not cook nicely, but it will still be a rabbit.' She ran the rolling pin lightly over the rabbit, it came out rather long and thin, but it was still indubitably a rabbit. Richard lifted it carefully and put it onto the girdle with Morag's more conventional three-cornered pieces. Then he went back to his stool near the stove.

Morag took up her knitting and sat down in the big chair. She kept one eye on the girdle as she worked—it was very quiet. Richard listened to the clicking of her needles in the quietness, it was a soothing sound.

He said at last, 'The fire is twinkling among your

neegles, Morag. I like it. I like your kitchen. I like everything in your house.'

' So do I,' Morag agreed, looking round the little room
lovingly. ' It is a very nice wee house.'

' When I'm grown up I'll have a little house just like
this,' continued Richard dreamily. ' It's much more fun
than a big house, much cosier and sort of—sort of safer
——'

' Och, but you will not!' Morag said. ' You will be a
gentleman when you are grown up, and a gentleman does
not live in a wee house like this.'

' Then I won't be a gentleman,' said Richard firmly.

' Och, but you will be a gentleman,' Morag told him
gravely. ' You cannot help yourself. You will be a gentleman, and you will have a fine wife, and a big house and
servants to wait on you, and you will be shooting and fishing
like gentlemen do. You will be too grand for Morag
then——'

' But I won't be like that a bit,' he told her earnestly.
' Mummy and I are very poor. We are going to live in a
tiny little house together, and I'm going to make money
for her when I'm grown up.'

Morag smiled, she did not think that Richard's life would
be like that. Everybody in Ardfalloch was sure that Mac-
Aslan would marry Mrs. Medworth—the thing had been
discussed in every cottage in the glen. MacAslan had saved
her life; they had been wrecked on the island together; and
they had danced together at the ball for all the world to see.
Alec and Gregor had seen them and had reported it to all
and sundry. Everybody was interested—vitally interested
in MacAslan's doings, and everybody was glad that he had
found a lady that pleased him at last—it was high time
there was an heir at Ardfalloch House.—She was a nice
lady, too—so they all agreed—there was a dignity about her,
and she had a kind smile for everybody—so she had.

Morag thought of all this as she smiled her enigmatic smile, but she said nothing—it was not for her to put ideas into Richard's head. She thought how nice it would be to have Richard at the Big House, he would grow big and strong in the fine air. He would come and see her sometimes, and she was glad to think of that, for she loved Richard very dearly. It would be nice to have a little son like that, thought Morag. She had thought so the very first time she saw Richard; and now she thought it again, even more fervently, for she knew Richard now. She sighed a little—she and Donald had been married for two years and there was no sign of a little son.

'Why are you sighing, Morag?' Richard enquired.

She replied quite simply, 'I was thinking I would like to be having a little son, chust like you.'

'Yes,' he agreed, nodding gravely. 'It would be nice for you, Morag. It would be company for you when Donald was out. Of course it would be a long time before he was big enough to help you like me. Babies aren't much good, just at first.'

'He would grow.'

'Yes, of course,' said Richard. 'Why don't you ask God to send you a baby?'

'I have asked Him, Richard.'

'I'll ask too,' said Richard. 'I'll ask Him to-night when I say my prayers.'

'That will be very kind of you,' Morag said.

There was a little silence after that; the fire glowed redly, and they heard the rain begin to patter gently on the roof.

'Morag,' said Richard suddenly, 'tell me more about the Little People.'

'I have told you too much already,' Morag said. 'It is not true, Richard, there are no Little People in your world.'

'Not in London, of course,' agreed Richard. 'But there are here. I nearly saw them this morning in the woods——'

244

He broke off suddenly, for there were footsteps outside on the little path, and, a moment later, a knock on the door. Morag rose and went to open the door. She found Mac-Aslan waiting on the step.

' Is Richard still here?' he asked.

' Yes, he is still here, MacAslan,' replied Morag, smiling. ' He has been helping me——'

Iain took off his cap and went in. He saw Richard sitting on the little stool by the fire, there was a peaceful happy expression on his small face.

' I've come to take you home, Richard,' Iain said. ' Mummy has gone on——'

Richard looked up and smiled. ' Now?' he asked, rather reluctantly.

' Would MacAslan not wait till the rain is past?' Morag suggested.

' It's only a shower,' Iain said. ' I think we had better go.' He knew that Linda would worry if they did not go at once, and she was worried and anxious enough already, but he had a feeling that he was an intruder in Morag's kitchen, he was interrupting something. . . .

It was a queer feeling, and it passed as quickly as it had come. In a few moments Richard had found his cap and his jacket, and they were walking back to Ardfalloch House together through the sweetly perfumed dampness of the woods.

When Iain got back to the cottage he found Donald waiting for him in the sitting-room. He was standing by the window, and Iain had a sudden impression of Donald's enormous stature. He seemed to dwarf the room. He turned as Iain came in and Iain saw that he was disturbed in some way, but he was too deeply sunk in his own grave troubles to spare more than a passing thought for Donald's unusual mien. He flung himself into a chair without speaking and gazed at the fire. There was no need to pretend to Donald—they understood each other too well. It was one of the good things about Donald that there was no need to explain one's mood. If Donald did not understand one's mood, he at least respected it.

Iain was so utterly wretched, so sore and angry that he wanted to be alone, but Donald's company did not irk him —to be with Donald was just like being alone, it was almost better.

'There is something the matter, MacAslan,' said Donald at last.

Iain laughed bitterly. 'There certainly is,' he replied. 'Everything is the matter——'

'Is there anything I can be doing to help?' Donald enquired anxiously.

'No, there is nothing. I can't even tell you about it.'

'Are you sure of that? There is nothing I would not do for MacAslan—nothing at all.'

'There is nothing to be done.'

'That is a pity, then,' said Donald.

There was a little silence between them, and then Iain began to speak. He spoke because he had come to such a pass that he could not remain silent.

'It's a strange world, Donald. You and I have been born in strange times. We have been born too late. If we had lived long ago we would have been free to follow our inclinations. It's nonsense to talk of freedom nowadays— we are bound. Civilisation has bound us with invisible bonds——'

He stopped suddenly and glanced at Donald. Donald must not guess the nature of his trouble—he had promised Linda—but Donald could not guess. Donald had no clue to what had happened, no means of knowing, and the thing was far too complicated for Donald to understand. It was perfectly safe to let himself go, to talk in this vague wild way; perfectly safe, and what an incredible relief! Iain felt as if the pent-up rage and bitterness was pouring out of him as he spoke.

' I have shared in your troubles many times, MacAslan,' said Donald a trifle wistfully.

' Nobody can share this,' replied Iain quickly. ' Nobody at all. I have given my word.'

' That is a pity.'

' Nobody can help me,' Iain continued with something like despair in his voice as the magnitude of the disaster which had befallen him and Linda came clearly before his mind. ' Nobody can help. I can't help myself. I see the trouble coming and I cannot avert it. I am bound. I must sit down and wait for the trouble to come, and that is a hard thing to do. Oh, Donald, this modern world is impossible for a natural man to live in. I was born with the instincts of my forefathers—their feelings and desires are in my blood. I belong to a bygone age. I would to God I had lived in the days when a man took what he wanted by force and held it, when a man swept his enemies from his path like so many flies——'

' They must have been good days,' Donald agreed. ' But even now——'

' You don't understand,' Iain told him. ' All is changed now, and, even if it were not changed, I am bound—I have allowed myself to be bound so that I may not even rid the world of a wild beast.'

That was the thought that was embittering him now. He had allowed himself to be bound. He had allowed Linda to bind him with promises so that he must not touch a hair of Medworth's head—so that Medworth must go free. *Medworth*—the mere thought of the man almost choked him with rage. His face grew dark with anger, and his hands were clenched upon the arms of the chair until the knuckles shone white. If he saw the man now, even his sacred promises to Linda would not hold him back. What right had Linda to tie his hands and render him impotent to deal with his enemy?

'A man is not a man nowadays,' he cried with passionate bitterness. 'Or at least he may not behave like one. He must bow his head to injustice, he must keep the law—even when he knows it to be false and unjust. Men fight with their tongues now, with lies and deceit. In the old days life was free and simple. A man followed his conscience and was answerable to God alone. He could right his own wrongs by his own power. A blow in the open is better than a lying whisper in the dark. Oh, it must have been good to be a man in those days!'

'Is there nothing I can do for MacAslan?' The grave words fell with strange significance into the little silence which had followed Iain's impassioned speech.

Iain looked up—he had almost forgotten that Donald was there, so quiet had he been.

'There is nothing,' Iain said. 'Nothing at all that you can do—or anybody else. I have spoken wild words, Donald—you must forget them. Nobody must know of this trouble.'

'Nobody shall know,' replied Donald firmly. 'It is not likely that I should speak of MacAslan's secrets to another person.'

Iain was content with the assurance. He knew that Donald was a safe repository for secrets, and, after all, what had he said? He had merely inveighed against the times he lived in and had voiced a futile—and somewhat childish—wish that he had been born in a manlier age. He sighed, and stirred in his chair, and his hands dropped slackly at his sides. He was suddenly very tired—more tired than he had ever been in his life.

'I must be going now,' Donald said quietly. 'There are things I must be doing, MacAslan.'

Oatcakes

'Did you come to see me about anything special?' Iain asked in a flat voice.

'It is no matter,' Donald assured him. 'I will not be troubling you about the small things——'

'Come to-morrow,' said Iain. He felt quite incapable of coping with anything more to-night—even with the small details of the estate—his mind felt heavy and blank.

'We are shooting the south moors to-morrow,' Donald told him, 'but I will come in the evening, if that will be suiting MacAslan.'

Iain nodded. He watched Donald cross the room to the door.

'Donald!' he said suddenly. 'Donald, you understand—don't you—I would have told you about this trouble if I could have done so—if I hadn't been bound by a promise. You are not hurt——'

Donald looked back at him gravely. 'I understand, Mac-Aslan, and I am not hurt. There is no question of that at all. It is only that I would serve MacAslan in the trouble——'

He waited a moment, looking at the limp figure in the chair with questioning eyes, and then—as Iain neither moved nor spoke—he went out and shut the door behind him.

CHAPTER XXI

Facing the Future

IAIN and Linda decided that there was nothing for them to do but wait—wait until the summons came. They were both a little hazy as to what form it would take. They saw each other more often and more openly now that Iain had made friends with Mrs. Hetherington Smith, but they scarcely ever saw each other alone. There were always other people there, and, even if they met in the woods, there was always Richard to debar them from a frank discussion of their position. (Linda could not bear to let Richard out of her sight for a moment.)

Linda went through the days in a kind of dream. Sometimes she was hopeful, pinning her faith upon justice—God's justice and man's. Sometimes she was sunk in despair. She had no illusions about Jack Medworth; he would do as he had threatened, nothing would turn him from his purpose. He wanted Richard for several reasons: partly because, as he had said, the child was his son, and partly because he enjoyed bullying Richard, but principally to revenge himself upon her. He hated her—Linda knew that—and, until now, she had always had the upper hand of him. She had loved him to start with, but very soon her love had died. Jack had killed her love, not only by his unfaithfulness, but by letting her see the underlying coarseness and brutality of his nature. He had come back to her from other women and she had turned from him in disgust. Her cold disdain had maddened him. Jack had called her an iceberg, but she knew that the ice was only on the surface; she was human underneath, human and warm, craving for love. When he found her cold he had tried to rouse her by tormenting Richard, until she had been forced to take action against him—the only action open to her. Linda thought of the divorce—the sordid horror of it all, the exposure of her life, the dreadful publicity. Jack had hated it, too, and had hated her for dragging him into it. This was his chance to revenge himself upon her, to wound her in her only weak spot—through Richard. Linda know that he would do it, there was no escape, and she saw clearly that it would be far worse this time because she would be arraigned. She and Iain would be questioned and cross-questioned, and their relations to each other debated, every action probed and pried into, until there was no beauty or privacy left— she had done this to Iain.

These were Linda's thoughts; they went round and round in her head all day and all night. She tossed and turned upon her bed, and sometimes her pillow was wet with tears of despair.

Iain was wretched, too. He marked the shadows beneath Linda's eyes and knew that she was not sleeping—neither was he for that matter. The tension was so great that Iain felt it would be a relief when the summons came, and they knew the worst. They would go to London, then, and pre- pare their defence. It would be better to have something definite to do. He watched Linda very carefully during those days, trying to read her thoughts (and her thoughts were not difficult to read). Sometimes he saw her glance fall upon Richard with a passion of protective love, sometimes she caught him up in her arms and held him as if she would never let him go. Sometimes it seemed to him that her love for himself had gone—vanished into thin air—she scarcely noticed him, all her heart was bound up in the child. Linda was not normal—he realised that—the strain was driving her mad. It was a further horror to Iain that the strain might injure her brain. He had his mother constantly before his eyes, a dreadful warning of how the delicate balance of a woman's brain may be upset. Linda was stronger than his mother, her moral fibre was more resilient, but she was being highly tried.

These thoughts and feelings boiled below the surface of life, but, in spite of that, life moved on from day to day, and Linda and Iain, in their different spheres, went about their usual tasks and pleasures, ate and drank, and spoke to their friends as if there was nothing much wrong. Mrs. Hetherington Smith guessed that Linda was unhappy, but she had no idea of the reason. She was more than usually kind and considerate to Linda, making her rest as much as possible and protecting her from the unwelcome attentions of Sir Julius with unobtrusive tact. Meanwhile the Ardfalloch house-party disintegrated. Greta Bastable left to pay another visit in the north, and Desmond Cray went with her. Mr. Proudfoot returned to London. Other people came for a few days' shooting and went away—Linda hardly noticed them. Of the original house-party, only Mr. Stacey remained, and Jim Wyllie and Colonel White.

One day, when the Ardfalloch house-party had gone to shoot the Cluan Moors with Mr. Finlay, Mrs. Hetherington Smith summoned Iain and told him to take Linda for a walk. She gave them a tea-basket and told them to make a long afternoon of it.

'Off you go,' she said, with her friendly smile. 'It will do you both a lot of good. Richard and I will be quite happy by ourselves.'

They went off in silence, somewhat dazed by the prospect of a whole afternoon alone together. It was a lovely day. The sun was golden, and a keen sweet breeze stirred through the heather. Their feet chose the path to Balloch-gorm. Linda had not been that way before.

'There's a bothy up there,' Iain said. 'We'll have tea there, shall we?'

'Yes,' said Linda.

She was feeling happier to-day. The moors were so beautiful, and the mountains were so clear and high, her own troubles seemed smaller for the time being. Iain realised that the shadow had lifted a little, and he was glad; he did not want to bring the shadow back, but there was something he wanted to say to her, something he wanted to discuss—a plan had been forming in his head. He thought: I'll wait a little, I'll wait until we are having tea.

The path climbed higher, the moor was vast and empty of all life, it was seamed with narrow gullies, peaty water lay in pools, stagnant with green slime. The sky was like an immense inverted bowl of clearest blue glass. The heather was waist high in patches. They came to a clear space of emerald green turf with two black-faced sheep grazing upon it; they lifted their foolish faces and looked at Iain and Linda as they passed. On this high moor the air was like wine, tingling through their limbs. Linda thought that this land was primeval, it was untouched by man's hand since the beginning of time, untouched and untouchable. There was nothing you could do with this moorland except enjoy it. They walked on and on, scarcely speaking—a grouse rose from beneath their feet with a harsh scream.

'It's ten days now,' said Linda suddenly.

'I know,' said Iain. 'I was just thinking that. It can't be long now before we hear—I think we ought to have some plan.'

'Some plan?'

'For Richard,' Iain explained.

They had reached a cluster of boulders. Linda sat down on one as if she were suddenly tired.

' I've thought of something,' Iain continued, sitting down on a lower stone and looking up into her face. ' We could hide Richard. I believe we could do it, Linda. Donald and Morag could take him—we could say he was Donald's nephew and that his parents were dead.'

Linda looked at him in surprise. The plan seemed the height of madness to her—a child's crazy idea. She said vaguely, ' But how? Everybody in Ardfalloch would know who he was.'

' But nobody would betray the secret,' he told her. ' I really think the scheme is worth considering. I've thought about it for days now, and I can't see how they would find him. No stranger coming to the glen would know that he was not Donald's nephew—how could they? Even Medworth wouldn't know the child in a few months. He would be browned and sturdy—altered out of all recognition.'

' It's—it's an extraordinary idea,' said Linda doubtfully.

' I suppose it *would* be to you—just at first,' Iain admitted. ' The idea grew gradually with me. I went into Donald's cottage that day after we had seen Medworth, and Richard was sitting by the fire. He looked so *right* somehow, so much at home, so happy and peaceful and comfortable. I couldn't help thinking what would happen if Medworth got hold of him; and, gradually—I can't explain very well—gradually the two ideas came together and I saw this plan.'

' Yes, I see,' said Linda. She began to believe there might be some sense in the wild scheme.

' He would be quite safe with them,' Iain continued earnestly. ' They are both fond of him—Morag worships him and Donald would do anything I asked him to do—Richard would come to no harm there, I am sure of that.'

' They are very nice people,' Linda agreed.

' You see, it's really a choice between that and Medworth,' Iain said, ' unless of course we win the case, which seems—I'm afraid it's rather doubtful.'

' I know.'

' Linda, we can't let Medworth have him—it's unthinkable. Richard would be ruined for life—his nerves shattered.'

' I know, I know.'

' I've thought out all the details,' Iain continued. ' We could leave Richard with them when we go south. Donald could pretend he was going to his sister's funeral and come back with Richard. They could say that their nephew was coming to live with them—it's often done. Everybody in the glen would know that it was not true, but nobody would say a word. In a few months he would be absorbed into their life. We could leave him there for a year, or even two years—it wouldn't harm him. By that time Medworth might have given up the search, he might have found some other interest. You told me he never sticks to anything for very long—anything might happen in two years.'

' Isn't there a policeman in Ardfalloch?' Linda asked.

He laughed. ' Mac Var!' he said. ' Mac Var is Morag's brother. We don't need to bother about Mac Var.'

' This is a most extraordinary place,' said Linda, smiling in spite of her misery.

They discussed the plan further. Iain saw that he had at least given her something to think about. As far as his own hopes went, they were finished. Linda would not be free, he could never hope to marry her. But if they could save Richard it would be something—the other things seemed to matter very little beside that.

' I wouldn't be able to see Richard,' said Linda at last.

' No,' agreed Iain. ' I'm afraid not—it wouldn't be safe.'

' I could bear that if I knew he was happy.'

' I think he would be happy,' Iain said.

She looked across the moor towards the mountains, and

tried to think the thing out. Was Iain's plan really feasible or was it a fairy tale? She had seen quite clearly from the very beginning, that, if they lost the case, her own life would be finished. She would still be Jack's wife—the wife of a man who hated her—the only thing for her to do would be to go abroad, to vanish off the face of the earth, and try to bear her misery in solitude. At one blow she would lose Richard and Iain—everything that made life worth while. It did not seem possible that she would be able to bear it, but she supposed that she would bear it. Other people bore heavy burdens and continued to live—or exist. People didn't die of broken hearts.

Her face was so unutterably tragic that Iain felt his heart turn over in his breast. He said, 'Linda, what are you thinking?'

Linda told him. 'You see,' she said, 'it would be the only thing to do—to go right away. I shouldn't do Richard any good by remaining.'

'Linda—couldn't we? Couldn't you?'

'No,' she said. 'How could we? You have your place here—your duties. We couldn't possibly. It would be an untenable situation. You must never see me again if we lose the case. You must forget me, Iain.'

'I couldn't—how could I?'

She looked down at him pityingly, her determined eyes looked softly into his, they were full of tears.

'You must—try,' she said brokenly. 'I'm not going to ruin you, Iain. That would make it worse—for me. I've thought about it day and night—day and night.'

'Oh, Linda,' he said. 'Oh, Linda—I love you so . . . I would lay down my life for you—is there nothing I can do?'

She gave him her hand, and he held it against his cheek. They were silent for a long time. Neither of them felt any passion, only an immense tenderness. They were too worn and weary with their anxieties, too shattered for passion.

After a little they rose and went on. The bothy stood in a little green hollow surrounded with boulders. It was a small hut, built of rough stones. Linda thought it looked right in the wild setting of mountain and moor. The eye, sweeping over the landscape, scarcely dwelt upon the bothy —it was part of the scene. There were no trees here, no bushes, nor any kind of cultivated plants; only the sweeping line of moor and mountain and rock with the small lonely building crouching in the hollow like a child's toy. It was strange to think that the place had been built by men's hands, and that people had lived here and called it home. The moor was so vast and so utterly deserted that she and Iain might have been the only people in the world, the only people who had ever been in the world.

The door was an aperture in the wall. Linda looked inside and saw that the walls were black with peat smoke; there was a hole in the roof which had served as a chimney; the floor was of trodden mud.

' It looks very old,' Linda said in a quiet voice.

' About three hundred years—possibly,' Iain told her. ' Prince Charlie slept here for a night after his defeat at Culloden. He was to have lain at Ardfalloch, but it was too dangerous to have him there. He was a hunted man with a price upon his head——'

' You were Jacobites, of course,' Linda exclaimed, looking at Iain with heightened interest.

' Some of us were,' Iain said. ' It was one of the most ghastly things about the Jacobite cause that it divided families, so that brothers found themselves fighting against each other. Our family was divided in that way. MacAslan himself was a far-seeing man (some people called him by a less pleasant name); he saw the futility of it all. He knew that the Stuarts had no real backing, no real friends, for all the high-sounding promises they had obtained. He knew that England would never acknowledge a Catholic king. All these things he knew, and he saw the end. He refused to call out the clan. His attitude was very unpopular—even with his own people. There was a younger brother who raised part of the clan and joined the White Standard—he was wounded at Culloden. He crawled home and took to the heather when the tide turned against the Highlanders. There were many like him, skulking in caves amongst the mountains, wounded and starving.'

Linda had known of all this, but it had never seemed real to her before. She forgot her own troubles for a little as she thought of those hunted men lying amongst the mountains. She could imagine the loneliness of their lives, the fear that stalked them. She could imagine the grim discomforts of their plight.

' How could Prince Charles have stayed here if the Mac-Aslan was not on his side?' Linda said at last.

' There is a difference between wanting a man as a king and handing over a hunted fugitive to his pursuers,' Iain pointed out. 'MacAslan was loyal to the Prince's person. He had no wish to see him taken and beheaded, and he was able to help him better because he was known to have held aloof from the rebellion. He was not the only big chief who refused to join the rebels, and yet had a warm corner in his heart for the rightful heir to the throne—there were others like him who saw the frightfulness of civil war, and refused to sacrifice their men. Civil war is a dreadful thing, it bites deep into a nation's heart. The bitterness of those days still lingers——'

' Still lingers!' exclaimed Linda in amazement.

' I believe so. It lingers subconsciously.'

' It was so long ago.'

' So long ago, but we have long memories,' said Iain with a sigh. ' The mountains shut us away from the world and we have time to brood upon old wrongs—upon hangings and stabbings and massacres. My people were oppressed, they were hunted like wild beasts, they were forced to bear injustice, and bound by cruel laws that they could not understand. Oppression breeds treachery.'

'Are they treacherous?' Linda asked—she thought of Donald as she spoke, and Morag, and Alec MacNeil.

'Treacherous to their enemies, and loyal to their friends,' Iain said, smiling a little as he read her thoughts. 'After all, treachery and loyalty *may* go hand in hand, for a man could be treacherous through intense loyalty. It all depends whether the action is performed in your service or in the service of your enemy,' he added, smiling a trifle sadly at the jest. 'But, perhaps, when I said that oppression breeds treachery, I really meant that it breeds secrecy. My people are secretive. You think you see them, Linda, but you can never read their hearts——'

'But you—' she whispered, half afraid of the strange things he was saying—' you aren't—like that.'

'I don't know what I am. The two strains in me are always at war, pulling me in different directions, making me helpless and useless. We should not be in this mess if I had been whole and powerful and free.'

'I don't know what you mean,' she said, looking up at him with an anxious frown.

'It's easy to explain. If I had been all Lowland, with the good sense, and the "look before you leap" attitude of the Lowlander, I would have foreseen what might happen, and avoided the danger; and, if I had been all Highland, I would have killed Medworth and not listened to you when you held me back.'

She gazed at him in silence, she could find no words to express the turmoil in her brain. Was it true that Highland blood was so fierce and reckless?

'It's no good talking about it,' Iain continued, trying to speak more calmly. 'Medworth has gone. It's no good saying what I might have done now—I didn't mean to speak of it, but, somehow or other, every subject I start upon leads back to this—let's have tea, shall we, Linda?'

They had tea, sitting with their backs against a boulder in the lee of the bothy. The sun shone bravely in its bowl of blue sky. Far away on the heathery slopes of the mountain a grouse called harshly to its mate. Iain and Linda were very silent. They were so near to each other that they could be silent without constraint. Their thoughts were busy with the same subject, but they had said all that there was to be said—each knew what the other thought.

Mrs. Hetherington Smith had given them an immense amount of food—they could not eat a quarter of it.

'She is a dear,' Linda said, as she repacked the basket. 'I can't tell you how kind she is to me. Sometimes I feel I should like to tell her the whole thing—she knows something is wrong.'

'There would be no harm in telling her,' Iain said.

'You wouldn't mind?'

'Why should I? She might help us—I thought her a very sensible matter-of-fact sort of person——'

'I'll wait a little and see,' Linda said thoughtfully. 'I'll wait until we hear something definite—we must hear soon——'

They walked back to Ardfalloch rather slowly, making the most of their time together. It had not been a happy time for either of them, but they were loath to part. It might be days before they saw each other alone.

As they neared the place where the path joined the main track from Ardfalloch House they saw a man coming up from the village. He was evidently on his way to the old cottage, but, when he saw Iain and Linda, he turned and came towards them. It was MacTaggart from the inn. Iain was surprised, for MacTaggart was no walker; it was said in the village—half in jest—that MacTaggart never put his foot outside his own door. What could the man want, Iain wondered.

'Were you coming to see me?' he asked, after they had met and exchanged greetings in the usual manner.

'I wass indeed,' replied MacTaggart. He took off his hat and passed his handkerchief over his head. He was hot, and very red in the face from his unaccustomed exercise. 'It wass yourself I wass coming to see, MacAslan, but now that I have seen you I will not be coming up to the house—no indeed—it wass chust a thing I wass wanting to tell you, so it wass.'

'You had better come in and have a drink——' Iain began.

'No, indeed, and thank you, MacAslan,' he replied. 'It is back to my place I will be going, for I do not like to be leaving it for long. It is chust that I wass thinking I would be telling you about the young man that is living with me chust now.'

'A young man?' Iain enquired.

'He is not so very young either, but not so old. And indeed he is harmless enough; but it is a strange thing for a young man to be living with me, and him neither shooting nor fishing, and I wass saying to myself I would be seeing MacAslan and telling him about it.'

Iain was used to the Highland manner of conveying information and found no difficulty in interpreting Mac-Taggart's news. He found it rather disquieting. Strangers sometimes came to Ardfalloch, and, finding the inn more comfortable than the usual run of Highland inns, stayed on for a little. They tried to obtain leave to shoot or fish, or climbed some of the hills if that was their line. But this stranger neither shot nor fished, and there was obviously something queer about him or MacTaggart would not have troubled about the man. Iain would not have paid much heed to MacTaggart's story in ordinary circumstances—he would have listened with feigned interest, and turned the whole thing into a joke—but the position in which he and Linda were placed was so precarious that the least suspicion of anything out of the ordinary was alarming. He determined to find out all he could from MacTaggart and proceeded to do so in his own way.

'Well,' he said, smiling, 'and I suppose the young man is waiting for an invitation to shoot my birds or to catch a salmon in Mr. Finlay's water—is that what it is, MacTaggart?'

'It is not then,' replied the landlord promptly. 'For the young man hass neither rod nor gun, nor even a pair of strong boots for the hills.'

At this information Iain became definitely alarmed. What on earth could a young man be doing at Ardfalloch if he had not come for sport?

'What has he come for, MacTaggart?' he enquired.

'And how will I be knowing?' said the landlord in reply. 'He is a nice enough young man and he is going about the place talking to people and asking about this and that. There is a great talk in the village about him—so there is—and nobody knowing what to be saying at all.'

'What is he asking?'

'He is asking about everything,' MacTaggart replied, throwing out his hands in a gesture of helplessness. 'He is asking about who is at the House and he is asking about MacAslan, but chiefly he is asking all about Mister Middleton.'

Iain heard Linda give a little gasp, and he put his hand on her arm to steady her.

'All about Mr. Middleton!' he said lightly. 'Well, I suppose he is a friend of Mr. Middleton's and was recommended to your inn by Mr. Middleton—there would be nothing strange in that.'

'It is what I thought myself,' agreed MacTaggart;

'chust at first it is what I thought. But if the two gentlemen are friends, then it is a queer thing that Mister Howles should be asking so much about his friend. Och, I cannot explain it, MacAslan, but he is asking things that he would not be asking if he did be knowing Mister Middleton well. And yet, if he does not be knowing Mister Middleton well, what interest can there be for him in the gentleman's doings. I cannot be making head or tail of the thing——' added MacTaggart with a sigh.

Iain could not make head or tail of it either. He questioned MacTaggart closely, but there was no more information to be gained anent the strange visitor who neither shot nor fished, nor even possessed a pair of stout boots for the moors. MacTaggart had already told all that he knew. Presently they parted from him, and he waddled off down the path to Ardfalloch village.

He walks like a duck, Iain thought, as he watched the corpulent figure of the landlord out of sight. He walks like a duck, and yet, in spite of that, there is something dignified about the man.

'Did he come all the way from Ardfalloch to tell you that?' Linda was saying.

'Yes,' said Iain, and then he added thoughtfully: 'It's a queer tale—who can the man be?'

'A friend of Jack's,' Linda replied. 'That's obvious. It gave me a shock when he mentioned " Mister Middleton," but of course I see now that it has nothing to do with us—how could it? You're not worried, are you, Iain?'

'No, of course not,' replied Iain, trying to sound convincing.

'A friend of Jack's,' Linda continued. ' Jack has scores of friends of all sorts and conditions—people he meets casually, I mean. He probably met this man somewhere, and told him about Ardfalloch, and that the inn was comfortable, and the man has come—why shouldn't he?'

'There's no reason why he shouldn't,' Iain admitted, ' except that a young man who neither shoots nor fishes would find Ardfalloch frightfully dull—there's nothing else to do.'

' I don't find it dull!'

' But you're not a young man, and you're not living alone at MacTaggart's inn.'

'That's true, of course,' agreed Linda, smiling a little in spite of herself.

They had reached the small bridge over the burn by this time—it had been agreed that they were to part here. They both felt it was better that they should not be seen too much in each other's company. Now that the moment had come to part they both felt that the hours had been wasted —there was so much that they might have said—but now it was too late.

As he went home through the woods he thought again about the young man at MacTaggart's. It was just as well that Linda had missed the point of the landlord's story—the part that he found so disturbing. MacTaggart had said that the young man had asked things about Middleton that he would not have asked if he had known him well, and yet if he did not know Middleton (or Medworth) well, why should he be so interested in his doings? That seemed to Iain the most significant feature in MacTaggart's story—and the most puzzling. Iain wrestled with the problem for the rest of the evening. Could he be a friend of Medworth's, sent to keep an eye on himself and Linda in Medworth's absence, and merely asking questions to throw dust in the eyes of the villagers? Could he be an enemy of Medworth's, prying into the man's affairs with some ulterior motive? Iain could not fathom the mystery to his own satisfaction.

Linda was already too full of anxieties and perplexities to trouble herself over this new complication. She had no room in her mind to think of anything except Richard and

Iain and herself. While she was with Iain she had been a little comforted, she had actually believed that his plan for Richard's safety might work. But, after she had parted from him, and the magic of his presence had faded from her mind, Iain's plan seemed childish and crude. She thought of it that night as she lay in bed—tossing and turning, sleepless with anxiety—and tried to decide whether Iain's plan was sense or madness. Was Iain as powerful as he thought? Could he keep Richard here, at Ardfalloch, if the law gave him to Jack? Was it possible to defy the law and to hide Richard in the glen, or was it only the dream of a man who was divorced from reality? Iain lived in a different world from the world she knew; he lived in a world where might was right, where a man took what he wanted and kept it. For centuries his forebears had been a law unto themselves—kings in their own domain—and their blood ran in Iain's veins. The inexorable strength of the law was not realised by Iain—how could he know the law's strength? At Ardfalloch the law was represented by Mac Var—Morag's brother—a mild-mannered man who spent most of his time digging in his garden or helping his neighbours to get in their harvest. Iain liked Mac Var, but he did not respect him as a potential force. He did not see the vast machinery behind Mac Var, the machinery that ground you into powder.

Linda remembered the conversation between Sir Julius and Mr. Hetherington Smith at the dance. She had scarcely heard it at the time, but now it came back to her. Sir Julius had said that the people here were decadent; that they looked backwards instead of forwards; that they lived in the past. Wasn't that true of Iain? Linda turned over in bed and thought about it seriously. Iain was not decadent, but she had sometimes thought that he lived in dreams. She had sometimes thought that he was not really living in the twentieth century. Iain's mind moved differently from hers, differently from anybody else's—it was a part of his charm that he was so different from other people—did this quality of *difference* make him a competent adviser? Linda sighed, she remembered how he had wanted to go after Jack and kill him. Was that a sign of an unbalanced mind, of the hysteria that Sir Julius had spoken of, or was it merely a sign that he was more natural than other men, less bound by convention? She supposed that it was innate in Iain, the desire to sweep an enemy from his path—that old brigand in the library (of whom Mrs. Hetherington Smith was so fond) would not have hesitated for a moment. He would have made short work of anybody who stood in his way. Linda had no illusions at all about Iain's seriousness and strength of purpose. He had not merely *said* he would kill Jack Medworth, as another man might have said it in a sudden burst of anger—Iain had meant it in deadly earnest. She had been terrified that she would not be able to prevent him from doing it. She had clung to him and reasoned with him until she was limp and exhausted with the struggle.

The whole thing came to this, Linda thought: Was Iain's strength real? Could he take Richard and keep him in spite of the law?

Linda could not make up her mind one way or the other; sometimes she thought: It is a mad plan, a crazy idea. How could they hide him here when one chance word would give the whole thing away? How could I bear to leave him here, with the MacNeils, in a peasant's cottage? How could I ever have thought of such a wild plan? And sometimes she thought of Jack Medworth and the sneer on his face as he spoke of ' licking the little rabbit into shape,' and she flung herself face downwards upon her bed and cried, ' No, no, I can't let him have Richard, anything would be better than that,' and she remembered that even *seeing* the man had upset Richard and made him quite ill; and she thought of all that Iain had said, and how Richard would be quite safe and happy with Morag, and that it would do him no harm to live with them for a little until Jack forgot, or found something else to interest him.

By this time it was getting light—the room was filled with a queer half-light that seemed to choose what it would illumine and what it would hide. The oval mirror shone like a silver shield, and, across the grey windows, the dark feathery branch of a fir tree moved up and down in the wind of dawn. Day had returned. Linda turned her pillows for the twentieth time and tried to forget her troubles in sleep.

CHAPTER XXII

The Inspector's Visit

THE mystery of the young man who was living at Mac-Taggart's Inn was solved a few days later. It was a Sunday morning. Mrs. MacAslan and Janet had gone for a walk and Iain was alone in the cottage. He was sitting by the fire, thinking as usual about the extraordinary muddle in which he and Linda had been involved, and wondering why they had heard nothing more of Medworth and his machinations, when there was a knock on the door. Iain went to open it and found a strange man standing on the step. The man was about his own age—or slightly older—and was dressed in a plus-four suit and a shabby but well-cut Burberry coat.

'Mr. MacAslan?' he enquired.

'Yes,' replied Iain. 'Do you want to see me?'

'Please,' said the stranger. He took off his coat and followed Iain into the sitting-room.

Iain looked at him critically, he was rather a nice-looking fellow, clean-shaven, with a long straight nose and good teeth.

'Won't you sit down?' he said.

'Thank you,' said the man. 'I'm sorry to bother you, but I want your help in rather a curious case—I am Detective-Inspector Howles—Scotland Yard.'

'Scotland Yard?' exclaimed Iain in amazement.

Inspector Howles showed his badge.

'That's interesting,' Iain said. 'Perhaps you won't

believe me when I tell you I have often read of a Scotland Yard badge, but never seen one before.'

Howles laughed. ' I believe you, all right,' he said.

Iain thought hard—surely Scotland Yard could have no interest in Linda's case—it was the King's Proctor, Iain knew that much. This man must have come to see him about some other matter. What could it be?

' I am told that you own this place,' Inspector Howles was saying, ' so I thought I'd like a talk with you. I thought perhaps you might be able to throw some light on my case. It's a strange case, very puzzling. I suppose you know that Mr. Jack Medworth has disappeared——'

' Disappeared!'

' Completely vanished,' Howles said. ' I see you don't know about it. He left here on the twenty-eighth August. Drove to Balnafin in the local taxi and took the Glasgow train—but he never arrived there.'

Iain was gazing at the inspector in amazement. ' Never arrived there,' he echoed stupidly. ' How d'you know?'

' I've made every enquiry,' the man replied. ' His luggage arrived, and was placed in the lost luggage depot, but nobody saw Mr. Medworth. I've searched the luggage, of course, but there was no clue to his disappearance—perhaps you are aware that he stayed here under the name of Middleton.'

' I know that,' Iain admitted. ' I knew him when he was here—I lent him my boat once or twice.'

' Perhaps you knew he was divorced from his wife—she is staying at Ardfalloch House, I believe.'

' Yes, I knew that.'

' You know Mrs. Medworth?'

' Yes.'

' Can you help me at all, Mr. MacAslan? Do you know if the man had any enemies?'

' Enemies? D'you mean *here*?'

' Yes.'

' I think he was *liked*,' replied Iain thoughtfully. ' He was amusing—very good company. I used to go down to the inn, sometimes, and it seemed to me he was popular. He had travelled, you see, and he had a fund of stories—rather doubtful stories, but they went down well. It's quiet here, you see, and the men rather like somebody new, somebody who has knocked about a bit and can tell them about the world. He used to have quite an audience sometimes.'

The inspector sighed. ' I know all that,' he said. ' I've been here nearly a week, making enquiries on the Q.T., but I haven't got any further—not a yard further. I thought perhaps you might have heard something.'

' What sort of thing?' enquired Iain cautiously.

' Well, do you think there was a woman he was after, or anything like that? Medworth was a bit of a devil with women—I found that out—I thought perhaps he might have interfered with somebody's sweetheart, and got murdered for his pains—something like that. Your people here have got the reputation for being wild and fierce—they don't *seem* so, I must say. I never saw people who were quieter, or kinder, or more law-abiding on the surface—what's under the surface, Mr. MacAslan?'

Iain could not help smiling. ' They're good and bad like other people,' he said. ' If Medworth had meddled with their women they wouldn't have liked it—but did he?'

' I can't find anything,' Howles admitted. ' Not a blessed thing. That's why I'm asking you.' He hesitated a moment and then added, ' Supposing he *had* meddled with their women, should you think it likely that they would kill him?'

Iain did not like the question—he scarcely knew why. He thought a moment and then he said, ' I can tell you this, if any of them had felt inclined to avenge themselves upon Medworth they would have done it *here*. They wouldn't

279

have waited until he left Ardfalloch. These people are primitive, in a way—they would have killed the man here, in their own glen, if they were going to do it at all—but it seems to me you have no reason to suspect the people here, have you?'

'No, I haven't,' said Howles with a sigh; 'and what's more I happen to know that there was nobody from here on the train. I'm afraid I shall have to rule out that possibility. I'm loath to rule it out because I haven't got anything else to work on—except suicide. What do you think of that as a solution, Mr. MacAslan? Was Medworth that sort of man?'

For a moment Iain was tempted to say he was—it would be such a nice easy explanation of the mystery—and then, suddenly, he couldn't say it.

'That was not my impression of the man,' he admitted.

Howles nodded. 'It couldn't possibly have been that, or we should have found the body. I just wanted to see what you would say.'

Iain had a feeling of panic. He didn't know why he was frightened, but quite suddenly he felt that this man was more clever than he seemed. He had set a sort of trap, and Iain had nearly walked into it. What did the man *know*? Did he know about Linda? Did he know that Medworth had intended to bring an action against himself and Linda? Did he—could he possibly suspect that Iain had wanted to kill Medworth?

'Did he speak to you of his reason for staying here?' enquired Howles, after a few moments' silence.

'Yes; the first time I saw him,' replied Iain, glad that this was a question so easily answered. 'It was in the bar-parlour at MacTaggart's; he told us that he was writing a treatise on birds. He also made enquiries about the fishing.'

'That is all correct, Mr. MacAslan,' said the inspector,

smiling. 'But was that the real reason he was here? Did he try to see Mrs. Medworth?'

Iain felt his forehead grow damp. He said, 'Medworth met her once—here in my house—by arrangement.'

'Were you present at the interview?'

'Yes.'

'What took place?'

Iain thought hurriedly, then he said, 'Need I tell you that? I mean, is it important—has it any real bearing on your case?'

'I understand your reluctance,' Howles replied in quite a friendly manner. 'You needn't tell me, of course. I can't insist upon you telling me anything, but if you could give me an idea of what took place at their interview it might save me from having to trouble Mrs. Medworth.'

Iain hesitated; the last thing he wanted was for Linda to be worried by Inspector Howles. 'Then you needn't see Mrs. Medworth—if I tell you?' he asked.

'I can't promise that,' replied Howles. 'But your account might satisfy me.'

Iain thought: That's nonsense. He's only saying that to persuade me to speak. I shall have to be damned careful with this man. 'They talked about the child,' he said aloud. 'Mrs. Medworth has the custody of the child. Medworth wanted to come to an arrangement by which *he* should have the child, but Mrs. Medworth couldn't agree to that. If you know anything about Medworth I needn't tell you why. Mrs. Medworth saw no reason to give him what the law had denied him.'

'I see,' said Howles slowly. 'He was angry, I suppose.'

'He was—annoyed,' amended Iain.

'Was that what he was going to see his solicitor about?'

Iain felt his hair rise in horror—*so Howles knew that.*

'He wrote to his solicitor, making an appointment,' explained the inspector. 'Rather an ambiguous letter. I take it he was a man who liked making little mysteries—surprising people. It was Medworth's solicitor who called in the Yard. The letter was urgent, and Medworth never appeared on the day appointed. Mr. Wales was worried. He thought it was odd after writing so urgently that the man should not turn up. I've got the letter here,' added Howles, touching his pocket.

' Could I see it?' Iain enquired, trying to make his voice sound as casual as possible.

' I see no reason why you shouldn't,' Howles replied. He took the letter out of his pocket-book and handed it over. It was a crumpled half-sheet of paper.

27th August.   MacTaggart's Inn,
                                          Ardfalloch.

Dear Wales,

Can you see me on Monday about 4? It's urgent. You'll be surprised when you hear my news. I've got a big job for you. No more now as I want to see your face when you hear my news.

Yours in haste,

J.M.

' Yes,' said Iain slowly. He folded the note and handed it back.

' Any comments?' enquired Howles.

' It's very like the man.'

' H'm. You mean breezy?'

' I suppose I do,' said Iain.

' But what was the big job?' Howles asked. ' That's the question. From what you tell me Mrs. Medworth refused to relinquish the child. Had he any hold on her? Was the big job something to do with her, or was it something quite different, something we know nothing about?'

Iain did not like this at all. The man was far too near the truth. It was most uncomfortable. He waited a few

273

moments as though he were considering the matter, and then he said, ' I suppose you are quite sure that Medworth really is dead?'

' I'm not sure he's dead,' replied Howles a trifle irritably. ' I'm not sure of anything. All I know is that the man has disappeared. He may have disappeared voluntarily, but that isn't likely in view of this letter—is it? Here's a man writing urgently to his solicitor about a " big job "—it was Wales who defended him in the divorce suit, of course— here's a man, I say, writing to London full of confidence, and then, suddenly, he disappears. What happened to him? Did something go wrong at the last minute? Did something happen to make him change his mind? Perhaps you think he lost his memory——'

' No, I don't think that.'

' Neither do I. You see what a mystery it is. I've worked at the thing till I'm tired and I can't find any clue. I started working at the other end, but I soon saw *that* was hopeless, so I came up here. I traced him quite easily as far as Balnafin and into the train. Quite half a dozen people saw him at the station. It's a small place and they all remembered him perfectly—the man in the booking office who sold him a ticket (a through ticket to Glasgow)—the station-master—a couple of farmers. The porter remembers handling his luggage. The station-master saw him into a first-class compartment—it was empty. The guard saw him get in. That's all right: the man got into the train; after that—*blank*. Nobody saw him get out at any of the stations where the train stops. Nobody saw him again as far as I know—the man simply vanished,' said Howles with a gesture of something like despair. ' The man simply vanished into thin air——'

' Most extraordinary,' Iain said.

' Most extraordinary,' agreed Howles. ' It's beaten me. The man was an easily recognisable sort of man—a big

man, a man you would not be likely to forget—people like
that don't vanish. If they've been killed you find their
bodies. I've had the line searched, of course. I thought he
might have fallen out of the train, or been pushed out, but
no—not a vestige of the man has been found. What d'you
make of it, Mr. MacAslan?'

'I can't make anything of it,' replied Iain truthfully.

'Neither can I,' said Howles. He rose from his chair.
Well, that's that,' he said with a sigh. 'I must thank you,
Mr. MacAslan. You haven't helped me much, but I am
grateful for the frank way you have answered my questions.
I must try another line, that's all. A man like Medworth,
with his reputation, may have had enemies. In fact, he must
have had enemies—women and racing—yes. One of his
enemies has done him in, and I've got to find who it is.
I'm on the wrong scent here. It's disappointing to have
wasted so much time to no purpose, but it's all in the day's
work.'

'Queer sort of work it must be!' said Iain in a friendly
manner.

'Yes, queer but interesting,' agreed Howles.

'Have a drink before you go,' suggested Iain.

'Thank you, sir—I don't mind if I do.'

Iain fetched the whisky and a couple of glasses; they sat
down and lighted cigarettes. Howles at once began to talk
in a different way; he was more casual and his eyes lost their
piercing directness. The inspector was 'off duty'; the
interview was over; they were merely chatting now. *But I
must still be careful,* Iain thought—although what he had
to be careful about was not very clear in his mind.

'It's funny how my ideas have changed in the last few
days,' Howles was saying. 'When I came up here I thought
I was coming amongst—well, amongst sort of savages—
wild Highlanders with kilts, and daggers in their stockings.
I thought I had only got to walk into this valley and find a

murderer—several perhaps. The only thing that worried me at all was in case I got a dagger in my own back.'

Iain laughed. 'You find Ardfalloch more civilised than you expected?'

'I find the people more civilised,' replied Howles. 'You could hardly call the *place* civilised, with the roads in that frightful condition, and scarcely a telephone in miles; no evening papers except a stray one from Glasgow if someone in the village happens to have come over from somewhere else; with no plumbing to speak of and no cinemas——'

'There's wireless,' Iain reminded him, somewhat amused at the inspector's indictment.

'Yes, there's wireless,' admitted Howles. 'What on earth did they do before wireless was invented? Those little farms amongst the mountains are cut off from everybody—so they tell me—for weeks on end during the winter. And yet the people living in them are better informed and more interested in world affairs than many a Londoner.'

'You certainly seem to have sized us up,' said Iain, smiling.

'Well, that's my job, sir,' replied Howles, with a kind of modest self-satisfaction. 'It's my job to size people up. I've gone about a lot amongst the people here. They were a bit suspicious of me at first, but I've made friends with them now—some of them—and a kinder, quieter, better-living set of people I've never met. There's practically no drunkenness—there's no theft. I made friends with Mac Var—your local P.C.—and if ever I want a soft job I'll exchange with him. The man doesn't know he's born. Spends most of his time gardening, and the remainder walking out with the best-looking girl in the village. I've poked about a bit, and talked to people in the bar, and round about the place, and I've met with the greatest kindness and hospitality. They're a great crowd. Take Mac-Taggart, for instance—I've been staying at his inn—he's a fine man, and well-read, too. Take Donald MacNeil—what a splendid type! I consider Donald MacNeil absolutely typical of the Highlander—am I right?'

Iain smiled. Was Donald typical? Was anybody typical when you really knew them?

'Donald and I get on splendidly,' continued Howles with enthusiasm. 'He's a little dour, at first, but his heart is gold. You'd think to look at him—with his huge shoulders and enormous hands—you'd think he would be wild and rough, but Donald's one of Nature's gentlemen; he's the kindest soul alive—wouldn't hurt a fly; and that wife of his is a *great* girl. I went up to Alec MacNeil's farm, they were having tea, and nothing would satisfy them but that I should sit down and have it with them—I never met with hospitality like it. There they were, sitting round the table with about half a dozen children—ragged as guttersnipes but with manners like kings and queens. They handed me butter and pressed me to eat as if I were their long-lost uncle, though it looked to me as if they had a pretty tough struggle to make ends meet without feeding chance strangers——'

'Yes,' said Iain. 'They have a tough struggle. I'm sorry for Alec and his wife.'

'Well, I must really go,' said Howles. 'I mustn't take up any more of your time—thank you again, sir.'

They shook hands, and Iain saw him out of the door.

'D'you live here all by yourself?' enquired Howles suddenly.

'No, my mother is here, and her maid.'

'I see,' Howles said. 'Well, good-bye, sir. Mustn't shake hands again, it's not lucky.'

CHAPTER XXIII

Iain and Linda

IAIN went back into the sitting-room and poured out another drink—a stiff one—he felt better after he had had it. He thought: *Medworth's dead. Good lord, how extraordinary!* I suppose he *is* dead. He must be—what other explanation is there? I ought to feel absolutely wild with delight, but I don't. Why don't I? *There's something funny about it.* The man left here alive and well and full of self-confidence —he never reached Glasgow—what happened? What could have happened? He must be dead, and if he's dead it's all right—marvellously all right—but it seems too good to be true—things just don't happen like that. I wonder what Linda will think about it. Richard is safe, anyway, and that's all that really matters to her.—He felt a sudden rush of relief at the thought that Richard was safe.—*I am wild with delight,* he thought—*it's just that I hadn't realised all it means.* It means that Richard is all right, and, if Richard is all right, so is Linda. It means that I shall get Linda after all—with no court case or anything. Good lord, of course I'm wild with delight! I may have to wait a bit until she recovers from the strain and the shock, but I can wait. I've waited five years for Linda. I can wait a bit longer if I know it's going to be all right in the end. I can be patient if I know. And then he thought: *But perhaps Medworth isn't dead.* He may not be. He may have disappeared— voluntarily. Something out of his past may have cropped up and made it necessary for him to disappear—money troubles, or a woman. If he just stays away until Linda gets her decree absolute I suppose it will be all right. It's only a month now. After that he couldn't do anything—at least I don't suppose he could. Why don't I know more about it all? Somehow I feel the man is dead. He was so determined to go to London, nothing but death could have prevented him.

Iain walked about the room to ease the tumult in his mind. He thought: *I wonder if Howles will go and see Linda.* He would have to see Linda if he wants to find an enemy in Medworth's past. I didn't believe Howles when he said perhaps he wouldn't have to see Linda—he won't leave here without seeing her. I ought to see her first—I must see her first, but I don't want Howles to think I'm rushing off to see Linda and warn her. It would look as if we had something to hide. Howles is convinced, now, that the secret of Medworth's disappearance is not to be found in Ardfalloch—and that's all to the good. We don't want him to ferret about here too much. He might came across the fact that Medworth was threatening Linda and me with an action—I don't see how he could find that out, but he might. It would be distinctly unpleasant, to say the least of it. *He would have found somebody who wanted Medworth out of the way*—there's danger there. What do I think about it personally? he asked himself, stopping and gazing into the fire. *Do I think that Medworth's disappearance has anything to do with us?* How could it have anything to do with us? Isn't it just coincidence that makes me think it might have? I wanted the man out of the way and the man has vanished. It can't be anything but a coincidence. It's a mighty lucky one for us—too lucky to be comfortable, somehow. . . .

He sat down at the table and drew a piece of paper towards him. 'Darling,' he wrote, 'Janet will bring you this. Burn it at once——' and then he stopped. He thought: *No, it's too dangerous to put on to paper—besides, how can I explain?* I simply must see her. I must see her before *he* sees her, but how? Where will she be? Perhaps Howles is on his way to see her now . . .

At that thought he was seized with panic. He snatched up his field-glasses and rushed out of the house. Howles was not in sight. Iain ran quickly along the path leading to Ardfalloch village. *What a fool I was!* he told himself. *I should have watched to see which way the man went.* How much start has he got while I've been thinking things over and wasting precious time?

Iain had not gone very far, however, before he saw Howles in front of him, picking his way rather carefully down the path. It had rained a lot in the night and the path was slippery and boggy in patches. Howles was more used to pavements than to Highland tracks full of tree roots and stones to trip unwary feet. Iain heaved a sigh of relief. The inspector was going back to the inn for his Sunday dinner. He would be safe there for at least an hour —probably more. MacTaggart did himself and his clients well; Sunday dinner was a substantial meal at the inn. After he had partaken of MacTaggart's Sunday dinner, Howles would want a rest and a pipe before he felt inclined for the long hot walk to Ardfalloch House.

Now that Howles was off his mind—temporarily at any rate—Iain turned his attention to the problem of finding Linda and getting her alone. How was this to be accomplished? He wondered if she had gone to church at Balnafin with the Hetherington Smiths. It was possible—it was even probable. If so, they would now be on their way back from Balnafin in the motor-launch. Would it be better to go out onto the Black Rock from whence he could see the loch, and watch for the boat, or to run back to Ardfalloch jetty and try to waylay her on her way up to the house? Of course, she might not have gone to church at all—there was that to be considered—but this looked like his best chance. It would be too risky to go up to the house and see her. Howles might easily find out that he had gone straight up to the house—it wouldn't look well.

After thinking the matter over Iain decided to run back to Ardfalloch jetty. It really was his only chance. Even if he saw Linda in the launch from the rocks it would do him no good. He turned and ran back along the path, running easily and not too fast, for he had a long way to go—all round the bay—and he must conserve his energy. He was very fit and in good training, his open-air life had made him hardy, and he considered it a man's duty to keep his body in good trim. He passed his own little cottage without stopping—Janet would wonder where he was, but that could not be helped.

The path mounted steeply between his cottage and Donald's. When Iain reached the top of the hill he stopped for a moment and looked out over the loch. A launch was coming from the direction of Balnafin—it was his own launch and there were several people in it, but he could not make out who they were—even with his glasses. He could get to the jetty before the launch if he hurried, but there was no time to waste. As he passed Donald's cottage a sudden thought struck him. Donald would not be there, of course—Donald would be in the launch—but there was Morag . . .

Iain jumped over the small fence, which protected Donald's small garden plot from the depredations of the rabbits, and ran up to the door calling her name.

' Morag—am beil thu ann? Morag!'

Morag was cooking the Sunday dinner; she dropped a saucepan lid with a clatter and clutched the table for support. Her face was as white as a sheet.

'Ciod e a tha ort?' she cried. 'Is it bad news, Mac-Aslan?'

He was too excited to notice her agitation. He stood by the door, panting. 'Morag,' he said, 'listen—I want you to do something for me. There's no time to explain—it's important. I must see Mrs. Medworth alone—it's—it's absolutely essential. I think she's in the launch. Will you run down to the jetty and tell her that I must see her—don't let the others hear.'

Morag was quick-brained—she was already rearranging her pots and pans on the stove, so that Donald's dinner should come to no harm in her absence. She caught up a shawl and flung it round her shoulders, and followed Mac-Aslan out of the house.

He took her hand to help her up the hill, and they ran together. 'You understand, don't you,' he said. 'I must see her either now, or directly after lunch—nobody must know.'

'I understand,' Morag told him, and then she added a little breathlessly, 'Is it trouble, MacAslan?'

'No, it's not trouble, Morag,' he replied. He looked at her face for the first time and marked its pallor. 'I'm going too fast for you,' he added, slackening his pace.

Morag pulled him on. 'It's not the pace,' she said, panting a little. 'It is chust the fright. I was thinking, maybe, it wass trouble—trouble for Donald.'

Iain laughed. 'Oh, that Donald of yours!' he exclaimed. 'Are there any other thoughts in your head but Donald? He's a lucky man, is Donald, to have such a loving wife.'

'It is not trouble for Donald, then?'

'No, it has nothing to do with Donald. Nothing at all.'

They had reached the edge of the trees by this time. Iain hid himself behind a convenient bush. The launch was coming into the little harbour, feeling her way carefully, for the tide was only about an hour past the ebb and there was scarcely enough water for her to cross the bar of sand. Donald was leaning over the side of the boat gazing down into the water.

From where he was hidden, Iain could see all that was happening; he saw Morag strolling down to the jetty; her red shawl made a brilliant patch of colour against the soft blues and greys of loch and sky; he saw, too, that Linda was in the launch, as he had hoped and expected. She was wearing a grey hat to-day, and, beneath its brim, her face was pale and strained. The field-glasses brought her very near, he could even see the small lines about her dear eyes —lines which had not been there at all a month ago.

Iain wondered how Linda would take his news. She could not help being pleased—and yet it was an uncomfortable thing to feel pleased at the news of a man's death. How queer we are! Iain thought. I would have killed the man myself without a qualm—yes, I would have killed him —and yet, now that I hear he is dead, I find it an uncomfortable thing to be pleased.

They were disembarking now. Linda, Richard, Mrs. Hetherington Smith, and Sir Julius were the four members of the house-party who had attended church this morning. Iain could not help smiling to himself at the constitution of the church party. The two women had gone because they liked it; Richard had gone for the pleasure of going to Balnafin in the launch, and Sir Julius, obviously, because of Linda. Iain did not think the London doctor was the sort of man to attend church for the conventional reasons. Iain watched Morag anxiously, she was leaning over the edge of the jetty speaking to Donald—that was a good move, Iain thought, applauding her cleverness. The others would think—as they were meant to think—that Morag had come down to the jetty to speak to Donald about something.

Richard had taken Morag's hand and was smiling up into her face; Linda jumped lightly from the boat; Sir Julius was helping Mrs. Hetherington Smith; Donald had one hand on the jetty to steady the launch. He saw Morag turn and speak to Linda—she had done it. Nobody could have heard—except perhaps Richard, and Richard didn't matter. They were all standing on the jetty, now. After a moment or two they began to walk up to the house, the three adults together with Richard running in front. Iain stayed where he was, waiting for Morag. He wondered what she had arranged.

' Well,' he said eagerly, as she came towards him.

' I told Mistress Medworth,' Morag said. ' She will come out and meet MacAslan after lunch—it would be difficult to get away before.'

' You've done splendidly, Morag,' he told her.

Her eyes brightened at MacAslan's praise; she was pleased that she had been able to do what he wanted, but she was rather curious to know the reason for the secrecy. It was pardonable curiosity; MacAslan meant so much to everybody in Ardfalloch; his affairs were of vital importance to them—and of vital interest. It seemed strange to Morag that MacAslan could not go up to the house and meet Mistress Medworth openly. He was going to marry her—everybody knew that—and Morag was glad. Mistress Medworth was a kind lady and pleasant. She had not so much money as Miss Finlay, and that was a pity, but you could not have everything. But surely, thought Morag, surely if they were going to be married there was nothing to prevent them from meeting openly? It was very strange, so it was. Perhaps Morag would not have troubled her head about the matter if she had not had another trouble on her mind, another secret thing that haunted her night and day.

She looked up sideways at MacAslan and smiled coax-

ingly. ' Mistress Medworth is a very nice lady,' she said.
' Kind and pretty, so she is.'

Iain smiled, too. He knew that Morag was dying to know
all about it, but she would never put her questions into
words. There was familiarity between Iain and his people,
familiarity such as southerners can never know nor understand, but there was also a strong barrier of etiquette beyond
which his people would not pass.

' I want to see Mrs. Medworth about something important,' Iain said. ' A business matter. I should never be able
to get her alone if I were to go up to the house.'

Morag nodded, half satisfied. What he said was true, but
she felt that there was more in it than that.

' Mistress Medworth will be staying at Ardfalloch?'
Morag said—it was half a question, half an assertion. She
made it significant by the smile—the enigmatic smile—
which accompanied it.

Iain sighed. ' I hope so, Morag—I think so,' he told
her.

' I am glad,' said Morag simply. ' We will all be glad.
She is a very nice lady.'

Iain went through the woods to meet Linda; he sat down
near the gate which shut off the garden from the woods, and
settled his back comfortably against a tree. He would miss
his dinner, but that did not worry Iain; he was used to
missing his meals when he was out shooting or fishing. It
was very quiet in the wood, quiet and peaceful. The sunshine fell in golden slants between the branches of the trees.
Presently a rabbit came out of its hole and looked at him
with cocked ears. The rabbit reminded him of Richard and
the picnic on the island—he smiled as he thought of Richard. It was nice to know that Richard was safe. It would be
interesting to see Richard grow up and develop; there was
good stuff in Richard. Iain thought: I shall be able to help
Linda with him, and the thought pleased him.

He did not feel impatient, waiting for Linda, there was so much to think of, and he began to feel happy. Medworth's death was now established in his mind, and he could turn his thoughts to the happiness that awaited him. He could see the future stretching out before him like a broad placid stream, with himself and Linda floating down the stream in a boat together.

There was so much to think of that the time passed quickly; he was almost surprised when he saw the side door open and Linda hurry across the garden towards him. He had not thought, until he saw her coming, of how he was going to tell Linda his news.

He went forward and took her hands. ' I had to see you,' he said gravely.

' Yes,' she replied. ' Morag told me—I came as soon as I could.'

' We'll go up the burn,' Iain said.

They went along the little path by the side of the burn. It was coming down fast to-day, tumbling from pool to pool, hurrying along between the rocks as if it were in haste to reach the calm bosom of the loch. On the banks grew hazel trees, there were nuts forming on them now, but they would not be ripe for another month. The path crossed the burn by stepping-stones, slimy with weed. Iain took Linda's hand, and he kept it in his as they went on. He did not want to tell her here; not until they had put a safe distance between themselves and a chance wanderer from the house. Iain knew the place where he wanted to tell Linda; it was quiet and secluded, they would not be disturbed.

In a little while they came to the place. The burn leapt over a rock in a miniature waterfall. Ferns grew in the crevices of the surrounding rocks, their pale fronds sparkled with drops of spray. An oak tree, stunted by the cold winds and unsuitable soil, hung over the cascade; it, too, had drops of water like diamonds upon its dark-green leaves.

Iain and Linda sat down on a sun-warmed stone, and looked at each other gravely.

' What is it, Iain?' she said.

He had been dreading this moment, wondering how he would answer the inevitable question, wondering how she would take the news he had to give her. After all, the man had been her husband, she must have pleasant memories of him as well as painful ones. Iain was suddenly jealous of those memories—jealous that another should share memories with her that he could not share. All those years that he had not known her rose up between them—she was mysterious to him. He felt—I don't know Linda—can you ever really know another person, even if you want to with all your strength, even if you both want it?

She said again, ' What is it? I can bear anything—anything but uncertainty.'

He still hesitated, wondering how he could tell her. At last he said, ' A queer thing has happened, Linda.'

' A queer thing?'

' Medworth has—has disappeared.'

' Disappeared?' she asked, looking at him in bewilderment.

Iain nodded. ' He has vanished. Nobody knows where he is. He never went to London at all.'

' But he must be somewhere—where is he?'

' They don't know,' Iain said. He waited a little. It was better for her to get used to the idea gradually; better to let her mind work in its own way. She would begin to ask questions when she was ready.

She sat forward on the rock. He could see the curve of her white cheek and the knot of dusky hair on the nape of her white neck. Her 'hands were clasped together rather tightly upon her lap.

In a little she turned and looked at Iain. 'Is he dead?' she asked in a low voice.

'Nobody knows,' Iain replied. 'He has just—just vanished.'

'You know nothing about it?'

'Nothing, except what I've been told. I have not seen him nor heard of him since that afternoon at the cottage. You know that, Linda. I should have told you if I had heard anything.'

She was satisfied with his reply. For a moment she had been afraid—but she knew that Iain would not lie to her.

'Tell me all about it,' she said.

He told her about the inspector's visit and all that he had said. He softened down the high-lights of the interview, and he did not allow it to appear that Howles had tried to trap him. He wanted to warn her that they must be careful without frightening her—it was difficult because her brain was so quick to catch impressions. She was too intelligent to be deceived.

'You think this man is dangerous,' she said quietly.

'He would be if we were not entirely innocent,' replied Iain quickly.

'Jack threatened us.'

'But he doesn't know that—and there is no way he could find out—if we're careful.'

'Yes,' she said thoughtfully. 'Go on, Iain.'

Iain went on. He glossed over the probability of Medworth's death and dwelt more on the known fact of his disappearance. She listened to it all quietly, sitting very still with her face turned away from him, so that he could not see how she was taking it.

At last she said, 'He must be dead, Iain—they would not have called in Scotland Yard unless they thought that.'

'People lose their memories——'

'Not Jack,' she said. 'He must be—dead.' There was a little silence and then she added, 'You think so, too.'

Iain did not answer. It was difficult to know what to say. She was upset, of course—it would not have been Linda if she could have heard of Medworth's death unmoved. Iain hated Medworth at that moment—hated him more deeply than ever before.

'Isn't it sad?' she said at last in a low voice. 'Isn't it dreadful to think that his life is finished, and he has made nothing of it—attained nothing—learnt no lessons? He has gone on—somewhere—with all that cruelty still in him. He hasn't learnt anything at all from his life here. He loved Life, you know; he was full of Life, full of confidence in himself. He thought he knew all about Life, but he knew nothing—nothing at all. He was not ready to—to go on.'

'Perhaps he never would have learnt,' Iain said, following her train of thought.

She looked round at him quickly. 'You think there is a Purpose?' she asked.

'We must think that, Linda. Otherwise everything is meaningless—a huge unhappy muddle.'

'I'm glad you think that. You think that lives are really complete—when they end.'

'Don't you?' Iain asked her.

'But—murder,' she said, in an awed voice. 'God couldn't intend—murder.'

'Why should you imagine it was murder?' Iain exclaimed. 'The man has disappeared—we know nothing more than that.'

'How could it be anything else? What other explanation is there? He left here to go to London. You know how full of confidence he was, how full of purpose—and he never went to London. Do you think he could have changed his mind so suddenly? You don't know him, Iain. He tires of things after he has got them—tires very quickly—but, until he has got them, he pursues them—avidly.'

Iain thought: *He pursues them as he was pursuing Richard*—but he did not say that. He said, 'Richard is safe. Have you thought of that, Linda?'

'I know,' she said. 'It's so difficult. I am feeling so many things all at once that I can't feel any of them properly.' She twisted her hands together. 'Richard is safe,' she said, 'and I am free, and we shall not have to go through the ordeal of the Law Court . . . all this . . . all because . . . Jack is dead. I haven't realised it yet . . . I can't. Death is always dreadful. . . .'

Iain waited in silence for a few minutes and then he began to talk of Inspector Howles. He wanted to prepare her for the inspector's visit. It was important that they should both tell the same story—the same in every detail. Iain had told the inspector the truth, but not the whole truth, and Linda must do the same.

'Do you think he will really come and see me?' Linda said. 'I can't see what he would gain. What could I tell him that he doesn't know already?'

'He may ask you if you know whether Medworth had any enemies,' Iain replied—it was better for her to be prepared.

'I see,' said Linda. She thought about it for a few moments with a frown of concentration on her brow. 'He had enemies, of course. He lived the sort of life that made him enemies. Racing and—and women are things that rouse passions in people. A lot of racing men disliked Jack, partly because he was successful and popular, and partly—partly because he was not—not generous in victory.'

Iain thought: I can imagine what he was like—how they must have hated him when he won! He said aloud, 'But I'm afraid that wouldn't be much use to Howles.'

'No, I suppose not,' Linda agreed. 'He will want something more definite. There was a man who came to the flat and—and threatened Jack. It was something to do with a woman. He came twice, and the second time they quarrelled —I wasn't in the room, of course, but I could hear them shouting at each other.'

'What happened?'

'Jack threw the man out—he was very strong,' she said simply.

It was a glimpse into her life, a strange horrifying glimpse. How she must have suffered! thought Iain. What indignities, what fears, what agonies of mind she must have endured! She was so fine in herself, her spirit was so delicate—how could she have borne such things?

Linda looked at him and smiled rather sadly. 'Don't look so miserable,' she said. 'These things hurt me at the time, but they taught me something. I don't quite know what they taught me, but it is valuable, I am sure of that. Perhaps they taught me to endure, and to be able to recognise goodness when I see it. I was very ignorant before. Try to think of it like that, Iain. I would not be as I am if I had not suffered these things—and you like me as I am——'

'Linda!' he said huskily. He laid his hand on hers as it lay on the sun-warmed rock.

'You have been very good,' she continued, pressing his hand. 'I do appreciate that. If you knew what it meant to me—your goodness, your consideration, your patience. Be patient just a little longer, Iain.'

He saw tears on her cheek, heard them in her voice. He felt as if his heart would burst. It was dreadful that she should be so unhappy, and that he could do nothing— he would have given his life gladly to protect her from pain.

'Oh, Linda!' he said again. His arm went round her and he drew her very gently against his shoulder. For a moment or two she stayed there, savouring his strength and gentleness. The peaty smell of his Harris jacket was in her nostrils, its rough hairy texture against her cheek—and then she unwound his arm and stood up.

'No,' she said brokenly. 'Not yet——' and turned and fled from him down the stony path.

CHAPTER XXIV

Ardfalloch House

ARDFALLOCH HOUSE was swept and garnished, there were fires in the rooms, and lamps shed their soft circles of light upon the polished surfaces of tables and furniture. Everywhere there were vases, filled with chrysanthemums—yellow and bronze and white. The front part of the house was very quiet, there was an air of expentancy about it. Mrs. MacAslan sat in the drawing-room near the fire, she was making a cross-stitch mat in gay colouring. Sometimes her small white hands paused in their task, and she lifted her head and listened.

In the kitchen premises there was a soft babble of talk. Janet and Donald, and Morag, and Alec MacNeil were sitting round the kitchen table—they had finished their tea and now they were waiting for the sound of a car in the avenue. The two young Highland maids moved about with their quiet tread, clearing away the remains of the meal, and chattering softly to each other in their own tongue.

The four at the table were speaking English out of politeness to Janet (she had never troubled to learn the Gaelic in all her long years' sojourn at Ardfalloch.) As a rule the mere sight of Donald was enough to rile Janet—she was inordinately jealous of MacAslan's affection for the sturdy Highlander—but, to-night, there was a temporary truce between them. Janet was too excited to be thrawn. Her excitement would not have been evident to a casual observer, nor to anybody who did not know her well; it was evident only in the unusual glitter of her eyes, as they darted about the kitchen after the maids, and in the unusual loquacity of her tongue.

' I was jist thinking the ither day,' said Janet in a conversational tone. ' I was thinking tae masel' it's changed days for Ardfalloch. There was naething ever happened in the place—but we've had oor share of excitement in the last wee while.'

She looked round at her companions for their agreement, but they were all three silent and withdrawn.

' You will be meaning the detectives, Miss Walker?' said Morag at last.

' Jist that,' nodded Janet. ' It was a queer-like thing—yon man's deith. I declare it gives me the shivers when I think on it. A fine stir it made, too—Ardfalloch in a' the newspapers, an 'pictures o' MacTaggart's inn where the man bided when he was here, an' pictures o' MacTaggart at the door. I'm thinking MacTaggart made a guid thing oot o' it, what with detectives drinking at the bar, and folks coming a' the way fra' Inverness tae see the place oot o' sheer curiosity.'

' It is an ill wind that blows nobody any good,' said Donald a trifle sententiously.

' You'll have seen the man, I doubt,' Janet asked him with interest.

' I saw him often enough,' replied Donald. ' He was often enough to be seen in the bar, or walking in the village. A big man with feet that turned outwards a little as he walked.'

' Och, and I, too, have seen him,' put in Alec eagerly. ' He was good company—so he was. He would stand a drink to anybody, and he was full of stories. Some of his stories were very funny. Did you be hearing the one about the miller's wife, Donald?'

'There's nae need tae blacken the man when he's deid,' said Janet quickly—it was obvious from Alec's grin that the story about the miller's wife was unfit for mixed company, and she was afraid it was going to be retailed.

'But maybe he is not dead,' Morag said quietly. 'They have found no proof that he is dead—it was in the newspapers I was reading that,' she added. 'They were saying that he may have gone away to America——'

'He's done nae such thing!' exclaimed Janet. 'It's just noansense saying that he's away tae America. Would the man be away tae America and leave his luggage lying in Glasgow?'

'It is queer,' Alec agreed thoughtfully. 'It is very queer that he did not be taking his luggage with him if it is to America he is gone——'

'There's naething queer aboot it,' Janet told him, 'for the man's not gone to America. The man's deid, an' doesna' need his luggage—he's deid, I'm telling you. They're just saying he's mebbe no deid tae clear themsel's. They canna find the murderer an' they dinna like tae look fules—an' that's a' there is tae it.'

There was nobody with sufficient temerity to contradict Janet's assertion, and a little silence ensued. Their thoughts veered from the mystery of Medworth's disappearance which had been more than a nine days' wonder in the quiet glen.

'They will be here soon now,' said Donald at last. He took his big silver watch out of his pocket and glanced at it as he spoke.

'Och, they will be tired!' Morag said compassionately. 'It is a long way to come—so it is—they will be very tired.'

'It is to be hoped they will be here soon,' put in Alec,

' for there is snow coming. I have been smelling snow in the air all day.'

' Dae you say so! ' Janet exclaimed. She had lived in the glen too long to disbelieve in such weather prophecies. Snow had no smell for her, and she was never aware of its imminence until the first flakes fell, but the Highlanders were seldom wrong when they smelt snow—Janet knew it to her cost. She went to the window and drew aside the heavy curtain; a few big flakes of snow had begun to fall, they floated past like feathers in the black darkness of the night.

' Aye, it's begun,' she said, frowning.

' It will not be much, and they will be here very soon,' Donald assured her with his usual optimism.

Janet dropped the curtain and went back to her seat. The young maids had withdrawn, there was a light clatter in the scullery to show that they were busy washing up the dishes.

Donald broke the little silence that had ensued.

' Does Mistress MacAslan *know*? ' he enquired in a low voice.

' Know! Of course she knows,' replied Janet with a truculent look. She was always on the defensive when her mistress's weakness was hinted at. ' She's been told that they're married and expected hame—how would she not know?'

' I was chust wondering if she had taken it in,' said Donald meekly.

' You and your wonderings!' Janet said scornfully. ' Could anybody fail tae see that MacAslan was expected? The whole hoose is prepared for him an' his bride. Mistress MacAslan kens mair than you'd think, she was as pleased as a bairn when Miss Finlay came over wi' flowers—helping her tae pit them in vawses——'

' Did Miss Finlay bring flowers, then?' asked Donald with interest.

' She did indeed,' replied Janet. ' Great bunches o' thae chrysanthemums—the hoose is like a wedding wi' them. Miss Finlay brocht them hersel' and dressed them—she was here the whole forenoon at it.'

' Och, and that is very nice—it is very nice indeed,' said Donald. ' MacAslan will be glad.'

' I'm no sae sure of that,' said Janet with sudden jealousy —what did Donald know of MacAslan's likes and dislikes— ' I'm no sae sure he'll be pleased. MacAslan likes fine tae see flowers growing, but he's no sae partial tae them in the hoose——'

' MacAslan will be glad,' said Donald with gentle stubbornness.

There was a threat of war in the air. Alec averted it with commendable promptitude.

' Will Richard be coming with them, Miss Walker?' he enquired.

' Richard!' exclaimed Janet, her attention distracted by this new foolishness. ' Richard's biding wi' Mistress Hetherington Smith. You never heard tell of a bairn going on a honeymoon, did you, Alec?'

' I did not,' admitted Alec meekly. ' But I do be knowing very little about honeymoons at all.'

' This puts me in mind,' said Janet in a more amiable tone —she had squashed Alec successfully and felt all the better for it—' This puts me in mind o' the time the old Chief brocht hame his bride. It's the waiting puts me in mind o' that, for it was a deeferent kind of hame-coming they had.'

' Tell us about it, Miss Walker,' said Morag.

' Och, there's little tae tell. The hoose was full then— *there's* the deeference—auld Mistress MacAslan was alive, and she was fond of company. There was a wheen o' tenants tae welcome the couple, and an airch on the drive, and there were folks from Cluan and Achnafettel and Balnafin in the drawing-room, an' pipers skirling forbye.'

' I could be giving them a wee skirl,' suggested Alec diffidently.

' Weel, an' there would be nae hairm in that,' agreed Janet with surprising graciousness. ' I'm no saying but what MacAslan might like a wee bit tune.'

Alec smiled with pleasure. He had brought his beloved pipes with him in the hopes that there might be a chance of playing a welcome for MacAslan and his bride.

' Weel, there we waited,' continued Janet. ' There was nae motors in those days, and the Chief and his lady had tae drive frae Balnafin in the carriage. We haird them coming in the distance, an 'auld Mistress MacAslan called us in tae the hall. It was dark as pitch an' the lamps o' the carriage were shining in the drive——'

Janet broke off. There were steps outside and a knock on the back door. ' Wha's that?' she said in surprise.

It was Calum Mor. He entered rather sheepishly with his pipes under his arm.

' I was wondering,' he said, looking round at the little group in the lamplight. ' I was wondering could I be playing for MacAslan when he is here——'

' I am playing for MacAslan,' said Alec, frowning at his cousin in annoyance. ' It is not the right thing at all that you should play for him, Calum Mor. I am MacAslan's man—I live upon his ground——'

' And what harm is there that you should both play for MacAslan?' enquired Donald peaceably. ' It will be all the better, and Calum Mor is MacAslan's man even though he is living at the other side of the loch. The MacNeils are all MacAslan's men—so they are.'

Calum looked doubtfully at Alec. He was anxious to play, but he did not want to offend against the laws of etiquette.

Alec smiled at him. ' We will both play for MacAslan,' he agreed.

' I was wondering,' Calum said again. ' I was wondering if I could be playing MacAslan's own tune for him. I was thinking, maybe, he would be liking to hear it. He was calling it "A May Morning".'

Alec's face fell. ' A May Morning!' he exclaimed. 'That would be a strange tune to be playing—it is "The Highland Wedding" we should be playing for Mac-Aslan——'

' It is MacAslan's own tune,' Calum urged.

' It is a foolish idea,' Alec said sullenly. ' A foolish idea to be playing "A May Morning" for MacAslan on a November evening with snow in the air.'

Calum's eyes blazed with sudden rage; he was about to reply, but Donald was before him:

' Och, do not be quarrelling, then!' he besought them. ' It is not a good thing to be quarrelling on such a day as this. And you are both in the right—so you are. This is what you will do, you will play "The Highland Wedding" for MacAslan, for it is the right thing to be playing and it is a good tune, so it is. But first you will play "A May Morning" as a compliment to MacAslan. It is his own tune and it will please him to hear it—I am thinking there will be a May morning in MacAslan's heart when he brings his bride home to Ardfalloch, whatever the weather.'

Donald's decision was diplomatic and psychologically sound. It appealed to the imagination of his hearers, to the vein of romanticism and sentiment in their Celtic blood. Alec and Calum were pleased and satisfied. They murmured their approval. Calum sat down and was provided with tea—all was peace once more.

A gust of wind rattled the window and moaned eerily in the chimney.

' Och, do be hearing the storm!' Morag cried.

' Whisht!' said Donald.

They all raised their heads and listened.

' Aye, it's them right enough!' Janet exclaimed.

They all rushed out into the hall—Donald flung the doors open. The little car (a wedding-present from Mr. Hetherington Smith) was just drawing up at the bottom of the steps. The ground was already white, and the snow was still falling softly. It was very dark, but the headlights of the car streamed out in front, lighting up the snow-covered ground and the bushes on the farther side of the drive with a queer artificial effect.

MacAslan climbed out of the car. He took his bride in his arms and sprang up the steps and across the threshold of his house—it was the age-old custom—they were both laughing happily and excitedly as he set her down.

' Ceud mìle fàilte!' cried the Highlanders.

' Gum a fada bèo thu!'

' May you live for ever in peace and plenty!'

' This is a good day for Ardfalloch!'

They were beside themselves with joy, showering blessings and good wishes on the bridal pair. It was a great moment for them—a moment after their own hearts—the Chief had brought his bride to Ardfalloch. They saw the romance of it, the historical importance—the torch of the MacAslans had been carried forward a step further. Soon there would be an heir—another link in the chain—their eyes strained forward into the future and backwards into the past. It mattered nothing to them that there was no arch in the drive, no company of guests and tenants such as Janet had described—they were there themselves, and Mac-Aslan had come. It was a moment none of them would forget.

Janet alone said nothing. She was no less moved than the Celts, but it was not her way to show her feelings. She thought, as she looked at the bride's flushed face and sparkling eyes: *This is no dwaibly body, MacAslan has chosen better than his father*—and she was glad that it was so. She

300

busied herself with their comfort, helping them to unwind
their scarves and to take off their coats.

Linda was excited and pleased with the welcome; she
shook hands with them all and tried to thank them, tried to
tell them how happy she was to come back to Ardfalloch.
She glanced at Iain—his eyes were shining with excitement,
he was unconscious of himself—as she could never be. She
saw that he was like these people beneath the surface, they
were his people in very truth. He could understand them,
could share their enthusiasms and express his feelings in
gracious terms. It was a great moment not only for them
but for Iain also, a moment for consummation towards
which he had been moving for months. It was perfect
happiness—this home-coming—Ardfalloch his own once
more, and Linda to share it—there was nothing more he
wanted in the world. Troubles might come later, money
was still scarce, but he would not look forward into the
future to find troubles, he would make the most of this
moment of pure joy.

The flood of greeting had scarcely abated when the
drawing-room door opened and Mrs. MacAslan appeared.
She was smiling happily and her small child-like face was a
little flushed. Iain put his arms round her, and kissed her
tenderly; then he pulled Linda forward.

'Linda is your daughter now. You know that, don't
you, Mother?' he said.

She nodded and held up her face for Linda to kiss. 'I
have a present for you,' she said in her soft fluty voice. 'A
present for Iain's bride. I waited up to give it to the bride,
but I am going to bed now, because you would rather be
alone.' She nodded gravely like a child that knows it is
being good and clever. Linda found a little parcel being
thrust into her hand.

'But, Mother—of course you must dine with us—how
absurd!' cried Iain, catching her arm as she turned away.

'Not to-night,' she said, smiling her little sad smile. 'Other nights I will, but not to-night. You will like it better alone. I remember I liked being alone best. It was clever of me to remember—wasn't it, Iain? It was so long ago—long long ago. But I can remember things that happened long ago better than things that happen now. I remembered when I was sitting in the drawing-room waiting for you to come—I remembered that I liked it best when we were alone—together. Janet will bring me my dinner in bed. I like having dinner in bed, don't I, Janet?'

They were all standing in the hall listening to her. None of them spoke. They were all—in their different ways—moved by her pathos, by the unconscious courage of her, and by the simplicity of her words. She had lost so much that she had almost lost herself. She was scarcely a denizen of their world, she was only a forlorn little ghost, remembering her past happiness in a former existence.

Morag's hand crept into Donald's. 'We will be going now,' she whispered. 'She is right, it is alone they should be—those two.'

They went out together into the snowy darkness of the night, Alec and Calum followed them; Janet ran upstairs after her mistress; Iain and Linda found themselves alone in their own home at last. They stood in the hall, scarcely realising the fact that the others had gone; the house seemed strangely silent after the chatter and bustle which had followed their arrival.

Suddenly there was a skirl of pipes outside the window, as Calum and Alec began to play 'A May Morning.' Iain lifted his head and listened, there was a little smile lurking at the corners of his mouth; he had expected a tune when he saw the pipes tucked under the two men's arms, but he had not expected that they would play 'A May Morning.' By playing his own tune they had paid him a very charming compliment, and the hidden significance which Donald had intended was not lost upon him. It was spring in his heart in spite of the softly falling snow. Iain marvelled afresh at the instinct of the Celt for the deeper things of life—the meaning that lay beneath the surface.

'They are playing a welcome for you,' said Linda softly. 'How happy they are to have you home again.'

'They are playing for you, too,' Iain said.

She shook her head smilingly. 'It is for MacAslan,' she said. 'And, perhaps, a little, for MacAslan's bride—they don't know me yet, but I love them already—your people.'

Iain did not answer—it was true, what she said, but some day they would know her and love her for herself, he was sure of that. They went into the drawing-room and stood there near the fire looking at each other gravely.

'I really believe it now,' Iain told her. 'It was all a dream before, but now that I see you here it is real—and you are real, Linda.'

'I am real, and you are real,' Linda said. She put her arms round his neck and drew his head down on a level with her own—she was no ice maiden now, no fairy woman; she was warm and living, and wholly mortal as she melted into her husband's arms.

CHAPTER XXV

Donald and Morag

DONALD and Morag walked home together; it was still snowing gently, and the ground was crisp under their feet, lightly powdered with pure sugary flakes. Far away in the forest a stag was bellowing. They could hear also the sound of the pipes, of Alec and Calum playing a welcome to Mac-Aslan—the sound grew fainter as they went through the trees.

Morag put her hand on Donald's arm, it was a strong safe arm, and she needed its support and the comforting feel of it. She said, ' My heart was sad for her, Donald.'

' Mine also,' Donald replied in his deep voice. ' He was a fine man—the old Chief—and he held her soul in his hand. She had lost everything when he was gone from her.'

' She had her son,' Morag said. ' Was her son so little to her, Donald?'

Donald did not reply to that; it was always a strange thing to him that her son meant so little to Mistress Mac-Aslan, but he would not criticise her. She was one of the family he revered, and was therefore above criticism.

After a moment's silence Morag added shyly, ' Would you be liking a son, Donald?'

' Morag!' he exclaimed, stopping and looking down at her with shining eyes.

' It is true,' she told him, nodding her head. ' A son—or maybe a little daughter. You would not be grieved if it were to be a little daughter, Donald?'

' It is a wonderful thing,' he said gravely, tenderly. ' It is what I have been wanting this long while—and you, too, have been wanting it. Och, Morag, it is a wonderful thing! '

They went on together, hand in hand, full of happiness at the consummation of their hopes, full of thoughts and fears and rosy dreams of the future.

After they had walked on for a little in silence, Morag said softly, ' Will you be telling me now what happened to Mister Middleton? '

Donald's face changed. ' Can you not be leaving that? ' he asked her. ' I have told you that I do not want to speak of it. It is not a good thing to speak of—it is not a good thing for you to be thinking of things like that.'

' I cannot help it,' she said rather sadly. ' If I knew what had happened I could put it away and not be thinking of it all the time. It has been a trouble in my heart since the day that MacAslan came to the cottage and called for me. I am afraid.'

' Na biodh eagal ort! ' Donald exclaimed. ' Why are you afraid, Morag? '

' I am afraid in case there is trouble in it—trouble for you.'

Donald sighed. He said, ' Why should you be thinking I know any more about Mister Middleton than other people? '

Morag did not answer that, but her grip on his hand tightened.

' What do you know about it, Morag? ' he asked.

' I know that you killed him,' she said softly.

' And is that not enough for you to be knowing? '

' It is too much—or not enough,' Morag said. ' The thing is a trouble in my heart all the time—a trouble and a fear.'

' A fear? ' he questioned. ' What are you afraid of, then? '

' I am afraid that they may find his body,' she whispered.

' They will not find his body,' said Donald simply.

They said no more until they had reached the cottage. Donald went round, closing the doors and snibbing the windows; Morag made up the dying fire, and pulled Donald's chair in front of it. She knew that he would tell her now, and she was half afraid to hear the story, but she felt she must know what had happened. She must know that Donald was safe, that he had left nothing undone that could trap him. She shivered a little with the fear and the excitement.

Donald came in and sat down in the chair; she drew the creepy-stool to his knees, and sat upon it, leaning against him and looking up into his face.

' I did not mean to be telling you,' he said softly. ' I do not know how you are knowing anything about it, Morag.'

' It is because I know you,' she told him.

There was a little silence, the fire was burning up now, the pine branches crackling, the room was full of warm red light.

He said at last, ' I will tell you, then—from the beginning. I will tell you how it happened. I met him in the woods, he was coming away from MacAslan's wee house and he was angry. I could see he was an angry man by the gait of him, and by the way he drove at the grasses with his stick, as though they were his enemies and he would kill them all. He has been quarrelling with MacAslan, I thought, and MacAslan has got the best of it or he would not be so angry; but MacAslan has made an enemy. He was almost on the top of me before he saw me—so full was he of his angry thoughts; but when he saw me he stopped and said in his English voice, ' Hallo, Donald, you are the very man I wanted to see!" " Good afternoon to you, Mister Middleton," I said. He began speaking to me then, sounding me about the way I was feeling towards MacAslan, sounding me very cautiously to see what I would be saying. " Och!" I said to him, " MacAslan is a hard master—he is a proud,

overbearing man, MacAslan is." " Proud, is he?" said
Mister Middleton, with a nasty look on his face. " Proud,
is he? I'll soon humble his pride. I'm going to drag him
through the mud, Donald. He won't like that, will he?"
" No, indeed, Mister Middleton," I said, laughing. " It
would be a fine thing to be seeing MacAslan in the mud."
He looked at me very hard at that. " But I thought you
were so devoted to your chief," he said in a sneering voice.
" I am living on his ground," I said. " I am his slave—or
little better. He is a hard master," and then I pretended
that I had suddenly become afraid, and I said, " But you
will not be speaking of this, Mister Middleton, or you will
be getting me into trouble. I do not want trouble with
MacAslan," I told him. " I will keep your secret," he said,
smiling in a nasty way. " Your secret is safe with me," he
said. We talked a little more, and then he told me that he
was wanting me to go to London, and go into the law-court,
and tell the judge about the morning that I went to the
island—the morning after the storm—and fetched Mac-
Aslan and Mistress Medworth. I would get money for it,
he said, and all my expenses, and we would have a good
time in London together. " Och, and that would be fine!"
I said. " It is very quiet here. It would be fine to see
London—so it would." " Then you will come," he said.
" That's great. I will have some pretty girls ready for you,
Donald. I will write and tell you when you are wanted and
send you the money ".'

' Och, but he was wicked!' Morag exclaimed.

' He was very wicked,' agreed Donald gravely. ' So then
I made out that I was frightened, and I said to him, " But
what will I be saying to the judge, Mister Middleton?"
" I'll tell you what to say," he said, laughing. " Don't
worry about that. All I want is for you to tell how Mac-
Aslan and Mrs. Medworth spent the night on the island
together, and how you went for them in the morning. By

the by, where were they when you went for them?" " They were waiting on the rocks," I told him. " That is a pity," he said. " But it is good enough with the other evidence as well." I told him that I did not understand, and he said that Mistress Medworth was his wife, and that she had divorced him, and that his name was Medworth and not Middleton at all. " But you can keep that to yourself," he said to me. I could not make head nor tail of the thing, and I could not understand why, if Mistress Medworth had divorced him, she was not free from him——'

' I do not understand either,' Morag murmured.

' It is difficult,' Donald said. ' It is very difficult to understand, but it did not really matter whether I understood that part of it or not. I understood very well that he was MacAslan's enemy and would do him harm. There was no doubt in my mind about that. If you had seen his face when he was speaking of MacAslan—och, he was dangerous—dangerous and bad.'

' How could he have hurt MacAslan?' Morag questioned.

' And that I do not know either,' replied Donald. ' A man like that has ways of doing harm. He was deep and sly and there was no truth in him, nor any scruples. But that was a thing I had to know, and the only way I could be knowing was to see MacAslan himself.'

' You saw MacAslan and spoke to him about the man!' Morag exclaimed. ' Then MacAslan knew——'

' MacAslan knew nothing of it.'

' Then how——?'

' If you would be letting me tell the story in my own way——'

' I will be quiet,' Morag promised.

Donald was silent for a moment, arranging his thoughts. He found the story more difficult to tell than he had expected. The thing had been done with haste and urgency, in a sort of cold rage that had left his brain very clear to plan the details of his self-appointed task. But, looking back, it was not so clear. He could see his own actions, but he could not see how his mind had worked.

Donald sighed; he continued: ' I saw the man was dangerous to MacAslan, but just how dangerous I did not know. I saw that the man must not be allowed to leave Ardfalloch until I knew more. I said to him, " I must think about all this, Mister Middleton." " You are not backing out of it, Donald?" he said quickly. " No, I am not backing out of it," I told him. " But there is much to arrange. I must have a little time to think." " You must think quickly, then," he said, " for I am going away to-morrow, to London, to see my lawyer about the case. Look here, Donald," he said, " I will give you ten pounds if you will come—as well as all your expenses—and another ten if you will say what I tell you to say about where you found MacAslan and Mrs. Medworth when you went to fetch them from the island." " That is a lot of money to me, Mister Middleton," I said. " But I have told you already where I found them." He laughed and said I had better think again. When I saw that he was bribing me to lie about MacAslan my anger rose, so that it was hard to keep myself from striking him as he stood. But I remembered that he was MacAslan's enemy before he was mine. So I stifled my anger and I said to him, " I will come and see you to-night, at MacTaggart's, and we can arrange it all comfortably." He was content with that—the more so because it had started to rain, and it was not at all to Mister Middleton's liking to stand and talk in the rain. He said he would expect me at the inn that evening, and went away. So then I went on to see MacAslan, and he was out.'

' You waited for MacAslan,' Morag encouraged him.

' I waited for him in the little room, and, while I waited, I thought about it all, and one moment it seemed to me that the man was very bad and very dangerous, and the next moment it seemed that I had made much out of little, and that the man could do no harm to MacAslan since Mac-Aslan had done no wrong. It seemed to me that all the talk of judge and law-court was childish talk and meant nothing, and that the man was talking to relieve his anger and no more. But, when MacAslan came, I saw that it was not so. I saw that the man's talk of how he could harm MacAslan was true.'

'MacAslan told you——'

'There was trouble on him,' Donald said, without heeding the interruption. 'There was great trouble on Mac-Aslan that day. He would tell me nothing, for he was bound with a promise, but there was no need for him to be telling me. He told me without knowing that he was telling me, for I held the key to his secret in my hand. So when he spoke of the old days when a man was free to follow his nature I knew what he meant, and when he spoke of the desire that was on him to kill his enemy I knew who it was that was his enemy. But I held my peace, for I felt that it was better that MacAslan should think he was talking to the air.

' I was watching him as he talked, and I could see, by the blackness of his face, that it would be an ill day for Mister Middleton if he should meet MacAslan. It seemed to me that no promise would hold MacAslan's hand.'

'I have never seen MacAslan in wrath!' Morag exclaimed.

' It does not happen often, nor for small things,' Donald told her. ' MacAslan is a man who keeps his anger for the big things and does not fritter it away on trifles as some men do. MacAslan's anger is like a storm. I was afraid.'

' Afraid!' echoed Morag incredulously.

' I was afraid that MacAslan would kill his enemy,' Donald explained patiently, ' and he was in no mood to be cautious. He was in no mood to plan the thing securely, or to be secret in his planning. There was such anger in Mac-Aslan that he would not count the cost if his enemy were before him—I could see that. There was only one thing to do—only one—I knew that I must kill the man myself.

' In a way I was glad when I saw my path clear, for the man was bad altogether. He was MacAslan's enemy and mine. There were plenty of reasons why the man should die, but the chief reason was that as long as he was alive MacAslan would be in danger. I knew that I must kill him, and I knew that I must do it before he left the glen, for, once he had gone away, it would be a hundred times more difficult. At first I could not think how I could do the thing —I would have liked to fight the man, for he was as big as I am, and strong, and it would have been a good fight. And I felt I would like to put my two hands round his throat and squeeze the life out of him—for I, too, was angry, though my anger was cold and deadly, and not hot like MacAslan's anger—but then I saw that I could not fight the man, for it would be too dangerous. It was not for my own satisfaction I was to kill the man, but for MacAslan's safety, and therefore I could take no risk. I must think of a sure way. I left MacAslan and walked into the village, and all the time I was thinking and thinking of how I could do the thing, and do it secretly.

' Mister Middleton was in the bar, and he called to me to have a drink, but I could not drink with the man when it was in my heart to kill him, so I said I had no time, and signed to him that I wanted to speak to him privately. We went upstairs to his bedroom and sat down on two chairs, and he looked at me and said, " Well, Donald, is it all right?" and I said, " It is all right, Mister Middleton, I will come to London when you say." " That's splendid," he said. " I'll write and tell you when to come, and send you the money. You won't regret it," he said. All this time I was hardly daring to look at the man in case he should see what was in my mind—and the hatred that was in me—and I was wondering and wondering how I could do the thing that I must do——'

'How did you do it, Donald?'

'Can you not be waiting for me to tell you, woman!' he asked her, smiling at her impatience. 'I am telling you from the very beginning, so that, when I have finished, there will be no more to tell, for it is not a good thing to be speaking of.'

He looked round the small cosy room and lowered his voice. 'And then suddenly I saw how I could do it,' he continued. 'It was an easy way, and a secret way, and there would be no danger in it at all. I said to him, "Och, it is a pity you are going away to-morrow, for we have never been out after the duck," and I asked if he would not be liking a shot at the duck in the morning before he left. He thought for a minute, and then he laughed, and said it would be good sport, but he was leaving Balnafin by the eight o'clock train. And, at that, I saw my plan, and how it could be done, and it was a very good plan,' said Donald complacently. 'So then I said to him, "The early morning is the best time for the duck—this is how to do it, Mister Middleton. You will order the taxi to call at the inn for your things, and to meet you at the bridge at seven o'clock, and I will call for you at the inn at four o'clock in the morning, and we will go up to the duck-bog together, and you will shoot a couple of brace of Mr. Hetherington Smith's duck to take south with you in the train." He was laughing to himself. "It will be good sport," he said again. "You are a rogue, Donald, but I like you. You will be expecting a big tip for the morning's work, I suppose." "I will be leaving that to yourself, Mister Middleton," I said politely.

'I left him then, for I had some arrangements of my own to be making. And in the morning I called for him at four o'clock as we had arranged. We walked up to the bog together. He had his gun, and a bag over his shoulder. He gave me the bag to carry. " That is for the duck," he said, smiling. " It is a poacher's bag, that." " Och, it is not the first time I have been carrying a poacher's bag," I said. " No," said Mister Middleton, " and it won't be the last, eh?" I was listening very carefully to all he was saying, and taking note of the way he walked——'

' And why were you doing that, Donald?' Morag enquired.

' You will be seeing why, in a little,' replied Donald. ' It was very misty and dark just at first, and once or twice he said, " We won't see any duck this morning, Donald. I would have been better in my bed "; but I told him it would soon clear and it would be just right for him, and, sure enough, in a little while the sun came through the mist, and the mist began to clear, so that you could see quite a long way. When we were coming near the bog, I stopped and said to him, " You will have to take off that coat, Mister Middleton, for the duck will be seeing you a mile away." He took off his coat—you will be remembering the coat with the big checks, Morag—and he took off his hat and his blue muffler and put them beside a bush. He had his gun under his arm. We went on together.

' When we got to the bog I said to him, " You will be needing big shot for the duck, Mister Middleton." " I have sixes," he said. " That is no good at all," I said to him. " It is fours you are needing." I had a bag of cartridges on my shoulder. He gave me the gun, and I loaded it with the big shot. He had gone on ahead of me, and I put the gun to my shoulder to shoot him. . . . And then, somehow, I could not do it—my gorge rose at the thought, for the man was so unsuspecting. I said softly, " Mister Middleton," and he turned and looked at me. " I am going to kill you, Mister Middleton," I said. For a moment he did not believe that I would do it. He thought it was a joke I was having with him, and then his face changed, for he saw that I was in earnest—and he turned and ran from me.'

Donald paused for a moment and drew his hand across his brow. He was surprised to find that his hand was wet. The telling of the tale had brought it all back to him—the stress and the strain, and the fear that he might make a mistake, and so ruin them all.

'Go on, Donald,' Morag urged.

'He ran from me,' Donald continued. 'It was strange, that.'

'You had the gun,' said Morag sensibly.

'I had the gun,' Donald agreed. 'But, even so, it was strange. A man's instinct is to go for his enemy, and I had thought from his speech that this man was brave—even reckless. I had listened to his stories at MacTaggart's, and in all his stories he was brave. He had tackled armed men and knocked them out with a blow—it was in America—but he ran from me. I had expected him to leap at me, and to try to wrest the gun from my hands—I was prepared for that—but, when he turned and ran, I was not prepared. All in a moment I saw that I had done wrong to speak to the man and tell him of my intention. I had been thinking of my own feelings, and I had not allowed my scruples to endanger my plan. MacAslan's safety was at stake. If the man escaped we were all ruined—I saw that. It was all clear in my mind. I saw that he must not escape whatever happened. If it had been necessary to kill him before, it was a hundred times more necessary now. All in a moment I saw this, it was all quite clear in my mind. He was running along the edge of the bog by now, and I was running after him. I gained on him, for I knew the ground and then I raised the gun and shot him. He fell without a sound.'

'Oh, Donald, it was dreadful,' Morag whispered.

'It was dreadful,' Donald agreed; 'but there was no other

way at all. I had to do it, Morag—it was for MacAslan, and it was the only thing. And you must remember he was bad —altogether bad—and very dangerous. You must remember that, Morag.'

' Tell me what happened next.'

' There was duck in the bog,' Donald said, visualising the scene. ' They rose up in the air when they heard the shot and flew away squawking, and after that it was very still. I knew there was no time to waste, for I had wasted time already. I had much to do—there was no time to waste.

' I took a spade I had hidden in that place the night before and I dug a hole. The ground was very soft, and soon there was water in the hole. I put him in the hole, and covered him up, and I put back the turf I had cut, and I stamped on it, and then I strewed some leaves about the place. There was hardly a mark to be seen when I had finished. Then I took the check coat and put it over my coat—he was broad in the shoulders, that one—and I put on the hat and the blue muffler, and I took a little piece of tow I had brought with me, and stuck it on my lip, and I went down to the bridge.

' Very soon Rory came along with the taxi. I spoke to him sharply in English, saying, " You are late, damn you. Get a move on or I shall miss my train." "Yes, sir," he said meekly. ' I got in, laughing to myself. Rory drove on quickly. Presently we got to Balnafin. I went into the station, and called loudly for a porter to fetch my luggage. I took a ticket to Glasgow. There were several people waiting on the platform for the train——'

' Och, it was very dangerous!' cried Morag. ' Were you not afraid that they would know it was not Mister Middleton?'

' I was not afraid,' Donald replied simply. ' Nobody at Balnafin was knowing the man well. They were knowing the coat and the hat and they were not bothering about who was inside them. It was Mister Middleton they were expecting to see and so it was him they were seeing. And then, too, it was early in the morning. In the morning people are dull, and they are busy with their own affairs—there was little danger in it, Morag. I bought a paper at the bookstall and read it, and I walked up and down the platform with small steps. The train was late in coming, but, at last, it came. They brought the luggage on a truck and put it in the van. The station-master was there—he was wanting a tip—he was fussing round the luggage, and then he came and opened the door of the carriage for me. I said to him, "Thank you, my man," and I gave him two and sixpence. The porter came and said the luggage was all in the van—I gave him a shilling. There was nobody else travelling first class, and I knew they would not forget me in a hurry, and that was what I was wanting.

'When the train started I took off the check coat and the hat and the blue muffler and the little moustache. I rolled them up together, and put them in the poacher's bag. I had my own cap in my pocket. When the train stopped at Dalnahuilish I got out at the other side of the carriage—the side away from the platform, and hid behind a truck until the train had gone. Then I walked back to Ardfalloch across the moors, and I threw the bag into the middle of a tarn.

'Mister Hetherington Smith was shooting the south moors that day. I met them coming up from the first drive. "Where have you been, MacNeil?" he said to me. "I have been making up the butts," I told him. "Some of them are needing a little patching after the rain." I showed him a butt that I had been patching the night before and he said, "That is a good piece of work—you must have been out early getting this done." You see, Morag, it is all quite safe.'

Donald and Morag

'It was well done,' Morag said slowly. 'It was very clever of you, Donald, indeed it was.'

Donald was pleased, but he would not admit it. 'Och, I am not wanting praise,' he said. 'It is enough that I have rid MacAslan of his enemy.'

'They will be very happy, I am thinking,' said Morag, nodding thoughtfully.

'I am thinking the same,' agreed Donald, reaching for his pipe.